DELHI
1857

THE SIEGE, ASSAULT AND CAPTURE
AS GIVEN IN THE DIARY AND
CORRESPONDENCE OF THE LATE
COLONEL KEITH YOUNG, C.B.,
JUDGE-ADVOCATE GENERAL, BENGAL

EDITED BY
GENERAL SIR HENRY WYLIE NORMAN
G.C.B., G.C.M.G., C.S.I.
AND
MRS KEITH YOUNG
WITH A MEMOIR AND INTRODUCTION BY
SIR HENRY WYLIE NORMAN

WITH ILLUSTRATIONS AND MAPS

The Naval & Military Press Ltd

Reproduced by kind permission of the Central Library,
Royal Military Academy, Sandhurst

Published by
The Naval & Military Press Ltd
Unit 10, Ridgewood Industrial Park,
Uckfield, East Sussex,
TN22 5QE England
Tel: +44 (0) 1825 749494
Fax: +44 (0) 1825 765701
www.naval-military-press.com

© The Naval & Military Press Ltd 2004

In reprinting in facsimile from the original, any imperfections are inevitably reproduced and the quality may fall short of modern type and cartographic standards.

Colonel Keith Young, C.B.
From a portrait painted when about 20 years of age.

TO

The People of Britain and of Greater Britain,

TO SECURE WHOSE INHERITANCE IN
THE INDIAN EMPIRE MANY
BRAVE MEN LAID
DOWN THEIR
LIVES.

Before and After.

'If nothing happens, all is right; but if it turns out a preconcerted mutiny, force must be met by force. The least concession would lose us India, and justice has placed us on high ground, thank God! Neither your Lordship nor myself would shed a drop of blood, if it could be avoided, but a thousand lives must be taken rather than let four hundred thousand men dictate to their government unjustly—or justly either for that matter. But woe to the government that places itself in so dreadful a position!'

Sir Charles Napier to Lord Dalhousie (1849).

To what is our success to be attributed? 'To the fire of the British Artillery exceeding in rapidity and precision all that the Brigadier-General has ever witnessed in his not short career; to the force of the Enfield Rifle in British hands; to British pluck, that good quality which has survived the revolution of the hour; and to the blessing of Almighty God in a most righteous cause—the cause of justice, humanity, truth, and good government in India.'

Extract from an 'Order' by Sir Henry Havelock (1857).

'There is indeed occasion for our deepest thankfulness, and how loud a call is there on us all, for the most humble and heartfelt gratitude, for the change which has come over the state of affairs generally, through the loving mercy of our Heavenly Father, who, though He has seen fit to try and chasten us severely—as severely as any nation, except, perhaps, the Jews, was ever chastened—yet has not allowed us to be overwhelmed, but has shown us a way out of all our troubles. May we all lay deeply to heart the solemn lessons which have been taught us by the mysterious and tremendous events of the past few months.'

Sir Donald M'Leod to Colonel Keith Young (1857).

Recessional.

'God of our fathers, known of old,
    Lord of our far-flung battle-line,
Beneath Whose awful Hand we hold
    Dominion over palm and pine;
Lord God of Hosts, be with us yet,
Lest we forget—lest we forget!

'The tumult and the shouting dies,
    The captains and the kings depart,
Still stands Thine ancient Sacrifice,
    An humble and a contrite heart.
Lord God of Hosts, be with us yet,
Lest we forget—lest we forget!

'Far-called our navies melt away,
    On dune and headland sinks the fire,
Lo, all our pomp of yesterday
    Is one with Nineveh and Tyre!
Judge of the Nations, spare us yet,
Lest we forget—lest we forget!

'If, drunk with sight of power, we loose
    Wild tongues that have not Thee in awe,
Such boasting as the Gentiles use
    Or lesser breeds without the Law;
Lord God of Hosts, be with us yet,
Lest we forget—lest we forget!

'For heathen heart that puts her trust
    In reeking tube and iron shard,
All valiant dust that builds on dust,
    And guarding calls not Thee to guard;
For frantic boast and foolish word,
Thy mercy on Thy People, Lord!'

                      RUDYARD KIPLING.

PREFACE.

THE motive that leads me to publish my Husband's Letters and Diaries is the desire that his children and friends may be able to read them. At first it was intended to print these papers for private circulation only, but now it is thought best to publish them, for, though a number of years—over forty—have passed since the great Indian Mutiny of 1857-58, many still live who took an active part in the brave endeavour to quell it and restore right and order; and many others, either connected with India or having friends who were in the country during that troubled time, still take a deep interest in those years of anxiety and suffering, followed by righteous retribution.

My warm thanks are due to Sir Henry Norman, who has so kindly edited this book and written an Introduction and Memoir.

The Index and the Map of India have been specially prepared by my daughter, Mrs Inglis, whose work of subediting her father's letters has been a labour of love.

F. M. Y.

EDINBURGH, 1902.

MEMOIR AND INTRODUCTION.

ALTHOUGH I had on more than one occasion met Colonel Keith Young before 1856, it was not until that year that I became intimately acquainted with him. He was then Judge-Advocate General of the Army, the Head-Quarters of which were at the time in Calcutta; and I joined as Assistant Adjutant-General of the Army in May of that year. Colonel Young was then forty-eight years of age. He had joined the Bengal Army in the year 1824, and was appointed to the 50th Native Infantry; and having passed the interpreter's examination in 1828, he was appointed Acting Interpreter to the 68th Native Infantry, but had in 1830 to proceed home on sick leave, and did not return until 1833. From that period until 1841 he seems to have done duty with his own regiment, with an interruption from 1838 to 1840, when he again had to proceed to England on account of his health.

In 1841 he was appointed a Deputy Judge-Advocate General of Division; and in 1843 he was selected for the post of Civil Judge-Advocate in Sind, an appointment apparently thought necessary, as the Governor of Sind, the famous Sir Charles Napier, was a soldier, and might need advice on points of law, in the course of his administration.

Colonel Young continued in this office under two successive Commissioners of Sind who followed Sir Charles Napier—namely, Mr Pringle and Mr Bartle Frere, afterwards Sir Bartle Frere.

In 1852 Colonel Keith Young was selected for the high post of Judge-Advocate General of the Bengal Army, and on the appointment becoming permanently vacant in 1854 he was confirmed in that office, and continued in it until he died at Simla, on the 18th May 1862. As Judge-Advocate General he served under four successive Commanders-in-Chief—Sir William Gomm, General Anson, Lord Clyde, and Sir Hugh Rose, afterwards Lord Strathnairn. There is ample evidence of the esteem he was held in by all the eminent officers, civil or military, under whom he served; and the last-named Commander-in-Chief followed his remains to the grave at Simla.

From May 1856 until October 1857 I was closely associated with Colonel Keith Young at Army Head-Quarters. I then had to go home on sick leave, and was followed by him after a few months, and saw him from time to time in England. After we both returned to India in 1861, I think I only once saw him—for while he continued in his old office of Judge-Advocate, I became Secretary to the Government of India in Calcutta. It would appear, therefore, that my close association with Colonel Young only extended over a period of about three and a half years; but it included a voyage of more than fifty days between Calcutta and Allahabad in 1856, when the Head-Quarters' Staff and their families were boxed up together in a river 'flat' towed by a steamer, and where we were in close association all day and every day, and had to work in the same cabin. It also included the period of the outbreak of the Mutiny, the march to Delhi, and the whole Siege of Delhi, during which our tents were close together, we messed together, and met at all hours of the day and night. We were also in Camp together during the months of January, February, March, and April 1858, which included the Siege and Capture of Lucknow; and we met together in 1859, when the course of action towards the white soldiers of the late Company's Army had to be considered, and measures taken to avert what threatened to be a serious disaster following closely upon the great crisis of the Mutiny of the Bengal Army. It may readily be imagined that in these circumstances acquaintance with a man like Keith Young ripened into warm friendship, and that there was every opportunity for us thoroughly to know each other. His letters from Delhi will enable the readers of this work to form a good idea of his character. Happily our communication with Simla, where most of our wives were residing, was open throughout the Siege, and these letters show what were his thoughts from day to day. Anxious, deeply anxious we all were for those poor ladies in the hills, who day by day, for months together, were never certain for a minute that they might not hear of the death of the one who was dearest. They could not but dread the occurrence of some disaster to our arms, which would have speedily involved them in cruel massacre; and they were constantly troubled by reports, and even by threats of coming evil; while they were without protection from a rise of the people or a visit of mutineers, except such as could be obtained from a newly raised company of European Volunteers, who could afford but little security to a large and scattered place like Simla.

It was therefore incumbent on the husbands who were before Delhi to be careful to give all the encouragement they truthfully could send to their wives, and it will be seen that Keith Young did this.

We all were hopeful, and I think that not one of us ever doubted our eventual success; but we could not tell who would live to see that success, or at what cruel cost it might not be purchased. We had, however, Christian Faith, and truly our wives had the same in quite equal measure. Without such Christian Faith, surely these wives could not have retained their spirits and written letters of encouragement to their loved ones at Delhi, whom they might never see again, and who were constantly exposed to death.

The feeling that they were helpless, and that they were necessarily filled with ceaseless anxiety, caused the letters of Keith Young and of other husbands to be letters of encouragement to the wives; and although the great body of officers at Delhi were hopeful, perhaps these officers almost went beyond their inmost convictions in those letters.

Many reports of the advance of British troops from below reached our Camp, which were quite untrue, but perhaps had a good effect in Camp for a time. Other reports came to us from the city, of misfortunes to the mutineers—such as a failure of percussion-caps, a want of ammunition, or of desertions by mutineers from the city. These stories were grossly exaggerated by our informants, but they probably did raise the spirits of our Force, even though some of us instinctively felt that they were not altogether true.

It must also be recollected that some of us who had heard very evil intelligence, had to keep it to ourselves, and much of this was, for a time, unknown even to Colonel Young. If he had always known what a few of us had heard, perhaps more than one of his letters would have been less hopeful than they were.

It will be seen that he was able throughout to take a cheerful view of our future, and thus help to sustain his wife's courage. She, I am quite sure, knew that her husband was exactly where it was his duty to be, and would not have desired him to be elsewhere. His letters to her will be read with interest, not only by the survivors of the period of the Mutiny, but by others who have been connected with India, either personally or through relatives, or who take an interest, through their large-hearted and patriotic sympathy with their countrywomen and countrymen, in the most critical period of our Indian History.

Colonel Keith Young was forty-nine years old when the Mutiny began, and I think he quite looked his age. His face and expression were always pleasant to look at, and it was impossible to think that any guile existed in him. He was most truly honest and faithful in all that he said or did. He had abilities of a high order, which were recognised by such good judges as Sir Charles Napier and Sir Bartle Frere, and he earned the confidence of all who served with him, including the General Officers Commanding before Delhi, whom he so often attended in the Field; and he was highly valued by his various colleagues in the Army Staff. In private life he was much esteemed and respected.

I may here mention an occurrence that I think shows the transparent honesty of his face. When he was living a little way out of London in 1860, he was hurrying through the streets to catch his train to take him home, when he became aware that he had lost his purse. He went up to the first policeman he saw and asked him to lend him half-a-crown. The policeman evidently thought that Keith Young looked like a man to be trusted, and immediately handed to him the coin he asked for. I think this is striking evidence of the confidence which Keith Young's appearance inspired.

I do not think it was possible to conceive any one more thoroughly upright, or to meet any one who was more liberal to all with whom he was brought in contact.

For his services at Delhi he received the Military Companionship of the Bath.

His death in 1862, at the age of fifty-four, may be attributed first to exposure during the war. He, as well as most officers who served throughout the Siege of Delhi, had suffered from the exposure, but the effects of that exposure were greatly aggravated by his mission to Meerut in the height of the hot season of 1859. When what was called the 'White Mutiny' broke out, consequent upon the transfer of the European soldiers of the East India Company to the direct service of the Crown, the prospect was very grave, and the Commander-in-Chief ordered a special Court of Inquiry to assemble at Meerut to hear what the Company's soldiers had to say. Every individual soldier was allowed to come before this Court, and the Inquiry was so important that Lord Clyde thought it expedient that it should be conducted by the Judge-Advocate General. Colonel Keith Young conducted this anxious duty with his usual ability; but it is believed that this employment at the hottest period of the year had a bad effect on his constitution, and led to his lamented death.

Mrs Keith Young has decided to publish the letters written to her by her husband during the first portion of the Mutiny (which included the Siege of Delhi), as well as a few letters received by him, or written by him to friends or relatives, in the same period; and I have esteemed it a grateful duty to offer this Introduction to these letters, mostly written by him who was my dear friend, and with whom I often took counsel concerning very difficult and perplexing questions.

H. W. NORMAN.

ROYAL HOSPITAL,
    CHELSEA, 1902.

CONTENTS.

CHAPTER I.

PAGE

OUTBREAK OF THE MUTINY.—24th February to 24th May.

The greased cartridges—Mangul Pandy—Mutiny of troops at Meerut—Native invaliding rules—Bad news from Delhi—Departure of General Anson from Simla—Colonel Keith Young ordered to join the Commander-in-Chief · · · · 1–15

CHAPTER II.

AN ACCOUNT OF THE OUTBREAK CONTAINED IN A LETTER TO LONDON.—14th May to 25th May.

Alarm about the Goorkhas—King of Delhi proclaimed—With the Rana of Kooyntal at Joonug—Return to Simla · · 16–23

CHAPTER III.

ADVANCE ON DELHI.—25th May to 7th June.

Massacres at Delhi—Camp at Umballa and Kurnaul—Death of General Anson—Waiting for the siege-train—The 'Army of Retribution'—Letters from Meerut—Escape of Sir Theophilus Metcalfe—March to Gurannda—News of Brigadier Wilson's victory—Brigadier Wilson's Despatch—Illness and death of Brigadier Hallifax—Wilson's second victory—In camp at Raie—Hodson of 'Hodson's Horse'—Arrival at Alleepore—News of fresh mutinies—Arrival of siege-train and of Brigadier Wilson—Fidelity of the Raja of Puttiala—Orders for advance · · · · · 24–46

CHAPTER IV.

FIRST BATTLE BEFORE DELHI, AND COMMENCEMENT OF THE SIEGE.—8th to 22nd June.

Battle of Budlee-ka-Serai—Death of Colonel Chester—In Camp before Delhi—Hindoo Rao's house—Arrival of General Reed—The

PAGE

'Gallant Guides'—Regiments leave England for India—Occupation of Metcalfe House—Flagstaff picket surprised—Repulse of enemy—'Orders' by the Governor-General—Intended assault on the 13th June—Departure of the Jullunder force—Should we wait for reinforcements?—Councils of War—Decide to wait for reinforcements—Good news from Peshawar—Successful attack on the enemy by Majors Reid and Tombs—Carelessness of the Engineers—The dead Fakeer and his mother—Enemy attack us in force, and are repulsed with loss—News of Major Olpherts' force—Colonel Baird Smith to be Chief Engineer   .   .   .   47-77

CHAPTER V.

SIEGE OF DELHI (*continued*)—ARRIVAL OF REINFORCEMENTS.—
22nd June to 4th July.

Arrival of Olpherts' force—Sir Neville Chamberlain arrives—Mutiny of the 4th Irregulars—Our losses and reinforcements since 8th June—Anxiety about Cawnpore—Commencement of rains—Arrival of Colonel Greathed and the 8th King's—Cawnpore reported safe—Bad management at the Bhagput bridge—Letter from Simla—'Delhi must soon be taken'—Fidelity of the Hindoo princes—Enemy again attack us, but are driven back with loss—Letter from London—Reasons for the Mutiny—Arrival of reinforcements at Calcutta—Sikhs and Poorbeahs—Arrival of Coke's Corps—News from Agra—Mutineers in Camp—Bareilly Brigade attack us—Alleepore plundered—Coke in pursuit of rebels   78-105

CHAPTER VI.

SIEGE OF DELHI (*continued*)—ILLNESS AND DEATH OF SIR HENRY BARNARD—GENERAL REED ASSUMES COMMAND.—
4th to 16th July.

News from Agra and Allahabad—Heavy rains—Raja of Bullubghur protests friendship—All well at Agra—'Delhi will be attacked on a dark night'—Large Force sent to destroy the Bussye bridge—Fenwick's Corps and the Carabineers—Tombs and Hills win the Victoria Cross—Fight with the enemy—Heavy losses on both sides—Hodson 'taken in' by the enemy—'Comforts' for the soldiers—Reported reinforcements from Cawnpore—9th Irregulars sent away—Uneasiness about Sealkote—Nicholson's Movable Column—'Cossid' news from Agra—The staunch little Goorkhas—Enemy pursued up to the city walls—Brigadier Wilson on the strength of Delhi—Letter from Mr Colvin at Agra—We lose heavily in the fight of the 14th—Brigadier Wilson to command the Force—General Reed goes to Simla on sick leave   .   .   .   106-132

CHAPTER VII.

SIEGE OF DELHI (*continued*)—BRIGADIER WILSON ASSUMES COMMAND.—17th to 31st July.

Reed, Congreve, and Curzon leave for Simla—Severe fighting at Agra—Conflicting rumours from Cawnpore—General Wheeler and party reported massacred—Another fight with the enemy—Captain Greensill shot by a sentry—Letter from Meerut—Brigadier Wilson is 'very careful'—Reinforcements being sent by Lawrence—Enemy attack our left—All well at Agra—Hodson to command a Cavalry corps—Nicholson leaves Umritsur to join us—A 'cheery' device for the Assault—News of insurgents' defeat at Futtehpore—Disarming of the 4th Irregulars—Anxiety for news from Havelock—Letter from Mr Bartle Frere—Dissensions in the city—Kemaon Battalion expected—General Penny assumes command at Meerut—Rumoured fate of Wheeler at Cawnpore—Enemy try a grand attack—Frustrated by heavy rain—Letter from London—Great anxiety in England—Numbers of troops being sent out - 133-168

CHAPTER VIII.

SIEGE OF DELHI (*continued*).—1st to 11th August.

Arrival of Kemaon Battalion—The Eed Festival—Attack by the enemy—Letter from a spy in Delhi—Enemy's losses on the 1st—Murder of General Wheeler confirmed—Letters from Colonel Tytler at Cawnpore and from Sir Henry Havelock—Death of General Lawrence on 4th July—Five hundred mutineering Sepoys cut up—The King of Delhi's Commander-in-Chief—Failure to destroy the Jumna bridge—Arrival of Brigadier Nicholson—Nicholson's Column expected on the 18th inst.—Delhi powder factory blown up—The 'terrific' Highlanders—Letters to London—Enemy's superiority in guns—Composition of our Force—Army officers not responsible for the Mutiny - - - - - - - 169-195

CHAPTER IX.

SIEGE OF DELHI (*continued*)—CAPTURE OF ENEMY'S GUNS, AND ARRIVAL OF NICHOLSON'S COLUMN.—12th to 18th August.

Massacre at Cawnpore confirmed—Heavy losses of the enemy—Arrival of Nicholson's Column—Havelock's 'Order' to his men—Waiting for the siege-train—Colonel Cotton to command at Agra—Camp 'shaves'—Special Service of Humiliation—Detail of Delhi Field Force—Hodson sent out on an expedition - - 196-218

CHAPTER X.

SIEGE OF DELHI (*continued*).—19th to 24th August.

Sepoys deserting from Delhi—An account of the Delhi massacre—News from Brigadier Neill—Mutiny of 10th Cavalry at Ferozepore—Lieutenant Delafosse's account of the Cawnpore massacre—Arrival of the siege-train at Umballa—Return of Hodson to Camp—Enemy reported in force near Nujufghurh . . . 219–232

CHAPTER XI.

SIEGE OF DELHI (*continued*)—VICTORY OF GENERAL NICHOLSON.—25th to 31st August.

Nicholson's Movable Column sent out to intercept the enemy—Letter from Cawnpore—The 'Mutiny speeches' in the House—Letter from London—Mistaken estimates of Delhi's strength—50th Native Infantry still staunch—Nicholson meets the rebels and defeats them—Return of victorious Column—Enemy attack us in force and lose many guns—Sir Colin Campbell to be Commander-in-Chief—Hodson at Nujufghurh—Siege-train at Kurnaul—Reinforcements at Calcutta and Bombay—Letters from London—Indignation at Home—Indian Mutiny Relief Fund opened at the Mansion House 233–254

CHAPTER XII.

SIEGE OF DELHI (*continued*)—ARRIVAL OF SIEGE-TRAIN.—1st to 13th September.

Letter from Mr Bartle Frere—The mutiny at Aboo—News of the evacuation of Herat by the Persians—Newsletter from Delhi—Preparations for the Assault—Much sickness in Camp—Arrival of the Rifles and Artillery—News of Lucknow—The batteries are commenced, and possession taken of the Koodsee Bagh—Arrival of the Cashmere troops—The Engineers too sanguine—Wilson defended for delaying the Assault—The telegraph established in Camp—Eve of the Assault 255–281

CHAPTER XIII.

ASSAULT AND CAPTURE OF DELHI.—14th to 24th September.

Letter from the Church at Delhi—Telegrams from Delhi to Simla—The Palace is shelled—Brigadier Nicholson dangerously wounded—Many mutineers leave the city—The magazine stormed and taken—Delhi 'plunder'—Death of Mr Colvin at Agra—Gradual occupation of the city—Our losses during the Assault—Burn Bastion and Lahore Gate taken—Palace and Fort evacuated and taken—Death of Mr Greathed—Colonel Keith Young leaves Delhi; his arrival at Simla - - - - - - - 282–301

CHAPTER XIV.

LETTERS RECEIVED OR DESPATCHED AFTER THE FALL OF DELHI.

The Mansion House Mutiny Fund—Ignorance at Home of the causes of the Mutiny—The King of Delhi—Letter from Sir Donald M'Leod - - - - - - - - 302–310

CONDENSED DIARY OF PRINCIPAL EVENTS OF THE SIEGE   313–319

APPENDICES.

A. JOONUG AND THE RANA OF KOOYNTAL - - - 321
B. ESCAPE OF SIR THEOPHILUS METCALFE - - - 324
C. THE FORTIFICATIONS OF DELHI - - - - 326
D. MUTINY OF THE 50TH NATIVE INFANTRY - - - 327
E. THE ORIGIN OF THE SEPOYS BEING CALLED PANDIES - 333
F. LORD LAKE AND DELHI - - - - - 333
G. THE KING AND PRINCES OF DELHI - - - - 333
H. THE MUTINY PREDICTED BY SIR CHARLES NAPIER - 334
I. TRANSLATION OF COSSID LETTER - - - - 335

GLOSSARY OF HINDOOSTANI WORDS - - - 337–340
INDEX TO REGIMENTS AND CORPS - - - 341–344
GENERAL INDEX - - - - - - 345–371

LIST OF ILLUSTRATIONS.

Portrait of Colonel Keith Young when about twenty years of age. (*Photographed from an oil-painting*) *Frontispiece*

Portrait of Colonel Keith Young. (*From a photograph by Mayall taken in 1861, when fifty-three years of age*) *To face page* xi

Portrait of General Sir Henry Wylie Norman, G.C.B., G.C.M.G., C.S.I., Governor of Chelsea Hospital. (*From a photograph by Elliot & Fry*) - - *To face page* 10

'Ellerslie,' Colonel Keith Young's home at Simla *To face page* 16

Portrait of General Sir Arthur Becher, K.C.B. (*From a photograph by A. Bassano*) - - - *To face page* 26

View of the Taj Mahal at Agra - - " 42

The ruins of Kutub Minar near Delhi. (*Showing the iron pillar said by tradition to reach to the centre of the earth*) *To face page* 50

The Purana Kila or Old Fort, near Delhi, on the road to Hamayoon's Tomb - - - *To face page* 64

Portrait of Sir John Lawrence, Commissioner of the Punjab; afterwards Lord Lawrence and Governor-General of India. He was called the 'Saviour of India.' (*From an engraving*) - - *To face page* 79

View of Simla, from a hill called Jakho " 91

Inside the Palace at Delhi; the Dewan-i-Khas or King's private Hall of Audience. (*Round the roof is written, 'If there be a Paradise upon earth, it is this! it is this!'*) *To face page* 103

Carved marble inlaid screen inside the Palace at Delhi - - - - - *To face page* 114

Portrait of Brigadier-General John Nicholson, who was mortally wounded in the assault of Delhi. (*From an engraving*) - - - - - *To face page* 125

View of the Fort at Agra - - - " 130

In the Fort at Agra, the Taj Mahal in the distance *To face page* 149

LIST OF ILLUSTRATIONS.

THE JUMMA MUSJID, OR GREAT MOSQUE OF DELHI *To face page*	158
PORTRAIT OF BRIGADIER-GENERAL SIR HENRY LAWRENCE, K.C.B., WHO WAS KILLED IN LUCKNOW. (*From an engraving*) - - - - - *To face page*	176
BUKTAWA KHAN, THE KING OF DELHI'S GENERAL. (*Facsimile of two humorous pen-and-ink sketches by Captain Maisey*) *To face page*	178
THE RUINS OF KUTUB MINAR, NEAR DELHI - "	194
THE CASHMERE GATE, DELHI - - - "	199
COLOURED PLAN OR MAP OF THE CITY OF DELHI AND SURROUNDING COUNTRY, SHOWING THE POSITION OF OUR CAMP ON THE RIDGE. (*From the original, drawn in the Quartermaster's office in Camp*) - -	
THE MEMORIAL MONUMENT AT CAWNPORE, ERECTED OVER THE WELL TO COMMEMORATE THE MASSACRE - *To face page*	226
FACSIMILE OF A 'COSSID' OR SECRET LETTER, AND OF IMPRESSIONS FROM THE KING OF DELHI'S SEALS. (*The seals were taken from the King by Major Hodson of 'Hodson's Horse,' and these sealing-wax impressions were made from them at Simla towards the end of the year 1857*) - - *To face page*	243
THE MOTEE MUSJID, OR PEARL MOSQUE. (*Inside the Palace at Delhi*) - - - - - *To face page*	262
SKETCHES OF SUGGESTED MUTINY MEDALS AND RIBBONS. (*Drawn by young officers in Camp before Delhi, and also in Camp before Lucknow*) - - *To face page*	274
THE CHANDNEE CHOUK, OR MAIN STREET OF DELHI "	287
THE LAHORE GATE, DELHI - - - "	293
THE DELHI GATE, DELHI - - - "	295
THE TOMB OF HAMAYOON, NEAR DELHI. (*Where the King and Princes took refuge after the capture of the city*) *To face page*	299
VIEW OF ELYSIUM HILL AT SIMLA - - "	308

The photogravures are by Annan of Glasgow, and the collotype illustrations by Frith of Gloucester. The engravings from which—by permission—the photogravures are taken, were published by Graves, of Pall Mall, London.

EXPLANATORY NOTE.

The following pages contain a direct and simple account of the Indian Mutiny, down to the Taking of Delhi, as set forth in extracts from Colonel Keith Young's diaries, in letters from and to friends both in India and in England, in official letters and telegrams, but principally in a series of daily letters written to his wife. The first mention of the rumour of a mutinous spirit shown by the Native soldiers is given in an extract from the diary dated the 24th of February 1857, with which the first chapter begins.

Colonel Keith Young's letters to his wife, which commence on the 25th of May, follow each other, without specially distinctive headings, in almost daily succession till the end of the volume. Most of the other letters and telegrams are placed under the dates when they were written; some, for reasons which explain themselves, appear under the dates when received. Colonel H. B. Henderson's letters from London are placed together at the end of each month.

With the exception of some of the official letters and telegrams, none of the correspondence has ever before been published.

At the end of the book is a Condensed Diary of the principal events of the Siege; also a Glossary, an Index to Regiments and Corps, and a General Index. These, it is hoped, will enhance the value of the book for purposes of reference.

The present volume is confined to the year 1857, and contains the Siege, Assault and Capture of Delhi. Should it be decided to publish more of Colonel Keith Young's Diaries and Letters, Volume II. will give an account of the Siege of Lucknow and the general progress and final suppression of the Mutiny during 1858-59.

M. K. I.

DELHI—1857.

*EXTRACTS FROM THE CORRESPONDENCE AND
DIARY OF COLONEL KEITH YOUNG.*

CHAPTER I.

OUTBREAK OF THE MUTINY.

(*Diary*) *Umballa, 24th February* 1857.—At home all day, except a walk to Chester's * to speak to him about the Barrackpore † disturbances. Sepoys there dissatisfied with the glazed paper used for the Enfield rifle cartridges, saying that there's pig's or cow's fat in it.

Simla, Ellerslie, 18th March.—The case of the 19th Native regiment ‡ to report upon this afternoon.

22nd March.—Write warrant for General Hearsay.§

General ANSON, *Commander-in-Chief, to Colonel* KEITH YOUNG,
Judge-Advocate General.

UMBALLA, *22nd March.*

MY DEAR COLONEL,—I think I cannot well demur to delegate my authority to Major-General Hearsay: Article 73 gives me the

---

* Colonel Chester, Adjutant-General of the Bengal Army.

† The 34th Native Infantry and the 19th Native Infantry were disbanded at Barrackpore on account of their mutinous conduct in connection with greased cartridges. See notes on pp. 2, 5, and 6.

‡ The 19th Native Infantry mutinied at Berhampore; they were marched to Barrackpore, and there disbanded by General Hearsay.

§ General commanding Presidency division. This warrant gave General Hearsay powers to deal at once with the mutinous Sepoys without referring to Head-Quarters.

power. I have not yet seen the warrant; when I have, I may perhaps find it necessary to ask you to come up to me.—Yours truly, GEORGE ANSON.

(*Diary*) 23rd *March*.—More papers about the 19th mutiny affair. Had Mitchell* possessed the confidence of his men, or had he acted judiciously in the first instance, there would have been no row. I am clear for letting the corps, if repentant, volunteer for Persia; but both the Chief and Chester say '*no*.'

General ANSON to Colonel KEITH YOUNG.

UMBALLA, 23rd *March.*

MY DEAR COLONEL,—The warrant to Major-General Hearsay has been forwarded to him to-day. The Governor-General had informed me of the attempt of the 2nd Grenadiers to seduce the Mint guard into the Fort,† but not of the delinquencies of the 70th, which have occurred since he wrote. There has been such an uneasy feeling in the depot here that I thought it right, after I had inspected it this morning, to address the Native officers and detachments on parade. It is a difficult and delicate subject to handle, but I trust that the course I have taken will produce some good. I am not surprised at the objection of the Sepoys, after seeing the quantity of grease (literally fat) which is upon the cartridges; they have not yet been used by the Sepoys, as they were to be made up at Meerut. In the meantime, I have given orders that firing should not be commenced by the Sepoys until I have ascertained whether there is any objectionable material used in the manufacture of the new paper for cartridges.—Yours truly, GEORGE ANSON.

* Colonel Mitchell, of the 19th Native Infantry.

† On the evening of the 10th March two Sepoys of the 2nd Grenadiers (Native Infantry), forming the Native detachment at the Calcutta Fort, appeared at the guard-house at the Mint and tried to persuade the Soubahdar of the guard—furnished by the 34th Native Infantry—to march his men into the Fort, where they were to be joined by the Calcutta Militia. The Soubahdar arrested them, and they were tried and sentenced to imprisonment for fourteen years.

Colonel KEITH YOUNG *to Colonel* H. B. HENDERSON,* *London.*

SIMLA, 24*th March.*

What think you of the mutinous proceedings of the Native regiments at Berhampore and Barrackpore? It is enough to make people open their eyes a little, and shows how frail is the tenure we have upon the—'affection,' I was going to say, but this word is quite misplaced, and I will substitute for it the 'fidelity' of our Native Army. So far as we know yet, the whole business has been caused by an idea that got into the men's heads that pig's and cow's fat was used in the preparation of the cartridges for the Enfield rifles, and I believe that there was some foundation for the report—hog's lard being the proper thing, I fancy, to use. Of course this was put to rights; but their suspicions once roused, the men took to examining the paper with which the cartridges are made up, and they found that some of the paper was highly glazed and would not take up water readily when soaked in it. This was enough—there must be fat of some kind in the paper, and it was found impossible to disabuse the minds of the men of this strange notion; and hence the disaffection, which it remains to be seen how Government will dispose of. I imagine it will terminate in the disbandment, at any rate, of the 19th; but if I had my way I would let them go to Persia or China, if they would come forward repentantly and volunteer.

The Commander-in-Chief is expected here on the 1st April, and by that time all the Staff will be congregated at Simla.

(*Diary*) 28*th March.*—At work all the morning at that mutiny case of the two men of the 2nd Native Infantry that came in this morning. Finish it, and get it off for the Chief by post-time.

31*st March.*—Letter from the Chief to say he will be in to-morrow to see me at noon.

1*st April.*—Getting papers ready for the Chief. Note from Curzon to say he (the Chief) will see me at half-past twelve.

---

* Late of the 9th Native Infantry—for some time Acting Auditor-General at Calcutta. He was the originator and organiser of the 'Mutiny Relief Fund.'

Go accordingly, and settle off the mutineers of the 2nd Native Infantry, and several other cases. The Chief is looking very well.

General ANSON *to Colonel* KEITH YOUNG.

SIMLA, 7*th April.*

MY DEAR COLONEL,—I have received an account of the proceedings at Barrackpore, and of the outrage committed by the Sepoys, though not in such detail. It's a bad state of things, but it is well that we should know it and thus be able to deal with it properly. I hope the trial will not be moved to Calcutta: it should be on the spot; and with the European force there present there would be no risk. However, this will be decided by the Government, who, I have no doubt, will act with firmness.—Yours truly, GEORGE ANSON.

(*Diary*) 8*th April.*—His Excellency spoke to me of the order disbanding the 19th—does not approve. Too diffuse, in my opinion. He says he thinks it's Lord Canning's own.

11*th April.*—The trial of the Jemadar of the 70th came in this morning. Work at it, and get it off to the Chief at about one.

General ANSON *to Colonel* KEITH YOUNG.

SIMLA, 13*th April.*

MY DEAR COLONEL,—Many thanks. Nothing can be worse than the Jemadar's case. I am glad to hear that the excitement in the cartridge question is subsiding. I hope it is so.—Yours truly, GEORGE ANSON.

Colonel HAMPTON, *commanding the* 50*th Native Infantry, to Colonel* KEITH YOUNG.

DINAPORE, 14*th April.*

I am truly glad in being able to tell you, in these days of trouble, that the good and dear old corps is in a perfect state of tranquillity and contentment; indeed, I never knew the men more orderly or more obedient to command. This you may easily imagine when I tell you that three men only have been sent to drill for the last month, and those only for very minor offences, such as dirty buttons and hair too long! Don't laugh —we all have a weakness, and you may recollect my dislike to 'curls!'

I am very sorry for old Mitchell. He could have known but little of either officers or men, and they nothing of him. I view the conduct of the men of the 34th Native Infantry in a far worse light than that of the 19th, and only trust they will get severely handled—the wretches! Wheler* ought to be made either to give up preaching or the command of a Native regiment—that's certain.

(*Diary*) 15*th April.*—Heard from Curzon this morning that His Excellency would not see me till half-past one; so took my time, and I need not have hurried, as he didn't make his appearance till about half-past two. Not much work for him. The trial of the man of the 34th who shot at the Adjutant,† submitted by me to His Excellency, disposed of before, however, by General Hearsay.

16*th April.*—Before I was dressed got a note from the Chief, with a telegraphic message from Government wanting His Excellency to give a warrant to General Hearsay to carry out sentence on Native commissioned officers. Found it could not be done, but His Excellency thought otherwise. He, however, came round to my opinion in the afternoon when I went over to him, and a telegraphic message was sent to Government accordingly.

General ANSON *to Colonel* KEITH YOUNG.

SIMLA, 16*th April.*

MY DEAR COLONEL,—What is the meaning of this telegraphic message just received? I thought that the warrant that was sent to Major-General Hearsay gave him all the powers he needed, and

* Colonel Wheler, of the 34th Native Infantry.
† The man was Mangul Pandy, whose name was supposed to be the origin of the Sepoys being called *Pandies*. (See Appendix *E*.) The Adjutant was Lieutenant Baugh. Pandy was executed.

that the execution of the Sepoy * had been carried out under them. If it does not extend to Native commissioned officers, I imagine the power must be given him, as the Government desire it. The message to say so had better be sent by express to Umballa and be forwarded by telegraph from there, and the warrant by this day's dâk.—Yours truly, GEORGE ANSON.

SIMLA, 19th *April*.

MY DEAR COLONEL,—It is most satisfactory to find that the Court have done their duty. I wish that the sentence could have been carried out at once without my confirmation. If you think it would be desirable that any remarks should be made on the enormity of the crime, it may be as well to prepare them. It may be difficult, however, to allude to anything but the facts that appear upon the evidence, with a general warning to the Army. —Yours truly, GEORGE ANSON.

SIMLA, 20th *April*.

MY DEAR COLONEL,—I think it will be better for me to confirm the sentence on Isurree Pandy, as it will be granted sooner than by warrant granted to General Hearsay. I think I can grant the warrant according to the meaning of the Act. If you have received the proceedings and come up *earlier* than two o'clock, I will attend to your business and defer any other.—Yours truly,
GEORGE ANSON.

SIMLA, 20th *April*.

MY DEAR COLONEL,—Telegraphic message just received. Did I see Section 6 of Victoria 7, Chapter XVIII.? The question is whether to send the warrant asked for, or to confirm the sentence by telegraph when the proceedings of trial are received. We ought to hear to-morrow at latest, and the last mode, if regular, would now be the quickest.—Yours truly, GEORGE ANSON.

(*Diary*) *Monday*, 20th *April*.—Woke up at about 3.30 this morning by the arrival of an express containing the trial of the

---

* Isurree Pandy, a Jemadar (Native Lieutenant) of the 34th Native Infantry, who forbade his men to aid their officers when Mangul Pandy mutinied.

Jemadar of the 34th. With the Chief about it; and His Excellency decides on sending telegraphic message to carry out sentence of death passed on Jemadar. I go to Chester's with it, and then to the post-office, sending it off by express—the first time, I fancy, that an execution has been ordered by telegraph.

22nd April.—To the Chief's at twelve, but little work for him. He read me part of a letter from Lord Canning, who, it appears, spoke to Mr Peacock * about ordering the execution of a sentence of death by electric telegraph, and he saw no objection to it; so we are all right.

General ANSON *to Colonel* KEITH YOUNG.

SIMLA, 23rd April.

MY DEAR COLONEL,—There seems to be no help for it in these cases. The sentence is certainly inadequate to their offence. I am rather of opinion that they might have been put upon their trials under Article 33. I think that the conduct of the prisoners was an 'insult to the religious prejudices of the Jemadar.' However, having been tried and sentenced to dismissal, I see no other course than to allow the sentence of dismissal to be carried out. I am not inclined to doubt their wish to be discharged, and it is therefore in fact no punishment; but they will be well got rid of.—Yours truly,   GEORGE ANSON.

SIMLA, *27th April.*

MY DEAR COLONEL,—I entirely agree with you that warrants should be given to officers commanding divisions to empower them to deal summarily with all such cases of insubordination as this in the 3rd Light Cavalry.† It is equally necessary in the event of the detection of an incendiary, which I hope is not so hopeless as Major Harriott ‡ predicts. The measures adopted seem to be judicious. If there has been no harshness on the part of the commander or other officers, and if this turns out to be a pre-

---

* The Legal Member of the Supreme Council.

† Commanded by Colonel Smyth at Meerut; the first Cavalry regiment that mutinied.

‡ Deputy Judge-Advocate at Meerut.

determined combination of the troopers of the 3rd Light Cavalry, it is unpardonable after the issue of the order on the disbandment of the 19th Native Infantry, and I am satisfied that the right way of dealing with it will be to order the summary discharge of the whole of the men who refused to take the cartridges. We have the 60th Rifles and European Artillery, which will render such a proceeding perfectly safe. The burning of the Havildar's hut simultaneously with this act of mutiny proves that it is an organised system of the Sepoys, and it *must be stopped.* You had better prepare the warrants at once for the Meerut and Sirhind divisions.—Yours truly, GEORGE ANSON.

(*Diary*) *28th April.*—To-day's *Calcutta* mentions that the Jemadar, 34th Native Infantry, was hanged last Tuesday afternoon, the 21st. The order only left here the day before about 3 P.M.

29th April.—Busy this morning with the 3rd Cavalry cartridge case—a bad business; hope they will be well punished. Order given for the trial of the offenders by General Court-Martial. Long talk with the Chief on the subject of the disaffection; he is very irate with Government apparently for having appointed an officer of the 19th—McAndrew—to the Staff. Call on Chester about the 3rd Cavalry affair, and then ride to post-office with telegraphic message to General Hewitt* to recall Harriott.

1st May.—All this morning busy with that case of Jemadar Salikram, which has come up from Calcutta; and though it is now nearly five o'clock, the Chief has not sent my man back yet who took the papers to him at about one. Get them at last, and he approves of my views.

General ANSON *to Colonel* KEITH YOUNG.

SIMLA, *2nd May.*

MY DEAR COLONEL,—Major Harriott will, of course, remain at Meerut. It will be advisable to tell him *not* to go until we are satisfied that he will not be wanted for any further cases of this description.—Yours truly, GEORGE ANSON.

* General Commanding at Meerut.

Colonel KEITH YOUNG *to Colonel* H. B. HENDERSON, *London.*

SIMLA, 2*nd May.*

Harry is well, and full of his homeward trip at the end of the year, and nothing so far as human eye can see is likely to interfere with his plans, unless we are all 'kicked out' of India before then by our mutinous Native Army. I suppose the late accounts received of their doings are making a great stir at home; and well they may. There is no little uneasiness felt in India on the subject, for the disaffection appears so universal that I am quite prepared to see it show itself at any of our stations. Barrackpore, they say, is now quieted down, and the neck of the Mutiny has been broken there by the late examples made. But we have the open refusal to obey orders to deal with in the 3rd Cavalry at Meerut, where nearly one hundred men point-blank refused to load their carbines with cartridges—the cartridges being just the same that had been in use in the regiment for the last thirty years; and to-day I understand that a party of Artillery recruits at Meerut have refused to use the common cartridges also. I have seen no official report of this latter affair yet; but as to the 3rd Cavalry, orders went off some days ago to try them all by General Court-Martial, and I hope to hear before the week is over that all are at work on the roads, or that some have been hanged—if there is any more open resistance to authority on their part than has yet appeared. I am convinced that sharp and severe measures are the only ones left to us if we wish to quell the mutinous spirit now so prevalent; and every general officer of division is being furnished with authority to deal with cases at once as they arise, without sending up the trials to Head-Quarters. My old Chief, poor old Sir Charles Napier, would be the man for the present occasion. Decisive action is everything in such emergencies, and he was just the man to act with energy.

All the Native troops in the Punjab are quiet and well-behaved at present; but there is no saying how long it may be so, for this business in the 3rd Cavalry was the last thing in the world to have expected, the Cavalry having hitherto always refrained from joining the Infantry in their mutinous proceedings. There is no doubt of the fact of the Enfield rifle cartridges having been served out in the first instance, reeking with all kinds of abominable grease stuff that was supplied to the Arsenal by contractors, and very much to blame are Government and all the authorities whose duty it was to have had things better ordered. These cartridges are made the rallying-point on the part of the disaffected; but there must be other causes for the wide-spread feeling of disaffection existing in the minds of the Sepoys, but what these causes are no one has been able yet to ascertain from themselves, and we are left to our own surmises on the subject. To my mind, the one great cause of complaint is the difficulty there now is for a man, Native officer or Sepoy, getting on the Pension Establishment, and there is no chance whatever of his being granted a pension as long as he can put one foot before another; so a commanding officer of a regiment, do what he will, cannot get rid of useless, worn-out men, who are sent back to him by the invaliding committees to become a source of discontent in the corps. Norman,* our Assistant Adjutant-General, who is a very smart young officer, told me of an instance within his knowledge of every man who was sent before the invaliding committee of a certain regiment having been rejected, except one, and that poor fellow died before his papers could be made out for pension. At Bombay, where the Army has always been in a more contented state than here, the invaliding rules are quite different, and men are admitted to pensions there—if pronounced unfit by the regimental authorities— who would be kept on the strength of the Army for years longer in Bengal. Another thing, I firmly believe, is that the Army is well aware of the secondary position their officers are made to hold, and of the little power they have and can exercise; and during the late régime, particularly of Lord Dalhousie, no pains were spared by him to show the paramount nature of his power at the expense of the military, and his Council, it strikes me, were walking much in the same direction. The well-being of the Army, in fact, and its officers, was a secondary consideration, and the Sepoys knew it; and the authority, particularly of commanding officers, has become much weakened in consequence. But I must quit the subject— though I could write a great deal more about it. In the end I have no doubt things will terminate satisfactorily, but we may have one or two awkward incidents yet to dispose of.

* Now General Sir Henry W. Norman, G.C.B., G.C.M.G.

(*Diary*) 6*th May.*—Talk with His Excellency about the indiscipline of the Army, and a necessity of a revision of the Native invaliding rules.

8*th May.*—Employed most of the day with the trial of the Umballa Jemadar, 5th Native Infantry, which I got the Chief to dispose of by the evening.

12*th May.*—Bad news in from Delhi this morning, which Chester, on his way from the Chief's, came to tell me of. Mutineers from Meerut have seized the bridge at Delhi; and, I fear, the men of the 3rd who were condemned to ten years' imprisonment with hard labour were under a Native guard, and escaped. Over at Chester's to take a walk, but stopped at the Chief's. A letter came from Waterfield, of 10th; fighting at Meerut, and it seems that the sentence on men of the 3rd had been carried out.

13*th May.*—An anxious time—no dâk in from Umballa. The 75th were to have marched yesterday evening, and to go on straight to Moohurckpore, about half-way to Umballa. Over at the Chief's and had a long talk with him; he appears to rather pooh-pooh the thing. We shall see.

14*th May.*—Bad news in—the Chief and Chester off in the middle of the day. A meeting at Mr Petersen's* to arrange for the defence of Simla. From the meeting I went to see Mrs Wyld, where I found F. The Goorkha corps at Jutogh said to be disaffected; and I wanted F. to go down to Umballa, and Mrs Wyld also. But no; she (Mrs Wyld) came and slept with us at Peskett's, where there were a great number collected.

15*th May.*—Got home soon after sunrise. An excellent letter from Maisey† giving an account of the Meerut and Delhi disasters. Everything apparently getting on as well as can be expected. Hear a rumour of the Goorkha corps (Nusseree battalion) in open mutiny, and refusing to march. Ride towards Boileaugunge— great alarm—many cutting off. At Peskett's garden, and then to the Rana's ‡ place.

16*th May.*—Home at sunrise. All quiet. Two Sepoys came to the house soon after I got there—very civil, and declared

* A large shop near the Simla Bank.
† Deputy Judge-Advocate at Umballa.
‡ The Rana Sansar Sain of Kooyntal, a hill Raja. See Appendix *A*.

they never intended to alarm any of the '*Sahib-Logue.*' The scoundrels! Determine after due consideration to go and sleep at the Rana's again, and to start at moonrise in the early morning for Joonug, his country-seat, some twelve miles off; arrange accordingly, send everything off, and go and dine at about four at General Gowan's, May Day Hill. Our old party and Mrs Daly came and joined us.

17th May.—Off with difficulty about 4 A.M.—dreadful scrimmage; reach Joonug about eight o'clock. Such a scene of confusion!

Colonel KEITH YOUNG *to Colonel* H. B. HENDERSON, *London.*

JOONUG, 17*th May.*

I write a line to tell you that there is not a word of truth in the reported 'Simla Massacre.' F. and I, and the dear *Babas*, are as well as you could wish, enjoying ourselves at this place, some sixteen miles from Simla. We came out here this morning—'fled,' you may say—for fear of the mutineering Nusseree battalion at Jutogh rising against us and resorting to deeds of violence. We are here under the protection of a friendly Raja, and shall probably remain two or three days longer, and then return to Simla or go on to one of the European hill cantonments as circumstances may render desirable. I haven't the least fear myself of the Goorkhas having recourse to violence under any possible contingencies, but the late dreadful excesses at Meerut and Delhi have made everybody over-anxious, and had we remained at Simla, F. would have been about the only lady there; and as all the rest of the Head-Quarter officers had left the day before yesterday, there was no use of my staying on in an official point of view. Any day, however, the Chief may send for me to go down and join him.

It is a very nice, pretty country where we are now located, and except that our accommodation is rather confined, we have nothing to complain of. Our party consists of Colonel and Mrs Greathed, and the wife of the Umballa Brigadier, Mrs Hallifax; and in the adjacent houses and tents there must be some forty ladies and gentlemen, and nearly double the number of children.

You will see by the papers much later and fuller accounts of what has been going on than I can give you. My own impression is that if we retake Delhi soon, everything will be satisfactorily settled with a little management; but there is no doubt of matters being very serious, and necessarily causing much anxiety. Very much depends on the fidelity of the Puttiala Raja, who is now assisting us, and it is generally considered that he is staunch; he has proved himself to be so before on other trying occasions. Under any circumstances, we are all quite safe so long as we remain here; but if everything goes on as satisfactorily as it has done lately (that is, within the last four or five days), we may expect to return to our own house at Simla directly—unless General Anson commands the Army advancing on Delhi in person, in which case I shall join him, leaving F. at Simla. I am very much afraid of the great change of climate having a very bad effect on Chester, who was far from well when he went down.

WM. DE RHÉ PHILIPE, *Head Clerk Judge-Advocate General's Office, to Colonel* KEITH YOUNG.

SIMLA, 19*th May*.

DEAR SIR,—All continues quiet. The Bank is open for business again. Mr Petersen's, Ford & Self's, Anderson's, and Crayden's shops open, but not doing much business, I suppose. Library and bazaar open as usual. A clothman upset his light in the night and set his goods on fire, but no alarm occurred.

The Kussowlie guard stopped our outgoing mail on Sunday night, and burnt it somewhere below Jutogh. On rejoining there was a bit of a scrimmage, which ended in twenty-four of them, or thereabouts, being placed in confinement, and six deserting. The runners now come up the valleys, so that great delay occurs and no dâk is in yet. The post-office *baboo* has been appointed officiating Postmaster in succession to Mr D. Colyear, absent without leave. Hindoostanee servants, taking advantage of the absence of residents, beginning to steal; two were apprehended by the police last night, I hear.

I am glad to hear that the troops are on the move from Umballa by this time. Delaying for a siege-train would have had a bad effect; a prompt blow will be half the battle. I heard to-day that the communication with Calcutta had been re-established, but no positive signs of it are apparent. I am told that guards have been sent out to Joonug, Solon, &c.—I am, dear Sir, yours obediently, WM. DE RHÉ PHILIPE.

(*Diary*) 18*th May.*—Very hot day in a wretchedly small outhouse. Colonel and Mrs Greathed and Mrs Hallifax join us there. But we are comfortable to a degree compared to the other house, where are the Pennys and some twenty others. Early in the morning Greathed goes in to Simla and brings out word of the Kussowlie treasury having been plundered by the Goorkha guard; but the regiment are making the guard prisoners. People talk of returning to their houses.

19*th May.*—Great preparations for returning to Simla. About three, or earlier, the people began to start; and such a confusion about coolies! I went to assist them in getting away with all the little children, and a great business it was. Lend Mrs Nicoll our *janpanees*, so have to wait here till they return. Pay a visit to the Rana's house and garden.

20*th May.*—Prepare for our leaving after *tiffin*, but do not get away till close upon five. Alarm on the road from Rana's son that there was heavy firing all Monday night (18th) and Tuesday morning at Umballa: this turns out to be false. Get into Simla at about 10 P.M. Find Ellerslie just in the same state as we left it.

21*st May.*—Out rather early—call on Penny, Lord William Hay,* &c. Everything said to be quiet. The Goorkha corps has consented — obliging scoundrels — to march on Saturday; it remains to be seen if they will go.

22*nd May.*—Go out before breakfast; meet Sir Edward Campbell,† and we call on Paton, the Postmaster-General. Dâks in this morning, but not much news except from the Punjab, where all seems going on well.

23*rd May.*—Dâk in early this morning, and letters from Chester at last telling me to go down and join Head-Quarters. Call on Lord William Hay about carriage. No mules to be had until to-morrow. The Goorkha corps were to march this afternoon; it seems they haven't gone, but will go to-morrow: they appear to have it all their own way. Out shopping in the evening getting things for my journey.

* Deputy Commissioner of Simla—present Marquis of Tweeddale.
† Of the 60th Rifles.

Colonel CHESTER, *Adjutant-General, to Colonel* KEITH YOUNG.

UMBALLA, 22*nd May.*

I have just returned from the Commander-in-Chief, who wishes you to come down and join him, as your presence would seem necessary for the 'trial and hanging of mutineers.' I mean to give advice in the matter. I told you yesterday you should have room in my tent, and you are more than welcome to this. Mrs Chester goes up immediately. I write this in great haste to go by the early dâk.—Yours ever,   C. CHESTER.

P.S.—The treaty of peace with Persia has been ratified, and the troops are returning from Bushire 'in full steam,' to be made available to repair our damage in upper India. British troops also ordered round from Madras, Ceylon, and Maulmein. This comes from the Governor-General. The Commander-in-Chief will push on to Kurnaul most likely to-morrow or next day.

(*Diary*) 24*th May.*—The Goorkhas have gone. Mules have come. Call on Greathed, &c. Start at nearly five, and reach Hurreepore.

CHAPTER II.

AN ACCOUNT OF THE OUTBREAK.

Mrs KEITH YOUNG *to her sister in London.*

ELLERSLIE, SIMLA, 14*th May.*

We are living here in strangely unsettled times. You will remember my having mentioned in one of my late letters that a mutinous spirit had been shown by many of the Sepoys on account of these over-greased cartridges. But this, seemingly, is merely the excuse for mutiny, for men who have not been called upon to use these cartridges have mutinied. When, on account of the Crimean War our Home Government withdrew so many British troops from India, it was said here at the time, 'How wrong! If the Natives should seize the opportunity to turn against us, what could be done with so few Queen's regiments?' It has proved only too true. On Tuesday morning, the 12th instant, Captain Barnard (General Barnard's son and Aide-de-Camp) came up from Umballa as fast as horses could bring him, with a report to General Anson, Commander-in-Chief, of an electric telegraphic message having been received from Delhi, dated the 10th, saying that the regiments there had mutinied, joined with others from Meerut, seized the bridge of boats, and that several officers had been killed.

On Sunday two regiments at Umballa were in open mutiny; but they were quieted, and went away to their lines without using their firearms, though they threatened their officers. On Tuesday evening we were dining at the Chesters', when the Commander-in-Chief came there with a message from Captain Waterfield from Meerut—brought by runners, as the electric wire had been cut—saying that the station was burning in all directions, several officers

(SIMLA.) "ELLERSLIE."
Colonel Keith Young's House.

killed, and the place in a state of siege. It seems most extraordinary, for at Meerut there are only three Native Infantry regiments. They must have attacked the European soldiers as they were coming out of church, getting between them and their arms; or else, perhaps, our troops had marched over to defend Delhi, leaving Meerut at the mercy of the Native Infantry regiments. There has been no news since from Meerut. No dâk came in yesterday either from Delhi or Meerut, which is a bad sign.

Late last night (we only heard of it this morning) a message came from Delhi saying that all the regiments there had turned against their officers. The magazine on the banks of the river was blown up, it seems, by one of our sergeants, who sacrificed himself to prevent all the ammunition from falling into the hands of the Sepoys. We hear that Mr Frazer, the judge, is killed. Captain Douglas, Mr Beresford (Civil Service), Colonel Ripley, who commanded one of the Native Infantry regiments, and other officers have all been killed—murdered. Is it not dreadful?

The Chief is going down to Umballa to-day—Colonel Chester, Colonel Becher, and Captain Norman go also—together with his personal Staff. Keith, I am thankful to say, has not to go down; at least he has received no orders as yet. This is no time for Judge-Advocates, but for summary vengeance.

It is said that all the city of Delhi have risen, with the King at their head, and that the Sepoys have joined them. The ladies and the children in the city have been murdered; those in cantonments have escaped to Kurnaul, and are now on their way to Umballa. Government will now, too late, see the folly of leaving a large Native city like Delhi without any British troops, with the magazine—I believe the very largest in India—in the heart of the city. Of course they have taken that, and seized upon all the arms.

I hear that there is a general feeling among the Natives that our Government is trying to make Christians of them by these unclean cartridges, and by mixing with their *attar* (flour) beef and pig's bones finely ground. Some months ago I was sending some whole wheat to a little mill on a stream a short distance from Simla to be ground—it makes such nice brown bread. We had often found our bread gritty with dust. My *ayah*, when she heard that I was sending this wheat, asked me to send some for her also, as there was a report in the bazaar that all the flour was mixed with the bones, finely ground, of cows and pigs. I laughed at her, and said, '*Ayah*, what nonsense! Who says so?' She replied, 'It is quite true; all the bazaar people say so.' I thought it meant merely that the *bunniahs* (merchants) did it to increase the weight of their flour.

Friday morning, 15th May.—I went yesterday to see poor Mrs Nicoll. She was in great distress. She says all her hope for the safety of her husband rests on not having seen his name among those killed. She had heard nothing of or from him. The Bechers also are in great distress. Colonel Becher's only sister married Mr Hutchinson, a civilian at Delhi: they can get no tidings of them. Yesterday another message came from Meerut, better on the whole than was expected. The two Native Infantry regiments had turned upon their officers, and killed several—among others Major Macdonald of the 20th, his wife, and three children. We saw them constantly when we were at Meerut. The Native Infantry lines are some distance from the European; but directly it was known, the 6th Dragoons and the 60th Rifles marched upon them and soon sent them flying on the road to Delhi. The Carabineers lost six men, and the Rifles seven; but it seems so extraordinary that they did not pursue the wretches and cut them in pieces as they did the little children. General Hewitt's house at Meerut has been burned; also Mr Greathed's (the Commissioner), and several others. Mr Greathed and his wife were saved by their servants, who hid them in the garden.

All the British regiments have left the hills, and the Goorkha regiment at Jutogh was ordered yesterday to start early the next morning (this morning, the 15th). At four o'clock yesterday there was a report that they had refused to go, and that they would attack Simla and loot it instead. Our Commissioner (Lord William Hay) and others said it was merely report, and that the regiment was staunch; however, some of the Goorkhas were seen in the bazaar laughing and talking about the Delhi business, and when an Englishman passed he was hissed at. Another report had spread that they intended to go down as ordered, but would join either Europeans or Natives, whichever was strongest. Most of the English here, therefore, became alarmed; a meeting was held at 4 P.M., and it was decided that pickets should be placed at distances all along the road. In case of an alarm two guns were to be fired, a signal that all the people were to collect at the Bank, which was to be defended by the gentlemen and tradespeople of the place. There are very few gentlemen now at Simla, as all on leave have been ordered to rejoin their regiments.

Thursday passed quietly, but many frightening reports were abroad. The general belief was that the Goorkha regiment from Jutogh would attack Simla that night, so there were meetings at the different houses, and also at the church. Ourselves and about seventy others went to Dr Peskett's. The house looked more like a crowded steamer than anything else. The floor of every room was perfectly covered: there were more than thirty children. None of us could close our eyes all night, we were all listening for the guns; but morning came quite quietly, and now I am writing from our own house.

This morning Keith received a long letter from his Deputy at Umballa. All quiet there. He sends copies that have been received of the messages from Delhi and Kurnaul. The King has proclaimed himself as King of Delhi, and all the people have turned against us, and they have been joined by seven of our own Sepoy regiments. Brigadier Graves from Delhi has reported himself to be at Kurnaul with seven other officers, all that are left of the large number that were at Delhi; Captain Nicoll is among the number, also twelve ladies.

2 P.M., 15th May.—I have just returned from seeing Mrs Nicoll and Mrs Cave-Brown. The former has received a letter from her husband, and is very happy; but the poor lady who is staying with her, Mrs Galloway, whose husband is in the Civil Service at Delhi, can hear nothing of him—he, Sir Theophilus Metcalfe, and Mr Hutchinson have not been heard of since the outbreak: the only hope is that they have been hidden by some faithful servant in the city.

The Chief is blamed. He has not been trained as a soldier, and seems unable to grasp the importance of the situation. When he first received the bad news on Tuesday morning, he ought to have started off at once. Colonel Becher, Quartermaster-General, did his utmost to persuade him not to lose any time: but he said *no;* he would wait for the dâk. What is the use of the electric telegraph if the news it brings is not at once to be attended to? When the Chief left, Mr Mayne rode part of the way down the hill with him, and begged and prayed him to send up fifty soldiers, and not to leave Simla quite unprotected. He refused, saying he could not spare a single man.

Thursday, 21st May.—Soon after I had left off writing on Friday last, Keith, who had been out for some hours to inquire into the state of affairs, came home, and I saw immediately that something was wrong. He said, 'The Goorkhas are up in arms against us; you must start at once for the Bank.' I rushed upstairs to have the children dressed, and ordered two *janpans* to be ready—one to be taken at once to a friend, Mrs Poulton. When ready, Keith told us to go on immediately and he would follow on horseback. The Bank is about two miles from our house, and the *janpan* was carried so slowly that I gave up all hope of ever getting there. We met heaps of Natives from the bazaar rushing past us. Some said, 'The Goorkhas are quite close;' others said, 'They have not yet left Jutogh.' Just as Keith had caught us up, I saw through the fluttering curtains of the *janpan* some one rushing towards us with a drawn sword glittering in his hand. For a moment I believed it to be one of the Goorkhas. It was Dr Peskett turning back all the *janpans*. He called out, 'Turn back; it is too late to get to the Bank; the Goorkhas are close by. The ladies had better go to my house; and, come along, Young—Greathed—we must have a stand for it at the entrance to the bazaar!' He was very excited. My first thought was for Keith's pistols, which were in a case at my feet. When I gave them to him I quite thought I was looking at him for the last time, for we knew well that a few men, brave and determined as they were, could not stand for ten minutes against five hundred well-armed Goorkhas. Dr Peskett advised us all (many other *janpans* had come up) to go down to a little garden-house of his, low down the *khud*,* as being safer than his house on the *mall*. Had it not been for the two little sons, I would have followed Keith and the others to see the result. If the Goorkhas had commenced to attack the people, not a soul would have escaped, and we might just as well have died together.

Soon after we had reached the little house Colonel Greathed made his appearance, and gave the good news that the Goorkhas, though

* A very precipitous bank.

in a state of open mutiny, were still at Jutogh. We heard some time afterwards that they were prevented from leaving by one of the hill Rajas who was faithful to us, and who told them that if they went to Simla to do harm he would throw his soldiers among their women and children.

Keith, Dr Peskett, and several other men joined us at the garden shed, and soon afterwards we heard the two guns—the signal of danger—and then servants came down bringing reports. They said that Major Bagot, the commanding officer, had been killed: we heard later that this was not true. I was trying to silence the servant who brought this news, for Mrs Hallifax, who was near, was the mother of Major Bagot's wife. She quietly said, 'Oh, I heard; and very likely my daughter has been killed also.'

The Goorkhas had pushed back their officers with their bayonets, and had placed a guard over them, but treated them otherwise with respect. When they heard the two guns fired, their yells, we were told afterwards, were heard two miles off like a continual roar.

We remained in Dr Peskett's little house until about 7 P.M.; and then we went to a sort of shed belonging to one of the hill Rajas, about two miles off, and there we spent the night. Early the next morning we went up again to our respective houses at Simla, packed up a few things, determining to go back to the same place in the evening, for the reports in Simla were anything but cheering. Two Goorkhas came up and spoke to us; they said we need not fear, they would not hurt the '*Sahib-Logue.*' The only person they wanted to make their *salaam* to was the 'Lord-*Sahib !*' *

In the evening we started for the same place, spent the night there, and at 2 A.M., when the moon was up, started for Joonug, from where Keith wrote to you. It is about fifteen miles from Simla; the road there is very bad. The Rana is loyal. We remained at Joonug for three days. We were at first shown into a large sort of hall, just crowded with people, and a babel of noise and confusion; so we quietly slipped out, and Keith asked one of the Rana's servants if we could have an outhouse of some sort; he took us to a little room up a narrow stair, over a stable or

---

* The Native troops thought that General Anson was commissioned to convert them.

hen-house. He had it made nice and clean; some rough matting on the floor, and two *charpoys* * were put in. Colonel and Mrs Greathed joined us there, and we had a fairly comfortable night —at least we ladies and the children (our two boys) had. Our husbands stood at the head of the little staircase quietly talking the whole night long, it seemed to me; but really the morning was dawning when we reached Joonug. We remained for three days in this little mud room, without windows, and one door that could be shut up like the shutter of a shop.

Some of the gentlemen, we hear, have behaved so badly, showing shocking cowardice—men who, one would have thought, would have braved anything. People are never known until they are tried.

When we were returning last night from Joonug we met the Rana's son, who told us that heavy firing had been heard all Tuesday, and Tuesday night, in the direction of Umballa. If this was really the case, we feared that the Puttiala Raja, a man whose assistance we could not do without, had turned against us; but, like many other reports, it proved to be quite false. Report killed four persons within three days, and buried one—giving all particulars; but they are all alive and well!

A number of people, we find, have gathered at Dugshai and Kussowlie. In the former place cholera has broken out; two little children died of it a few days ago. But no wonder, people are so crowded together—forty in one house; and the barracks are full. Rations are served out to the women and children, meals for all being cooked together.

The particulars of the massacre at Delhi are most dreadful. Mr Frazer, the Commissioner, was wounded in the right arm; he immediately had it amputated, and then went to the Palace to try and pacify the King. He had an interview with him, and as he was coming out the Palace guards cut him down. Mr Beresford of the Delhi Bank, his wife, and three children were attacked and murdered in their own house. Two grown-up daughters, young girls of seventeen and eighteen, escaped to an outhouse. The brutes followed them; some went into the house and forced them to go out, while others shot them as they passed through the door. Mr Jennings, the clergyman, and his young daughter, a beautiful

* A small Native bed.

girl, just engaged to be married to Mr Thomason, son of the former Lieutenant-Governor of the Punjab, were murdered. Many others were killed. Sir Theophilus Metcalfe cut his way through the city at full gallop, and escaped just before the gates were closed. His beautifully furnished house, containing many rare and valuable things, was plundered and destroyed.

It seems that when the regiments mutinied at Meerut, after killing their officers they went over to Delhi. When their approach was known at Delhi, Brigadier Graves ordered the 54th to stop their progress over the bridge of boats. The wretches, instead of doing so, got ready, and then turned round and shot their officers. Only one escaped: he was saved by his own company. All the regiments in Delhi turned upon their officers, and they had it all their own way, for there were no European troops in the place. It is hearing of all these horrors, and of what these creatures can do, that makes us all so nervous. Every day some frightening report reaches us. We have nothing, we believe, to fear from the Goorkhas; they evidently like their own way, but seem inclined to no acts of violence.

Monday, 25th May.—Have just time to add a few lines. I am really unhappy now, for Keith has gone; he started yesterday evening to join the Commander-in-Chief. They were to march from Umballa yesterday—our Queen's birthday—a good day for a commencement. The Goorkha regiment marched from Jutogh yesterday, at last obeying orders, though now they say they will not go farther than Kalka—the foot of the hill. I am very anxious to hear of Keith's safe arrival in camp. He is to share a tent with Colonel Chester, Captain Norman, and Dr Mactier, so will be well taken care of. May God guard and protect him!

CHAPTER III.

ADVANCE ON DELHI.

Colonel KEITH YOUNG *to his wife.*

KUSSOWLIE, *Monday, 25th May* (3 P.M.).

Here I am quite well, having arrived this morning without any trouble or annoyance. The rain overtook us at Boileaugunge; but, with the assistance of the waterproof, I escaped a ducking. We were only, however, able to get as far as Hurreepore last night. The Goorkhas have gone down the hill to Kalka, and no further apprehensions need be felt about them now at Simla.

I write this from Mrs James Becher's, where I am going to *tiff* (lunch); and purpose leaving for Kalka this evening, and probably shall go with Dr Faithful to Umballa by buggy-dâk in the morning. The road is perfectly open and safe, and ladies continually coming.

Mrs Chester is very well, and Chester much better than she expected. Mrs Arthur Becher also here, very well. Mrs Chester will remain here for the present. Dr Nisbett has been detained at Umballa, there not being a single medical man in that place. Mrs Norman is also here, but I have not seen her yet; and many other ladies. Mrs Chester would go to Simla at once, but she promised Chester not to leave Umballa until she heard from him. The Chief was to have left for Kurnaul yesterday, and expected to remain there some days; so I have plenty of time to join. All officers are ordered to join their regiments.

(*Diary*) *25th May.*—Off as soon after daybreak as I can manage it—go through Sabathoo; the Goorkhas just precede us as we reach Kussowlie, and go through gently. See Bagot; full of complaints of the treatment of the Goorkhas—the scoundrels!

UMBALLA HOTEL, *Tuesday, 26th May.*

I have not loitered long on the road; by my letter of yesterday, from Kussowlie, you would have had tidings of me so far. I came down as I had intended in the evening after paying Mrs Norman a visit: she was very amusing about the flight on Friday afternoon to Solon and Dugshai. I reached Kalka in time to have a little dinner with Bagot, who declares his regiment to be a most orderly set of men considering the way in which they have been tried. They halt at Kalka to-day, and perhaps longer, having no carriage to bring them on to this their first place of destination. Where they are eventually to go I know not. They were not allowed to take charge of the Treasury again at Kussowlie, at which Bagot is very irate; but the men, it seems, made no objection when the decision was communicated to them, but marched cheerfully on to Kalka. I spoke to several of the men along the road, and they said they would willingly go on to Delhi with me to punish the ruffians there; but I am not so sure after all that they would do so.

I came in here this morning in the mail-cart, arriving soon after eight. It was delightfully cool, so much so that my *puttoo* coat was in requisition; it is so cool that I have determined to go on in the mail-cart when the Loodianah dâk comes in. The Chief went yesterday. My baggage must follow the best way it can; they have promised to forward it from the post-office.

They have just come to tell me that the mail-cart is ready, so I must say good-bye. The siege-train is expected to-morrow or next day. All is quiet here, and everything seems looking up.

(*Diary*) 26*th May.*—Called at about half-past three—not long in getting ready. A cup of tea and off. Dreadful storm soon after daybreak; dark as pitch, and then heavy rain. First two miles of road covered with people going to Kussowlie; every woman and child from Umballa ordered up. Get to hotel at Umballa at about eight. On to Kurnaul by mail-cart; very hot; no adventures; reach at six.

CAMP, KURNAUL, *Wednesday*, 27*th May* (8 A.M.).

I got here all right about sunset yesterday, and do not feel at all the worse for the journey; though I must confess the sun *was* rather warm at one time. I found Chester, Norman, &c. located in the dâk-bungalow, and they managed to make me as comfortable as circumstances will admit; but it's a terrible crush, every room having some half-dozen in it.

The first thing that greeted me was the intelligence of the Chief having been attacked with cholera; and he died, poor man, early this morning in General Palmer's house, where he was staying. His death has thrown a gloom over the party, the rest of whom, including Becher,* Congreve,† and Mactier, are all well; and, in fact, there is very little sickness about. The illness of the Chief is not to be wondered at, for they say he was quite unequal to his position in the present state of affairs. General Reed will be Acting Commander-in-Chief; and General Barnard, who is now here, commands this force.

Everything seems to be going on well. They are pushing on troops to Paniput, and beyond; and good accounts are received from almost every station of the state of the troops—Native, I mean. The 60th Native Infantry is the only Native regiment here, and it is to march this morning towards Rohtuck. We shall remain here till the siege-train arrives, and it is expected at Umballa to-day or to-morrow, so I suppose we shall be here some five or six days.

Brigadier Hallifax is here with his brigade; tell Mrs Hallifax he is looking very well indeed. I gave Plassy's (his little son) letter to him.

Bagot's Corps is ordered to Saharunpore, the very place, I believe, that Bagot was anxious to take them to. I hope you have had no more alarms at Simla; there ought to be no cause for any there. Arthur Becher sent out a couple of elephants last night to bring on my traps.

(*Diary*) 27*th May.*—Poor General Anson! Chester returned about three in the morning to say he was dead, poor man. Chester tells me that he must have felt himself quite unequal to the present emergency; and anxiety of mind has had much to do with his fatal illness. He seems to be popular with very few; and the Native troops have apparently a great hatred for him,

* The late General Sir Arthur Becher, K.C.B.—then Quartermaster-General of the Bengal Army.
† Acting Adjutant-General of Queen's troops.

honestly thinking that he was commissioned to convert them.—
Quite a private funeral in the burial-ground in the evening,
Chester reading the service.

CAMP, KURNAUL, *Thursday*, 28*th May* (8 A.M.).

All well here, and were my traps up I should be as comfortable as possible—that is to say, as comfortable as one can be with the third or fourth of a room which is full of visitors the whole day long, from the General (Sir Henry Barnard) downwards. You would be very much amused to see our arrangements: but we all keep our health, which is everything; and as to Chester, he is infinitely better than I have seen him since his return from England. He is out and out the best officer with the army, and works like a horse. He and Norman and Becher do everything. As to Congreve, he appears to have nothing whatever to do, and passes most of his time lying on his bed smoking.

I shall be very glad to get my things, if only for the decent writing materials, as it is quite a task writing with this scratchy pen and bad ink, for which I am indebted to Norman!

We all attended poor General Anson's funeral last night, Chester reading the service.

You remember the dâk-bungalow we stayed at here on our way up to Simla, and the little mice that were running about the rooms—there are several in this room, and as tame as ever. All the 75th officers are in this bungalow, and a host of others besides.

Tell Mr Philipe I will write to him in a day or two when I can see my way a little clearer. I think we shall stay here a couple of days or so longer, and then move on to Paniput. All the news we get is good, and no doubt is entertained of our soon putting matters to right at Delhi.

Arthur Becher sends his love, and says you might have put up a bottle of curaçao for him!

I forgot to tell you that Charlie Hall and Mrs Martin are expected here to-day, and are to go on to Simla. If Mrs Poulton does not come you might offer rooms to them. Major Martin is here.

(*Diary*) 28*th May.*—No troops yet—getting anxious about them. Very hot in the daytime. We are at the dâk-bungalow,

Chester, Norman, and myself in one room; the others equally full, except Congreve, who has a large one to himself. He is anything but well or comfortable apparently. Delightful to get a decent night's rest. Her Majesty's 75th officers keep us awake for some hours singing; they seem a jolly set.

CAMP, KURNAUL, *Friday, 29th May* (8½ A.M.).

I was made very happy last night by the receipt of yours of Monday and Tuesday, the 25th and 26th, and I quite hope now to hear pretty regularly from you, though the Simla post does not appear very much to be depended upon, and you must not be anxious if you occasionally don't hear from me. There is not, so far as I can judge, the least possible cause for any further alarm. As to our putting down the rebellion when we advance, there is not the shadow of a doubt; in fact, it is not truly a rebellion, but merely a gathering of the disaffected Sepoys, the people of the country not being at all with them. It is a pity we cannot advance at once; but now the siege-train is so near it is not considered politic to go on without it. We expect it will be sufficiently near to allow of our moving on to-morrow evening.

I wish you could look in upon us here, and you would be much amused at the happy appearance of the party occupying the dâk-bungalow. In the centre rooms are all the officers of the 75th, who amuse us in the evening singing glees, which they do very well. The costumes that we all wear are diverting enough; scarcely any one thinks of dressing in proper style, unless General Barnard, who, compared to all of us, looks as if he had jumped out of a bandbox. Curzon and Lowe and Mactier are staying with him in General Palmer's house; the two former are very much cut up at General Anson's death. If Pat Grant* comes round here as Commander-in-Chief, very likely Mactier will remain as his surgeon. Brigadier Hallifax started last night for Paniput to join his brigade, and looked in upon us on his way out. He seems to be now in excellent health.

My things have not arrived yet; I fear Maisey has detained them to bring on with him, so I must not expect them until to-morrow morning. It is of no great consequence, however, as Norman has a *dhobie* who washes for me sharp. Don't trouble

---

* General Sir Patrick Grant, Commander-in-Chief at Madras.

to stamp your letters to me; no postage is collected here. I wish my writing-things would come; I can with difficulty write with Chester's paper and pens, and the *punkah* blows everything about in a most uncomfortable manner.

How is Mrs Daly? Her husband is a first-rate officer,* and will be at Delhi almost before us.

(*Diary*) 29*th May*.—Things in at last, after breakfast; just as well, as we start to-morrow. A grand panic in the bungalow. Some one, I believe, cried out in his sleep—nightmare, I fancy—and all rushed out, half-asleep and half-awake, with pistols, guns, swords, &c.; it was an absurd scene. Troops moving in now; 60th Native Infantry gone to Rohtuck to get them out of the way. Walk to canal this evening.

CAMP, KURNAUL, *Saturday*, 30*th May*.

I have made a rough sketch of the composition and movements of the Army of Retribution, and you can show it to Mr Philipe or any one you like; though I dare say there will be a much more complete account of the force in the *Lahore Chronicle*.

Rough Sketch of the Composition and Movements of the Army of Retribution.

1ST BRIGADE.—Brigadier Hallifax, Brigade-Major Simpson: 1st Fusiliers, Money's troop Horse Artillery, and three squadrons 9th Lancers one march beyond Paniput. The 60th Native Infantry two marches beyond Paniput, on the road to Rohtuck.

2ND BRIGADE. — Brigadier Graves, Brigade-Major Nicoll: Her Majesty's 75th, with Head-Quarters of the 4th Irregular Cavalry, march to-night towards Paniput, and will be joined to-morrow by Turner's troop Horse Artillery one squadron, and Head-Quarters' 9th Lancers. The 2nd Fusiliers and one squadron of the 4th Native Cavalry Lancers coming on with the siege-train, which ought to be at Piplee to-night or to-morrow morning. The rest of the 4th Cavalry have been detached to Moozafernugar and other places.

* The late General Sir Henry Daly, G.C.B.

In addition to the above are some Native contingent Horse in advance with Lieutenants Hodson and McAndrew, and some with the siege-train under Native commandants. The whole of the above Force will concentrate some two marches from Delhi, and then be joined by Brigadier Wilson, now at Ghazeeoodeen-Nugar, who will cross the Jumna at the Bhagput bridge of boats (which has been put in excellent order) with his Column from Meerut, consisting of a wing of the Rifles, ditto Carabineers, one troop Horse Artillery, one company Artillery with heavy guns, and some Sappers — part of the Sirmoor battalion and some Irregular Cavalry taking his place at Ghazeeoodeen-Nugar. Colonel Hope Grant commands the Cavalry of the Force, but he has only with him, as stated, one squadron of the 9th Lancers. Colonel Mowatt commands the Artillery; Major Laughton, Chief Engineer; and Dr Tritton, Superintending Surgeon. It is expected that if all goes right we shall be at Delhi on the 8th June, or at latest the 9th.

Letters this instant in from Meerut of the 28th and 29th. All well at Meerut and with Brigadier Wilson's Force; and all the news good except that some eighty Rampore Horse had joined the insurgents. Major Reid,* commanding the Sirmoor battalion, was at Bolandshur, and his little Goorkhas were doing excellent service. A newsletter also in says that the insurgents are quarrelling together at Delhi, and that the large majority of the Sappers and the Artillery are quite ready to desert them on our reaching Delhi.

One of the letters that came to-day had an enclosure, copied by Harriot, and signed by him in his usual neat hand; he is at Meerut with General Hewitt. Poor Mr Johnson, the civilian there, a friend of the Chesters, who escaped the massacre at Meerut, died from a fall from his horse; Captain Garstin had a letter to-day mentioning this. Another letter received to-day says that there are several prisoners, fugitives from Delhi, at a village called Belaspore, close to where Brigadier Wilson is to be to-day, and he will of course have them released at once. I do hope poor Mrs Galloway's husband may be with them, but I fear there is little hope. Every one I have seen from Delhi says it is impossible he could have escaped. Metcalfe,

* The late General Sir Charles Reid, G.C.B.

to whom I spoke when he was here, said Galloway was in the city when the 3rd Cavalry arrived. Metcalfe himself had a most narrow escape, having been three days concealed within a mile of Delhi.* Mr Thomason is also here, and Mr Le Bas, who escaped. Metcalfe has gone on to Paniput with the advanced force to render assistance to the military.

A Sepoy was caught here yesterday with lots of plundered rupees, &c., on him, and a silver mug, belonging, it is believed, to Mr Le Bas. I fear, when we get beyond Paniput, it will be found necessary to utterly destroy some six of the villages which are said to have harboured plunderers and ill-treated the fugitives. Little mercy will be shown any villages in which this can be proved. I made out a proclamation yesterday at the request of General Barnard, which has been translated and circulated, stating that all offending villages will be destroyed.

You never saw such a busy scene as is going on in the room we occupy—Chester, Norman, Maisey, and myself are sitting round the table writing, and every ten minutes or so comes in a telegraphic message or despatch of some kind or other, which brings in Becher and Congreve to hear the news. The telegraph is invaluable. The signalling apparatus goes on with us this afternoon, and will be set up at our new halting-place, Guraunda, so that when we arrive at our ground we shall know at once what is going on at Umballa.

It was awkward having to disband the men of the 5th Native Infantry yesterday, though nothing much is thought of this, or of the misconduct of the men of the detachment at Rampore yesterday. All will most likely soon get their deserts; and as for Simla, now that the Nusserees have marched quietly to Saharunpore and their brother Goorkhas are all behaving so well, you need be under no further alarm of disturbances in the hills.

All our party are very well except Congreve, who groans away. There is no sickness here, but at Piplee Colonel Mowatt is reported very ill. Chester is very jolly, and drinks his beer daily; he sends his kind love. I don't know what ——— means by saying Chester and Becher have lost their heads. Chester is the best man in camp, and has come out wonderfully;

* See Appendix B.

and though there has been great delay in advancing and much vacillation, the former was unavoidable for want of carriage, and for the latter he is not, so far as I can judge, to blame. He and Becher had a grand row yesterday about the siege-train having been left without any European guard. It was a great mistake sending on the Europeans, and had the Goorkhas attacked the train yesterday it might have been serious. He is a real good fellow, Arthur Becher, and we all like him much, but he is too easily excited. I do not think Chester and he will fall out again.

(*Diary*) 30*th May.*—March this evening about five o'clock to Guraunda. Terrible confusion; no tents or anything up for a long time. Ride with Mactier, and come on with General's party.

CAMP, GURAUNDA, *Whitsunday*, 31*st May* (1½ P.M.).

We arrived here last night about eleven o'clock. We have at present the advantage of having the electric telegraph working in the camp; two or three men belonging to the department came on with us, and in the course of an hour or two a tent is pitched close to the wires and a repeating station formed. Mactier and I went into the tent early this morning, and at our request a message was telegraphed to Umballa to ask if all was right; in a minute the answer came, 'Yes, all right here.' They can't telegraph down towards Delhi; but it's everything if they can continue telegraphing upwards, as at present.

We had rather an unpleasant night of it last night, every one's tent and every one's traps being behind. The General gave us all some tea. At last, about 2 A.M., I was able to turn into bed comfortably, having bought a light little *charpoy* at Kurnaul. All the servants are behaving very well; and Soobhan (*chuprassie*), who gave me a deal of trouble on the road down, having stayed behind at Kussowlie without leave, is now making himself useful in every way and doing all he can to regain his lost character.

Frank Turner's troop Horse Artillery and a squadron 9th Lancers came in this morning, and we all, including the 75th, go on to-night to Paniput. It has been decided, however, not to leave this until one or two in the morning, which will allow of our getting a little sleep before we go, and of our reaching our ground at daybreak. It is a great thing for us the Horse Artillery having come, as they will always be with us now, and we are honorary members of their mess.

General Barnard appears to be a very good, gentlemanly little man, and I dare say he is as good for the work as most others. He does not apparently want for pluck, and this, I fancy, is nearly all that is required.

We have not been able to find out how poor Colonel Mowatt is. He was left behind at Piplee yesterday morning very ill with cholera; curious his being attacked, for it seems to have been a solitary case, the whole troop, Turner told me this morning, being in excellent health. I am glad to hear that Mrs Hallifax is so cheerful: remember me very kindly to her. I hope to-morrow or next day to be able to send some account of Brigadier Hallifax; his brigade ought to be two marches beyond Paniput to-day.

Becher has lent me a very nice single pole-tent. With the assistance of a *tattie*, * the temperature is bearable enough, and altogether I am very comfortable.

It is a great comfort indeed Chester being so well. He bears up bravely, and, I hope, will continue to do so, for we cannot spare him. Yes, I saw the *Lahore Chronicle* giving me by name as one who 'bolted!' The accusation has not disturbed me; I am quite satisfied that I did right, and that there was nothing dishonourable in leaving Simla as I did.†

Shute and Maisey I saw to-day, looking well, as indeed are all our party, Head-Quarters and Divisional Staff. Hope Grant ‡ is here, but I have not seen him; he goes on to-night by mail-cart to join the Advance Brigade, where there are three squadrons of his regiment.

Open all letters that come for me. No tidings yet of Colonel Mowatt, so I trust he is recovering, as bad news travels fast. I saw Dr Paton yesterday, looking well. No home mail in yet. Tell Mrs Norman that her husband is very jolly.

CAMP, PANIPUT, *Monday, 1st June.*

All is well with us, and we have been gladdened to-day with the news of the Brigadier's most opportune victory. I have given

---

* A screen of wet grass or straw. † See pp. 12, 13, and 21.
‡ The late General Sir Hope Grant, G.C.B.

the substance of his despatch, which was a very short one, on a separate piece of paper, to allow of your circulating it to all interested in your neighbourhood.

Substance of Brigadier ARCHDALE WILSON's *Despatch of 1st June* 1857.

A despatch was received from Brigadier Wilson this morning stating that on the 30th, about 4 P.M., he was attacked at Ghazeeoodeen-Nugar by a large party of the insurgents from Delhi, who have heavy ordnance with them. The enemy were driven back, and entirely defeated; the Brigadier capturing four of their heavy guns and one large howitzer, with trifling loss on our side. The troops, he states, all of them, behaved most admirably. The despatch was written at 8 P.M. of the 30th, and further particulars are promised to-morrow. Nothing is said of any officer having been killed or wounded, and the casualties that took place were principally from the accidental explosion of a tumbrel after the capture of the ordnance. A Native letter received this morning prior to the Brigadier's despatch says that the insurgents were completely defeated, the Delhi people who went out being the first to fly; and many had reached the city wounded with sabre cuts, evidently showing that the Carabineers had done good service in the conflict. The same post brought a letter from General Hewitt at Meerut, where all was quiet.

This victory must be a great blow to the insurgents, and will no doubt have a most depressing effect upon them, and show what little chance they have when all our force is congregated together; this we expect it will be on the morning of the 4th, when Brigadier Wilson is to cross at the Bhagput bridge, close to Raie, where the Advance Column was to be this morning.

We go on this evening a double march, the European Infantry being conveyed on the spare carts; and this will take us within nine miles or so of Raie, to be at hand in case the enemy should come from Delhi on this line of road; but after their defeat by Brigadier Wilson, it is most unlikely they will leave Delhi unless to try to get away to their homes—which, in fact, it is said they are doing in great numbers.

I am sorry to say that accounts were received this morning of the death of Colonel Mowatt. He, it seems, gave up at once—made up his mind that he was to die, and this, poor man, had a good deal to say to his non-recovery. I am very sorry also to say that Brigadier Hallifax has been pronounced as too unwell to accompany the force, and he went back the day before yesterday to Kurnaul, and I hope by this time is at Umballa. I saw a medical statement of his case this morning, and pray tell Mrs Hallifax, with my kind regards, that there is nothing the matter with the Brigadier that the quiet and rest of Simla will not remove. It appears he had, among other ailments, an attack of ophthalmia, but the principal thing the matter with him was a tendency to apoplexy, which would have endangered his life had he passed another day in a tent. All our party are as jolly as possible, except Congreve, who has fever, liver, and severe cough. I fancy he will not go on with us from here; but nothing has been settled yet.

Chester is, happily, as well and plucky as ever, and he, Norman, and I have taken up our quarters to-day in one of General Barnard's large double-poled tents; there are *tatties* and a *punkah*, so that we are very comfortable. The General is very kind and considerate—coming over to Chester's and finding his tent small, insisted on our coming over here. We are also now members of the Artillery mess, and, judging from the dinner last night, we are likely to fare most sumptuously in future.

There is a report that Hansi and Hissar have been plundered, but it wants confirmation. From other quarters the news is good, and the only contretemps we know of is of a small party, a Havildar and eight of the 60th Native Infantry, with two officers, who went to collect boats on the Jumna, having been obliged to cut and run into camp on account of the villagers rising. I think it is likely enough that they were taking boats without paying for them. All got into camp without damage, losing some of their things. Better, perhaps, say nothing of this unless to give a correct version of the affair if you hear an exaggerated account of it.

The telegraph wire was found cut here, but it has been repaired, and is in full operation again. The people of Paniput are very civil, and have come forward with money and stores. Mrs Chester is not to return to Simla until we have taken Delhi, and, please God, this we shall do before a week is over, unless we have to wait for the siege-train, which is not likely.

No cholera at all in camp. The 9th Lancers haven't had a fresh case since they left Umballa; and, except Colonel Mowatt, Turner tells me there was no case in the Artillery.

(*Diary*) 1*st June.*—A party of eight Sepoys (60th), with Captain Fagan and Mr Martin, came rushing in just as we had finished dinner, and said they had been attacked by thousands, and had just escaped with their lives!—Spend the day in Chief's tent, and dine there at five, sleeping at the Artillery as before. People here civil, they say. Colonel Mowatt died of cholera.

CAMP, LUSSOWLEE, *Tuesday*, 2*nd June* (10 A.M.).

Poor Mrs Hallifax, there is sad news to communicate to her. Dr Tritton joined us this morning, and brought in word that the Brigadier died last night at Kurnaul. Dr Tritton has promised me that he will himself write to Mrs Hallifax; but I have thought it as well to write a few lines also, which will you read and give her?—and I know how well you will console and comfort her under her heavy affliction.

All is going on very well here. We had a fearfully long march last night, some good twenty-two miles, but nobody appears the worse for it, and we are now in a most favourable position, being only nine miles from the Advance Column at Raie, where we join them in the morning; and the next day Brigadier Wilson is expected there, and then 'Hurrah for Delhi!' The bridge at Bhagput, close to Raie, is in good order; Brigadier Wilson will cross the Jumna by it. The promised despatch with further accounts of his victory has not come in yet; but there has been a letter from Meerut stating that all was well there, and that Her Majesty's 84th were beginning to arrive at Cawnpore; and things must be quiet all below there, as the letter which mentions the arrival of the 84th talks of the telegraphic communication being open the whole way to Calcutta.

You would have been much amused could you have seen our proceedings of yesterday evening. We all (of our party, I mean) congregated at the Artillery mess, where, after having a cup of coffee, we lay down on the ground till about 10 P.M., when the trumpets sounded, and when all was ready off we started at the head of the troop, except Chester, who accompanied Dr Brown in his buggy. At half-way the Artillery had made first-rate arrangements for tea, &c., and there we pulled up for nearly an hour, taking a snatch of sleep on the ground after we had refreshed ourselves. Frank Turner, Norman, Bunny, Mactier, and myself were sharing the same blanket. The two latter galloped on with me as the day broke, and we got in soon after sunrise. The 75th, which had started at sunset, were most of them in before us. It was a good lift for them getting conveyed here in carts.

The siege-train was at Kurnaul last night, and is expected at Paniput to-morrow morning. Tell Mrs Shute, with my kind regards, that I saw her husband this morning. He is quite well, also Maisey; there is, indeed, no sickness in camp, and Congreve is better. I fear it is true that Hansi and Hissar have gone. There was a letter to-day, of 24th May, from Colonel Seaton, with 60th Native Infantry—all well.

(*Diary*) *2nd June.*—Very hot. Breakfast at General Barnard's—a good, kind little man. Another victory by Brigadier Wilson; but it is an anxious time without him. The question is—Ought he to join us? I think he ought.

CAMP, RAIE, *Wednesday, 3rd June* (6½ A.M.).

Chester is hard at work with his letter; he writes most regularly every day to Mrs Chester, and I can imagine her delight at receiving his letter, for she must indeed be most anxious about him. He bears up most wonderfully; and I trust he may be spared to receive the reward of his exertions—our speedy success.

We have very good accounts of Brigadier Wilson's force; but, in consequence of his having been attacked a second time, he has not yet commenced his march to join us. I suppose he will do so to-night, which will bring him in the day after to-morrow. In the last attack which took place, I think on Saturday, he gave the insurgents, it is reported, a tremendous thrashing, killing upwards of five hundred of them, and they are said to be much dispirited in Delhi in consequence. A party of two hundred tried to make off to their homes, but were intercepted by the Bullubghur Raja and thirty thousand rupees taken from them.

I have not seen Brigadier Wilson's official despatch, but I understand that he mentions two officers as having been killed—Lieutenant Perkins of the Artillery, and Captain Andrews of the 60th Rifles.

All in camp are in the best health and spirits, and the only fear appears to be now that the insurgents have been so thrashed that they will not venture to make a stand at all when our force advances. There is a very respectable force here now: the 1st Fusiliers and 75th, two troops of Horse Artillery, and the whole of the 9th Lancers; but I imagine that there will be no onward advance until General Wilson joins, unless there should be news from Delhi rendering an onward move at once desirable.

As we approached our camping-ground this morning, we saw evident signs of the insurgents having been at work about here. For the last three miles or so the telegraph wire is carried off, and many of the posts removed. This is very annoying, and I fear they will hardly get the wire up to work to-day. It was close to this that the lady fugitives from Delhi were maltreated; and five men who were concerned in these outrages were hanged last night by the civil authorities, and they have several more under trial this morning. We met a party of the Jheend Raja's troops, Cavalry and Infantry, with two guns, who were on their way to chastise a village some three or four miles off, where a large quantity of the Delhi plunder is said to be stored. I have no doubt the work will be done satisfactorily. Metcalfe, McAndrew, Maisey, and several others were accompanying the force.

Was it not sad my having to write to poor Mrs Hallifax of her husband's death? How is she? When he left Kurnaul I thought he was looking very well, and was not at all prepared to hear of his death; but it seems the extreme heat of the tents had quite upset his head, and brought on a species of apoplexy.

I can't particularise every one you know in camp, but all are quite well. Becher is a little pulled down by the heat and hard work, but he seems to have excellent health, as have Norman and Mactier. Of course Mactier was with the late Chief when he died, and Coghlan, the doctor of the 75th, a clever man, was in close attendance also. I must really say good-bye, or I shall be late.

CAMP, RAIE, 3rd June (later).

I was able to tell Hodson * just now of the 'strong-minded woman,' his wife, from whom he said he had not heard for some time. He is a first-rate officer, one of the very best in camp. He is attached to Colonel Becher's department, who has also two other assistants, Shute and Garstin.

I hope I have been premature in mentioning the death of Captain Andrews of the 60th. It was from an account of the business received in a private letter from Meerut; and Brigadier Wilson's despatch of the second fight, which I have since seen, only gives the name of Lieutenant Perkins, Artillery, as having been killed. The names of Lieutenants Light and Elliot, of the Artillery, are stated as having done good service. It seems the second fight was merely one of Artillery, the scoundrels not venturing to come much nearer than a mile of Brigadier Wilson's position; and as soon as he had silenced their guns and began to advance upon them, they bolted like a shot, and our men were too much knocked up with the heat to be able to carry on the pursuit. I fancy the scoundrels were too much frightened at the way they were cut up on the previous occasion to put themselves in the way of the Carabineers again.

We are in orders for the whole force to march at 1 A.M. to Alleepore, which is only ten miles from Delhi. At Alleepore I suppose we must remain for some two or three days for the siege-train, which it seems it will be necessary to take on, as there is little prospect of the rebels venturing outside the walls to meet us when all our force is congregated there.

There has been considerable discussion as to whether Brigadier Wilson's force is to come over and join us, and it is decided in the affirmative, and I think rightly so. Our object is Delhi, and everything must be sacrificed to this; and with Delhi once in our possession the rebellion must cool down. But the civilians on the Meerut side, Messrs Greathed and Williams, are most anxious that Brigadier Wilson should remain where he is, and they talk of all manner of disasters if he is removed. They are wrong; and as to Meerut itself, they have fortified

---

* Major Hodson, of 'Hodson's Horse.'

the school of instruction and can hold their own against any number. Time only will show whether General Barnard or the civilians are right.

(*Diary*) 3rd *June.*—Dine last night at the Artillery—pleasant party and good dinner. Have my bed there, and sleep; but there was such a row I made little of it after eleven, and we didn't start till one o'clock. Reach Raie soon after daybreak—find the leading column here. Anxiety for Wilson's joining us; the civilians protest against it, but the move has been positively ordered. Dine at the mess, and very glad after dinner to lie down to sleep. Several men hanged and shot.

CAMP, ALLEEPORE, *Thursday*, 4*th June.*

Here we are at Alleepore, within ten or eleven miles of Delhi, having arrived this morning at sunrise. We marched with all the baggage in the rear, and with every precaution to be prepared to receive the enemy in the event of their showing themselves on the road; but there was nothing to be seen of them, though a party of Lancers, after our arrival here, went on some four or five miles in advance to look about. We remain here until joined by Wilson's force, expected on the 6th, on which day the siege-train may also be here. It left Paniput this morning.

On our march from Raie we found unmistakable marks of the enemy's proceedings: the telegraph posts down for some six miles and the wire removed, and villages and roadside bungalows in ruins. One dâk-bungalow, however (the one we stayed at), was standing with the roof entire, and several bullock-train wagons, two or three uninjured, were at the door. Many of the villages are full of plunder. At one o'clock this morning I saw a whole lot of things being brought, by some of our people, into camp; they had evidently belonged to some *boxwallah*—cases of spectacles, dolls, toys, and small penny books: of these I have taken possession of two as 'prize property' for Keith and Arthur.

Your letter of the 2nd June has just reached me on my return from a good breakfast at the Artillery mess—a first-rate beafsteak-pie! You may imagine from this I am not very ill—indeed, I never felt better in my life; and though the sun is rather hot, it doesn't affect me. Norman or Chester will write at once if I get ill, which please God I shall not. Chester tells me to give you his love; he is a fine old fellow, Chester. Do not be surprised if you are for days without hearing from me. I shall always write; but, as I told you before, the postal arrangements cannot be depended upon.

(*Diary*) *4th June.*—Marched this morning in fighting order; were to have started at one, but it was two o'clock before we were well off—tedious work. The old General very kind with his cold tea, which was very acceptable. Reach Alleepore soon after sunrise, and our tents came up pretty quickly. Eleven miles from Delhi. Fine open plain for a fight, but no enemy to be seen. Very hot day; mess in a garden.

CAMP, ALLEEPORE, *Saturday, 5th June.*

Nothing from you to-day, but I am not at all anxious, for there is no Simla dâk at all; and everything, I am sure, must be going on well there—at least, there is no reason why everything should not go on well. You must not believe one-tenth part of the reports that, I understand, reach Simla. All goes on prosperously here; the 2nd Fusiliers came in this morning, and Brigadier Wilson's force is to join us to-night. Everything will then be ready for the advance on Delhi, and, as I told you before, not a doubt is entertained of an immediately successful result. Disunion is known to exist amongst the insurgents; a party of some three hundred of the Gwalior contingent, who had gone over to the enemy, having sent in word quietly that they are willing to come and lay down their arms and give up their horses on promise of pardon, which will no doubt be accorded them.

Mrs Stafford is living in camp. I saw her husband just now; he is looking well. It is a great pity that she did not go back to Kurnaul. Besides Mrs Stafford there are several other women, wives of patrolling officers here, and I suppose they must all remain now. Stafford told me that Sergeant Larkin's friend, the Quartermaster-Sergeant of the Hurrianas, had escaped, and is now in camp, but he is very anxious about his family, who had left the bungalow and could not be found, and he is consequently ignorant of their fate.

Excellent accounts to-day of the good conduct of the Nusseree battalion at Saharunpore, who are making up for their late misbehaviour by trying to settle the country.

I hope Gowroo continues to behave well: give my *salaam* to him. The servants with me are behaving very well, and with the assistance of the mess I find the three men I have quite enough. I enclose a letter from the *bheestie* (water-carrier) to his brother.

The enemy are said to have advanced out of Delhi to within some six miles of this; but, if true, they will not venture farther, as we are all prepared for them, and they would have to fight at great disadvantage. The more they collect together the better, as when Wilson's force arrives there will be nothing to prevent our advance, and it is better that the insurgents should be outside than inside the walls of Delhi. We expect the Guide Corps the day after to-morrow.

(*Diary*) 5*th June.*—Very bad news came in during the night: Nussereebad troops mutinied, Muttra treasury looted, and Bhopal Cavalry false; and no despatch from Wilson, who will, I fancy, find the bridge broken at Bhagput. Lots of rumours all day. A storm, with a few drops of rain, cools the air.

CAMP, ALLEEPORE, *Saturday*, 6*th June* (1 P.M.).

I write a line to say that all is quiet up to the present hour, and there seems no intention on the part of the enemy of being so foolish as to advance in this direction farther than they now are; and as Brigadier Wilson's force is only about twelve miles off, it has been decided by General Barnard not to move onward until they arrive. Carts and elephants have been sent to help them in, and they will arrive in the course of the night.

Greathed, of the Engineers, arrived an hour or two ago from General Wilson's camp at Bhagput—or, rather, on this side of the river opposite Bhagput. He says the road is quite open beyond Meerut; he himself left Agra only two days ago, having travelled without any molestation on the dâk-cart. So much for the stories in circulation about the disturbed state of the Doab. He mentions that all was quiet at Agra, but after the plunder of the Muttra treasury it was deemed desirable to disarm the Native

(AGRA.) THE TAJ MAHAL.

regiments. Tell all friends what I have heard from Greathed about the state of the Doab.

(*Diary*) 6*th June.*—All right with the train, which came in this morning; and, a few hours later, in came Greathed of the Engineers from Wilson's camp at Bhagput. Bad news, however, from Rohilkund: all the troops there have risen, it is said; but as Greathed came in a dâk-cart from Agra two days ago, it can't be very bad. The enemy entrenching themselves five miles off; we go at them in the morning, I believe.

CAMP, ALLEEPORE, *Sunday*, 7*th June.*

I was delighted this morning by getting your long letter of Wednesday and Thursday last, which ought, properly speaking, to have reached me yesterday; but, as we have advanced, the dâk appears now to take a day longer than it did. I also received by the same dâk a very nice letter from Mrs Chester, thanking me for writing to her about her husband. Poor, kind Mrs Chester, she has indeed great reason to be thankful that Chester keeps his health so well; and I trust he may be enabled to carry through to the end. At the present he continues in the best health and spirits. What a pleasure it will be to her to have him back again! It is strange that with the great heat and exposure every one really looks better than when quietly enjoying themselves and doing their work at home.

Brigadier Wilson's force marched in this morning, and I can't tell you how well they all looked, the Brigadier himself in high health. He came on last night, and slept in my tent. Edwin Johnson the picture of health; and Colonel Jones, of the Rifles, as fat and rosy as ever. I went out to see the force march in, and a very nice little addition they are to our small army. The Rifles in particular, though they had had a long march, came along stepping out merrily and singing in chorus. The little Goorkhas too seemed very jolly, and they are believed to be very staunch—this is the Sirmoor battalion. The Goorkhas at Jutogh, the Nusseree battalion, behaved as they did from not knowing what their brethren in the plains intended to do—whether to be faithful to us, or to join the insurgents. These are the only Native troops, except a few Sappers and about fifty of the 4th Irregulars, that we have in camp now. A party of the 60th Native Infantry were sent away yesterday to rejoin their regiments, and a squadron of the 4th Lancers were got rid of by sending them to Meerut; they might have proved faithful, but a mistrust of them had got about, and our troops did not at all like their being in camp.

We are encamped just as we were yesterday, and everything seems quiet on ahead and we have had no alarm whatever, so that we were able to get a good sleep last night; and it was deliciously cool, there having been a violent storm about sunset. I don't know what the order of the day is for to-morrow, but I fancy there is little doubt of our moving forward—driving back the enemy's post that I told you they had established on the road some five or six miles off, and taking up a position sufficiently near the city to bombard it.

You mistake Chester in supposing that he is anxious to rush on imprudently. He is not at all this way inclined. He wants to go to work very systematically, and to save the troops from exposure as much as possible; had it not been for him I think there would have been an advance yesterday. Hope Grant was all for going on, but I am sure he was wrong; and we have now got Brigadier Wilson, who is equally wary and careful, and him and Chester I look upon as our great mainstay in camp. With our small army we cannot afford to be anything but careful; a rush might bring quick success, but it might end in serious disaster. As I have said to you often before, no one doubts for an instant the ultimate result of the contest, and ere this reaches you all confidently expect that Delhi will be in our possession, and with very little loss on our side; and, once Delhi is ours, serious as matters are in several quarters, there is every reason to hope that all will quiet down in time. The worst news is from Rohilkund, where it is said all the regiments have at last mutinied. And I fear it is too true; and that the European community from Bareilly, Moradabad, and Shahjehanpore have fled to Meerut. It is most unfortunate; but, Delhi ours, Chamberlain's* column from Lahore will be available for Rohilkund.

I told you, I think, that Chester had a letter from his son

---

* General Sir Neville Chamberlain, K.C.B.

at Saharunpore, dated the 4th instant, and that the Nusserees (Goorkhas) were doing good service. I am anxious about Arthur and his wife. A corps at Nussereebad, which is in his direction, has mutinied. I have not heard from him since I left Simla.

He is a nice person, P——, to try and frighten you all as he does. Did I think there was the least cause for being alarmed I would tell you at once to go down to Kussowlie; but in my opinion you are entirely safe at Simla, unless any of the hill Rajas should take it into their heads to rise—an event altogether improbable so long as the Puttiala Raja remains faithful, and no doubts are entertained of his fidelity or of the Naba or Jheend men, whose contingents are with us. Don't you allow, therefore, any croaking rumours to distress you, and by God's blessing, before this week is over, you and all will be satisfied by hearing of our being triumphant in Delhi, and of our having read the mutineers such a lesson that there will be no further rising anywhere. Measures are being adopted to destroy the bridge across the Jumna so as to prevent the escape of the rebels. I hope Daly's Guides will be with us to-morrow or next day; they will be invaluable. There are still accounts of dissensions at Delhi among the different parties.

Dr Nisbett has been ordered back to Simla, Dr Waghorne taking his place at Kussowlie. I met Dr Batson this morning on his way into camp: he was disguised as a Cashmere mendicant, and looked one to the letter. He stopped and gave us a most romantic history of his adventures. Mrs Stafford has, I believe, gone back to Meerut. General Reed is expected in camp to-morrow.

CAMP, ALLEEPORE, *Sunday, 7th June* (5 P.M.).

It is settled that we march to-night towards Delhi, taking up our position to-morrow at Hindoo Rao's house—the place you may remember we went to see, and where there were lots of deer and a tiger, and where you had a swing in the veranda.

George Hall came in a little while ago, and begged me to send his love to his wife and to you, as he would most probably be quite unable to write himself. He is looking very well, but complains of being dreadfully hard-worked, and says he has not had his boots off for several days. He is a very good officer. I think

I told you that Brigadier Wilson spoke well of the conduct of his men; they and the men of the 4th Irregulars are, it seems, considered staunch, and are to be employed with the Army, being kept, however, as far as possible out of harm's way in the event of their being inclined to join the enemy.

There will not be an opportunity for me to write to-morrow, but the day after I hope to be able to send you a long letter. The news of the Nussereebad regiments' mutinying is, I am sorry to say, true—the 15th and 30th. I trust we shall have finished Delhi long before they can get there, and they will have but little hope of escape then. The 8th Irregulars are staunch, it seems, at Bareilly, so things are not quite so bad there after all. I am sorry to say poor Howell is very unwell, but his is the only case of sickness I know of in camp.

I saw Dr Mackinnon, with his kind, smiling face, this morning. I expect we shall have a very large party at the mess to-night, as all the Meerut Artillerymen are, I believe, coming. I did not see either of the Pembertons, but I think they are both here—Duncan certainly. They will most likely be at mess to-night.

Greathed, the Commissioner, came in last night. He is the Governor-General's Agent with the Army. It was high time he came; for Metcalfe, though a particularly nice, gentlemanly fellow, is rather harum-scarum, and better calculated for an irregular horseman than political adviser to the General.

Good-bye till the day after to-morrow. Heaven bless and preserve you and the little chicks.

(*Diary*) *Sunday, 7th June.*—Wilson going on this morning;* large party at mess. Orders for advance at 1 A.M. to-morrow.

* Every one advanced together on the 8th of June.—H. W. NORMAN.

CHAPTER IV.

FIRST BATTLE BEFORE DELHI, AND COMMENCEMENT OF THE SIEGE.

Colonel KEITH YOUNG *to his wife.*

DELHI CANTONMENTS, *Monday, 8th June* (11 A.M.).

Happy indeed will you be to hear that the Almighty has preserved me unhurt throughout to-day's battle. We have gained a glorious victory, but there is one sad, sad tale to tell—poor Chester has been killed! You may imagine the gloom which this has thrown over us all. Had it not been for this we should have been so happy, for our loss has been comparatively trifling, and poor Chester is the only officer, I believe, known to be killed, though Russell of the 54th is very dangerously wounded. Chester's death must have been instantaneous, a round-shot tearing through his side, and killing also his white horse, 'Sir Walter,' which he was riding at the time. There were two fights this morning, the first about five miles from Alleepore, the second at the Ridge on which Hindoo Rao's house is situated. Chester was killed at the first, which took place soon after five o'clock; his body is being brought in, and will be interred in the cantonment burial-ground this evening. When Chester fell I was on the opposite side of the road with Mactier, and I cannot tell how shocked we were, on coming across the road, to find him lying dead.

To-morrow we shall probably commence bombarding Delhi, which we can do with heavy guns from the Ridge we now occupy with our pickets. This will be altogether an Artillery affair, and I shall have nothing to do with it, so you must not imagine me in any more danger.

We took all the enemy's guns—twenty or more; the scoundrels ran away from us as hard as they could into Delhi. The little Goorkhas behaved admirably, as did also the Sappers and Miners.

George Hall and Major Martin were detached to the left with their men, and I have not heard yet what they did. Mactier sends his best regards; Shute is quite well.

(*Diary*) *8th June.*—Off about 2 A.M., and a sad though victorious day of it. Enemy in position at Budlee-ka-Serai, about five miles opposite, and at daylight three guns opened on us a terrific fire—poor Chester killed. We carried their guns, and then advanced, driving the enemy from the Ridge on which stand the Flagstaff and Hindoo Rao's house; these we occupy in force. All over at about 9 A.M., and at 4 P.M. or earlier we get up our tents. Funeral of poor Chester.

Notes from Captain SEYMOUR, *Her Majesty's 84th, Assistant Adjutant-General Queen's, to Mrs* KEITH YOUNG.

SIMLA, *June* 1857.

Some people have been spreading reports here which have caused alarm, and lest any should have reached you I would mention that I have just seen a public notice from Lord William Hay that there are no grounds for the least apprehension, that he has taken the necessary steps to keep peace in the bazaar, and, if necessary, that he could bring in any number of armed men; and lastly, he requests that the residents will bring to his notice all cases of insolence, either on the part of servants or the people of the bazaar. There are some terrible croakers in this place; do not believe anything they say.

In case you have heard that a body of mutineers had reached Budlee, which has caused some alarm in Simla, you will be glad to learn that they marched towards Umballa on the 11th, and reached a place called (as it was pronounced to me) Leisuarm. I can't find it in the map, but the report is from Lord William Hay, who received a letter this morning.

Thank you very much for sending me the account of the victory. I knew you would have so many notes to write to answer inquiries that I did not like to trouble you with one. I received yours on the road on my pilgrimage to the Reading-room at Burra-Simla.

Colonel Chester's death is a sad blow, just, too, at the time when he had rendered such valuable services and been so conspicuously useful. He was always exceedingly kind to me, and I shall ever regret him.

All the passengers in the P. & O. Company's steamers coming to Bengal were bundled out at Madras, and the 43rd Light Infantry placed on board and brought up to Calcutta.

Many thanks for the extracts from Colonel Keith Young's letter. The troops coming round the Cape are arriving in fast steamers; but none are coming by this mail overland; the delay in getting an answer from the Sultan, and the uncertainty of steamers being ready at Suez, prevented it.

Sir Edward Campbell to Mrs Keith Young.

SIMLA.

MY DEAR MRS YOUNG,—The enclosed is from Shute. The dâk left apparently very early in the morning, which accounts for your getting no letters.—Yours, E. F. CAMPBELL.

Captain SHUTE *to Sir* EDWARD CAMPBELL.

DELHI CANTONMENTS, 9*th June.*

I wrote to you yesterday in pencil after our engagement, and forcing these wretches from their position and taking their guns, &c., with the loss on our side of poor Colonel Chester and others by cannon-shots, which were thickly put in.

Everything quiet last night, though all day yesterday round-shots were coming in from the city. To-day we have two heavy guns in position, which they do not seem to like, and they are quieter.

Buried poor Chester and others last evening. More in my letter by-and-by. I am very well, and all right; and I hope we shall bring Delhi to its senses soon. Bunny, I should have told you, is well.

Colonel KEITH YOUNG *to his wife.*

CAMP, DELHI CANTONMENTS, *Tuesday,* 9*th June* (10½ A.M.).

We are getting on as well as we possibly can. The enemy were quite quiet last night as far as disturbing us, but firing was heard to a great extent in the city, and it is supposed they were fighting amongst themselves. It is fortunate they let us alone—

not that they could have done any harm; but everything being so quiet the men got a good night's rest, of which they were all much in need. This morning the enemy commenced firing again from the city; but during the night a battery of heavy guns had been erected by our people on the heights, and they have now quite silenced their fire. These heights (on which Hindoo Rao's house and the Flagstaff are situated) are nearer the city than was supposed, and our batteries completely command the gateways, and I fancy shells can also be thrown into the Palace from these batteries, which will simplify matters very much. Our camp is on the parade-ground, quite out of reach of the enemy's fire. You never saw such a scene of devastation in the cantonments, only the walls standing, and things lying about the roads in every direction—broken dinner-sets, music-books, &c.

I went to look at the public garden this morning, near which the Head-Quarters' tents are: the summer-house in it burnt down, but the trees and shrubs uninjured.

Wasn't it sad news I wrote you yesterday about poor Chester? I have since heard more accurate particulars of his death. It seems he lived for a minute or two after he was struck down, and young Barnard, the Aide-de-Camp, jumped off his horse and went to his assistance, holding his head until he died. He was quite sensible at first, and spoke to Barnard, asking him to raise his head that he might look at his wound; and seeing—as well he might, poor fellow—that he couldn't live, he wanted Barnard to leave him, which he would not do, but gave him some water to drink, on which he said, 'What's the use of giving me water?' But it seemed to revive him a little, and he died without apparent pain. His remains were interred in the burial-ground yesterday evening, Mactier and I having had the body bound up in blankets, and we got Mr Rotton to perform the service. That poor fellow Russell, also, whose wound proved mortal, was laid by Chester's side in another grave.

I am sorry to say that two more officers were killed that I had not heard of when I wrote to you yesterday: Harrison, Her Majesty's 75th, and Delamain, 56th Native Infantry; and poor Howell, I regret to add, died of cholera the night before we left Alleepore. Light, of the Artillery, slightly wounded in the forehead; Greville, 1st Fusiliers, slightly in the hand; and

(NEAR DELHI.) RUINS OF KUTUB MINAR.
Inlaid arch and iron pillar said by tradition to reach to the centre of the earth.

young Davidson, of the Artillery, very severely burnt by the blowing up of a tumbrel. I don't think there can be any more casualties amongst the officers, or I should have heard of them. Bunny was in great distress yesterday evening at not having sent his letter in time. Tell Mrs Bunny he is in high health and spirits. I spoke to Duncan Pemberton for an instant. He is very well; his brother is not here.

The Guide Corps came in this morning under Daly, to whom I spoke. He is quite well. His corps has made a wonderful march. George Hall and Major Martin are occupying a post some four or five miles off. One of their men was in just now with a letter for Arthur Becher, and I spoke to him; they have remained staunch, and after the lesson the enemy got yesterday there is little chance of their proving traitors now.

General Reed arrived in camp yesterday, and came on here after the fight. He is in very infirm health. I was able to give him my *charpoy*, the only one that was up. Soobhan manages well.

(*Diary*) 9*th June.*—The enemy behaved very well last night, allowing us a good night's sleep, which was much needed by the troops. Took a ride into the garden just across the canal; not much damage done to it apparently. In the morning early the Guides came in—a most soldierlike-looking set of fellows. In the afternoon, about two, grand attack on the Ridge, and all troops out; drive the enemy back. In the evening another attack: the Guides did good service.

DELHI CANTONMENTS, *Wednesday morning,* 10*th June.*

The dâk-man, I understand, reports the road as quite open, and as long as our troops continue to move along there is every prospect of its remaining so. This is a great comfort; but if by any mischance you happen to be for a day or two without letters, you must attribute it to some obstruction on the road and not to anything going wrong here, for nothing can be progressing more favourably with us than matters are at present. Our guns are playing away from the heights on the devoted city, and a large mortar was got into position last night, and it is to be hoped they will be able to throw shells from it into the Palace; but I have not heard yet whether that can be done. Our guns that are in position are at Hindoo Rao's house, and the enemy are evidently most anxious to get us out of it if they can; and yesterday they came out in great force to the attack, but were repulsed at every point. Our men, however, suffered some loss, principally from foolishly pursuing them too far; and the gallant Guides, who had only come off a thirty miles' march in the morning, were foremost in the fray: they are a noble lot of fellows.

Norman is a very gallant and intelligent young officer, and, I hope, will some day be Adjutant-General of the Army.* We don't know who is likely to succeed poor Chester, but Neville Chamberlain is spoken of.

The Calcutta dâk of the 29th is in to-day; at least I have got a packet of that date, and there may be more later. I have heard nothing from Agra or Meerut. Of course the road is open now from Delhi to Meerut, but the insurgents will hardly venture to go to Meerut to attack it; and if they do, it is known that they are strong enough at Meerut to resist any attack that can possibly be made upon them. General Wilson's force joined us, because Delhi is our grand object, and, that taken, our task afterwards will be an easy one. Wilson's force arrives very opportunely, and he himself is worth anything. He is, in fact, *the* head in camp. As to the new Chief, he is very sick, and never leaves his tent; and General Barnard, though a good, kind man, is not quite up to the work required of him.

There was a very good account of the 60th Native Infantry from Rohtuck yesterday—I forget the date. I saw Shute this morning, and Hodson; both quite well. I sent Mrs Hodson's letter to her husband.

Norman has just been with me. He says there are good accounts of late date of all the Saugar troops, and from Mooltan; and that the Nusseree battalion was doing good service on the 8th.

(*Diary*) 10*th June*.—It seems that there was no flag put up at the Flagstaff after all, so got Becher's people and had the General's put up this morning. A fine view of the city; fellows firing away.

* He became Acting Adjutant-General in May 1859, and again acted as Adjutant-General in 1861, but in January 1862 was made Secretary to the Government of India in the Military Department.

Take another ride to the gardens; warmish day. Nothing doing last night, but firing going on all day from our batteries and the enemy's, and we don't appear to have much the best of it; people looking rather gloomy, and talking of the necessity of an assault. Dine at the Artillery mess; and no sooner in tent and in bed than there is an alarm, and all turn out—great confusion. Nothing, however, came of it.

CAMP, DELHI CANTONMENTS, *Thursday*, 11*th June*.

I had just dated this when your letter of the 9th was put into my hand, and I am distressed to find that you should have been so needlessly anxious about the non-arrival at Simla of the dâk from this of the 6th. You must not indeed make yourself unhappy when there is no dâk in: it is only surprising to me that, considering the way in which our rear is exposed, the mail-carts are able to get on at all; and both Mactier and I have fully made up our minds, as the dâk was late this morning, that it had been plundered on the road, and this we must expect ere long, though everything should go as right with us as it is doing at present.

We are occupying the same position still, and shall not move from here, I imagine, until the assault is made upon Delhi, and when this is to be is not yet decided. A man who came from the city this morning describes the place as a perfect pandemonium. All the people (soldiers as well), frightened at our shells and shot, are rushing away from this side; and as none, I believe, are allowed to leave, the place must be in a dreadful state of confusion. A party of the insurgents of the Gwalior contingent (Horse) came into camp and gave themselves up this morning, and they say there are many anxious to do the same, but they can't get out of the city. I suppose we shall be able to make some arrangements with them before long. I saw Major Martin this morning, who has come in with his party near here—they being considered quite staunch now.

Mr Greathed had a letter just now to say that three regiments had left England on an account being received of the first row at Barrackpore. The 88th and a battalion of the Rifles are two of the regiments; the third I can't remember.

We don't find it particularly hot in tents, and the nights and mornings are quite cool; this morning I was glad to put on my *puttoo* coat. There is no present appearance of rain, and I trust it will hold off until we are in possession of the city. I am very glad to hear the servants are behaving so well: this is a great comfort to me; and if Mrs Hall does not like the *janpanees*, I would still keep them on until the fall of Delhi.

What a capital corps the Guide Corps is! They are invaluable to us, and Daly is a first-rate officer. His Adjutant, poor fellow, died yesterday evening. Daly was with me five minutes ago having a cup of tea. All our party are quite well, and I have seen nearly every one of them this morning—Becher, Norman, Shute, and also Hodson, who was very thankful for the letter you enclosed to him. Metcalfe was with me too just now, looking well. Mactier sends many kind messages to you: it is pleasant having him as my chum.

The enclosed is from Mungroo (*syce*). Tell the servants all are well here. Soobhan has told me to ask you to pay the old *khansamah* on his account. Will you settle about this?

(*Diary*) 11*th June.*—Firing again this morning soon after daybreak, and some of the shell came into camp about two or three hundred yards from my tent. The best news to-day is that some half-dozen of the Cavalry, Gwalior contingent, came in last night and gave themselves up; the worst is, the mutiny at last of the 60th, at Rohtuck. All officers safe in camp. Change the position of the Head-Quarters, going more to the left, near the 2nd Fusiliers.

CAMP, DELHI CANTONMENTS, *Friday*, 12*th June* (10½ A.M.).

I found your letter of the 10th June waiting for me on my return to my tent just now. How regularly our dâk comes, and how very uncertain our letters are in reaching Simla! On the 10th you ought to have received my pencil letter of the 8th giving an account of the fighting of that day, and telling the sad story of poor Chester's death. I wish he had been here now, brave old man, to see how gloriously we are progressing towards the capture of Delhi. We have made a move in advance to-day, occupying Metcalfe House, and I hope in a day or two matters will be in train for taking the city. In the interim our position is on the Ridge, to drive us from which the enemy made another most determined attack this morning soon after daybreak, but they were repulsed everywhere with great slaughter, particularly in the direction of Hindoo Rao's house, where some three or four hundred of them were killed. The Guides are said to have behaved particularly well. The loss on our side has been small: some six or eight killed, and thirty or forty wounded; amongst the latter one officer, Curtis, 60th Rifles, slightly wounded. Captain Knox, Her Majesty's 75th, was killed; he commanded the left picket, and, poor fellow, owes his death to the careless lookout he allowed his men to keep—they got close up to his post at the Flagstaff before he was aware of it, and some of the enemy were actually killed between our camp and his post. It is said, but I know not with what truth, that this was a last desperate effort of the enemy—that they have only three days' provisions, and that there is dreadful sickness in the city; probable enough, but we shall know in the course of the day.

I was speaking to some of the men of the Gwalior contingent that have come over, and they say that the Sepoys are committing all kinds of atrocities in the city, and that the city people are all ready to rise on them when we go in. The Sepoys have lots of money; one man killed to-day had eighty gold mohurs on him, and another thirty-three.

From what we hear of the Jullunder mutineers, in all probability they will be intercepted, a force having marched after them on the morning of their flight, with guns, Infantry, and Irregular Cavalry. Our Irregulars and the Goorkhas are behaving as well as men can behave. I had a letter just now from Bagot, of the 9th—all well.

Daly is now sitting in my tent, and I saw this morning Bunny, Shute, Norman, Hodson, Becher, and Nicoll all well, and many others; indeed, I have heard of no casualties except those I have mentioned, and I have seen officers from all the posts. George Hall I saw yesterday afternoon quite well, and he and Major Martin could not have been in the way of the fighting this morning, no Cavalry having been engaged. Norman, too, who was with me a little time ago, is looking as well and cheerful as ever.

Many kisses to the dear children. May God watch over them and you, as He has hitherto done, is my constant prayer.

(*Diary*) 12*th June.*—Just as I was dressed and going out, heard fire of musketry, and messengers came hurrying down to say that the enemy had got on the Ridge. Alarm sounded, and great confusion. Went up to the Flagstaff—found it too true; the enemy had crept up, and the picket had allowed itself to be surprised. The relieving officer, Captain Knox, killed; and also two or three men of Her Majesty's 75th. Some of the enemy killed on the Ridge, and on our right great slaughter made of them. A quiet day afterwards.

The following ORDERS *by the* GOVERNOR-GENERAL *are sent for your information and guidance:*

Sir Henry Somerset to assume command of Her Majesty's and the Honourable East India Company's Forces in India until further orders; Sir Patrick Grant to proceed to Bengal as Provisional Commander-in-Chief of that Army, pending the appointment of a successor to General Anson; Major-General Reed, C.B., to assume command of the Bengal Army till Sir Patrick Grant arrives; Major-General Sir Henry Barnard to command the Field Force proceeding against Delhi; Brigadier Cotton, Her Majesty's Service, to be Brigadier-General, and command the Peshawar Division for the present.

The above message came by telegraph from Bombay this day, 12th June 1857.

(Signed) J. R. COLVIN,
Lieutenant-Governor, N.W.P.

JAMES NOWELL YOUNG *to Colonel* KEITH YOUNG.

MEAN MEER, 12*th June.*

MY DEAR COLONEL,—As these three trials—viz., Boral Sing, trooper; Dhawkul Sing, trooper; and Fagwa Mahomed Khan— in 8th Light Cavalry, will not stand scrutiny by legal spectacles, I write a few lines accompanying them to acquaint you with the General's reasons for not disposing of the trials as would have been done in ordinary times.

On the 3rd instant, when the horses of the 8th Cavalry were being taken from the regiment, there was much confusion. The regiment was first paraded, four guns were unlimbered before them, and the men were threatened that a squadron of Irregular Cavalry on the spot would be ordered to confine every trooper dismounted, and every man was ordered to mount himself as best he could. The horses were at last got off with the assistance of some spare *syces* from the Artillery. On the whole, the General thought there had been too little systematic arrangement as to what each man was to do to justify his bringing any man of the corps to trial before a General Court-Martial. The three men tried were brought forward as the worst behaved on the occasion, to be made examples of as far as practicable. By the ruse of 'getting themselves thrown,' the men succeeded in defying authority as far as it was in the power of disarmed men to do.

I send by this post the first proceedings on deserters. Twelve more of the 9th, and nine of the 16th, have since been tried, and of them, two from each corps—old Sepoys—are to be transported for life.—Yours truly,

JAMES NOWELL YOUNG,
Deputy Judge-Advocate General.

LIEUTENANT-COLONEL YOUNG,
Judge-Advocate General.

Colonel KEITH YOUNG *to his wife.*

CAMP, DELHI CANTONMENTS, *Saturday*, 13th *June.*

I feel very much the anxiety I know you are suffering, and wish to Heaven it were in my power to relieve you by telling you with any certainty when we are to be within the walls of Delhi. That we shall be so soon, and make a triumphant entry, no one in camp doubts for an instant; but the *when* is not yet settled, and the delay is caused, as I told you before, by a wish to avoid the loss of men that there must necessarily be on our side if we advance to the attack without a breach being made and other necessary preparations. These are all, I believe, going on quietly. The enemy have not attempted to molest us since the terrible lesson they got yesterday, and they have scarcely even fired a gun from the city since.

I told you of the 60th Native Infantry having at last mutinied and fired on their officers, none of whom were hurt, as they escaped into our camp. It seems pretty certain that the men of this corps have not come into Delhi, but are making off to their homes across country. A party of ten was met by the 9th Lancers yesterday, who cut up eight of them; and a large body was seen higher up crossing the river.

It is the most sensible thing that Sepoys when they mutiny can do, to cut off to their homes, for their situation in Delhi must be anything but an agreeable one, and the addition to their numbers will hardly be an additional source of strength in their present confused state. I told you—did I not?—of the recent quantities of money some of the Sepoys are said to have; and one of the 75th, I think it was, got eighty-eight gold mohurs from one of them the day after the first fight, and yesterday several bags were taken by our men.

It is a pity the Jullunder force has got away unhurt, but I have no doubt their day will come. A report was received to-day of their marching towards Delhi *viâ* Hansi, but whether they will enter Delhi remains to be seen. Should they do so, their numbers, as I before remarked, will add little or nothing to the real strength of the insurgents, cooped up as they are within the walls.

Poor Mrs Chester, how I feel for her! And yet I don't know that it was not a happy release for poor Chester. His life must have been a continual burden to him; and though he bore up manfully and was really wonderfully well considering, yet he must, I think, have sunk eventually under the excitement in which he was living for the time. I told you that his grey horse, 'Sir Walter,' was shot down by the same shot that killed him. Maisey's horse was also killed that day; and Hamilton (Pension Paymaster), who is here acting in the Quartermaster-General's Department, had his horse's leg broken by the same shot that killed Chester.

I suppose you have by this time had at Simla a detailed account of the killed and wounded; of the latter several are at their work again. I saw Colonel Herbert yesterday morning with his regiment apparently none the worse; and Light was at mess last night eating a good dinner. General Reed has bought Chester's other horse, 'Miss Haliday,' but there is very little chance of his ever riding it; he is still confined to his tent, and looking very ill. I went over to him just now to do a little work; he is a poor, infirm old man, and seems as if a puff of wind would carry him away. It was a terrible trip he had down here, and he was sick when he started; I almost wonder at his surviving it.

Major Martin was at my tent this morning for news; he and his men, with George Hall, are encamped about a mile or two to our left rear, guarding the camp. A large convoy came in this morning, supposed to be in danger last night from a report by Fenwick at Alleepore that the enemy had crossed in force at Bhagput to attack it. No truth whatever in the report. There were rumours this morning of an attack from the Fort, but none came off.

We are very comfortable, Mactier and I, in our tent. It is not quite so cool as you have it at Simla; but, with the assistance of a *tattie*, we have nothing to complain of.

(*Diary*) 13*th June.*—Wake up about 1 A.M., and get ready. Arrangements made apparently for assault;* but, after an hour or two's delay, decided that it was too late, the pickets not having been withdrawn in time. Most fortunate, I think, that we did not attack, for failure would have been death—and success was not quite certain; and we are not reduced to such a desperate state yet as to risk all. My own idea is—wait till the Sikh corps comes. Very hot day—attack on the heights again; about five, go to Flagstaff. A party of the enemy's Cavalry got round to our left; Congreve very excited about it.

CAMP, DELHI CANTONMENTS, *Sunday*, 14*th June.*

Your two letters of the 11th and 12th reached me a few minutes ago, and very glad indeed I was to get them, as I hardly expected to see your handwriting again for some time, there being a report in camp that a party of the enemy's Cavalry had got back to Alleepore and stopped our communication. It must, however, be a mistake; but a detachment, with some of the Jheend Raja's troops, has been sent out to see, and if the enemy were actually at Alleepore they will no doubt soon make themselves scarce. It is supposed that there is a party of only about a hundred. It seems very strange to me that, now the country is so disturbed, our dâks continue to come so very regularly; and yesterday Becher told me that the bullock-train came in without meeting any interruption, and bringing property of all kinds. I fancy the Sikh corps, which we understand are on their way down to reinforce us, go a long way in keeping things quiet in the direction where they are marching.

* See *Forty-one Years in India*, pp. 167–168.

We still continue to occupy our old position on the Ridge, and the enemy occasionally make faint efforts to dislodge us, always ending in their discomfiture and loss. But it is annoying to think that there seems little prospect now of our entering Delhi until the Sikh corps join us, or until the Bhurtpore, or Jeypore, or other contingents make their appearance; or until there is such a decided schism in Delhi as to show that the two parties are pitted one against the other.

News of a reliable nature came in yesterday to Greathed to the effect that the Hindoos were becoming quite disgusted, finding they were being made complete dupes of by the Mahomedans, who wish to make a religious war of it. Hopes were expressed that the Sappers and Artillery might be brought over to our side. One of the contingents on which we can depend is said to be at Pulwal, about twenty-eight miles from here, but it is a very difficult thing to obtain information from any quarter except from the main road to Lahore and Simla.

We had service in camp this morning, Mr Rotton, the clergyman from Meerut, officiating. There was a very small congregation; he merely read prayers—no sermon.

I am very glad you wrote to Mrs Chester. Yes; I have his watch, jewel-case, &c., all safe, and a large lock of his hair, which Mactier cut off for Mrs Chester. I hope she will come up and stay with you.

George Hall was at church this morning, quite well, as are all his men, he said. Daly is now writing in my tent; and I have seen nearly all the Simla people this morning, or rather those in whom the Simla people are interested—Hodson, Shute, Becher, &c.

(*Diary*) 14*th June.*—Service in 2nd Fusiliers' mess, but at home all day. Attack on Metcalfe House, and Cavalry said to have got round left flank.

CAMP, DELHI CANTONMENTS, *Monday,* 15*th June.*

I was unavoidably interrupted this morning while writing to you. I had finished the extract of the newsletter * when General Barnard came into my tent with an express announcing the departure of a large force from Jullunder (some four thousand) to join us here; and after a long conversation as to the ex-

* See page 62.

pediency of waiting for these troops before making the assault on Delhi, he asked me to go over to Greathed, the Governor-General's Agent, and see what his idea now was on the subject of an immediate assault, which he had hitherto strongly advocated at all risks. His views, however, are now somewhat modified. We then went to talk with General Reed, and had a long conversation as to the advantages or disadvantages of waiting till reinforcements arrive : the result is, if Brigadier Wilson agrees —and I have no doubt he will—that we shall wait quietly in our present position until a larger force is collected. The truth is, poor General Barnard has been so badgered by Greathed and one or two others about him to move on with his present force, that against his own conviction he had determined to do so, and in all human probability the attack, though rather a desperate one considering our limited numbers, would have been successful; but it *might* have failed from some unlooked-for accident, and then 'Good-bye!' not only to our little force, but to India itself. With the reinforcements now on their way to join us—and we reckon they cannot all be here till the 25th or 26th instant—risk of failure would be avoided; and the only thing against the delay is the bad political effect it may have, but this will be put to rights again immediately Delhi falls; and as to other mutineering regiments joining, the only force we are anxious about is that from Bareilly, which has guns with it. But we hear there is every prospect of this force remaining in Rohilkund to watch events; and, besides this, the bridge at Gurmukteesur has been destroyed, which would render their crossing the Ganges a difficult operation.

There must be sufficient European troops now at Cawnpore to keep Oude quiet; and from Agra we hear that all is getting on well, notwithstanding P——'s croaking.

I have told you all this that you may see exactly how matters stand with us, but you must not say a word about it to any one. The two Generals talked of having a Council of War to discuss the question, but I advised them just to speak quietly to Greathed and Brigadier Wilson, and decide the point of waiting or not waiting themselves. In our present position we are perfectly secure; every effort that the enemy have made to dislodge us has ended in their discomfiture and loss—they have not gained a single advantage over us of any kind as yet. This must necessarily make them dispirited, and they are not likely to become a bit more courageous when they know that a large force is on its way to join us. With our present little Army, after taking the city we could not prevent the mutineers escaping; but with the force advancing we should be able to spare a strong brigade to go in pursuit of the wretches.

It is not very pleasant the prospect of being in tents for another ten days or so, but you would be surprised to see how comfortable we are—with *tatties* and a *punkah*. As to our living, we could not dine more luxuriously than we do if we were quietly located at Simla, and I have not seen better *gram*-fed mutton anywhere; and you will be amused when I tell you that the pastry at the mess is about the best I have come across in India—it seems that the Artillery mess cook or confectioner is famous for his skill. I give you all these little details that you may know we are not utterly miserable! Of our party, Norman, Mactier, and myself always dine at the mess; and Becher sometimes. Our *tiffin*, Mactier's and mine, is a biscuit and a glass of wine or brandy and water. We are nearly at the end of the two boxes I got from Anderson's; but Mactier has picked up another box somewhere, which will last us, I hope, until we get into Delhi.

(*Diary*) 15*th June*.—Attack by the enemy in force this morning about seven, on right flank; little execution done on them, I fear. Saw one of their colours flying. They were driven back, however, and have not ventured to show themselves since. Go to Greathed, by General Barnard's wish, to talk of waiting for reinforcements. Agree on Council of War, so decide; otherwise there was to have been an assault in the morning.

Extract from NEWSLETTER *of* 15*th June* (*written by a* SPY *inside* DELHI).

On the night of the 14th Mahbook Ulee Khan died, and will be buried this morning. A petition from the Sepoys of Nussereebad and Neemuch reached the King to the effect that they were coming up with the treasure and magazine stores. 'Doun Sing plundered us; if you send us assistance we can come on.' The King wrote in reply that no such assistance could be afforded, that he himself was prepared to die, and that any others prepared for a like fate might come on. On account of the death of Mahbook Ulee Khan there is a difficulty to-day about provisions; it is not likely that effective arrangements will again be made for supplies.

The mutineers who first came to Delhi have grown heavy on account of their being laden with plunder, and are no longer fit for action, and on being ordered to fight set forth excuses. The day before yesterday the King said, 'If you do not go out, I will blow up the powder-magazine and die.' On this some of the troops went out to fight; and on their return at night, when it was found they also were dispirited and that defeat was only delayed on account of the protection afforded by the gates and walls, the force were still more dispirited. Replies have come to the King from Bhurtpore, Dholpore, and Gwalior. Gwalior says, 'When you are really King I will come to your assistance.' Dholpore was first going to kill the messenger, but let him go; and Bhurtpore said he was always disloyal to Delhi, and would remain so.

CAMP, DELHI CANTONMENTS, *Tuesday*, 16*th June.*

After all, they decided to have a Council of War yesterday afternoon, and, as I expected, it was almost unanimously resolved to wait in our present position for reinforcements; and Brigadier Wilson, I was glad to see, was quite of opinion that this is the right thing to do. He says we are perfectly safe here, that nothing can harm us, and with fresh troops we shall be able to take Delhi with but little loss and with a certainty of destroying the mutineers.

Young Greathed, of the Engineers, was present at the Council, and was the great advocate for a forward move at once; but his talk was too fiery and wild for any one to listen to. Here therefore we remain for the next eight or ten days, and in that time it will be surprising if the dissensions among the mutineers do not increase.

Two villagers came in this morning from Allyghur, bringing an extract of General Orders appointing Patrick Grant Provincial Commander-in-Chief.* I questioned the men, who said they left Allyghur two days ago, when all was quiet there, and the road and telegraph open to Agra. The collector was at

* See page 56.

Allyghur, and some European troops were also arriving—pushed up, I suppose, from Cawnpore. There was a letter also to-day from Nynee Tal, giving an account of the fugitives there from Bareilly. Brigadier Sibbald is the only one known to have been killed; but several officers of the 18th Native Infantry have not turned up, amongst them young Stewart who married Miss Maul. She was at Nynee Tal. At Almorah the Goorkhas were quite staunch, and Colonel M'Causland has taken the precaution of disarming the Native Artillery, who are said to have plotted the murder of the officers of the 66th.

Hodson was in my tent just now. No dâk in to-day; your last letter is that of the 13th June. What an unnecessary alarm you appear to have had! These alarmists ought to be tried by a Court-Martial of ladies; consult Mrs Hodson and Mrs Norman about this!

(*Diary*) 16*th June.*—A very quiet day; hardly a shot fired by the enemy all day long; and we are comparatively quiet, entrenching our positions. Another Council of War this afternoon, when it was decided to wait for all the reinforcements coming up before the assault is made; this will allow of the insurgents being completely followed up and destroyed, and is the right plan.

Major MORRIESON *to Colonel* BECHER, *Quartermaster-General.**

BHURTPORE, 16*th June.*

MY DEAR BECHER,—The bearer is a *hurkara* of the Bhurtpore regiment, and one of thirty despatched by me to be posted on the road to bring your correspondence. They have bungled the matter, however, and have been fleeced of my letter, so that the communication cannot be maintained till you receive this. I sent another note—two notes—enclosing copy of General Order appointing Sir H. Somerset to temporary charge of the office of Commander-in-Chief in India, and our old Adjutant-General, Patrick Grant, to be Commander-in-Chief of the Bengal Army before Delhi.† I hope these may reach; but if not, and this

---

* This letter and others from Major Morrieson, Captain Eden, &c., came by secret letter-carriers called *cossids*.

† See page 56.

(DELHI.) PURANA KILA.
or Old Fort.

does, then let me have your communication, on the thinnest paper and the smallest space, for Agra or Calcutta.—Believe me, yours very sincerely, R. MORRIESON.

Colonel KEITH YOUNG *to his wife.*

CAMP, DELHI CANTONMENTS, *Wednesday,* 17*th June.*

I wish with you that we were in Delhi, but of the wisdom of remaining where we are until reinforcements arrive there cannot be a question. We shall then be able to act effectually, and pursue with vigour those of the mutineers who escape from the city, which, with our present small force, would be a manifest impossibility.

Nothing of the least moment has occurred since my letter of yesterday. The enemy have hardly fired a shot for the last twenty-four hours, and must be getting more and more disheartened and uncomfortable; and as to the mutineering regiments from Jullunder and other places joining them, we scarcely look upon these additions as any great advantage to them, for there is no proper leader to organise their forces, and the more men they have the more difficult will be their organisation. It seems very doubtful, however, if either the Jullunder or Rohilkund mutineers are making for Delhi, but parties of ours and of the Jheend Raja's are on the lookout for the former; and as to the latter, it is said that one, Bahadoor Khan, a descendant of the old Rohilla Chiefs, has set up the standard of independence at Bareilly—and this being the case, he will of course endeavour to keep the mutineering regiments with him.

Nothing is known of the 28th at Shahjehanpore yet, but it is feared they would go with the rest. No more Rosa sugar or rum for milk punch! I hope you have been manufacturing plenty of apricot jam!

We continue to receive the best accounts from Peshawar, where General Cotton * has arranged a first-rate force, mounting some of the Europeans who can ride on the 5th Cavalry horses. Of the 64th Mrs Poulton will have later accounts from the *Lahore Chronicle* than I can give. The impression here appears to be that, however mutinously inclined, they would dare to do nothing

---

* The late General Sir Sydney Cotton, G.C.B.

after hearing of the severe examples that have been made in other corps in Peshawar.

George Hall came and sat with me this morning for half-an-hour; he is very well, but is rather disgusted at being ordered back to Paniput with some men of his regiment to secure the communication being kept open. Another officer goes with him, and there is also a civilian of the name of Richardes, so that he will not be alone; and besides, with the fresh troops that are daily coming up, he will meet with many friends; but he does not like being away from Delhi and Head-Quarters. He is an excellent officer, and is allowed to have done very good service; and this is perhaps the reason why he has been selected for this duty, as he will exercise a kind of independent command.

CAMP, DELHI CANTONMENTS, 17*th June (later)*.

There is an interesting letter just received from M'Causland at Almorah, saying that all was right there, the Goorkhas behaving admirably, and an expedition being organised to retake Bareilly. The Goorkhas' four guns, manned with European Volunteers, and about four hundred Horse would, it is supposed, be sufficient. The Nawab of Rampore is favourable to us, and has taken charge of Moradabad, so that I hope soon we shall have good accounts from Rohilkund.

Word has come in from the city that the inhabitants there are willing to guarantee to us thirty lacs of rupees if we agree to spare the city.

I saw Hodson this morning, and he has asked me to mention to Mrs Hodson that he had not time to write as he intended. I have never come across Duncan Pemberton since the first day of his arrival; I fancy he is always at Hindoo Rao's, in the batteries there.

Poor Dr Hay is one of those murdered at Bareilly. Mrs Hay was at Nynee Tal.

There was an attack this afternoon in two columns, under Reid and Tombs, on a battery being erected on our right flank: a quite successful capture of a 9-pounder gun, and many men killed. Tombs had two horses shot under him. General Barnard is very excited about it, and came over to the mess to thank Tombs.*

* The late General Sir Harry Tombs, K.C.B.

CAMP, DELHI CANTONMENTS, *Thursday*, 18*th June.*

Your letter of 15th reached me rather late yesterday afternoon. We had begun to fear that the dâk was plundered; and it seems, from what the postmaster says, that there was an attempt on the part of some Sowars to seize the dâk horses, and this in some measure was the cause of the delay. It is wonderful how the dâks come along so regularly as they do; but there are so many of our troops now moving along the road that I trust any of the insurgent Sowars there may be about will think twice before they try anything on the Trunk Road. George Hall, too, moving up with his men will have a good effect. He started last night.

Major Martin, I believe, remains here; but the doctor (Allen) went off last night with the wounded, and such ladies as there were in camp, to Meerut. Amongst the latter we have at last got rid of Mrs Laughton (the Persian), wife of Major Laughton. Fancy the absurdity of his being allowed to bring her with him from Umballa; and she must have had some twenty or thirty camels and half that number of carts in her train!

The enemy have again been firing at us, but they do not harm us much, as their gunners are not very good marksmen, which is fortunate, as otherwise our outposts might suffer considerably. However, a sad casualty has occurred, which ought not to have happened, and our Engineers are blamed for not being as careful as they might be. There has consequently been rather an outcry against them generally, though the young hands, including certainly Chesney, are liked, and known to be good men. Yesterday an unfortunate shot from the enemy's battery in the city found its way near Hindoo Rao's house into an open doorway, and killed an officer (Lieutenant Wheatley, 54th), two Carabineers, two Goorkhas, and wounded four men besides; all which might have been avoided had a few sand-bags been put up by the Engineers, as they have been ordered to do. General Barnard was very vexed and angry about it, and I understand he pitched into Major Laughton furiously this morning. It is a great pity that this should have occurred, as with this exception the enemy's guns have done no damage for the last two days; but they fire very seldom now, and seem to have given up attacking us. Yesterday afternoon, however, it was found that they were erecting a fresh battery on our right, and a party was sent to destroy it, which was done, and one of their guns captured and brought into camp, many of the enemy being killed; whilst on our side the only casualties were three or four wounded, including one officer, Captain Brown of the Fusiliers. It would be a good thing indeed if the enemy would attack us in force; but there is no prospect whatever of this.

I can imagine Hodson having a very good opinion of himself, but he certainly is a first-rate officer. He and Daly and Reid are about the best officers in camp; but none of them were present at any of the Councils of War. The General, however, goes about consulting every one; he is a very good little man, but not a Sir Charles Napier.

The rains still keep off, and they are making arrangements for putting the camp in order to be prepared for the rain when it does come.

Our shells occasionally find their way into the Palace, and by a newsletter received this morning one fell within a few feet of the enemy's powder-magazine, which has since been removed. There will be no effectual shelling of the Palace until the city is taken, I fear, and then we shall be able to overwhelm them with shells from our small mortars.

We hear there is bad news from Jhansi, in Bundelkund, and, I much fear, notwithstanding the way Colonel Hampton writes of them, the 50th will not remain staunch. Good accounts to-day from Saharunpore of the Nusseree battalion. Arthur Becher was in my tent just now; he and Mactier always send some kind message to you. Congreve also desired me kindly to remember him; he is quite well again.

(*Diary*) 18*th June*.—In the tent all day, and kept it tolerably cool. Very quiet in the evening; a shell fell close to the mess tent, but did no damage.

Major REID *to Captain* S. BECHER.

Dated 18*th June* (*before Delhi*).

That was a satisfactory business last evening. I destroyed the two batteries in Kissengunge, burnt the village and all the timber used in forming batteries and magazines, destroyed the gates of two *surrais*, and killed between fifty and sixty men—thirty-one bodies counted in one place, and nine in another; a great number of wounded men were taken away. Our loss in the two columns (Reid's and Tombs') was two privates, 1st Fusiliers, killed, and Captain Brown wounded; also four or five men of the different regiments employed. Major Tombs had two horses shot under him, and his jacket was rent by a musket-shot.

Colonel KEITH YOUNG *to his wife.*

CAMP, DELHI CANTONMENTS, *Friday,* 19*th June.*

There is little to tell you since I wrote yesterday. All is as quiet as possible, and while I write there is not a single gun being fired, either from our side or by the enemy. They fired away a great deal yesterday, but I only heard of one casualty—a man of the Carabineers slightly wounded in the face by a shell when going up to Hindoo Rao's batteries. Our shot and shell must do them much damage, though we do not know the amount, but falling in the confined space they do they cannot fail to do injury. I fear, however, there is little chance now of our blowing up their magazines—at any rate, until we can establish ourselves very much nearer the Palace—most of the mortars with the siege-train being of very small calibre. Of these there are a great many, and our fire will be overwhelming, it is said, when our batteries are sufficiently advanced; but this they will not be for several days yet, until fresh troops arrive. Metcalfe House is one of our most advanced posts, and it is occupied in force, but more as a picket at present than as a post of attack.

Some people from the Jeypore and Bhurtpore contingents came into camp last night, and a party of Sirdars are to arrive here to-day with some Cavalry, but the main body of the contingents will probably remain where it is, or thereabouts, to keep the country quiet and cut off the insurgents when Delhi is taken. It is of immense political importance to us these contingents being where they are, as it reassures the villages, and shows the mutineers and the people of Delhi that these Hindoo states adhere and are faithful to our cause.

There is a most distressing report from Shahjehanpore, of all the people there, except two, having been murdered while at church on the 31st May; the report comes in a letter from Simpson from Meerut, and wants confirmation. As to Jhansi, I fear the report of the massacre of all there is but too true. What a fearful retribution will yet fall on those infernal scoundrels! And as to Delhi, when we get in there I don't think our men will spare a single life; they are perfectly infuriated.

I do not think I told you of rather a touching incident that occurred on the day of the fight, on the 8th, when we got up to Hindoo Rao's. In an old ruined mosque there we found an old woman with the dead body of a Fakeer, a fine young man, who had been shot by our advance party; and she was mourning over the body and caressing it when two or three European soldiers came in, and one of them put up his musket and was going to shoot her, swearing that the women were worse than the men and did more mischief. I told the man not to disgrace himself and us by killing a defenceless old woman, and that we must not imitate the butchers of Delhi and Meerut, and become like them. One of the party chimed in with me, and spoke to the same effect; the would-be murderer sulkily drew off, and the poor woman's life was spared. She was alive when I left the place about half-an-hour later, and I hope escaped uninjured. I had a long conversation with her; she told me she was a Native of Cashmere, which she had left many years ago to reside near Delhi, and the young man was her only son. She of course declared that he was a harmless individual, with no evil designs on us; but her being found at such a juncture, in the entrenched position of the enemy, didn't say much in his favour. She seemed quite to understand that it was not our custom to make war on women, and spoke with apparent horror of the atrocities committed at Delhi on unoffending women and children.

I was at Major Martin's tent this morning; he was well. Hodson, too, I saw a little while ago; he had been suffering from cold, but was right again.

(*Diary*) 19*th June.*—Serious attack on our right rear in the afternoon—the Neemuch and Nussereebad regiments, and a troop of Native Horse Artillery; very serious affair.* Stay on the Mound with General Barnard. Attack repulsed; but night came on, and result not known. People looking very serious. Dine at mess about ten. Go and see Daly—wounded; also Becher.

CAMP, DELHI CANTONMENTS, *Saturday, 20th June.*

I fear it will be some time before this reaches Simla, for the enemy are evidently trying to cut off the communication with our rear, and, until Olpherts' force arrives, which ought to be here in four days, the dâks will certainly be very uncertain.

The troops from Neemuch and Nussereebad, which consist of three regiments and a troop of Horse Artillery, made an attack on us yesterday evening on our right rear, and, as usual, got well thrashed, losing two of their guns; but I am sorry to say we lost also several men, some thirty, perhaps, killed and wounded; and amongst the former, I am very sorry to say, was poor Major Yule of the 9th Lancers. He was shot in the thigh, and then received a mortal wound in the head and neck. Arthur Becher, too, is slightly wounded in the right arm—a musket-ball went through the fleshy part of it below the elbow; but as the bone, Mactier says, is not broken, I hope he will soon be well again. He has just been writing a left-handed letter to Mrs Arthur. If you write to her, or when you see Sep. Becher, you may assure them that the wound is a very trifling one and not likely to be productive of anything more than a little temporary inconvenience. He himself is very cheerful. Daly, also, of the Guides, was wounded yesterday evening in the left shoulder by a musket-ball, which passed clean through without doing any material injury; but it might have been a very serious affair had the ball penetrated an inch lower.

At Daly's request I wrote a few lines to Mrs Daly this morning, and, to show her that he was not so very ill, he directed the letter to her with his own hand. It would be kind were you to go over and see her, and say you have heard from me that he is getting on as well as he possibly can; and with reference to his not writing himself, it was thought desirable that he should remain

---

* As far as I have ever heard, the troops which arrived at Delhi from Nusseroebad and attacked our rear on the 19th June were the two (not three) Native Infantry regiments from Nussereebad, a Native field battery—not 'a troop of Horse Artillery'—and a few of the 1st Bombay Lancers.—H. W. NORMAN.

as quiet as possible for a day or two. The enemy suffered very considerably—some four or five hundred killed and wounded. One prisoner was taken, a man of the Bombay Lancers, who were at Nussereebad. He says almost a dozen of his regiment, including himself, deserted with the mutineers; that there were three * regiments, and when they reached Delhi the gates were shut upon them and they were told they must go out and fight first. Hence yesterday's affair.

This morning part of the same force came round again, but were soon driven away without any loss whatever on our side. It most unfortunately got quite dark yesterday evening before the enemy were driven back; had it not been for this, we should probably have taken all their guns. Hinghan (*kitmutghar*) is most bellicosely inclined, and went out this morning to where the Jheend Raja's troops are, in our rear, guarding the camp; they fired away, too, at the enemy, who, Hinghan says, cut off as hard as they could when they saw our troops coming. Hinghan then went over the field of battle of yesterday, which, he says, was covered with the dead bodies of black people, but not a single white one. Our killed and wounded had been brought in.

I was with the General yesterday at a place called the Mound, where we were out of fire and could see all that was going on. With the exception of Becher, who should not have been where he was, there is no one else hurt that you know. Shute, Bunny, Hodson, &c. all well. This fighting is all very horrid, and I hope to be able soon to tell you that the business is satisfactorily terminated. When Major Olpherts joins, our force will be nearly doubled. All the detachments that are ahead of him will be ordered to halt till he comes up, so that he will march in here with an imposing force.

Norman has just come in to our tent to have a little sleep, and I think I shall have one also, as I have just finished this. There is a glorious wind blowing, and, with the *tattie* well watered, the tent is quite cool and comfortable.

Perhaps the dâk may come in after all, as a man has just returned from Alleepore, sent by Hodson, to say all is quiet there; and a convoy of two or three hundred camels with grain came in this morning without molestation.

* See note, page 71.

(*Diary*) 20*th June.*—A large party went out, under Hope Grant, before daybreak to the scene of last night's action—brought in two * captured guns, driving off small parties of the enemy; but Grant was hardly in camp before two guns again opened on the camp, driving in all the followers and cattle. All the disposable force out again. Hard work, poor fellows, but no loss on our side. There were, however, forty or fifty killed and wounded last night; † amongst the former, poor Yule. Some four hundred of the enemy, they say, *hors de combat*.

CAMP, DELHI CANTONMENTS, *Sunday,* 21*st June.*

The dâk, it seems, was brought in yesterday on horseback; the coachman, hearing that the road wasn't quite safe, took a circuitous route with the mail. He properly got a present of twenty-five rupees for his carefulness. Precautions having been now taken to have parties of Cavalry along the road, I hope there will be no further fear for our letters. Letters were received from Major Olpherts yesterday, when he was to be at Guraunda, and he expected to reach here by daybreak on Tuesday morning, the eventful 23rd—which day, it is thought at Simla, is to decide the fall of India!

The addition of Olpherts' force, which, besides Cavalry and Artillery, consists of a regiment of Sikhs—a first-rate regiment, he says—and between three and four hundred European Infantry, would be a very nice increase to our force; but so far as thrashing the enemy goes, they have not the least chance if they attack us again, and some heavy guns have been put in the battery, to protect our right rear, if they try to get round that way again.

The principal thing we want fresh troops for is to give those in camp a little rest, as when there is an alarm the whole of the Infantry is called out, and it is rather hard work for them; but still their health is excellent, and the weather is far from being as disagreeable as one would think.

You ask me what Hope Grant's opinion was about making an immediate assault on Delhi, without waiting for reinforcements.

* In point of fact, only one gun was captured.—H. W. NORMAN.

† When returns came in the loss proved much heavier than is here stated. Three officers and seventeen men were killed, two men were missing, and seven officers and seventy men were wounded. No less than sixty horses were killed and wounded in our force.—H. W. NORMAN.

He was not present at either of the only two Councils that I attended, but I am pretty sure that he could not have voted for an assault. It would have been a desperate enterprise, and, if not successful, everything would have been lost. When the first attack was fixed upon—and I don't think I ever told you of this, it was on the morning of the 13th—it would have been in the nature of a surprise, and much more likely to succeed. The attack did not come off on account of some dilatoriness on the part of Brigadier Graves in bringing in the pickets, and after that day the enemy were on the alert. Depend upon it, it has been a wise decision resolving to wait for the troops now coming up—the 8th, 61st, and Coke's* regiment—which we look for in eight days or so; but if favourable opportunity offers—and there is a talk now of a split in the city amongst the enemy—we may still go in before the 8th, &c., arrive, but no risk of failure will be run, depend upon it: there is too much at stake.

Your letter of the 19th has just reached me. Tell your friend from me, with my kind regards, that I do not think any one in camp shares her fears of our losing India and of our army being annihilated; there does not seem the least possible chance of such a contingency, and she may rest happy with (*D.V.*) the certain consciousness of our being masters of Delhi before many days are over. The delay is unfortunate, but it can't be helped.

Becher is getting on very well, but there is some doubt now as to whether the small bone of the arm is not broken; Mactier, however, says it is a matter of trifling consequence. Daly is getting on well also. He is a very good fellow, and a first-rate soldier.

We had service this morning at 6 A.M., and such a long, sleepy sermon.

Captain EDEN, *Political Agent, to Colonel* BECHER, *Quartermaster-General.*

MITRALL, 21*st June.*

MY DEAR BECHER,—I've been obliged to move from Pulwal; my men were deserting, though quiet. Shall be near Hodul to-morrow, and stay as long as I can. I'm sorry and disgusted

---

* Now General Sir John Coke, G.C.B.

I can't be of more use ; I'll do all I can to keep open the communication, nevertheless. You *must* be in Delhi to-day. Give me a line to send Lieutenant-Governor. This is the third messenger I've sent you.—Yours sincerely, W. F. EDEN.

Colonel KEITH YOUNG *to his wife.*

CAMP, DELHI CANTONMENTS, *Monday,* 22*nd June.*

I have just had Oree's (*bearer*) letter read to me, and I find it is a very proper one, without a particle of treason in it. He is very particular in asking after Soobhan's health ; tells him that all has gone on well at Simla since we left, that grain is selling at the usual price, and that there is no cause whatever for any uneasiness up at Simla. Oree is evidently no croaker. He gives also an account of the weather, which, he says, is unpleasantly hot, no rain having fallen. The little boys, too, he mentions as being very well.

Nothing has occurred of any moment since I wrote to you yesterday. We had a false alarm in the afternoon, and all the troops turned out, but instead of an attack being meditated it seems that a party of Cavalry were escaping from the city and trying to get across the river, when they were fired at from the Fort—Irregulars, most likely, who were tired of the work and trying to get away to their homes.

Maisey told me this morning—and I hope it will prove true—that word has been brought in by a Native servant from Bareilly that the officers of the 18th Native Infantry who were supposed to have been murdered had been escorted out of Bareilly by some men of their own regiment, and had reached Nynee Tal. The report wants confirmation, but is very likely to be true, as the man corroborates the story we had heard of Dr Hay and others having been taken into the city and there murdered.

We have heard nothing more of Shahjehanpore, and no authentic intelligence has been received yet of what has actually happened there. All that I have seen came in a private letter from Tooney Simpson, in which he said that the regiment had mutinied on the 31st May—and here's the 22nd June.

It is most unfortunate our communication being so completely cut off towards Culcutta. We hear regularly from Meerut, and there was a letter in from Allyghur yesterday of the 18th instant, I think, when all was well; and to-day letters have come in from Mr Harvey and Captain Eden of the 18th, 19th, and 20th from Pulwal, where the Jeypore and Bhurtpore contingents are—some four thousand Foot, one thousand Horse, and seven guns. They are all right, but I fancy they will remain there until Delhi falls, when they will be of essential service in scouring and quieting the country.

You may have heard, perhaps, that the bridge at Bhagput had been broken; this is the road by which we communicate with Meerut. It seems the report is true. It was done by some Goojur disaffected villagers; but a large party of the Jheend Raja's troops are now there, and have recovered nearly all the boats, and as the bridge is one that could not have been kept up in the rains, it won't be put together again, and boats will be quite sufficient to take across stores and things required.

I wrote again to Mrs Daly this morning. Mackinnon and Mactier examined Daly's wound, and pronounced very favourably of it, and I hope he will soon be right again. There is not a better or more gallant soldier in camp than he is. Arthur Becher's arm is getting on very well, but he does not at all like the confinement. Hodson has got the temporary command of the Guide Corps till Daly gets well; certainly the fittest man in camp for it.

We are going to lose Major Laughton—whose wife was in camp with such a large retinue—he returns to Umballa—Lieutenant-Colonel Baird Smith coming from Roorkee as Chief Engineer in his place. I don't know about Chamberlain making a good Adjutant-General after the war is over, but he will be invaluable now, and his presence here will be worth more than a thousand men. We expect him either to-day by the mail-cart, or else he will come in with Olpherts' force in the morning. I hope when the force arrives they will pick General ―――― up with it on arrest, and bring him to a Court-Martial for his imbecile conduct.

It is just twelve (noon), and the dâk not in yet, so I will detain this no longer.

(*Diary*) *22nd June.*—All quiet to-day, but the talk is of a grand attack on our position to-morrow. Olpherts' force is at Raie, two marches off, and will join us in the morning. Bad news from

Gwalior—a letter from Pulwal says the Gwalior contingent has mutinied; the Gwalior man himself true. Troops ordered to be in readiness early in the morning.

P. H.* to Colonel BECHER, Camp, Delhi.

HODUL, 23rd June.

MY DEAR BECHER,—These blackguard troops began to bolt, and set up a separate standard, and we were, to save the regiment, obliged to take ground to the rear. D—— them! they are all alike; as for soldiering, a *tom-tom* and a *lattee* is all that should be allowed them as equipment.

Many thanks for the brandy and baccy. This awful heat! I have been very sick, but better to-day.

The Raja of Bullubghur, a scoundrel, sent me the enclosed last night: 'There are unknown covered ways running all through to north part of Delhi;' but Metcalfe should know about these, one being supposed to run from Hindoo Rao's house to the Palace. However, punch these *cossids;* and give me an early line, for they are in great anxiety at Agra, and it would be a vast relief to them to get a conclusive note.

That wretched Bhurtpore force kept me, by their mutiny, from joining Head-Quarters, for I left Agra with full credentials, and should have enjoyed the campaign; but what we have had to undergo has been distressing, useless, and disgusting. I hope this will get to you safe.—Yours, P. H.

COLONEL BECHER,
       Quartermaster-General.

---

* This letter is probably from Mr Harvey, although only initials are given. See Captain Eden's letter, page 96.

CHAPTER V.

SIEGE OF DELHI (*continued*)—ARRIVAL OF REINFORCEMENTS.

Colonel KEITH YOUNG *to his wife.*

CAMP, DELHI CANTONMENTS, *Tuesday, 23rd June.*

I assure you I have had the best of health, I am thankful to say, since joining camp; and as to the heat—it isn't cool, certainly, but there is nothing at all to complain of. Hodson had caught a little cold; he was living in a wretchedly small tent, and felt the heat in consequence. He has now moved into a larger tent, and, as his cold has nearly left, I suppose he won't complain any more. The universal remark is, 'What a remarkably mild hot season!' Yesterday was, I think, one of the hottest days we have had; to-day the wind is a little cold again.

The grand attack of the enemy on the eventful 23rd June * has been made, and, as usual, they have been unsuccessful at every point, so I hope we are good in India for another hundred years. I don't think that they have ventured to come to close quarters anywhere, having been kept at a distance by our Artillery, which has been playing away at them in grand style. They endeavoured to get to our right rear, as they did last Friday evening, but they were met by Olpherts' force and soon driven back. His party, consisting of about four hundred European Infantry, a Sikh corps, some Cavalry, and eight guns,† with a large convoy of stores and ammunition, is now safe in camp, baggage and everything; and a welcome addition they are to us.

I have not heard of any casualties this morning on our side, and as we have had it all our own way they must, if any, be very

---

* See *Forty-one Years in India*, pp. 172–174.

† Only six guns came—not eight: four guns of a European troop, and two guns of a Native troop—all from Jullunder. —H. W. NORMAN.

trifling. Young Anson I saw just now: he came in with Olpherts. Chamberlain, the new Adjutant-General, has not arrived, but he will most likely be here in the course of to-day or to-morrow. We shall be very glad indeed to see him, for we sadly want a head to direct. Norman is a very gallant and good officer, but he has not the experience of Chamberlain, nor would his opinion carry the same weight with it. I was glad to hear from Norman yesterday that there was a letter from John Lawrence yesterday approving of all that had been done here, and expressing his opinion that we ought to make sure of taking the city before risking an assault, and saying what I have always advanced myself, that the continual defeats of the enemy must necessarily serve to cow and dispirit them, and will render our attack on the city a more easy task.

The 8th, I understand, are coming up on camels, so I dare say the attack will not be very long delayed. Soobhan said he would write to-day, but he tells me his letter is not ready. Becher is getting on very well, and if he only keeps quiet—which he doesn't seem much inclined to do—he will soon be able to go about again, with his arm in a sling. Daly I saw this morning; he, too, is going on well. You might mention this to Mrs Daly in case she has not heard from him, but he sent me a letter for her addressed by himself to put in the post.

I saw a letter yesterday to Thomson from Tooney Simpson, dated the 20th. All were well, and they were half expecting the mutineers from Rohilkund to attack them. The Meerut party have heavy guns and have entrenched themselves, and, if attacked, ought to be able to hold their own against any force; but nothing is yet known for certain of the Rohilkund mutineers, and the general impression appears to be in favour of their not leaving Rohilkund at all.

(*Diary*) 23rd June.—A wretchedly anxious day this has been. Olpherts' force in all right, with convoy, by about eleven; the enemy tried to attack him, but the bridge over the canal having been destroyed in the night, they couldn't get guns over. Fighting all day almost on our right to try and take some guns of the enemy; we lost many men, and all faces very long about it. Not much generalship, I fear.

CAMP, DELHI CANTONMENTS, 24*th* June.

The dâk came in a little earlier than usual to-day, perhaps owing to the new Adjutant-General, Chamberlain, being on the mail-cart! We are all so glad in camp to hear of his safe arrival, and hope there will be some generalship now, for there has been little hitherto, except, perhaps, on the 8th; our movements that day were planned by poor Chester. The truth is, General Barnard, though a very nice, kind-hearted, and brave old man, is no more fit for his present post than he is to be Pope of Rome; and as to General Reed, I fancy he is no better, but he very wisely abstains from interfering. We have safely weathered the eventful 23rd June, and I hope there was truth in the report that the Natives looked upon it as the day that was to terminate our Rule; for if so, they may now superstitiously feel inclined to despair altogether of success—and nothing is more likely, considering the thrashings they have had.

I am sorry to say that after I wrote yesterday a party of ours on the right followed up the enemy to try and take some guns, and we lost a good many men without effecting our object. The enemy were, however, completely driven off, and with terrible slaughter. The Native report was two thousand killed and wounded; but I believe there is little doubt of their having between four and five hundred killed, and perhaps double the number wounded. One young officer, Brown,* a cousin of Mactier's, was killed; Colonel Welchman, wounded in the arm; and Captain Jones, of the Rifles, in the fleshy part of the thigh.

It is a pity to think that we should have had so many casualties yesterday; but the letters from the city this morning talk of the enemy being most disheartened at the result of their attack, at which all the men they could get to fight were present. They may try it again when they get fresh mutinous regiments; but each day strengthens our position and renders it easier for us to resist their attacks, and without exposing our men so much as hitherto. This letter I speak of says that there are not above two hundred of the Jullunder mutineers now left, that a great many of them were killed yesterday, and that numbers have died from cholera. Major Olpherts was here just now: looking rather fagged, but otherwise well. Fancy, the Sikh corps that came in

---

* The officer killed was Jackson.—H. W. NORMAN.

with him yesterday were sent, after a twenty-mile march, to fight on the right, and they acquitted themselves admirably; our Europeans were quite delighted with them.

The detachment of George Hall's corps that were on the other side of the Jumna (at Moozafernugar, I think) have mutinied, plundered the treasury, and, it is said, murdered their officer, Lieutenant Smith; but this, I trust, may turn out not to be true. George Hall is, with some fifty of his men, at Lussowlie, some two marches this side of Paniput. They have always behaved very well; and as they have no treasury to plunder, and our troops are constantly going along the road, they may remain staunch, especially after hearing of the thrashing the enemy got yesterday. But it will be an anxious time both for Mrs Martin and Mrs Hall when they hear, as hear they must eventually, of the defection of Lieutenant Smith's detachment.

It is all Major Martin's own fault that his men were not disarmed long ago; the order was given for its being done, but he felt so sure of the fidelity of his men, and begged that it might not be carried out, and George Hall seconded him so strongly when he came into camp, that the order for disbandment was not carried out. I sincerely trust no calamity will befall them.

Becher is getting on famously. I will give him your message when I see him, and he will have something kind, I know, to say in return. I was sitting with him for some time this morning; also with Daly, who is able to write to his wife now. I have just posted his letter to her.

(*Diary*) 24*th June.*—Matters were better than anticipated. The guns we didn't get; but it seems the enemy suffered very great loss—some fifteen hundred men killed and wounded—and they are much depressed. The Bareilly mutineers said to be on their way here, and the detachment 4th Irregulars have murdered their Adjutant, young Smith, and joined the mutineers. Chamberlain, our new Adjutant-General, came in to-day; it is to be hoped he will be able to instil a little more energy and decision into our councils.

CAMP, DELHI CANTONMENTS, 25*th June.*

What a creature that man ——— is, going about apparently trying to frighten people out of their wits! I am afraid he will have been going his rounds with a false detail of the last affair of the 23rd. It was bad enough our losing so many men as we did, but with this exception the results were most satisfactory, and all the accounts from the city agree in saying that we inflicted a terrible blow on the enemy; and one or two wounded Sepoys who have been brought in, mutineers of the 61st, say the slaughter amongst them was very great, and that they had no chance against the Europeans. I made a mistake in calling Mactier's cousin, who was killed on the 23rd, Brown; his name was Jackson, a son of Dr Jackson in Calcutta—not the one you know, but an older celebrity.

The enemy are quite quiet to-day, hardly firing a shot. I suppose they are waiting for reinforcements. We have no certain intelligence yet as to whether the Rohilkund brigade is coming on here or not; by the last accounts they were entrenching themselves at Gurmukteesur Ghat, so perhaps they intend to remain there for the present and wait events.

We are still without intelligence from Cawnpore and down below, but the *cossid* that came in last night from Agra came round by way of Allyghur, and said that all was quiet there. I think it must be a mistake to suppose Her Majesty's 84th to be there; they are probably still at Cawnpore, where Sir Hugh Wheeler is organising a force. There was a letter to-day from Mr Eden, with the Bhurtpore and Jeypore contingents. All was quiet with them, but they give no news of matters towards Gwalior, Bundelkund, or Saugar, all of which places we are anxious about—I mean as regards the conduct of our Native troops, for the Hindoo princes of these parts are all faithful to us. I saw Hodson this morning; he seems quite right again. It is all very well his abusing the authorities in camp, but I don't know that we should have done wisely had we acted altogether upon his view of what was correct. Of the extreme unfitness, however, of Brigadier Graves for command there can be no question, and I hope to hear of his being superseded. I am glad to hear Greathed is coming down from Jullunder after all; he is expected the day after to-morrow.

There seems little doubt of Lieutenant Smith of the 4th Irregulars having been murdered; but Major Martin still declares that his men on this side of the river are staunch, and that it was the plunder from the treasury that set Smith's detachment wrong. George Hall has been ordered to join Head-Quarters, leaving his men where they are; he is expected in camp to-day. Arthur Becher is improving so fast that I expect he will be insisting on getting on horseback again before long; he sends every kind wish and message to you, as does also Mactier. I must write to poor Mrs Chester, which I have not been able to bring myself to do yet, to tell her that we (the Staff) are going to erect a monument to her husband in the burial-ground here. All at Head-Quarters have subscribed, and I have sent up the paper to Sep. Becher for his and Seymour's names, and there will then remain only Mayhew to ask.

I am glad to hear such good accounts of the servants. Soobhan does not appear to wish to carry on a correspondence with Oree, but tell Oree his letter was duly received, and I was pleased to hear all were so well; and tell him we are all well here, for he appears to doubt it.

P.S.—Any letter from Arthur? I have had nothing since leaving Simla, but I trust all is well, as he is near a European regiment at Deesa, on the Bombay side.

I am very glad I mentioned Norman the day after the fight. Give my kindest regards to Mrs Norman, and say her chivalrous young husband is quite well. Hodson, too, I saw a little while ago; he did not seem the worse for his exertions yesterday.

Give my kind love to Sir Edward Campbell, and say his regiment is keeping up its old reputation—'Celer et audax,' their proper motto.

(*Diary*) *25th June.*—All very quiet. Met the General (Barnard) as he was returning from reconnoitring our position with Chamberlain, who, he says, does not give him much comfort. I told him we were sure to win, and he said he was very thankful to me for saying so. Brutal conduct to a Sepoy last night the topic of conversation; Congreve upheld it. Quiet all day; rain keeping off. Attack contemplated to-morrow.

CAMP, DELHI CANTONMENTS, *Friday, 26th June.*

I generally breakfast in my own tent now, the Artillery mess being so far off, and besides, the hot weather has at last given me a distaste for the heavy meat breakfasts we have there, and my morning meal now is mostly restricted to *soojee* (porridge of coarse flour); and Mactier often joins me. We are always constant attendants at the mess dinner in the evening, when there is generally a large party discussing the events of the day.

The enemy made a faint attempt to come out to attack us again to-day, but the arrangements made to receive them soon drove them back again, and all is quiet now; and I do trust, and think, too, that there is little prospect of any further loss of life on our side until the assault takes place, and then even, if well managed, the loss will probably be but small.

You ask me to tell you what has been our total loss, including the 8th. It is very difficult to learn exactly how matters stand, they are so dilatory in sending in returns; but I should think the total must be somewhere about five hundred killed and wounded, not much more or less. It is a large number in our little army, but some of these who are slightly wounded have again joined, or are rejoining; and as our reinforcements amount altogether to some two thousand since the 8th instant, you see we shall be in rather a better position than we were.

How very wrong of Dr P—— to set about such reports! I shall recommend his being officially written to if I see Chamberlain to-day, and told that he will be ordered forthwith from Simla if he is not more guarded in his behaviour.

I quite agree with you about Hodson taking the command of the Guides, and tell Mrs Hodson from me that everybody will admire her husband the more for sacrificing his private feelings to the public benefit. I saw him this morning looking very well. I had a letter from Bagot yesterday of the 21st, when all was well with him and the Nusserees; he is anxious to bring them over to Delhi to join us, but we are not anxious to see them! There were letters from Meerut yesterday which still talked of the Bareilly mutineers as halting at Gurmukteesur Ghat. I suppose we shall know in a few days whether they are coming in this direction or not; it seems after all that they do not number more than about two thousand. We are very fortunate in the weather; the rain still keeps off, and to-day the sky is almost cloudless again.

The mess to which we belong has plenty of everything, wine and beer included; but the unfortunate Rifles are entirely out of beer and wine, so, as some one remarked yesterday, they make up for it by keeping up the strictest etiquette at the dinner-table, and prohibiting smoking till the cloth is removed. They are always very particular, too, in wearing their green uniforms. Little Dr Innes looks as if he had always just jumped out of a bandbox, so neat and clean—very different from the Staff, who go about in all kinds of disguises and strange coats; and such a thing as uniform, except the helmet and sword, is not to be seen amongst us.

(*Diary*) 26*th June.*—The assembly sounded about sunrise, and the enemy were said to be leaving the city; but if they intended to attack they thought better of it, having gone back again. Very anxious this afternoon about the Bhagput bridge, which a party is said to have gone out to attack; also about Meerut, regarding which we are in a great state of uncertainty and distress.

CAMP, DELHI CANTONMENTS, *Saturday, 27th June.*

There is not much to tell you since I last wrote. This morning the enemy have been trying another attack on our position, but with their usual luck; they have been driven back at all points, and I have heard only of two or three casualties on our side, men of the 75th and Fusiliers. Norman is my authority, and is now sitting with us. No officer hurt. Their grand attack to-day appeared to be on our left, on the picket, near Metcalfe House. They also came out during the night; but Norman says our guns drove them back without there being any necessity for employing the Infantry, and killed a good many of them.

Light's heavy battery is the one that generally does most execution on these occasions; he is a capital, fearless officer. It is satisfactory to think that we are beginning now to expose our men much less than we did at first. We are still without news from below, and are very anxious to hear what has been going on at Cawnpore. At Allahabad we understand that the 11th Native Infantry mutinied,* and were attacked and dispersed by the Sikh regiment. A letter of the 20th was received from Mr Colvin last night, but no Cawnpore news in it, Mr Greathed told me.

* The 6th, not the 11th, was the Native Infantry regiment at Allahabad. The 11th mutinied at Meerut.—H. W. NORMAN.

As bad news proverbially travels fast, we may hope that all was going on well there.

On the evening of the 25th all was well at Meerut, and it was still unknown then whether they were to be attacked by the Rohilkund mutineers or not. It seems that they have many heavy guns mounted at Meerut, and they do not fear any attack. A large convoy of about two hundred camels, with rum and stores, arrived here from Meerut this morning, having left on the evening of the 25th. With what is coming from Umballa, there will be two months' supply of rum in camp, a good thing for the Europeans, and for the Sikhs and Goorkhas too, all of whom drink rum and have it served out to them.

Now that this convoy has arrived from Meerut, the Bhagput bridge, which is never kept up in the rains, has been broken up, and the boats brought to this side of the river, where are also now the Jheend Raja's troops. He got alarmed on hearing there was a large party of the enemy coming to attack him, and came across the river without waiting for the convoy; this is the report, and I believe there is some truth in it. His troops are very fine men; but he is not much of a soldier himself, and likes to be as near as he possibly can to our Europeans. As to his fidelity, it is undoubted.

The rains have at last come upon us. It began to rain about an hour ago, and there is every prospect of its continuance. It has made a very agreeable change in the atmosphere, and the doctors seem to think that, as we are in a nice high spot, a little rain will rather be a good thing than otherwise. It is not till the end of the rains that Delhi generally becomes unhealthy. Norman desires me to send some kind message to you.

(*Diary*) *27th June.*—Up at Flagstaff, and firing all the morning until rain came on, and then ceased on both sides. The regular rains have begun apparently. Attack this morning, and some four hundred killed and driven back; but, since rain, all quite quiet.

CAMP, DELHI CANTONMENTS, *Sunday, 28th June.*

I went down to see Martin and George the day before yesterday: they seem comfortable enough; the latter is dreadfully disgusted at the murder of their Adjutant, Smith; but there is reason to think he was killed by men of another regiment.

The rains, as I told you, set in yesterday, and it has made the atmosphere very pleasant. It is still thundering away, with an occasional shower. We are on nice high ground, and, except in one or two spots, the camp is quite dry.

Greathed came in this morning with his regiment, four guns, and a large convoy of stores of all kinds; all well. Colonel Hartley was also with the corps; he is full of ardour, but I fear a hard day's work on a hot, sunny day will go far to quench it. Her Majesty's 61st (wing) and Coke's corps are expected the day after to-morrow, and then we shall have received all our principal reinforcements; but John Lawrence, it is said, is raising some forty thousand Sikh Infantry, some of which are, indeed, already fit for service.

The people in the city don't appear to like fighting in the rain, as they have been perfectly quiet since it commenced. We are not sorry, as it allows of our men having a little rest. We lost more men, it seems, yesterday than Norman thought: some twenty-five to thirty killed and wounded, amongst the latter Lieutenant Chalmers, of the Guides, and Harris, 2nd Fusiliers, both slightly; but the enemy, a newsletter says, had some four hundred killed and wounded. It seems that, as usual, our loss, principally in the Guides, was from the men rushing forward and exposing themselves. The General (Barnard) told me this morning that he is trying to do his best to induce the men to hold back when these attacks take place. I hope when the city is assaulted, which I suppose it will be some time towards the end of next week, that due precautions will be taken to restrain the troops, and I believe all commanding officers are going to speak to the men upon the subject. We have too small a force to allow of its being scattered.

A man came into our tent just now, and said, 'This is bad news, the enemy having burnt the bridge at Bhagput!' The same story may probably have reached Simla, and have been re-tailed with many additions by P——, &c., but it is not the case. The truth is, the boats of the bridge were removed to this side of the river by the Jheend Raja's troops under McAndrew, on, it is supposed, a false report of the enemy coming in force to attack Bhagput. There is reason to believe that the enemy have no force in the neighbourhood at all, and that McAndrew was precipitate in breaking up the bridge; but whether they have a force or not, they will be able to do nothing now beyond destroying villages on the other side of the river, and as they are mostly inhabited by plundering *Goojurs*, their doing so will be a service to us.

McAndrew is not, I fancy, the man for his post, and I should not wonder to hear of his being superseded—as has been Brigadier Graves, who has, I hear, decided to apply for four months' leave. Quite right! This is no time to stand on ceremony, and keep inefficient men in important posts.

Mr Philipe will show you my letter to him of to day's date. You will see by it that Cawnpore and Lucknow are said to be safe, but I wish Major Morrieson had given the date of his latest letter from these places. His own letter was dated the 22nd instant from Bhurtpore. He says nothing of Agra, but as he mentions the road being open from there, and even to within six miles of this, we may conclude that all was well at Agra up to the date of his letter.

We were very much amused at Mr Mayne's account of Colonel C—— eating up the little children's dinner! Norman was here, and I read that part of your letter to him and Mactier. Mactier says he can easily imagine it.

It seems Norman has written to Sep. Becher about people spreading false reports, intimating that if P—— offends in this way he will be removed at once from Simla. I saw Major Brooke this morning, looking very well. Sir Edward Campbell has been, or is to be, ordered to join his corps: sad news for poor Lady Campbell.

Major MORRIESON to Colonel BECHER.

BHURTPORE, 22nd June.

MY DEAR BECHER,—I have been very unfortunate in my *cossids*, for I have written you by five different messengers, and now try a sixth. All the information we have at Agra is through Greathed, and that is precarious, I hear, and therefore Mr Colvin has asked me to try and help him. I have a dâk of *hurkaras* laid, but the non-receipt of any of my notes prevents these men having access to you. The bearer of this will bring you other *hurkaras* to supply his place, and once the country is opened I suppose we will get on well. It is only within three *coss* * of Delhi that any difficulty now exists in carrying on a regular dâk, and when this is overcome my own *hurkaras* will be needless, as the entire road will then be free.

Intentions of the Gwalior mutineers not yet known. No impression made yet on Cawnpore, where Wheeler hadn't lost a man. What the mutineers are about I can't imagine; they have a band of about ten thousand horsemen, but we know not where they are. Lucknow all safe; and, it is supposed, Allahabad also. A band of one hundred and fifty Europeans are arriving daily at Benares, and in two months we shall have a force six thousand strong there. Course of Neemuch mutineers not known, but beginning to be supposed this way.—Yours very truly,

R. MORRIESON.

Colonel KEITH YOUNG *to his wife.*

CAMP, DELHI CANTONMENTS, *Monday,* 29*th June.*

I hear P—— gives out that Nisbett is likely to be sent away from Simla, but there is not the slightest reason to think so. If any medical man is sent away from Simla, it will most likely be P—— himself. He also gives out, I hear, that he is under the Governor-General's orders and cannot be sent away by the Commander-in-Chief, though he professes that he would like to come down here and join the Army. You may be sure that if the Commander-in-Chief orders him away, he will not venture to disobey.

There is little to tell you from here since I wrote yesterday. The enemy have been ridiculously quiet, and we can only account for it by supposing that they don't like the rain. It is, however, now quite fine, near twelve o'clock, and they are doing nothing. Perhaps it may be that they were taken aback this morning by finding the supply of water to the city from the canal had been cut off by us during the night; but they must have plenty of water for drinking from wells and tanks, and the only way in which cutting off the canal water would particularly bother them is that it would stop all the mills in the city for grinding *attar*, and thus put them to much trouble. The damage was done last night by our

---

* Native miles = 1½ to 2 English miles.

Engineers, who went out with some Sappers and a party of Lancers, and met with no opposition.

It seems after all that though the enemy did not destroy the bridge of boats at Bhagput, they managed to get hold of some of the boats that had been brought over to this side of the river. Hodson went over to Bhagput yesterday to ascertain exactly how matters stood, and he told me this morning the mischief was all caused by great mismanagement on the part of McAndrew, the officer with the Jheend troops. He cut off without seeing the enemy, who were thus emboldened to come on—a small party of them; and they ran away again immediately the boats were burned. Except for the name of the thing the matter is not of much importance, as the bridge at Bhagput is never kept up during the rains; the bridge here is constructed so as to remain up the whole year round. I suppose Captain McAndrew will be superseded in his charge; he can't be a good man, as he has failed in almost everything that has been entrusted to him. The Jheend troops are first-rate men, and it is a great pity there is no one with them to inspire them with confidence. Your friend, Herbert Edwardes,* would be the man for the post.

We have no later news from Meerut than that I gave you yesterday. It must be an anxious time for those who have friends there; but no one who knows anything about the place doubts for an instant their being able to repel any attack that may be made upon them, though it is still expected that no attack will be made, and that the mutineers are just waiting at Gurmukteesur to see how matters terminate here. There is no news in from the city to-day, nor have we had letters from any quarter except up above.

That's a strange thing, if true, Mr Colvin being superseded by Sir Hugh Wheeler as Lieutenant-Governor. Mr Colvin certainly appears to have done very little to assist us; and as to his representative here, he seems to me perfectly useless, and such is the general opinion.

Colonel Greathed keeps the command of his corps, Longfield being appointed a Brigadier in the place of Graves, who, I told you, had got a hint to apply for sick leave, which he has done. Nicoll remains Brigade-Major as before.

* The late Major-General Sir Herbert Edwardes.

SIMLA FROM JAKHO (a hill.)

I went over to see Major Martin and George Hall yesterday evening, and this morning George Hall was with me in our camp. He had just got a letter from Mrs Hall, and he says the other day she got a packet of some dozen or more of his letters.

No firing going on at all. Colonel Hartley goes to Umballa to command the Sirhind division.

Mrs KEITH YOUNG *to Colonel* H. B. HENDERSON.

SIMLA, 29*th June.*

. . . . . .

In the midst of all the troubles that surround us, I look on the bright side of things, and hope we shall all before very long have a happy meeting in Old England. Some people here expect never to see home again; they think India is lost to us, and that before the end of this year every European who has not the opportunity of escaping by ship to England will be murdered. But this is a dreadfully gloomy view to take. I agree with those who believe that our rule will be more firmly established than ever, before very long, and that these wretched Natives will be well punished for their unfaithfulness and wickedness.

I wish we could have told you by this mail of the fall of Delhi. Our little army is still before the city; the assault has not yet been made. The city is much stronger and much better fortified than was anticipated, and the mutineers fight like devils. General Barnard says he did not see such heavy or sharp firing in the Crimea as he has seen here. They have plenty of guns and mortars, and ammunition in abundance—guns of a larger calibre than ours. Delhi was the largest magazine in India.

A number of Artillerymen have gone over to the enemy, taking their guns with them, and they serve them beautifully. Artillery officers say that our own men do not serve the guns so well, or manage to load them so quickly. It is dreadful to think that all the teaching and training they have had from us, and our own guns, should be turned against us. From below Delhi the dâks are all cut off: occasionally a letter from Agra is received; the only communication with Cawnpore and Benares is *viâ* Calcutta and Bombay, and nothing has been heard from Calcutta of a later date than the 5th June. One report says that five regiments have arrived in Calcutta; another, nine; and a third report received yesterday in a Bombay extra says that not a single regiment from England has yet arrived. The hands of our rulers are fettered for want of troops; as it is, they are obliged to take away regiments from stations where they are much required.

Every day brings some fresh, sad reports of regiments mutinying and murdering their officers—and not only their officers, but every man, woman, and child with a white face they can come across; often putting them to death with the most refined cruelties, worse than anything that has ever been written of the massacres of olden times, too dreadful to speak of or to dwell upon. And some of those poor people we saw, happy and bright, only last March, on our way up from Calcutta to Simla, how little they knew the fate that awaited them! And, if God is not very merciful, it may still be ours. But we do not expect it.

We soon hope to hear that Delhi has been taken by our brave soldiers, and that the rebels have received such a lesson as will strike terror in the heart of every Native in the country. God surely is with us. He will lead our army and scatter our enemies, if He commands, it does not matter what numbers are against us. Many people blame the authorities before Delhi for not having made the assault on the city long ago, instead of waiting for reinforcements; but every officer with the army who had a voice in the matter thought it would be madness with such a handful of men to attempt to enter a fortified city, defended by thousands of armed men, and with a populace besides of one hundred thousand, who might, and very likely would, rise against us; if they saw that things were taking a bad turn with us, they certainly would rise.

The enemy have constantly attacked us since the first engagement on the 8th, but have always been repulsed with great loss. Our loss altogether, killed and wounded, since the 8th, that day's loss also included, is estimated at about five hundred; not many more or less. I don't know how many the insurgents have lost. On the 23rd alone, the last time they ventured to attack us, they left five hundred dead on the field and twice that number supposed to be wounded.

Monday evening, 29th.—After writing the above, I received Keith's letter of the 27th. He is quite well, and has been so, I am most thankful to say, ever since he left Simla. I hear from him regularly every day, and write to him as often; I should be very unhappy if I did not receive his letters. You cannot think with what eagerness we look for the dâks: one of my servants each day waits at the post-office until the letters arrive, and then brings them to us as fast as possible. I say *us*, for Mrs Martin and Mrs Hall are staying with me; their husbands are also at Delhi. Another lady, Mrs Poulton, is also living with me, and her two little boys. Her husband is Adjutant of the 64th Native Infantry at Peshawar; the regiment has been disarmed. Every Native regiment in the country ought to be disarmed, but many cannot be, for there are no European troops to enforce it; and if they were ordered to lay down their arms, it would in many cases have the effect of bringing things to a crisis.

Poor Mrs Hall was in great distress two days ago: she received no letter from George Hall; and Major Martin, who commands the regiment, wrote to say that a detachment of the 4th Irregulars who were at Moozafernugar, near Meerut, mutinied and plundered the treasury, and had gone off to Delhi. George Hall, who was also on detached employ with a party of his men, had received an express from Head-Quarters to leave his men with the Native officers and to ride into camp as quickly as possible. He was about thirty-two miles on this side of Delhi; the next day his wife was made happy by hearing that he was safe in camp.

The last of our reinforcements were expected to be at Delhi on the morning of the 30th (to-morrow), and then there will be nothing to detain them from making the assault. How I wish we could hear that our troops were coming up from Calcutta, and would attack Delhi on the other side at the same time!

The Hindoo princes are all faithful to us—Gwalior, Jeypore, Bhurtpore, the Jheend Raja, and several others. There is a report, wanting confirmation, that the Gwalior contingent has mutinied; the Prince himself will certainly remain staunch.

I hope I shall receive my usual letter from camp before the dâk closes, that I may tell you Keith's news of the 28th.

Tuesday, 30th June.—I have received my daily letter, dated 28th; all well generally in camp. In that engagement of the 27th, four hundred of the enemy were killed and wounded; and five on our side were killed, and twenty wounded. Amongst the latter two officers, but only slightly. The 8th (Queen's) and

Rothney's Sikh regiment had arrived that morning (28th), and the 61st and Coke's Sikhs were expected on the morning of the 30th.

I wonder when the assault will take place; it is a most anxious time for us all. There are upwards of twenty ladies at Simla who have their husbands at Delhi, and perhaps as many more at Kussowlie, at the foot of the hills. Poor Mrs Chester is still there: her sister-in-law, Mrs Faithful, is with her. Poor Mrs Chester, I feel very much for her; but still, those poor people whose relations—husbands, wives, and children—have been murdered are still more to be pitied. It is glorious to die in action, fighting for your country.

Did not our cousin, Miss Willock, marry Mr Wedderburn of the Indian Civil Service? I hear they have both been murdered. Many now will be anxious to go home, when able to do so. To quiet and reassure the country, a number of our regiments must be sent out. Our guns must never again be in Native hands; all the Artillerymen must be British. Fancy those wretched creatures running off with our guns, and turning them against us!

We heard from Donald M'Leod* this morning; he was well, and all was quiet at Lahore. I have not heard from Harry or his wife for a long time; but it is their fault, for all is quiet at Mooltan, and the dâks come in from there regularly. I wish they would write. There is no regular communication from any station below Delhi; occasionally a *cossid* brings in news.

Will you tell Captain Bacon, when you see him, that we can hear nothing of the 50th, and trust that it has remained staunch? It seems so dreadful and strange being so completely cut off from Calcutta. Nothing has been heard of Sir Patrick Grant since he left Madras, which was on the 17th instant.

Colonel KEITH YOUNG *to his wife.*

CAMP, DELHI CANTONMENTS, *Tuesday*, 30*th June.*

The wretched mutineers were quiet all yesterday; but to-day I suppose they must have had fresh arrivals in the city, as they have been trying another attack on our right. As usual, they have been repulsed with great loss; but we also, I regret, have

---

* Sir Donald M'Leod, K.C.S.I.

had a few casualties in the Sikh corps and Goorkhas—from fifteen to twenty, I am told, killed and wounded; and amongst the wounded, two officers, Lieutenant Yorke of the 3rd, and Packe of the 4th, both doing duty with the Sikhs. The scoundrels have also, I am afraid, boned three or four of our elephants, and, if so, our *mahouts* must be very much to blame. To counterbalance this, however, we were delighted to see this morning that the bridge of boats is completely broken, and it is supposed that they will not be able to put it together again; it must have been done by the rise in the river last night.

You amuse me very much about Mrs Martin, but there is some excuse for her, as she has been sorely tried lately. As to disarming her husband's corps, it was finally determined upon in poor Chester's time, but the General allowed himself to be talked over by Martin, and I dare say there is no chance of their going wrong so long as they are in our camp and we meet with no reverse; but disarming them was, of course, the proper measure; and a pretty army we should have if we were to act upon Mrs Martin's ideas of what is right, and keep regiments in our pay that we could not send out on detachment for fear of their mutinying! The Jheend Raja, before we reached Alleepore, gave one or two quiet warnings that Martin's regiment was not to be trusted. You should hear George Hall speak about the men of his corps now; he is dreadfully disgusted.

In the last newspaper that came in was our friend Colonel Tucker's marriage. Johnson was at the mess last night, but did not mention it. He (Johnson) is looking uncommonly well—much better than when at Simla. Young Darling is also married, I see. Hodson told me yesterday evening that Mrs Hodson has taken The Priory—rather an out-of-the-way place to live in, in these times. She will, I think, not hear from Hodson to-day, as he has gone out again to Bhagput to make arrangements for securing the safety of the boats there. I wrote yesterday to Mrs Chester, telling her about the monument that the Staff were to erect in memory of her husband. Of course tell Sep. Becher, from whom I heard to-day, that nothing will be done until we have taken Delhi. Young Harry Chester came into camp two days ago, and has been appointed, at his own request, to do duty with the Goorkhas.

No rain to-day, and the weather pleasant enough; in the morning it was quite cold. It is now about 2 P.M.; the firing has ceased for about an hour or more, so I hope it is all over for the day.

(*Diary*) 30*th June*.—The alarm and assembly sounded soon after daybreak, but hardly anything done. An attack on the right, and we lost some thirty or forty men, killed and wounded. Bad this, and I fear the enemy scarcely suffered so much. Quiet after one o'clock.

Captain EDEN *to Colonel* BECHER.

HODUL, 27*th June.*

MY DEAR BECHER,—The accompanying from Harvey was never taken, though given to a villain three days ago. Hope you will give us the best intelligence, and that you are all right again. We are holding together yet! Mutineers from Neemuch, *en route* seemingly for Agra, about Biana to-day—probably strengthened by some Cavalry of Mahidpore contingent. Pray give bearer, Ram, to-day *cinquante* rupees. He wishes to leave the money at his village, near Delhi; he has done us good service. Pray do this if you can.—Yours sincerely, W. F. EDEN.

Colonel H. B. HENDERSON *to Colonel* KEITH YOUNG.

GRESHAM HOUSE, LONDON, 20*th June.*

The next accounts from India are most anxiously looked for. At the India House they are evidently much alarmed, and not without cause. An opinion seems to be growing here that our present red-tape and pipeclay system with our Native soldiery is not the 'all perfection' we had been led to believe. The old system of commanding officers with more power, and fewer officers, and somewhat more of the Irregular corps system, begins to be favoured. Even in my day, when Lieutenant-Colonels could discharge unfit men and promote deserving ones more easily than at present, and were more looked up to by the men, there was evidently an advantage over the present helpless situation of commanding officers. There were abuses, no doubt; but the men themselves liked it better. When on service with my Light company in the old 9th, nothing could exceed the devotion of the men. In Nepaul the fellows would not leave me till my tent was pitched, and till they saw me comfortable; they would have gone anywhere for the *Sahib-Logue* then. It may be the same now on service; but certainly we knew more of our chaps then, and were more among them than now would seem to be the case from what I hear from our young fellows on furlough.

Colonel H. B. HENDERSON *to Colonel* KEITH YOUNG.

LONDON, 26*th June.*

There was nothing in your letter which might not be seen at the India House, and, as it was of a date that made it valuable, General Vivian asked for extracts from it. Since that, however, they have private information of the outbreak or row between Ghazeepore and Dinapore, in which a small Artillery party were obliged to fire on an armed body who collected beside them, accompanying them, and evidently desirous to get hold of the guns. Of this you will have had particulars months ago; but of course here they are most anxious for the arrival of the next mail, expected daily.

It would seem that the feeling of disaffection is more general than it was believed here to be, and that, considering the hitherto favourable announcements from the Home authorities, the truth will much disappoint the English public.

You will see a strong letter from Tucker in the *Times* on the subject. No wonder he is sore, for I have heard him blamed for the way in which Commanding officers have been shorn of their authority with regiments, and their hold on the men weakened by the interference of Head-Quarters; and, if this has reached him, he must be additionally annoyed with Leadenhall. In casual conversation with people there, I fancy that a feeling in favour of Irregulars is becoming stronger. The cry for more officers is not much listened to, or liked. More European troops are apparently thought of; the officers with these may probably be kept up to the fullest number, so as to have some always ready to draw upon for other duties. I repeat what I *casually* hear from people in the India House, or those who hear from others, therefore am a poor authority; and even these plans, if thought of, may be largely altered. But it is certain some general changes will be introduced.

I quite agree with you that our restrictions and harsh manner of dealing with those who are entitled to go on the invalid establishment must be doing us great harm with the Sepoys. Originally, when we held out the benefits of retirement to the Native soldiery, the cost was small; but of late years the pensioners have increased to a terrible extent, and the non-effective charges are getting beyond what was ever contemplated. Still, it was this boon that created our Native Army, and is the grand hold we have on its fidelity. If men are sent back to their regiments rejected wholesale by the examining committees, we must expect they will be discontented, and spread the disaffection throughout the whole of the army. Our seniority system also is distasteful to good and young soldiers, and the promotion of old, worn-out men by mere rule of service renders the non-commissioned class a useless one, and our Soubahdars and Jemadars still worse. But I must drop these subjects; it is rather farcical that I should write on them to you out there, who must know everything practically connected with them a hundred times better than I can possibly do.

Colonel KEITH YOUNG *to his wife.*

CAMP, DELHI CANTONMENTS, *Wednesday,* 1*st July.*

There is not much to tell you that has happened since I wrote yesterday. As I told you, the enemy were driven back between twelve and one yesterday, and since then they have done nothing to molest us; but perhaps they are busy to-day receiving their Bareilly friends, who arrived this morning on the other side of the river and are crossing over in boats, the enemy not having been able to mend their bridge. I wish the scoundrels were a little nearer, for the distance is too great to allow of our guns molesting them in their transit across the river. I am sorry to tell you that, in addition to the officers I mentioned as being wounded, I heard in the evening that Lieutenant Blair, 2nd Fusiliers, was wounded dangerously—shot through the liver. Mactier has written to his father, Colonel Blair, to tell him of it.

We were taken by surprise this morning by the arrival of two men from Hodul, where the Bhurtpore contingent is—Mr Ford of the Civil Service, and Captain Stewart * of the 9th Native Infantry. They bring late news from Agra, where all was well; and European troops were said to be marching up to Agra from Cawnpore, under the command of Sir Hugh Wheeler: there is no truth in the report of his superseding Mr Colvin, it is said. All right at Lucknow, the troops that mutinied having been cut up by Sir Henry Lawrence. The latest news from Calcutta is of the 8th June: four Queen's regiments had arrived in Calcutta— 35th, 37th, 64th, and 78th; two of them on the 3rd, so that they must have reached Cawnpore some days ago; and these, with the 84th, are probably the troops that Sir Hugh Wheeler is marching to Agra with. The China force is said to have been heard of, and, in this case, must have been in Calcutta soon after the 8th.

Your letter of the 29th has just been given me. Yes, it is quite true, as you will have seen from my former letters, that the Gwalior contingent had mutinied; but it seems from what Captain Stewart and Mr Ford say that we are not to have them at Delhi, as they had not, by the latest accounts, left Gwalior, and the Raja there, who is staunch to our cause, was in hopes of coercing them with his own particular troops—Mahrattas. What a strange medley of affairs it is! Stewart also mentions, and Captain Eden writes the same from Hodul, 29th June, that the Neemuch mutineers had taken possession of the Fort of Khooshalgurh; and as they have mounted their guns on the walls, there they will probably remain. Stewart brought some late papers with him, and in one I see that part of the Joudhpore contingent had marched to Nussereebad, and that all were faithful. I suppose the contingent is composed of men of that part of the country, which accounts for their remaining firm, as it seems only to be the Oude men, or the *Poorbeahs*, as they are called, who take any share in the mutinous movement.

You may perhaps hear a story, with exaggerations, about some men of the 4th Sikhs. It seems there are about one hundred and fifty *Poorbeahs* in the corps, and they have been more than once half suspected of not being quite trustworthy; two of them

* The late Field-Marshal Sir Donald Stewart, G.C.B., G.C.S.I.

were overheard using seditious language, and they are to be tried for it, and will probably be blown away from guns, if it is proved. The Sikhs quite hate them, and Daly and all tell me that they use the word *Poorbeah* as a word of reproach, utterly despising them. In Daly's corps and in Coke's there are no *Poorbeahs;* all are Sikhs.* But I am sorry to say that in the regiments at Allahabad and Benares—Gordon's and Brasyer's regiments—there are a great many *Poorbeahs;* but I hope there are sufficient Europeans at both these places to keep them in order if mutinously inclined. All well at Meerut on the 27th.

Her Majesty's 61st† came in this morning, band playing in grand style. Coke's corps is at Alleepore, and will be here in the morning: a report has just come from there. Hodson not yet returned from Bhagput.

P.S.—I am glad you have written home. I have not done so by this mail, and must now wait until Delhi is taken; but this will not be till next week at earliest. Captain Robertson, Her Majesty's 8th, is coming here from Roorkee. All well at Saugar on 17th June, 1 P.M.

(*Diary*) 1*st July.*—Her Majesty's 61st (wing) came in this morning. Band playing—rather enlivening. Went up to the Ridge; lots of troops on opposite bank, supposed to be Bareilly mutineers. All quiet to-day, except considerable firing from the batteries on both sides: ours said to have destroyed the Moree Bastion, but Macleod (Artillery) says the damage can be repaired in two hours. Coke's corps comes in to-morrow morning. Stewart in from Hodul to-day.

CAMP, DELHI CANTONMENTS, *Thursday,* 2*nd July.*

You don't mention any more rumours of risings and intended murderings at Simla, so I conclude all are reassured again now.

---

* This statement as to Daly's and Coke's corps of course includes as 'Sikhs' a large number of frontier Mahomedans, and in the Guides one of the six Infantry companies were Goorkhas. There were also a very few *Poorbeahs* who were of undoubted loyalty. The Native Adjutant of the Guides and the Havildar-Major of Coke's corps were Hindoostanee soldiers taken from my regiment, the 31st Native Infantry. The Havildar-Major was killed on the 14th July, and the Native Adjutant was twice wounded.—H. W. NORMAN.

† Only half the 61st came at this time.—H. W. NORMAN.

The capture of Delhi cannot be very long delayed now; some time next week, I should say, there is a certainty of our being inside the walls. The day must depend upon the way in which it is intended to take the place. I do not know whether it is intended to batter down the walls first or not; if it is, an advance battery must be made, which will take a little time. Coke's corps came in this morning, and they were played in by Her Majesty's 61st band, sent out to the Garden by Colonel Jones. The men seemed to feel the compliment. They are a fine, rough-looking set of fellows, and upwards of eight hundred strong—a very valuable addition to our force.

A wing of Fenwick's regiment of Irregulars also came in; the other wing was here before. It is expected they will prove true, and they have behaved well hitherto; but if they show any symptoms of disaffection they will be disarmed at once. The few men of George Hall's corps (4th Irregulars) that are here, also those on the road, are behaving well. I told you of the distrust that the Sikhs had of the *Poorbeahs* in the Sikh corps. They are to be disarmed this afternoon; there are only one hundred and fifty of them, and they will be sent back to Huzara, where they left all their property. Once quit of these men, there are no infantry in camp on whom we cannot depend to the last. I spoke to Coke on the subject this morning, and he says his men and all the Punjab regiments are to be entirely trusted. How strange—the very men that were fighting against us only a few years ago!

The enemy have been very quiet to-day, except firing a few guns. One of their batteries at the Moree Gate is stated to have been knocked to pieces by our fire; but, though silenced, I doubt the damage done them being so irreparable. Murray-Mackenzie and Fagan were both slightly wounded this morning by part of a shell; the former had his knee slightly grazed, and the latter a cut on the forehead—his helmet saved him.

Mactier went to see Blair this morning, and he says he seems better, but the doctors declare that his liver is shot through; perhaps they may be wrong after all. One of those young officers of the Sikh corps, Yorke of the 3rd, is dead, poor fellow; the other, Packe, wounded in the ankle, is getting on well. There is some suspicion, from the nature and position of their wounds, that they were shot intentionally by the *Poorbeahs* of their own regiment. One of the scoundrels is sentenced to be hanged, and I fancy the sentence will be carried out for sedition. You can tell Mr Philipe, if he hears of it, that the man was tried by *Military Commission* and not by General Court-Martial.

As to the Bhagput bridge affair, it was a bad business and ought not to have occurred. It was as I said: the bridge was not destroyed in the first instance; but after the Jheend Raja and Captain McAndrew left, the enemy came and burnt many of the boats. Those that escaped were brought down to near this yesterday evening by Hodson, who is undoubtedly a first-rate officer. He was in here just now, and is quite well. He was asking me about some letter for Chesney (Engineers) * that he says you were to have sent me; I have never received one.

A letter was received in camp from Mr Colvin this morning, dated the 28th, when all was well at Agra, and he confirms what I wrote you yesterday about matters below, the Gwalior contingent not having left Gwalior. He mentions a communication to him from the Governor-General, of the 9th June, so that the report of his supersession by Sir Hugh Wheeler must be incorrect.

Those Bareilly mutineers have managed to make good their entrance into Delhi, but their numbers are said to have much diminished, and there is a report now in camp that the 29th Native Infantry is still holding Moradabad for us: strange, if true.

I am sorry to say the scoundrels have contrived to put their bridge of boats together again; I would the Engineers could manage to destroy it. Don't send any quinine—I hope not to require it; but if I do, there is plenty in store, Mactier tells me.

Daly has come to our camp for change; he is getting on well, as is also Arthur Becher. It is now 1.30 P.M., and everything quiet, not a shot being fired either from our batteries or from theirs. I met Captain Burnside at the General's last night; he was very well.

---

* The late General Sir George Chesney, K.C.B., then the Brigade-Major of Engineers with the Delhi force. He was M.P. for Oxford when he died. He was the first President of the Cooper's Hill College of Civil Engineering, and afterwards Military Member of the Viceroy's Council.—H. W. NORMAN.

(DELHI.) IN THE PALACE: THE DEWAN-I-KHAS, or King's private hall of Audience. Round the roof is written, "If there be a Paradise upon Earth, It is this! It is this!".

(*Diary*) *2nd July.*—Went to near Budlee Serai. On the road near the Garden saw lying the skeleton of a man, said to be the Havildar-Major of the Native troop, killed in the action on the 19th—his jacket still on him. Quiet all day, and no firing.

CAMP, DELHI CANTONMENTS, *Friday, 3rd July.*

I quite agree with you as to the absurdity of disarming people's servants unless the order can be carried out most stringently in the bazaar; but trust there is no fear of any disturbance at Simla, and, this being the case, it is of little consequence whether these have arms or not.

We hope you will not have much longer now to wait for the fall of Delhi, but no day is fixed upon yet for this happy consummation of our wishes. They are all quiet in the city again to-day, and the report is that the Bareilly people will only give up one lac of their treasure to the King (they are said to have seven), and fighting and disputes are going on amongst them in consequence.

Our camp is very healthy, all things considered. There was heavy rain last night, but it is now clear and cloudless again. Not only was that man of the Sikh corps of whom I told you hanged yesterday evening, but also a Ressaldar, Jemadar, and Duffadar of Nicholson's party of Irregular Cavalry, for trying to get Coke's corps to mutiny and turn against us.* They spoke to the Native Adjutant, who informed against them, and they were all tried by Military Commission for sedition—tried, found guilty, and executed; and the *Poorbeahs* of the detachment, some sixty or eighty, were sent away with the *Poorbeahs* of the Sikh corps, their arms and horses first being taken from them. It is hoped that the example will have a good effect on George Hall and Fenwick's corps; the latter came in yesterday.

Young Blair is getting on very well; Mactier went to see him this morning. I was surprised at his being so well; the doctors must have been mistaken as to the nature of the wound.

Colonel Baird Smith arrived last night, and with him our friend Robertson,† who has just been paying me a visit. He came across by Saharunpore. He gives an excellent account of the behaviour

* I think these men were shot by an execution party of the Carabineers—not hanged.—H. W. NORMAN.
† The late General Robertson, C.B., of the 8th King's.

of the Nusseree battalion there, who are doing first-rate service, he says, in quieting the country, which was all upset again by those Jullunder mutineers. He mentioned an instance of the Goorkhas attacking a body of some two or three thousand *Goojurs*, and totally routing them.

It is nearly two o'clock, so I must say good-bye. Arthur Becher, Mactier, and Congreve all send kind messages.

(*Diary*) 3*rd July*.—Very muggy weather; all quiet again to-day. Commissariat *baboos* came in from city; lots of intelligence, and say King is anxious to make terms—the villain! About five large bodies of troops seen on right flank, said to be intending to attack us in rear and to plunder Alleepore.

CAMP, DELHI CANTONMENTS, *Saturday*, 4*th July*.

No dâk in to-day, and I fear we can hardly expect one, as a party of the enemy managed to get to Alleepore last night and partially plundered it. All the plunder was, however, recovered from them this morning; but still the mail people will, I fear, hardly like to come on until they receive intelligence of all being right again. The miscreants belonged to the Bareilly Brigade, who came out in great force yesterday evening with the intention, they gave out, of annihilating us; but part of our little army (wing, Her Majesty's 61st, Coke's corps, six * troops 9th Lancers and Carabineers, Guide Cavalry, some of 9th Irregulars, twelve guns Scott's battery, and Money's troop), at about 7 A.M., came in sight of the main body of the enemy, who had been joined by the Alleepore party. It seems they never allowed us to get very near them, and they very soon ran off into Delhi, taking, unfortunately, their guns (six) back with them. On our side there were only one Native officer (Coke's corps) and one *syce* driver killed; and two men, Carabineers, and one Coke's corps wounded. No European officer hurt. The enemy are supposed to have lost from two to three hundred; and amongst the killed were observed some men in the clothing of the 29th Native Infantry, from which it would seem that the story we heard of the 29th Native Infantry still being at Moradabad is untrue. So much for the valiant

---

* Four troops, not six: that is, one squadron (two troops) each from the 9th Lancers and the Carabineers.—H. W. NORMAN.

Bareilly Brigade, who have proved the veriest cowards of any of the mutineers. Our men got lots of plunder this morning, and I saw Irregular Cavalry coming in just now, their horses loaded with all kinds of absurd things: one man appeared to be bringing in a small tent, another a Hussar saddle.

I have no news from any quarter to give you, and we are indebted to the *Lahore Chronicle*, of the 1st, for such information as we have of passing events below. The worst piece of news of the whole is that about the Sikh corps at Benares joining the mutineers; but it seems that Gordon, who commanded them, was very unpopular with his men, and both Daly and Coke, who know the Sikhs well, assure me that when they come up here there is no chance whatever of their remaining with the *Poorbeahs*, whom they hate most cordially; besides, too, the whole regiment didn't join, and it is said also that the majority of the corps were not Sikhs. I wish we had a few more Sikh corps in camp; they are first-rate, willing fellows, always ready for anything.

Sir Edward Campbell arrived yesterday, and came and paid me a visit. I was delighted to hear from him a good account of you and the dear *Babas;* the latter, he said, were the most sturdy, jolly little fellows possible. Campbell himself is looking jolly and well. I went in and sat with him and the other officers of the corps at their mess breakfast this morning; the short diet on which they are appears to have had no effect on their colonel.

I went to see Murray-Mackenzie this morning. He makes light of his wound; it is outside the knee, but it will be some time before he is well again. Mactier says he does not think young Blair can be hit in the liver, he is getting on so well. I have not seen Major Martin or George Hall for some days.

(*Diary*) 4*th July.*—Troops off very early under Coke, and it seems the enemy plundered Alleepore, driving away Younghusband with a small party of Punjab Cavalry. Coke's Column, however, got at the enemy about 7 A.M., but they scuttled away so fast that little harm was done them, and they succeeded in taking away all their guns; two on our side killed, and six or eight wounded. In the afternoon another alarm from them, and guns were sent out.

CHAPTER VI.

SIEGE OF DELHI (*continued*)—ILLNESS AND DEATH OF SIR HENRY BARNARD.

Colonel KEITH YOUNG *to his wife.*

CAMP, DELHI CANTONMENTS, *Sunday, 5th July.*

We have been very quiet since I wrote to you yesterday, and are so now. I dare say you received at Simla a very exaggerated account of the attack on Alleepore, making out all kinds of misfortunes to us. It was bad enough our allowing the enemy to get there at all; but beyond their partial plunder of the place, and obliging a party there of the Punjab Irregular Cavalry (1st,* I think) under Lieutenant Younghusband to withdraw, no damage was done. It is supposed that the enemy went to Alleepore in the expectation of finding the 17th Irregulars there with treasure, some two and a half lacs, and lots of ordnance stores; but Lieutenant Hockin (whom we met at Shumsabad) had been warned from here to halt at Lussowlie, which he did, and he is now coming on with the Jheend Raja's force, whose guns have been manned by Europeans † coming down, and a large party of Lancers, &c., are going this evening to meet the convoy and bring it in. Some went so far as to say that the 17th Native Cavalry had sent on emissaries to Delhi to arrange with the mutineers to join them and bolt with the treasure. It is quite possible enough, for I have not the same faith in any of these men that Mrs Martin has; but if such were their intention it

---

* The detachment belonged to the 5th—not the 1st—Punjab Cavalry.—H. W. NORMAN.

† This is a mistake. No guns of the Jheend contingent were ever manned by Europeans, nor did the Jheend force come to Delhi until September.—H. W. NORMAN.

has now been effectually frustrated. The only unsatisfactory part of yesterday's business is our not getting possession of the enemy's guns. We got one or two of their ammunition carts, but the general impression appears to be that had we managed properly we ought to have secured their guns; but it is not perhaps right to say so, for our Artillery are a first-rate set of fellows, and Norman, who was out, did not blame them. I only tell you what they say in camp, and the truth is that when the enemy bring out guns and we go after them, no one is contented unless they are taken.

You ask me the particulars of Lieutenant Smith's death; there can be no doubt whatever of it, I fear. Dr Scott, whom Mrs Martin and Mrs Hall know, got a letter some days ago from Meerut saying that he was wounded by a Sowar, whether one of his own men or not was not known. He was put into a *doolie ;* he was some distance from his house when this occurred, and on his way home. Some of his corps rode up and asked if it were the Adjutant-Sahib, and on hearing that it was they fired into the *doolie* and killed him. The letter did not, I think, say how this intelligence was received, but it was looked upon as the truth. Dr Scott comes across every morning to our tent for a cup of tea; he told me that George Hall was quite well, and Martin, he said, complaining a little as usual.

You will be shocked to hear that poor General Barnard is very ill with cholera, and from what Mackinnon and Mactier told me just now there is not the least chance of his recovery. Doctors Brown and Tritton are also in attendance on him, but they hold out no hope. The truth appears to be that the poor General has been ailing for the last ten days, but it has made no difference in his way of going on—always in a state of excitement, rushing about all day in the sun and exposing himself in everything. It is no wonder that he has been quite unable to bear up against the attack. He is the kindest, most amiable old man that ever was, but most utterly useless as a general, and altogether misplaced in his present position. Congreve is the next senior officer in camp, but it is arranged, I believe, that in the event of General Barnard's death General Reed will himself assume the command of the force—that is to say, Chamberlain will really command; and he is, perhaps, the best man in camp for it. I was in church this morning, and the text was most singularly appropriate to this case of General Barnard's—'Teach us to number our days, that we may apply our hearts unto wisdom'—and the discourse would seem almost written for him, but at the time it was not known that he was ill. It will be a sad blow to young Barnard, the Aide-de-Camp. He is a very nice young fellow, and so kind and attentive to his father. I hope I mentioned Hodson's name yesterday, as he tells me he did not write to his wife; he is very well.

Sir Edward Campbell was dining at the Artillery mess last night, and sat next to me. He was giving me a long account of the Simla doings, and told me also of ——— going about with exaggerated reports of our losses, &c.

It is half-past one, and Doctors Mackinnon and Brown, who have just left General Barnard, say he is dying, and cannot live more than an hour or two. Very sad, is it not?

5th July (later).

It is half-past three o'clock, and as it seems the post is not yet closed, I write a line to tell you that it is all over with poor General Barnard: he died about a quarter of an hour ago. How awfully sudden it has been, for though, as I told you, he has not been well for many days, he was out walking this morning a little before breakfast-time! His seems to be a solitary case, as I have not heard of any other in camp. When Mactier came in to tell me of the General's death, I was busy writing a reply for Arthur Becher to a letter he received a little while ago from Lieutenant Pearse at Hissar, dated 1st July. Pearse is employed settling the country; he gives a good account of everything. I extract the following paragraph from his letter, as it may be interesting to Mrs Martin and Mrs Hall: 'I have been able to save Mrs Jeffries and head clerk from destruction. Donald, assistant to Superintendent Lira, and seven others have reached here.'

What nonsense they are telling you about the dearness of supplies here! In the Artillery mess they have a two months' supply of beer, they told me a night or two ago, and we are charged merely the cost price and the carriage.

All quiet in camp. It is settled that General Reed assumes the command of the Force.

CAMP, DELHI CANTONMENTS, *Monday,* 6*th July.*

No dâk in yet, but I dare say it will be here before I finish this. It is most likely coming in with the treasure party, which was to be at Alleepore this morning; and a force of Artillery, Infantry, and Cavalry went out from here an hour or two before daybreak to make all sure in case the enemy should wish to have another try for the treasure. A newsletter from the city said that the mutineers had gone the day before to Alleepore to murder our wounded, and to secure the treasure coming here—eleven and a half lacs! There happen only to be two and a half. The men that were killed on Saturday all belonged, it was said, to the Bareilly Brigade, and buttons were observed on them (and they had their new clothing on) of the 29th, 68th, 18th, and 28th—a set of wretched scoundrels and cowards.

Except a few shots occasionally from the batteries, all is quiet in camp, and the reports from the city are that the Sepoys now tell the King that none of them will come out to fight again unless all come; and there is no getting the Delhi mutineering regiments (38th, &c.) to stir. I fancy there is no doubt of the truth of this, we have heard it from so many quarters. Another thing, too, which appears certain, is that they have expended all their gunpowder and are now manufacturing it for themselves; but this must be a difficult task this damp weather, and at the best it can never be so good as what they got from our magazines.

You ask me if we do not know more here about the intended plan of operations than we are willing to communicate. I assure you not: and indeed nothing is, I believe, definitely settled about the way in which we are to get inside the walls of Delhi; but that we shall be there before very long no one, I think, in camp entertains a doubt. It is confidently reported that there are dissensions among the mutineers, and this will be a great thing in our favour. There was a letter from Agra yesterday, of the 1st instant, when all was well. The Neemuch mutineers were expected there on the 4th, and the troops from Agra were to go out some five miles to meet them, fully confident of giving them a good thrashing— which, I have no doubt, would be done. All was safe at Allahabad, and a force was being organised there; and most probably, I should think, the new Commander-in-Chief, Patrick Grant, would come up there and assume the command of it. Nothing was said of a force moving from Cawnpore to Agra, but there was nothing more likely, as he must have had three European regiments with him upwards of a fortnight ago.

I had a letter also from the Jeypore contingent at Hodul dated the 3rd, when all was well. Eden, who writes, says: 'The report of the murder of Major Morrieson and Captain Nixon is unfounded.' We had never even heard of it here, so there was no occasion to contradict it. There was a letter, I think I told you yesterday, from Hissar, giving favourable accounts of the doings of Colonel Cortlandt's force, the main body of which was at Sirsa. Altogether, you see, we are getting on very fairly everywhere; and Hodson this morning, in talking over the news from the city, said all was very encouraging—and it is not often he admits so much. The Hodul letter said the Gwalior contingent was still at Gwalior, and that the Chumbal was full. No news whatever about the Native regiments in the Saugar brigade, 50th inclusive, so we may hope they are still right.

Sir Edward Campbell was giving me a very amusing account of Mrs ———. He says she takes a most desponding view of matters, and has fully made up her mind not to see her husband again. So much so, said Campbell, that it was his opinion she had another in her eye!

You ask me what command General Johnston is to get on joining camp. He will get no command here, but we know nothing of him for certain: and a report came in yesterday that he had died at Kurnaul; but don't mention this; it may not be true. I heard it from Nicoll and Metcalfe.

I was at General Barnard's funeral this morning. There were a great many people present. He was buried just opposite where poor Chester's remains were deposited.

We had very heavy rain last night. It commenced while we were at mess, and lasted until near daybreak. It has made the air very cool and pleasant, and in the early morning a puttoo coat and equally warm *continuations*, as Seymour calls them, were not uncomfortable. All well at Meerut, I think, on the 2nd; but the dâk is longer coming than it used to be. It is 2 P.M., and the dâk not in, so I will not wait longer. It seems the treasure party were detained by the rain, but are coming on all right.

Captain EDEN *to Colonel* KEITH YOUNG, *Camp, Delhi.*

HODUL, *3rd July.*

MY DEAR COLONEL YOUNG,—Thank you much for your two notes of 29th and 30th; the first I got this forenoon, latter yesterday, and sent them on at once to Lieutenant-Governor. We are all anxiety about yesterday's affair. Neemuch rebels are said to be at Futtehpore-Sikree, as yesterday, and disposed to march on Agra this morning. They may have been strengthened by troops from Tireh, but I doubt it; otherwise they consist of 72nd, a Gwalior contingent regiment, two troops 1st Cavalry, some five hundred Sowars Mahidpore contingent, a Horse battery, and two guns they brought away from Doab. I wish I could give you some news from Cawnpore and Lucknow.

The report current of the murder of Morrieson and Nixon at Bhurtpore is unfounded. Bhurtpore Sirdars gave them a hint to quit. Nixon went into Agra; Morrieson stays at Bhurtpore. Heard nothing of the other Gwalior contingent men; report has it that the Maharajah is keeping them quiet.

Mrs Eden writes me from Ajmere, on the 1st, that the dâk from Bombay and Indore was open again—it had been closed for three or four days. It is rumoured that Mhow is up too—only one regiment, the 23rd, and wing of 1st Cavalry. Kind regards and best wishes to Becher, please. Good-luck to you all.—Yours very sincerely, W. F. EDEN.

HODUL, *4th July.*

MY DEAR COLONEL KEITH YOUNG,—Thanks for yours of 30th again. I sent a man to you yesterday; my old friends Oodeyram and the Sikh go with this, and please introduce them to Mr Greathed, for whom they have notes. We have no news. Gwalior contingent detachments at Hatrass and Allyghur have mutinied. Alexander and officers of 1st Cavalry have gone into Agra; but it was not known what had become of the officers of 2nd Cavalry, or of Watson (magistrate of Allyghur) and those with him.

Neemuch mutineers at Futtehpore-Sikree still disposed, it is said, only to divide the money (they had three lacs) and go to their homes! It is also said they look for reinforcements from Gwalior before attacking Agra! Morrieson at Bhurtpore; Nixon at Agra. M'Sharpley, of the Road Survey, was killed by his own *chuprassie* for the money he had about him. Colonel Dixon died at Ajmere on 25th June.

Kindly inquire if Barry is all right; Oodeyram will know, and tell you about him. I sent his family to Muttra; thence they went to Agra. I hope Becher is doing well. Oh that this chivalrous force had been of better material, and I could have gone up! *Mais que faire?* Pray go in and win sharp! If Delhi still holds out, you had better send one of these men back at a time.—Yours sincerely, W. F. EDEN.

HODUL, 5*th July.*

MY DEAR COLONEL YOUNG,—I only send this bearer to bring news!—though hope it may be unnecessary. Neemuch mutineers yesterday still at Futtehpore-Sikree—so I learn from Dashwood at Muttra. The loyal 6th gone to the bad, and said to have murdered a number of officers at Allahabad. Symptoms of insanity displayed at Nagpore, Hyderabad, and Aurungabad. My men are homesick; but I hope to hold on till you take that wretched place Delhi. I hope Becher is doing well; my regards to him, please.—Yours truly, W. F. EDEN.

Colonel KEITH YOUNG *to his wife.*

CAMP, DELHI CANTONMENTS, *Tuesday,* 7*th July.*

It is near 1 P.M. All is well in camp, and the mutineers are as quiet as the most nervous person could wish. It was reported yesterday from the city that they had intended a grand attack on us to-day; but, as it has not come off, the impression with those best informed in camp is that they are unable to get up their courage sufficiently to come out again; and what convinces me that there is something very wrong with them is that a letter was received from the Bullubghur Raja this morning, who is known to have been assisting the King with supplies and men, swearing that he is a staunch friend of our Government, and waiting to come into camp. Becher brought the letter to me to read, as it was not wished to employ a *moonshee.* I succeeded in deciphering it, and it contained most humble protestations of fidelity; and he would never have committed himself in this way had he not seen that the King's cause was a failing one. In addition to the want of powder, it is now said there is a scarcity of percussion-caps in the city, and that they are altering the locks of the muskets for flints, as caps they can never manufacture.

How very imprudent of Colonel ——— to communicate to his wife the particulars of the intended assault, and much more so of her to mention it! It would compromise her husband very seriously were it known; pray tell her if she hears anything again about an assault not to say anything till it is all over. The reason of the assault having been put off was the arrival of the Bareilly mutineers, who were supposed to be on the alert to attack us, which would quite have frustrated our plans. If all is true that we now hear about the temper of the mutineers and the state of the city, our task will be a much easier one than it would have been a week or two ago.

What nonsense Mrs Martin and Mrs Hall talk about their regiments! If George Hall has written one-half to his wife that he has said to me, she must see that he looks upon his men now as a set of brutes. Dr Scott is now in our tent, and I asked him, without telling him why, what he thought would have been the result had the whole regiment been left at Hansi. 'Why,' he said at once, 'I am confident we should all have been murdered, ladies and all. We should not have been able to get away at all; had the whole of the 4th been there in a body they certainly would have mutinied.' The idea of blaming poor General Anson for the mutiny of the 4th—the scoundrels!—is absurd. He had faults enough of his own to answer for, poor man, without fixing on him fictitious ones. And Arthur Becher, too, how is he to blame? or how is anybody to blame but the wretches themselves? I never said anything against sending a detachment of them to Moozafernugar.

Robertson, Her Majesty's 8th, has just come in. He is very well, as he says is Greathed, who is living with him. Poor young Barnard left here yesterday afternoon on his way home, viâ Umballa and Sind. I was surprised to see Briggs from Simla walk in yesterday; he has come to organise a land transport-train between here and Umballa. A letter from Agra yesterday of the 2nd; all well there, at Cawnpore, Lucknow, and Allahabad.

Captain EDEN *to Colonel* KEITH YOUNG.

HODUL, *7th July* (6 P.M.).

MY DEAR COLONEL YOUNG,—I hope the party I now send will find its way to your camp, and display less of discretion than Bhopal Sing! The Ressaldar now sent is Gopal Sing, and the entire party belongs to Ulwar, who has behaved very well to us and lent us many men—howbeit, unhappily, in the instance that occurred here when with the Bhurtpore troops! As it is, I fear this man will be longer in reaching you than is necessary; he has in charge a formidable packet for the Commander-in-Chief, and two letters for General Barnard. Give him a *maulchit*, and send him off sharp, please. I have given this packet, by-the-by, to my *chokedar*, Koona Sing, a sharp fellow, who goes under escort of Gopal Sing.

We are in an agony of suspense about your proceedings, not having heard from you since yours of 30th! My men are together as yet, behaving well, spite of rain, cholera, fever, and want of forage! They are anxious to go home, though! I must shift my ground to-morrow a few miles. I don't like the Agra news. I send a note from Mr Dashwood; I wish he had confirmed the native report of the near arrival of European regiments at Agra! The Mhow Regiment (23rd) and wing of 1st Cavalry are said to be moving up *viâ* Neemuch. Will you kindly make inquiries about Ford and Stewart in your camp? We should be glad to hear they are *sains et saufs*. I hope Becher is improving; very kind regards to him, please. If you don't take Delhi speedily I must come up with my *Nagas*.—Yours very truly,

W. F. EDEN.

Captain DASHWOOD *to Captain* EDEN, *Political Agent Jeypore Field Force, Camp, Hodul.*

MUTTRA, *Sunday, 5th July* (8.30 P.M.).

MY DEAR CAPTAIN EDEN,—We have heard to-day that the Kotah contingent have turned rusty, and have kicked up a row and joined the insurgents; that the Gwalior contingent are marching upon Agra, and will arrive there the day after to-morrow or to-morrow night. All three forces out, including the Neemuch force, will

(DELHI.) IN THE PALACE.
White Marble inlaid and carved.

besiege the Fort. Under these circumstances, Thornhill and the rest of us have come to the conclusion that there is no use in staying on at Muttra, and we intend going into Agra, or, at all events, making the attempt; Thornhill and his clerk are going by land, the rest by water. This is, therefore, to give you notice that you will no longer get information from this place from me; but I will tell the settlement officer to keep you informed of what goes on.—Yours sincerely, H. M. DASHWOOD.

Colonel KEITH YOUNG *to his wife.*

CAMP, DELHI CANTONMENTS, *Wednesday, 8th July.*

Never mind about the loss of the money that was stolen from the store closet; but it's very annoying to think that one of our own servants should be the thief. The kitchen servants you might suspect—perhaps the *masaulchee*, as we know less about him than the others; or perhaps Gyanee. Or are there any of your guests' servants who were ever in the store-room and knew where the cash-box was put? You might offer a good reward, say fifty or a hundred rupees, for the apprehension of the thief; and glad indeed shall I be to hear that he has been discovered.

I am going to write to Mr Philipe to say that Sergeant Larkin had better sleep in the house until Delhi is taken. I will ask Mr Philipe to arrange for a *janpan* for Sergeant Larkin in the event of its raining; and you might let him have Doddy's pony to ride backwards and forwards—it will do the pony good, and keep him quiet.

No, Delhi is not yet taken, and I begin to think that I was premature in saying we should be inside the walls this week. It is not a bright moonlight night that will be chosen for the attack, but a dark rainy one most probably, so that we can get up to the walls without being discovered; and there will be a bright moon for many nights yet. It is clear that it cannot be to-morrow under any circumstances, as half the force has gone out on an expedition to a place some nine miles off to blow up a large bridge there, the more effectually to prevent the mutineers from getting on the Trunk Road without making a circuit of some twelve miles or more—which they are not likely to attempt.*

* The bridge was called the Bussye bridge, and crossed the Nujufghurh branch canal.

The force, some twelve hundred Infantry, with Cavalry and lots of guns, started about three this morning under Colonel Longfield. Hodson is with them. Some of the enemy were supposed to be somewhere in the direction of where our force was going, and it is to be hoped it will fall in with them; but I doubt it. It is now near 1 P.M., and we have heard no firing yet; and the bridge cannot have been yet blown up, as the noise of the explosion would have reached us. The people in the city are as quiet as possible again to-day, and except for an occasional shot from the walls, we should not know that there was any one there.

Some of General Anson's things were sold yesterday by auction, and several articles brought a very absurd price. Bacon (English), for instance, five rupees a pound, and candles three; other things, again, sold below cost price.

They are going to get up a Head-Quarters' mess, or rather have got it up—for it commences operations to-day. Everybody has joined; but Mactier and I, though members, remain on with the Artillery mess for the present, and are not to pay for the new mess until we commence dining at it—which I don't think I shall do for some time yet. I like going to the Artillery mess: they are a very nice set of fellows, and have excellent food too; but I dare say this will be pretty well attended to at the Staff mess, as Congreve is one of the leading members of it! He and many others had been living at General Barnard's table up to the day of the kind old General's death. It was rather an infliction having to feed so many strangers, and he got no allowance whatever for it.

Captain Briggs, I told you, was down here, having come, he says, to organise a land transport corps (*alias* a bullock-train) betwixt this and Lahore. He left this morning.

Hodson has just come back in advance of the returning force, which, he says, have done nothing but blow up the bridge, and have seen no one except the villagers, who came out with expressions of devotion and *ghuras* of milk—the latter the more acceptable of the two. I expect there will be a great outcry in camp, especially amongst the Artillery, at so large a body of troops going out and doing nothing beyond superintending the destruction of the bridge.

Chamberlain certainly will never be *pucka* Adjutant-General, and he does not wish to be so, I believe, himself, as he hates office-work. The best man in camp that I know for the appointment is Colonel Seaton, unless they would appoint young Norman, who is the fittest for it, to the best of my belief, in the whole army. His getting it, however, is altogether out of the question at present.*

CAMP, DELHI CANTONMENTS, *Thursday, 9th July* (2¼ P.M.).

I had only just returned to my tent and changed my clothes—for it has been raining 'cats and dogs'—when your letter of the 7th was put into my hands. I am very glad you have recovered the tin box with the rupees, but it is annoying, as you say, not knowing who the thief is; but I have very little doubt that the rest of the servants will find him out. If they don't, I will try what I can do when I come up to Simla (which I hope to do some day) by making them go through the ordeal of chewing rice. The money-box having been put back as it was,† I think this plan will be infallible. I fear it is Tajie. Had you not better give the *kotwal* a present for helping to recover the money? Ask Lord William Hay, and give, say, from twenty to fifty rupees.

Really you are as bad, by your own account, in not suspecting Tajie, Oree, or Gowroo, as Mrs Martin and Mrs Hall are about the wretched 4th Irregulars. We had a pretty specimen this morning of the faith to be placed in any of these brutes of Sowars; but, perhaps, better say nothing about it till you hear of it from other quarters. It is not the 4th, however, but the 9th that have been misbehaving this time—Fenwick's corps: the picket from which, on our right flank, joined a party of the mutineers and rushed into camp past a picket of the Carabineers, who are stated not to have behaved so well as they might have done. The object of the mutineers appears to have been to persuade the Native Artillery-

---

* See page 52.

† The box was returned in this way. One of their wise men in the bazaar came and spoke to the people, pretending that he knew who the thief was, and could have him punished and put in prison, but would give him an opportunity of returning the tin box with the rupees without being discovered. He said that during the night each servant was to take a large flower-pot filled with earth and empty it on a particular spot, the heap thus made not to be touched by any one until he (the wise man) came in the morning and removed from the midst of it the tin box with the money all right; then, with the *Mem Sahib's* permission, the matter would drop. This was done, and the box was found in the heap of earth as he said.

men to join them and make off with their guns; but this they refused to do, and it terminated in some thirty or more of the mutineers being killed, and the rest driven out of camp. It was some distance from where we are that all this happened; but it is a stupid piece of business allowing them to get into camp at all, and arrangements have now been made to guard against anything of the kind occurring again. Two *golundaz* and several camp-followers were killed; and one officer, Hills of the Artillery, got a sabre-cut on the head, and would have been killed had it not been for Tombs, who came to his rescue just in time, getting himself a cut through his helmet, but killing his opponent.* I trust that the consequence of all this will be the disarming of every Sowar in camp, except the Punjabees; and I believe this measure is pretty well decided upon, and with our Artillery it can be easily done, and the whole of them annihilated if they dare to lift a finger. Just before this affair took place it was reported that the enemy were going to attack us in force, and I went out with General Reed on the Mound; but the attack was a very feeble one, and our troops soon drove them all back into the city, with, so far as I can learn, little or no loss on our side. The only one I heard of as being wounded was Lieutenant Kemp of the 60th, or 5th † Native Infantry, I don't know which. He was shot through the hand and thigh, but not, I think, a very severe wound, as he stopped and spoke cheerfully as he was passing in the *doolie*.

I saw George Hall about an hour ago; he is getting rather infatuated about his men again, and will hardly allow yet that the men of the picket joined the mutineers. He says they merely galloped in to give notice of their approach. Our officers, however, who were at the battery close by, declare to the contrary, and say they saw them plainly making signs to the mutineers, whom they actually joined when they charged. I trust and think there will be no question raised about disarming not only the 9th, but the 4th also; and, as I said, with our guns they dare not stir. It will be a very different business from the disarming of the 14th Native Infantry at Jhelum.

* Tombs and Hills both received the Victoria Cross for their gallantry in this affair. A full account is given in *Forty-one Years in India*, Vol. I., pp. 187-189.
† The 5th.—H. W. NORMAN.

You ask me why I did not tell you of the intended attack of the night of the 2nd July. I knew nothing of it till afterwards, and if I had I don't think I should have told you, for these are matters that ought really to be kept as secret as possible; and if the intended plan of attack should reach the enemy, which I dare say it will now that it has been so freely spoken of, it is not likely to assist our ulterior operations. I fear, however, as I said yesterday, that I was premature in telling you that Delhi will be taken some day this week; we must put this off a little longer, but that it will be ours in good time we all feel very certain.

A large convoy of stores came in this morning, and, I believe, two or three hundred Sikh Artillerymen. It is a grand thing the Sikhs proving so staunch; they hate the *Poorbeahs* most cordially.

General Hewitt has been *allowed* leave to the hills, and General Penny succeeds him at Meerut. All was well at Meerut on the 7th.

(*Diary*) 9*th July.*—Alarm soon after breakfast. Enemy coming out in great force at the old place, the right and right flank; but the business began by a party of Cavalry rushing into camp on our left flank, the pickets rushing in with them, and, it is thought, the 9th Irregulars joining them—the Carabineers bolting. After this our troops swept all the left and left front and drove the enemy into Delhi, their loss said to be fifteen hundred; but ours very great—two hundred and twenty-three killed and wounded. Wretched rainy day. At the Mound with General Reed until all was over.

CAMP, DELHI CANTONMENTS, *Friday*, 10*th July.*

The dâk is not in yet, so I will commence at once by giving you a more correct description of yesterday's proceedings, of which I had received a very garbled account when I wrote to you. One knows very little at first of these fights except what comes under one's immediate observation, and I was with the old General on the Mound, with most of the rest of the Staff, having only left him once or twice to take messages to Coke's regiment, which was on the extreme left.

Well, let me first tell you that the result of the day's work was most satisfactory. The enemy were pursued to within three or four hundred yards of the walls of the city, and their loss is said not to be less than a thousand; and they are reported to have brought all the troops that they had out of the city to make an overpowering attack on us. Major Reid, who has a good opportunity of judging from his position at Hindoo Rao's, says they must have had about eight thousand men, and it is his opinion, from the punishment they got, that they won't venture to attack us again. It must be very disheartening to the scoundrels to find themselves always beaten in this way. I have not heard any news from the city yet, but I may before I close this, and will tell you what it is if I do. I am sorry to say our loss has been severe—about one hundred killed and wounded. Amongst the latter six officers: Lieutenant Mounsteven, Her Majesty's 8th, mortally—since dead; the rest slightly: Pullen, 36th Native Infantry; Lieutenant Hills, Artillery; Kemp, 5th Native Infantry; Murray, Guides; and Eckford, 69th Native Infantry, with Sirmoor battalion. Colonel Greathed was not with his regiment; several of his men were knocked over. Greathed's brother, of the Engineers, had his horse shot. All day, to-day, the enemy have been very quiet, not firing a shot. I should like very much to be at the council in the city to-day, and hear what they think of matters now.

As to the business of the 9th Irregulars, it is now being inquired into by a court sitting for the purpose; and whatever may be settled on the question of the picket having joined the enemy's Cavalry, or at best tacitly permitted their entering our camp, I trust the termination at the least will be the removal of all the Irregular Cavalry from camp, except the Sikhs.

Did I tell you how Hodson was taken in yesterday by a party of some hundred or more of the enemy, whom he met when on the lookout for these very men? He was quite convinced they were our own Sowars on their coolly telling him so, and they managed to get clean off without his finding out the mistake till too late to follow them up. One man of the 8th Irregulars was the only one killed, his horse having run away with him into our picket. The scoundrels, as Hodson observed, deserved to get away for their coolness and cleverness!

As I told you yesterday, there were some twenty or more

killed in and near the camp. It rained almost all day yesterday, and most of the night, and to-day, too, it has been drizzling a good deal; it is very cold in consequence, so much so that *puttoo* is very agreeable.

I think I shall ask you to send down a box of 'creature comforts'—some curaçoa, which, as Arthur Becher observed, would have been very acceptable yesterday when we were all dripping wet. Mactier, Norman, and I, however, got some brandy and hot water, of which we all much approved. We are well off for brandy, having got a dozen cases from M'Donald shortly after our arrival here.

I think I told you of the very high price some things fetched at an auction a few days ago, clothes and provisions that had belonged to Generals Anson and Barnard: flannel jackets, ten rupees each. It would be a great thing, certainly, if the poor soldiers could be provided with flannel shirts; but I fear there is no chance of the ladies making a tenth part of those required in time, and it is proposed to buy some on account of Government: they would have been invaluable yesterday.

A letter from Meerut, of 7th, says all well at Cawnpore, Futty-ghur, and Lucknow on 27th ultimo. Mr Saunders, Civil Service, has just arrived from Meerut; I hope he will be of more use than the other civilians here. I have just seen Hodson, who tells me there has been only one man in from the city as yet, and he gives little news beyond the fact of their being a good deal cut up at their losses of yesterday, and it seems they lost fifty of their Sowars, some Soubahdars, and the leader of the party, a Ressaldar.

I have just seen Mr Saunders; he left Meerut the day before yesterday, where he says all was well, and he met with no impediment on the road.

(*Diary*) 10*th July.*—Another very rainy day; and in the afternoon disgusted to find, on going to the General's to speak about the Court of Inquiry on the 9th Irregular business, that the enemy were said to be coming out again. It seems, however, that they soon returned, and our troops were not turned out. The enemy lost, it is said, five hundred killed yesterday, and, I suppose, some ten or fifteen hundred wounded; we had forty-three killed and one hundred and eighty wounded—bad lookout.

CAMP, DELHI CANTONMENTS, *Saturday*, 11*th July.*

The dâk came in very late yesterday afternoon, bringing me your letter of the 8th, No. 45. What nonsense Mrs F—— makes John Lawrence write! Depend upon it, though he is annoyed, as we all are, at our not being inside Delhi, there is no despondency with him; and as to its being folly keeping Lower India, we couldn't hold Upper India long without it. Mrs F—— must have altogether misunderstood him. I dare say what he did say is that when there is sufficient force collected at Cawnpore there ought to be an attempt made to reduce the country thereabouts to quiet and order; but Sir Hugh Wheeler ought to march up at once towards this, and I shall be much surprised if we do not very soon hear he is doing so with at least four European regiments. There is a report, indeed, to this effect, and I suspect that hearing of this has something to do with the delay in the attack. Here is the end of the week, and nothing done towards it yet. Talking of Lower India, I think I mentioned that by the last accounts both Behar and Bengal were quite quiet.

Nothing has happened here since I wrote you yesterday: the enemy have not bothered us at all, and there is reason to suppose, as was said before, that they will hesitate a long time before they attack us again. I am sorry to say that our loss the other day was much greater than any of us had any idea of: two hundred and twenty-three killed and wounded, of which forty-one were killed—rather more than half Europeans. With so many wounded in comparison to the killed, there must be a great many with only slight wounds. The loss of the enemy is said, by letters, to be fully as many as was supposed—five hundred killed; and the wounded were most likely not less than twice or three times as many. It seems that the scoundrels paraded four of their own guns through the city, giving out that they had captured them from us. Of course the mutineers and others whom they attempted to impose upon would soon find out the deceit practised upon them.

We hear no fresh news from the Jeypore contingent, or from Agra or about the Neemuch mutineers; but there is a report that the Raja of Gwalior has set up for himself. This very likely is not the case, but were it so, it would do us good in this way, that all the mutineers in his direction would flock to his standard instead of coming up here.

The Court of Inquiry on the 9th Irregulars' affair on the 9th has resulted, I believe, in an order being given for the march of the regiment out of camp, and back to Hooshyurpore; but they are not to be disarmed, there being no satisfactory proof, it is thought, of the complicity of the picket with the mutineers. The regiment was to have marched yesterday evening, but the men were detained on account of the rain; and the feeling is so strong against them in camp that I should not be surprised to hear of their being disarmed yet.

I am sorry to say that it is an undoubted fact that the picket of Carabineers and the 9th Irregular Cavalry disgracefully fled, though they were called upon by Tombs to charge the enemy—which they were quite strong enough to do, some forty of them; but except the officer in command—Lieutenant Stileman I think his name is—and one man, they all ran helter-skelter into camp, some of them getting thrown from their horses. Tombs and his Subaltern, Hills, were in great danger for some time, and killed some four or five of the enemy. I don't know what the General will do in this Carabineer affair. Greathed, who was here just now, says one or two of them ought to be shot; but I fancy the matter will be allowed to drop by the General telling them how they have disgraced themselves, and giving them an opportunity of wiping out the stain. Many of the men are very young. I don't envy these fellows—the abuse they will get from their comrades and from the 9th Lancers.

(*Diary*) 11*th July.*—Rained heavily all night, and a foggy, misty morning. The 9th Irregulars sent away to-day, but with their arms and horses. The general impression appears to be that they ought to have been disarmed; but the regiment was formerly commanded by Chamberlain, hence his partiality for it.

CAMP, DELHI CANTONMENTS, *Sunday,* 12*th July.*

Nothing has happened worth telling you since my last. All has been quiet, which may be in some measure accounted for by the heavy rain. It rained most of last night, and we have had a shower or two to-day, but there have been also a few glimpses of sunshine. Fortunately we are on good high ground, and the water runs off at once down to the canal in rear of our camp.

The most interesting piece of news from the city is that they have heard there that a European force is marching up here from Allyghur, and they propose going to the Hinden River and breaking down the bridge there, which had been repaired by the enemy for the passage of the Bareilly mutineers. This is the first time the city news has said anything about a European force moving up, and I think there can be very little doubt of the correctness of the intelligence, and that it is Sir Hugh Wheeler coming on with some of the European regiments which must have reached him from Calcutta. In a day or two we shall probably obtain reliable information on the subject from Meerut; and I am perfectly certain, from what I see of affairs here, that nothing will be done in the way of assaulting Delhi until these Cawnpore troops arrive, and the Kemaon battalion must also be here by that time. It is now, I believe, on this side of Umballa.

To counterbalance this good news of the approach of the Cawnpore force, there is a report that the Meerut mutineers have released the prisoners in the Agra jail, and that they may be expected here with three hundred of the prisoners in four or five days. As to the prisoners, it would be rather an advantage, perhaps, their getting into the city: they would certainly plunder all the Sepoys they could; and the Neemuch people have been reported to be coming so often, that there must be some great influence at work to prevent them, and if the Gwalior Raja is setting up for himself, the best thing that could happen for us would be for the Neemuch troops to join him. I think I told you that there is a rumour of the Gwalior Raja intending to make himself King of Central India, and it is to be hoped it is true, as we have nothing to expect from him in the way of troops that can be depended upon, and the more parties that try to assert their independence instead of rallying under one head the better. At Jhelum it seems that the Sikhs in the 14th took part against their *Poorbeah* comrades and fired upon them. I am very anxious now to hear about Sealkote; I fear there will be some great disaster there, as they have no European troops except a little Artillery.

I was in Becher's tent this morning when Mactier and Mackinnon had a final examination of his arm, and it was pronounced that the small bone was broken after all; they could not be certain before because of the swelling. He is in no pain, but he must have his arm in a splint now, and it will take about three weeks before it is well.

I had a letter yesterday from M'Causland at Almorah, of the 2nd. All well there.

CAMP, DELHI CANTONMENTS, *Monday, 13th July.*

Major Martin called on me this morning. He is always full of reliance on his regiment; he has only got about forty of them here, and as I believe they are the best men in the corps, it is possible enough they may remain staunch.

I saw George also to-day; I understand from Norman that he was offered the command of the 9th Irregular Cavalry (the regiment whose picket behaved so ill on the 9th), but he has declined the honour. Fenwick now commands, but it is intended to supersede him. It was half-resolved upon before, but yesterday evening he sent in a note from Alleepore (where his regiment now is) to say that he was informed that the enemy had crossed the river in force at Bhagput with the intention of attacking a convoy of ammunition, stores, &c. that was to come in from Raie this morning. The report wasn't much believed, but it gave some little uneasiness as the convoy was a valuable one; proper precautions were taken, and the convoy came in all right this morning, the force at Bhagput being altogether a myth.

Bad news this from Sealkote. Poor Mrs Brind! Is it true that her husband has been killed? The Movable Column must, however, be after the mutineers, and it is to be hoped will be able to give a good account of them; and Nicholson,* the officer in command, is just the man to do the thing well. We have had accounts, too, from Agra to-day, but not worse than we have been every day anticipating, as we well knew that the small force they have there could not defend the station if attacked and must retire into the Fort, which they have been obliged to do, and there they are quite safe against anything that can be brought

* Brigadier-General Nicholson.

against them. It appears that the Neemuch mutineers at last came down upon Agra, and our force went out to meet them, and found them posted in a village some five miles off. It seems our valiant allies, the Kerowlie and Ulwar contingents, deserted us, going away to their homes, and the Kotah contingent actually went over to the enemy, so there were only our own Europeans to depend upon; and we thrashed them and took two guns, but lost one of ours, which was disabled, and, running short of ammunition, we were obliged to leave and eventually to go into the Fort and abandon cantonments and the civil lines. The only officer I have heard of as killed is Lieutenant D'Oyly of the Artillery; neither our loss nor that of the enemy is stated. Except the loss of property at Agra, and the bad effect it may have upon the natives thereabouts, it is almost an advantage our being in the Fort, as it is well provisioned, and there is no force that can be brought against it likely to make the least impression on it.

The 64th and 78th were, I fancy, being sent up country about the time that letter you speak of as being in the *Telegraph* and *Courier* was written; they were probably the last of the first batch of regiments that arrived in Calcutta, and all were being sent up by driblets. The Madras Fusiliers and 84th were, we know, well up the country a month ago.

The *cossid* who brought the news of the fight at Agra (which took place on the 5th) said that there was a European force at Allyghur. We shall probably know particulars of it from Meerut in a day or two. I fear it may have gone on towards Agra, where it can be of no use now; but it will not be long in getting back here, *viâ* Meerut.

We have been all quiet in camp to-day, and no appearance of the enemy. I am sorry to say there were several cases of cholera yesterday and the day before in the 8th and 61st, but Greathed, who has just been here, says it has now left them; he attributes it to the fatigue and exposure they underwent three days ago.

(*Diary*) 13*th July*.—Large convoy came in this morning, supposed to be in danger last night from a report by Fenwick, from Alleepore, that the enemy had crossed in force at Bhagput to attack it; no truth whatever in the report. Rumours of an attack from the Fort, but none came off.

CAMP, DELHI CANTONMENTS, *Tuesday*, 14*th July*.

There seems to be no intention at present, as far as I can learn, of our assaulting the city just yet, but whether we are to wait for Sir Hugh Wheeler or not I don't know; there is no further intelligence of him, but we are all quite confident that he is on the road somewhere. By this time also, or before the end of this month, some of the troops which will no doubt have been sent overland, as soon as they hear of the Delhi business, will arrive here.

Norman has just been sitting with me, and we have been calculating that they ought to have heard in London of our disaster by the mail that would reach London by the 8th or so of June. From what Norman says, the news of the Delhi and Meerut massacres may have been telegraphed to Bombay on the 12th or 13th, in time to reach there by the outgoing mail.

I saw George Hall and Major Martin this morning; they are both well. Their regiment, of about forty men, are the only Irregulars now in camp, the 17th, Hockin's, having been sent off on an expedition somewhere to get rid of them. It seems that Fenwick has been removed from the command of his Irregular corps, the 9th, and ordered to rejoin his regiment, the 5th; his second in command, Lieutenant Campbell, succeeds him. All the camp is crying out because the 9th men were not disarmed; but it seems it was formerly commanded by Chamberlain, and he is weakly anxious to believe they are loyal. I don't think I told you that the Native Artillerymen, about forty, were disarmed two days ago. It was merely a precautionary measure: there was nothing known against them; they had behaved, indeed, particularly well, but disarming them was the right thing. I agree with you that all the Native troops should be disarmed if possible, except the Sikhs and Goorkhas; we cannot do without them, and as far as we know they are entirely with us. Fancy, the poor little Goorkhas have somewhat less than half the number of effective men that they had on the day of their arrival here, and yet they are always as jolly and cheerful as ever, and as anxious to go to the front when there is an attack.

Of the men *hors de combat* now, of course, there are a good many sick and wounded, who will eventually recover. There has been a good deal of firing going on for the last hour or two on our right and front, where the enemy have come out to attack us, but I have heard of no casualties, and from what Norman says, judging by the messages that have come down, there has been little damage done on either side. Our men have had strict orders to keep within camp, and for the last few days the Engineers have been employed in throwing up small embankments to protect the Infantry and allow of their firing at the enemy without exposing themselves unnecessarily.

Twenty minutes past three, and I must send this off. I have just been to Becher's tent: he has heard of no casualties; and Dr Scott, who has come in from the right flank, says he saw no *doolies* coming in with wounded, so I pray that the only loss will be that of ammunition.

Daly is getting well fast, and was walking about to-day. He is not going to leave, that I have heard.

P.S.—You might perhaps make up a box to send me with half-a-dozen of port wine and two bottles of curaçoa, to entertain Arthur Becher with when his arm is well! And will you put up also a small canister of the hill tea—a pound or so.

CAMP, DELHI CANTONMENTS, 14*th July* (8 P.M.).

I have just heard that there is another dâk going out, and there is time to write a line to give you the result of to-day's fight. It was after I had finished my letter that it began in earnest.

We drove the enemy back, but nothing could restrain our men from pursuing them close up to the walls of the city, and the consequence has been that we have had a great many hit. No officers killed, or even dangerously wounded; and Colonel Seaton, who has been inquiring, told me just now that he thinks very few of our men can be killed, and of those wounded, which may probably be about sixty, he thinks some forty are so slightly hurt that they may be fit for service again in a day or two. Of the officers wounded, Chamberlain is hit in the arm and young Chester somewhere in the leg; and there are some three or four others.

(*Diary*) 14*th July*.—Soon after breakfast firing commenced on the right front, and has been going on all day. It is now nearly 5 P.M. I fear we must have suffered considerably, though strict orders were given for our troops not to expose themselves. It has been a coolish day, fortunately. Chamberlain wounded.

Colonel KEITH YOUNG *to Colonel* H. B. HENDERSON, *London*.

CAMP, DELHI CANTONMENTS, 14*th July*.

F—— has, I hope, written to you pretty regularly, and told you of her welfare and of our doings here. Delighted you will be to find that we have been mercifully protected through all the sad horrors that have taken place in India, the long lists of which it is sickening to think of. How many a happy home must have been saddened by the perusal of them! I trust now that you have heard the worst in England; and as I do not doubt that every energy has been at work to send out reinforcements, we may soon expect to see matters take a more cheerful turn.

I wish we were inside Delhi; but I almost despair of this now until Sir Hugh Wheeler, or some one else, comes up with troops from below—and we hear he is now at Allyghur. People are altogether mistaken as to the strength of Delhi, and I heard Brigadier Wilson say the other day that it was the third strongest place he had seen in India, and that we had made it so by adding a glacis which quite protects the walls.*

What is Parliament going to do with Lord Dalhousie for bringing us to our present straits? I hope Patrick Grant is to be Commander-in-Chief; our present Acting Chief is about bedridden, and Chamberlain is actually commanding.

Colonel KEITH YOUNG *to his wife*.

CAMP, DELHI CANTONMENTS, *Wednesday*, 15*th July*.

It is the regret of all in camp that our troops were so rash as to follow up the enemy, yesterday, in the way which they did close to the walls; had it not been for this we should have lost scarcely a single man. Up to three o'clock, indeed, there was not, I believe, a single casualty, while the enemy had suffered severely; and

* See Appendix *C*.

now, when all our losses are reckoned up, they amount, it seems, to close upon twenty killed and one hundred and thirty wounded —a great many of the latter, however, as I mentioned yesterday, very slightly. A great many officers are also wounded—no less than sixteen, I am told, but most, indeed nearly all of them, slightly. The exceptions are : Pollock, 35th Native Infantry, very severely; Daniell, 1st Fusiliers, severely; Walker, Bombay Engineers, rather severely—his namesake, of the Bengal Engineers, died a few days ago, poor fellow, of cholera; and Chamberlain, whose arm is broken below the shoulder (left arm). Thompson, of the Artillery, is one of those wounded—a ball in his thigh, which has been cut out and no bone broken.

The enemy are all quiet to-day, and I suppose it was the arrival of fresh mutineers that induced them to try their luck again yesterday. Their loss is said again to have been great, but I have not heard the extent of it. I do trust that if they attack again, our men will be made to keep within cover. I fancy Chamberlain had a good deal to say to their going on yesterday; but it must be quite contrary to his own conviction of what was right. He is a fine, gallant fellow, but something more than that is required from a man in his position. He will not remain long Adjutant-General of the army after Patrick Grant arrives. We have heard nothing of him yet beyond what we saw in the paper that he had arrived in Calcutta on the 17th of last month. He ought, I should think, to be well on his way to join us by this time. Of Sir Hugh Wheeler's movements, too, we know nothing beyond common rumour, which places him somewhere about Allyghur.

There was a letter from Agra yesterday of the 8th, saying all was well in the Fort, where they had ensconced themselves. The burden of Mr Colvin's letter—for it seems he has sufficiently recovered to write—was, 'Come up here as quickly as you can after taking Delhi, for it is very uncomfortable with so many people in the Fort;' not an item of intelligence about the Neemuch or Gwalior mutineers, or anything else that was likely to be of use or interest to us here.

The 9th Irregulars have not mutinied yet, and there is perhaps not much chance of its doing so unless we meet with some reverse. I hope you will have no alarming reports about the mutineers from

(AGRA.) THE FORT.

Sealkote going up to Simla—there cannot be the least chance of
it; the very last place they would wish to go to is the hills, and
besides two of our columns are now after them, and one, I am
told, has already come up with them.

(*Diary*) 15*th July.*—Our loss appears to have been great
yesterday, upwards of twenty killed and some one hundred and
sixty wounded. Sixteen officers, but not one killed; and all, it is
said, might have been avoided had we not rushed down to the
walls of the Fort and got within reach of the enemy's grape.
Chamberlain and Reid are blamed for this.

CAMP, DELHI CANTONMENTS, *Thursday,* 16*th July.*

I read Norman and Becher that part of your letter in which
you recommended that the little Goorkhas should have the horses
of the 4th and 10th Cavalry to ride. We were all much amused
at the idea. Fancy a little Goorkha on one of those great large
horses! It would carry three of them at a time!

The Kemaon battalion will not be here for some time now;
they have been detained at Jullunder, or somewhere thereabouts,
and incorporated with a small Movable Column to look out for
the Sealkote mutineers in the event of their escaping Nicholson—
which it appears they have not done. There seems little chance,
I think, of many of them making their escape after the thrashing they have already got. In case of any of them getting across
the Ravee, there are still the Beas River and the Sutlej to stop
them.

All has been quiet here since I wrote to you yesterday, and the
only news of interest we have is that a *syce* had reached Meerut
from Cawnpore in seven days, and he said that Sir Hugh Wheeler
had left there with his force; but where he had marched to he
could not say. I dare say it will be some days yet ere we receive
reliable intelligence of his movements. We are anxious, of course,
to hear where he is; but the authorities in camp have evidently
made up their minds that a few weeks' delay more or less now is
of no consequence.

More changes again in the command of this force. I told you
that poor old General Reed was almost bedridden. That day

he was out exposed to the rain for so many hours quite knocked him up apparently, and it has at last been settled that he shall leave here to-morrow evening for Simla with a party of sick and wounded that are being sent to Umballa. At Simla, perhaps, he may be appointed to the command of the Militia.

I understand that Brigadier Moule is serving in the Militia at Nynee Tal as a private; but he is such a martyr to the gout that he is obliged to go to parade in a *janpan!*

Brigadier Wilson is to succeed to the command of this force, passing over Colonels Congreve and Longfield, neither of whom is, I believe, over anxious for the honour and responsibility. Congreve indeed it was who told me himself this morning that Wilson was to succeed General Reed. It is the wisest selection that could be made, and it is thought that the new Commander will get on very well, better than he has done as Commander of the Artillery here, his plans not having succeeded very well; but as Commander of the whole Force it is generally believed that he will do the thing much better. He can't do much worse than his predecessor, though General Reed would, I think, have got on very fairly had he been in rude health.

Curzon leaves here too to-night or to-morrow, the arrival of Patrick Grant having put him out of the coach; he will go to Simla in the first instance, I fancy, and then home.

Until General Grant comes up here it is intended, I believe, that General Gowan should assume command of the Army in Upper India, and perhaps he will think it necessary to come here and join. I don't think he will get any of us from here to go up and join him. Becher and I both agree that if he will go up to Simla we shouldn't so much mind running up and reporting ourselves to him!

(*Diary*) 16*th July.*—A very quiet day, nothing at all stirring. Gloomy accounts from below, and great fears are entertained that Wheeler has been destroyed at Cawnpore with his little Force; but this I trust and think cannot be true; but still it is pretty clear, by a letter from Lord Canning, that there is no assistance coming up to us from below. Shells unpleasantly close this evening.

CHAPTER VII.

SIEGE OF DELHI (*continued*)—GENERAL REED GOES AWAY SICK, AND MAKES OVER THE COMMAND TO BRIGADIER-GENERAL WILSON.

Colonel KEITH YOUNG *to his wife.*

CAMP, DELHI CANTONMENTS, *Friday, 17th July.*

Nothing new here since I despatched my letter yesterday. The enemy talked of coming out again to-day to attack, which it was thought probable they would, as they got an accession to their force yesterday of the Jhansi Force—eight hundred Infantry, they say, some Cavalry, and three guns. I suppose they are going to wait until they get further reinforcements; or, it may be, perhaps, that they are too much taken up fighting amongst themselves, as it is reported to be a grand ground of quarrel the Bareilly mutineers not having given up their treasure to the King, and there was a talk of coercing them with the other troops. This would be a grand *tomasha* if it could be got up. I am afraid your friend who tells you of the mutineers burying their dead and wounded in one pit is not much to be depended upon. They leave a good many of their wounded behind, I dare say, but still a great many get into the city; and we heard a week or ten days ago that there were fully three thousand wounded men there, and the number can't have much diminished, as there have been two skirmishes since then. They have one native doctor, it is said, who looks after all these unfortunate wretches.

About one hundred and fifty of our sick and wounded are to be sent off to Umballa this evening, amongst them Colonel Welchman and some other officers. General Reed also goes, and Brigadier Wilson has already assumed the Command of this Force. Colonel Congreve likewise leaves us this evening by mail-cart— not sick, but because, he says, he will be in a false position here and cannot act under an officer (Wilson) junior to him. I fancy he is very glad to get away; you will see him at Simla.

Curzon left here yesterday evening; he promised to call on you at Simla and tell you what a merry life we are leading. He has long been anxious to get away, and I don't much wonder at his now going, as by the arrival of Generals Grant and Havelock he has no appointment whatever.

I am with you at a loss to know what women and children Major Goad alludes to as being in Delhi. We have heard of none that I am aware of.

I called on Murray-Mackenzie this morning. He is getting on well; but his wound, which is one that requires rest for its cure, still confines him to his bed.

I met Brind * at the tent, who is very loud against Sir John Lawrence for leaving the Sealkote force without any Europeans. I should think, from what we hear, there cannot be much chance of many of these mutineers escaping. Brind was telling me that our position on the right, and right front, has been very much strengthened within the last two days, and that if the enemy do come out again in that direction they ought to be annihilated without our losing a single man; and now that Wilson is commanding (he is made a Brigadier-General), good care will no doubt be taken to prevent our men from leaving their cover and putting themselves in the way of grape-shot again from the walls of the city.

I fancy, from what you say, General Penny would just as soon stay quietly at Simla, and I should think he would be about as much use there as he will be at Meerut. He is certainly not the man for such a command.

Chamberlain's wound is getting on pretty well; it is a very severe one, and it will be long ere he is able to mount a horse again.

Your letter of the 15th has just reached me. What a real snob that fellow ——— must be to go about frightening the ladies in that manner! He ought to be turned out of Simla.

As to the pistols, &c., belonging to Mrs Hall's servant, depend upon it they were only put in the *almirah* to keep them out of the way of the Commissioner's people; but it is very annoying this

* The late General Sir James Brind, K.C.B.

kind of thing happening, and I am much vexed that the servants should think of talking in the way they must have evidently been doing before the children. I feel half inclined to run up to Simla (just to put them to rights), which, I dare say, I might very easily do and be back again here in full time to be present at the taking of Delhi; for I really begin to think that it will be a very long time yet, perhaps another fortnight or three weeks, before we take the place. During this long interval we shall be really far better off here than you all will be at Simla or elsewhere, looking to the state of uncertainty and anxiety you will be in. Were the delay double this, however, we should be all right here, and if we only keep on the defensive—which, I think, we really shall do now—we need scarcely lose a single man.

The camp generally is very healthy, and you need be under no anxiety on my account. I am quite well now, and we suffer no inconvenience except that it is a little hot sometimes in the daytime; and the flies are rather an abomination unless we keep the tent dark. We are pitched on nice high ground; but by way of ensuring the tent being kept dry we have raised the veranda some six inches or so, which effectually prevents any water getting in were it so inclined. It is a great comfort there being no mosquitoes; and at night it is almost cold enough for a blanket before morning. Nearly 3 P.M., and all quiet.

(*Diary*) 17*th July*.—Went to bid Welchman good-bye—find him tolerably cheerful; he goes to Umballa with a party of sick and wounded this evening. Nothing stirring to-day. In the afternoon pay a visit to General Reed, who also goes away this evening, having made over command yesterday to Brigadier (now Major-General) Wilson. Congreve also off to Simla this morning: Curzon went yesterday; both have, I think, shown rather indecent haste in leaving.

CAMP, DELHI CANTONMENTS, *Saturday*, 18*th July*.

I have thought it as well to write a few lines (herewith enclosed) to the servants about the theft that took place in the house, and warning them that I intend to come up to Simla again before very long, and that they had better behave themselves properly. It is just as well, I think, to write to them, as they

may perhaps have an idea that I have taken my farewell of
Simla altogether. I expect the arrival of Congreve will have
rather a good effect amongst the servants at the Chota-Simla end;
he says he will see you soon after he arrives. He started by
mail-cart yesterday afternoon. General Reed also left about the
same time in a dâk-carriage; he is to go to Arthur Becher's house,
he told me. He is well away from here, as he is not well, and
fit for little more than lying on his bed all day. Brigadier Wilson
has come and taken up his quarters now in the big tent in the Head-
Quarters' camp. There it still stands, with the large *shamiyana*
and the Flagstaff in front, but the grand street is a very different
affair from what it used to be in our old marches with little Sir
William;* now any one that likes comes into it, and it is made a
regular thoroughfare for horsemen, footmen, and what not.

There is little to tell you since yesterday. The enemy remained
quiet all this morning, and they have come out again now to
attack us at the same point, the right and right front. I was
out for half-an-hour with the General on the usual place of
assembly, the Mound battery; but all appearing to be going on
well, we returned two or three hours ago, and since then, from
the accounts that have been sent down, the enemy are keeping at
a respectful distance and our men are remaining well under cover.
And now that Brigadier Wilson is commanding, I have no doubt
but that the orders will be properly attended to—to be content
with driving the scoundrels off without following them up to the
walls of the city.

The fighting party of the enemy to-day are probably those that
came in the day before yesterday from Jhansi. The next to come
are the Neemuch mutineers; but by the last accounts they had
gone to Muttra. I suppose when they come they will have to
fight; but from all accounts they will not be brave at it, as at
Agra they ran away from our small force of Europeans like
driven deer. There was a letter yesterday from Agra, of the 11th,
giving an account of the fighting there; there were two days of
it, the 5th and 6th, and it seems to have been very severe. We
were unfortunate in only having about fifty Cavalry, and the consequence was that we were quite unable to follow up their Infantry,
who made off as hard as they could towards Muttra, fancying we

* Sir William Gomm, the then Commander-in-Chief.

were after them. The Agra letter says that since the mutineers
left all was quiet at Agra; that a party had gone out every day
through the city and round about with a couple of guns, but
fell in with nothing. Most of the Mahomedans are stated to have
left Agra. The letter mentions that all was well at Lucknow on
the 2nd instant, when Sir Henry Lawrence had six hundred of
Her Majesty's 32nd and a party of Her Majesty's 84th. No fears
were entertained for Lucknow; but about Cawnpore the accounts
were very conflicting. You need not say anything about it to
any nervous person, but there is every reason to think now that
the story we had heard of Sir Hugh Wheeler being at Allyghur, or
thereabouts, with three or four regiments is not the case; and some,
indeed, go so far as to say that he and the few Europeans he had
with him—which were, after all, little more than a hundred, the
regiments sent to join him having been detained at Allahabad—
have all been cut up. This, however, surely cannot have been the
case; and the real solution of the difficulty appears to be that he
had gone down to Allahabad, some friendly Native chief having
agreed to hold Cawnpore for us, and that Sir Hugh had left
Allahabad with a European force towards the end of last month.
The Agra letter states that all was well at Allahabad, and that
there was no doubt of there being a European force at the
beginning of this month or the end of last between that place
and Cawnpore; and a letter of the 15th received yesterday from
Meerut mentions, on what is considered good authority, and quite
independent of that from Agra, that General Wheeler had gone
down to Allahabad, and that he was to be at Cawnpore (which a
kindly chief was holding for us) on the 4th of this month with
four thousand Europeans. Supposing this to be true, and I
think we may assume it as very nearly so, it will still be a long
time before we can expect to see him here—say a fortnight or
three weeks, perhaps, from the present time—for Sir Hugh Wheeler
would probably make a demonstration with a large part of his
force in the direction of Lucknow before he came on here. All
this delay is very unfortunate, but it seems unavoidable; and
except in a political point of view it is of very little importance,
for our men seem really healthier than they are in cantonments.

Provisions of all kinds are in the greatest abundance and very
cheap. I happen to know, as I went with Thomson this morning

to look at the Sudder Bazaar, in the Government Gardens on the other side of the canal; it was crowded with people from the villages with everything for sale in the greatest profusion.

Our troops who escorted the sick and wounded out last night have brought in a large convoy of ammunition and stores. A strong party of Sikh Cavalry also came in, so that we are now well off for reliable Native Cavalry—a very good thing, as it will save exposing the Lancers and Carabineers very much. Fortunately to-day is a nice, cool, cloudy and windy day, so our men who are obliged to be out are not likely to suffer.

You asked me about the Puttiala Raja; there is no doubt about his sticking to us to the very last. My servants here are behaving as well as possible. Soobhan was very anxious this morning to go up to the batteries to see the 'fun;' but as Mactier and I told him he would be shot, he agreed to stay at home!

Tell Mr Philipe the Agra news. It is a pity there should be such absurd reports about, but there seems no helping it. Have you heard anything of a mine that the enemy were said to be making up to Metcalfe House? It seems to be all nonsense; but in case there should be anything we are quite prepared. As General Wilson has not considered it necessary to leave camp (3 P.M.), there cannot be much of importance going on. A village of plundering *Goojurs*, &c., was destroyed near Kurnaul a few days ago by Captain Hughes,[*] who killed several hundred of them, losing only two men himself.

(*Diary*) 18*th July*.—Out before breakfast with Wilson at the Mound—the enemy attacking the right, and right front, as usual. Nothing much doing, so came back to breakfast. The Brigadier went out again in the middle of the day, but knowing nothing of it I did not join him. It seems we followed up the enemy again as before, and our loss, sixty men, was much more than it ought to have been. Bad news from Cawnpore; Wheeler and all his party treacherously murdered.

CAMP, DELHI CANTONMENTS, *Sunday*, 19*th July*.

The dâk arrived about a quarter of an hour ago, the postman blowing his horn in a most frantic way as he drove into

[*] The late General Sir W. T. Hughes, K.C.B.

camp. The letters will be delivered presently; and Soobhan has gone to the dâk to bring Mactier's and mine. Mactier generally gets a letter from Simla every day from one or other of his numerous correspondents.

You will be anxious to hear the result of yesterday's attack; it is much more satisfactory as regards ourselves, but still we have lost more men than we ought to have done, Brigadier Wilson having about four o'clock, contrary altogether, it is said, to his declared intention, ordered an advance upon the enemy. Their loss was great; but we have had sixty killed and wounded. One officer, Lieutenant Crozier, of Her Majesty's 75th, killed; and one officer doing duty with the Fusiliers, Ensign Walter, died from sunstroke. Lieutenant Jones, Engineers, lost his leg in the morning early by a cannon-ball. I saw the returns a few hours ago at Dr Tritton's, so you may depend upon my not understating the casualties this time. Many of the men are wounded slightly, and I think of those killed there were only five Europeans, the rest being natives. We had an alarm soon after breakfast to-day of another intended attack, but it turned out to be unfounded, and the troops who had turned out were soon ordered into their tents again; and there has been nothing but a little cannonading from the heavy batteries going on, probably without much damage to either side.

Make the flannel shirts, please, as they are generally made; I have never worn any yet, so do not know whether it would be best to have them made with collars or not. Mactier and I have both agreed that a few jars of hill preserves will be very acceptable. I think you said that you had some apricot jelly made by the old *khansamah*. We always have some jam or other for breakfast, and the stock, Mactier tells me, is rather low. We two still adhere to the Artillery mess, but breakfast at home.

I am very sorry that I cannot give you anything more cheering than I told you yesterday about Sir Hugh Wheeler. It is certain that he had not marched upwards from Cawnpore towards here with any force, and our only hope now is that he may be safe with his little band, for it seems that on the 27th of last month no help had reached him from below, and that he had with him only some hundred or two European soldiers, and with these he had been fighting for upwards of a fortnight. The state of things at

Allahabad must have precluded the troops marching away from there so early as was intended. But it is a very great thing the force having arrived in time to save the Fort; it would have been a terrible calamity had this been lost to us, with its large arsenal.

On the 27th June all was safe at Lucknow, and Sir Henry Lawrence, whose letter I saw of that date, is under no apprehension of not being able to hold his own; he has with him Her Majesty's 32nd, he says, and a small detachment of Her Majesty's 84th. In all probability now if we wait for reinforcements to take Delhi they will be sent us from the Punjab; and now that the Sealkote mutineers have been disbanded they may be able to spare us one European regiment, a corps of Sikhs, and the Kemaon battalion; then we should be quite strong enough to ensure the safety of our large camp while the city was assaulted. A letter I saw from the city to-day says the residents are all with us, and that with four European regiments we should be certain of succeeding in our attack.

CAMP, DELHI CANTONMENTS, *Monday, 20th July.*

Nothing of any interest has occurred here since I wrote to you yesterday. The alarm was sounded for an attack again this morning, but nothing came of it, and we have been quiet all day; and just as well, for though the morning was cool it has turned out a very hot day, and the men would have suffered greatly from exposure had an attack been made. It is curious, but we were remarking yesterday that the mutineers have never attacked us on a Sunday—not from any delicacy to us, I dare say. We had service in the morning before the alarm was sounded yesterday, and I think none of us were sorry that Mr Rotton gave us no sermon, his discourses being generally more soporific than edifying; but he is a very good, zealous man notwithstanding.

We have no further intelligence about General Wheeler or the European troops from below; but it is of the less consequence, as I fancy there is no doubt, now that the Sealkote mutineers have been disposed of, that it is intended to send down a sufficient force to make matters secure here. Nicholson himself telegraphed to-day that he is most anxious to come down with his Column, there being nothing now for it to do in the Punjab.

Have you had an account at Simla of the doings of a small

portion of the Meerut force in attacking one Shah Mull, or some such man, an insurgent Chief who has been the chief leader in all the late disturbances? We have had no written report yet, but our expedition is stated by some Native Sowars who came in to have been wholly successful, some six hundred of the enemy, they said, with their leader, having been killed, and his son taken prisoner; but probably accounts of the business have reached Simla direct from Meerut.

Tell the old *khansamah* to write another letter, and you enclose it to me, and I will take care it reaches its destination, and will ask Major Harriott to secure an answer. When you come across Pyloo Das, you can tell him that there was a *goomashta* from the city a few days ago, whom I asked about his (Pyloo Das's) family; he appeared to know them, and said they were well, and that they had shut themselves up in their house. If he likes to give you their address, tell him I shall inquire about them myself when we go into Delhi.

(*Diary*) 20*th July*.—False alarm again early this morning of intended attack, and troops turn out. It is just as well there was none, for though morning cool, day very hot. In my tent all day writing. Nothing further yet about Cawnpore. In the afternoon it seems a part of the troops turned out again and went after the enemy. I went to the Mound : great excitement. Only two of our men wounded.

CAMP, DELHI CANTONMENTS, *Tuesday*, 21*st July*.

I have just got your letter of the 19th, and am sorry indeed to see that so many are so dejected at Simla at our having not yet taken Delhi. Here there is, I may say, no feeling of uneasiness at all on the subject, and though there are no doubt some croakers in camp, I haven't heard a single one express a doubt as to our success; and as to Miss Smith's brother writing to her that the general impression in camp is that Delhi will not be taken till October, he must be giving his own crude ideas on the subject. I should say that the general impression is that from a fortnight to three weeks will see us within the walls, as before that time we must receive our reinforcements either from above or below, or perhaps both.

Nothing more has been heard of Sir Hugh Wheeler, and we are

still in great hope that the ugly reports we heard—and they are still only mere reports—will prove untrue. At Meerut, on the 18th, they were still in expectation of seeing him soon; and there is no doubt of some European force being on its way up. But even supposing any untoward delay in their reaching us, we are now promised a large addition to our little army by Sir John Lawrence, from whom Chamberlain received a telegraphic message to-day saying that, in addition to the Kemaon battalion and Henderson's regiment of Sikhs,* now *en route*, he was sending nine hundred European infantry, and that he could push down Beloochee and Sikh levies to the number of twelve thousand men if required. Two or three thousand of these latter would, I am sure, be very acceptable for guards and escorts, &c.; but twelve thousand would be rather an encumbrance, I fear. You will see from the above that there can be little fear of our having to wait so long as October to take the place. The authorities here are well aware of the unhealthiness of the place in September, and you may be sure that there will be no unnecessary delay when once there are sufficient troops to make sure work of Delhi. It was wished to send off the women and children from Meerut up to the hills, and to get the greater part of the troops over here; but I doubt whether this can be effected.

I got a letter this morning from Major Harriott, dated the 17th. He tells me that by Native letters from Delhi they hear, as we do here, that the mutineers are much dispirited at their continual want of success, and know not what to do. It is a pity our reinforcements are not already with us; but the enemy are not likely to have their spirits raised in the interim by any advantage they can gain over us. Yesterday they again made a faint attempt at an attack, but ran away immediately our men showed themselves. I don't know what their loss was, but ours was only two men of the Guides slightly wounded. To-day, too, it was said they had determined on making a grand attack, but nothing has come of it.

A sad and unfortunate accident happened last night. Captain Greensill, Her Majesty's 24th, doing duty with Her Majesty's

---

* This is a mistake. Henderson's regiment of Sikhs—3rd Punjab Infantry—never left the frontier; Green's—2nd Punjab Infantry—is probably meant.—H. W. NORMAN.

75th,* was shot by one of our own sentries, and died a few hours later. He was at one of the outlying pickets, and had gone out after dinner to look about him, and on his return, not answering the sentry's challenge (a man of the 75th), the man shot him. I don't know whether the sentry is considered to have been over hasty; but it is a sad occurrence anyhow.

Did I tell you that they took a woman prisoner the other day, who they made out was leading a charge of Cavalry and who killed two of our men with her own hand? I believe the greater part of this to be a fiction; and as she is old and ugly, not much romance attaches to her, though she is wounded!

I hope, as you say, it is true that we have accepted the services of five thousand of Jung Bahadoor's men. I wish we had them here now.

I suppose now that Colonel Havelock is appointed a Brigadier-General we shall have Colonel Curzon Acting Quartermaster-General down here. He ought not to have left; and Colonel Congreve too, might, I think, have stayed, as he will probably find out to his cost. I hope he will speak to Lord William Hay about completely disarming the bazaar people.

I send Harriott's letter, as you may like to see it. Near three o'clock a nice shower has come on, making it very cool.

(*Diary*) 21*st July.*—Took a ride to our left. What an immense place the camp is! After breakfast alarm again, but nothing came of it. Rainy day and cool. Sad accident last night—Captain Greensill, Her Majesty's 24th, shot by mistake by one of our own sentries, not having answered the challenge. Talk of large reinforcements coming from Punjab.

Major HARRIOTT to Colonel KEITH YOUNG.

MEERUT, 17*th July.*

MY DEAR COLONEL,—I have just received, and hasten to reply to and thank you for, your letter of 15th. A letter from Brigadier Wilson to Hogge, some ten days since, informing him that you were the besieged party and could not advance your batteries without being annihilated in five minutes, dispelled our notions of the early

---

* Captain Greensill was attached to the Engineer Department.—H. W. NORMAN.

fall of Delhi—indeed, of its falling at all until reinforcements arrived. We have therefore ceased to expect anything but accounts of outside skirmishing until Wheeler or the Commander-in-Chief puts in an appearance with fresh forces. We cannot hear anything certain regarding Wheeler's movements; indeed, our chief reason for supposing him near is the evident fright they are in at Delhi regarding him.

A Persian letter received by Williams, the Commissioner, from some natives in Delhi, and dated the 14th, gave us an account of the action of that day; this man estimates our loss in killed and wounded at two hundred, the killed being about thirty or forty. He was not far out, it appears; so that when he states that the mutineers lost on the 14th upwards of one thousand killed, he, I dare say, may be very near the mark. He describes their dejection of spirits to be extreme—says that they went out at 8 A.M. ten thousand strong after binding themselves by a solemn oath not to return unless victorious. Other spies, indeed, all agree in stating the mutineers to be in the greatest state of fear and apprehension, that there is no *bundabust* (organisation), and that they seem perfectly aware that their sole chance now consists in annihilating the force with you before Wheeler joins.

A party of about two thousand of the mutineers are said to have come out three days since and destroyed the bridge over the Hinden, at Ghazeeoodeen-Nugar, to prevent Wheeler's junction, so that it is supposed he must be on the Meerut side of the Jumna, and may possibly find it necessary to reach Delhi *viâ* Meerut and Kurnaul. In the absence of bridges and boats if the force here were to move it would, I imagine, take the Kurnaul route; but we are hampered with about five hundred women and children, for whom we could procure no sufficient carriage, and to give up this place, as some talk of, seems to me perfect madness—the loss of prestige would be great, the loss in barracks and other property enormous. So that unless the very existence of our troops at Delhi was jeopardised, the abandonment of Meerut would, I think, be a most serious evil. I only hope it is not contemplated by those in authority. We are still fortifying and entrenching to an immense extent, but for what purpose I cannot make out: the time for such work seems to me to be quite past.

Can I do anything for you here, or are you well supplied from

Umballa? I could, if you wished, send you a coolie-load of wine, brandy, &c., by the first opportunity. I have not despatched a single public paper since the outbreak, nor, indeed, have I received one, the first communication from the office of any kind being a demi-official from Mr Philipe with form of charges for deserters; all the papers are ready for despatch at a moment's notice.

By the way, now that Hewitt has been superseded and Penny not arrived, we have no power to assemble District Courts on Europeans. The warrant is addressed to Major-General Hewitt, or Officer Commanding the Meerut Division; this at the present moment is Brigadier Polwhele, with whom we cannot communicate. I am therefore at a nonplus in regard to an apothecary who has been insolent to a medical officer; I cannot possibly proceed against him regimentally.

Of course nowadays I have little or nothing to do here, and should like much, when the time for action arrives, to be at Delhi. Could you then, on Wheeler's or the Commander-in-Chief's arrival, procure me fifteen days' leave? A demi-official note from you saying the officer commanding at Delhi would not object to my coming would, I imagine, be quite sufficient: the Adjutant-General's permission would do. I hope you receive good accounts from Simla. —Very truly yours, FRED. HARRIOTT.

Colonel KEITH YOUNG *to his wife.*

CAMP, DELHI CANTONMENTS, *Wednesday, 22nd July.*

I am glad Curzon has been to see you, and has given you so favourable an account of me. What does he intend to do? He ought, I think, to return to Delhi if he remains Quartermaster-General; both he and Congreve have, in my opinion, been rather premature in leaving here.

Matters go on much more quickly and smoothly in camp now that Brigadier Wilson is commanding. He is a gentlemanly, quiet, steady 'old fellow,' looks to everything himself, and gives clear and distinct orders, and all feel much more at their ease than they did under their late commander, in whom no one had confidence. He (Brigadier Wilson) is rather over-careful, perhaps, but this is a fault quite on the right side; though the troops don't like turning out so often when perhaps it may not have been actually necessary. This morning, for instance, the alarm was sounded at four o'clock, just before daybreak, heavy firing having been heard, and it was thought our pickets were attacked. It turned out, however, to be the enemy themselves firing furiously from the walls, thinking we were attacking them, and the wind setting from that direction made it seem that the firing was much closer to us than it really was. Since then all has been quiet to-day, and a news-letter that I saw just now from the city says that they have little heart now left for fighting, and very probably they may not come out again to attack us in any force unless they are joined by fresh troops: and there seems little chance now of their getting any more except the Neemuch mutineers; but these appear to have been so well thrashed at Agra that they will not have much wish to try their luck again.

It is a great pity that we have not a few more men at Agra so as to have followed up the mutineers, who, later letters from there state, have been completely beaten, though we did not know it at the time, and had we been aware of it we couldn't have followed them up for want of cavalry.

We hear nothing here about the horrible stories of the streets being undermined and the houses all loopholed. It cannot be the case: and there are grave doubts also of any of the gateways being undermined, as was at one time reported; but of course all this will be properly inquired into before the city is assaulted. We have no further news from below, but the reports are strong of the European force having silenced Lucknow and Cawnpore and Futtyghur, and being on its march up. The newsletter from the city to-day talks of the European army that is advancing.

I was wrong when I told you yesterday that Sir John Lawrence had offered twelve *thousand* men; it should have been twelve *hundred*, which is perhaps as many as we really want. It was a mistake of the telegraph. Altogether he is to send nine hundred European Infantry, the Kemaon battalion, Green's regiment of Sikhs, and the Belooch corps—about two thousand Natives altogether. The two first corps are near Umballa by this time, and all perhaps will be here in about a fortnight or so, by which time, probably, we shall have the European force from below very near us. We shall with either force be quite strong enough to take Delhi; but with both we shall be able to do what we like.

(*Diary*) *22nd July.*—An alarm very early this morning—at 4 A.M.; but it turned out that the firing which caused the turn-out was all on the enemy's side, who fancied apparently that we were attacking the city. A packet of letters, and amongst them an English one of 26th May, from H. B. Henderson, came from Captain Eden. Quiet all day, but warm in tent; slight rain. Dine with Becher at the Staff mess—not such a good one as ours of the Artillery.

CAMP, DELHI CANTONMENTS, *Thursday, 23rd July.*

We are still without any authentic intelligence of Sir Hugh Wheeler, or of the European force that is moving up. A letter received yesterday evening from Agra, of the 17th, where all was well, says that six European regiments had left Cawnpore, and a *cossid* who came in this morning says they are this side of Allyghur; while the newsletter from the city to-day talks confidently of a European Army coming up. We are satisfied in camp that there is no doubt of this; but it is a great nuisance our getting no intelligence from the officer commanding the force, whoever he may be. Several messengers have been sent to him lately, and in a very few days now we shall have them returning, and learn exactly how matters stand.

There has been more fighting again this morning. The enemy made an attack on our left—the first, I believe, they have ever made. Of course they were driven back, losing a good many of their men; but we have not escaped, and in trying to take some guns, which we *all but got*, our brave fellows went close up to the city walls and several were knocked over. One officer, Captain Law, 10th Native Infantry, doing duty with Coke's corps, killed; and Colonel Seaton, Captain Money (Horse Artillery), Major Drought, and Frank Turner wounded. Frank Turner's is very slight, merely a graze on the shoulder; Money, I believe, is hit on the knee; and Colonel Seaton's, it is hoped, will not prove serious —and I am sure I trust not, as he is one of the best officers in camp. Some thirty men are reported killed or wounded; but most of them, from what I hear, belong to Coke's corps. Only one Artilleryman was wounded, and they must have been in the thick of it. Bunny had a narrow escape, I am told—a shot grazing his cheek. No one from this camp is hurt except Colonel Seaton.

Norman, Hodson, and others have just been in here with me. Everything is quiet now, and the cowardly scoundrels, having been driven into the city, are not likely to make their appearance again to-day. Our men can never get within four or five hundred yards or more of them, and the advance of our troops is the signal for their firing off muskets and running away helter-skelter as hard as they possibly can.

Letters have just come in from Meerut of yesterday's date. All well there; but I do not hear that they give any certain intelligence of the approach of the force from Cawnpore. The idea of sending away all the ladies and children from Meerut has, I believe, been abandoned on account of the extreme difficulty that there would be in getting carriage and providing a sufficient escort for them; and now that forces are moving here from above as well as below, it is not considered so necessary as it at one time was.

I think I shall take Harriott at his word, and get him to send me over a coolie-load of wine and beer. Fancy some brandy yesterday selling at auction here for eight rupees a bottle! There were only two bottles of it; had there been more they would have fetched a more reasonable price.

Harriott's brother-in-law, Saunders, Civil Service, is over here, having come about a week ago. He goes, I believe, to Paniput in a day or two, to keep the district quiet. Mrs Saunders is still at Meerut.

Fancy poor Goldney being killed—at least so the papers say: we know nothing more of the Fyzabad mutiny than the information contained in them. Mrs Hall must be very anxious about her sister, of whom George Hall tells me nothing has been heard since the first outbreak. We can only hope that she is safe at Benares, and that the report about poor Goldney's death may prove untrue.

It is feared that Major Drought's wound is very dangerous; but none of the others.

(*Diary*) 23rd *July*.—Alarm about 7 A.M., but, having a good deal of writing to do, didn't turn out myself. The attack this time was on our left front, but it was rather a feeble one. We lost, however, I am grieved to think, some dozen men killed and forty

(AGRA.) IN THE FORT.
The Taj Mahal in the distance.

wounded; and one officer killed—Law, 10th Native Infantry. Very rainy afternoon.

CAMP, DELHI CANTONMENTS, *Friday, 24th July.*

I believe I overrated the number of our casualties yesterday. It is difficult to find out exactly, but they say now it was only twenty-five.* What an unusual number of officers were wounded in proportion! I am glad to say they are all doing well; and Frank Turner was dining at mess, so you may suppose that he was not very hardly hit. Bunny, who was here this morning, has just the slightest mark on his face.

The scoundrels in the city have been very quiet all day, and there is no talk of their making another attack. I have strictly told Hodson and Becher what you say about not going into the city until we get reinforcements! Our spies and people are, I dare say, rascals enough to be in the pay of the enemy, and to misrepresent their strength; but there is no chance now of our assaulting the city without fresh troops, and when the attack does come off, it will not, you may be sure, be made without our having better intelligence of what we are to expect inside than is to be obtained from common spies. Tell Sep. Becher he is altogether wrong about there being heaps of muskets in the magazine: they were all sent away to the Ferozepore magazine (I think it was) shortly before the outbreak.

Where did Mr Mayne get his information from about Chamberlain's arm? There is certainly no present intention of amputating it, and it is fully expected that it will be saved unless an unfavourable turn takes place, which is not anticipated.

There were letters from Agra last night of the 18th instant, when all was well there; and a daughter of Colonel Herbert's, who is married to Toby Glover, writes, I understand (for I did not see the letter myself), that they are as merry as possible, and she and Mrs Machell are, she says, managers of one of the messes in the Fort: and altogether they appear to think it very great fun, and are quite ready to thrash any party of mutineers that may come to attack them.

It is difficult, from the various accounts, to learn with accuracy

* The actual casualties in this affair were one officer and eleven men killed, five officers and thirty-four men wounded, and one man missing.—H. W. NORMAN.

where the European force is that is coming up here. One portion of it, Mr Colvin himself says, consisting of three or four regiments, was at Futtehpore on the 4th July; and then again the *cossids* who brought the letters, and whom I questioned myself, said that two regiments and a Sikh corps were only two marches from Agra, and that there were three more a short way behind them; and then Meerut letters received this morning say that six European regiments had reached Cawnpore about the 8th. The real truth we shall probably learn in a day or two; and that there is a large force on the way somewhere seems quite clear. As to any number of mutineers stopping them, it is altogether out of the question; but there is not likely to be any large force for them to come into collision with. The Gwalior people, as I told you, are remaining quietly at Gwalior.

Has Mrs Becher mentioned to you that Arther Becher has written to Sir John Lawrence, through his military secretary, about disarming effectually the people at Simla? I wrote the letter, and Becher signed it. I don't think Sir John can fail to give some stringent orders on the subject; but say nothing of the matter unless you hear of it elsewhere.

I saw Colonel Greathed this morning looking very well, also Sandy Robertson; they live together. Young Anson goes up to Simla, leaving this evening by mail-cart; he is going, he says, to look after some of his uncle's property, and hopes to be back here in a week. He has promised to call and tell you how anxious we all are to get away on sick certificate; but Mactier we find inexorable! Octavius Hamilton is going away sick to join Mrs Hamilton at Mussoorie; I fancy he is very tired of it, and, for the matter of that, perhaps we all are a little. Hodson has given up the command of the Guides, having got a Cavalry corps of his own now to get into order; he is indeed a good officer.

All is as quiet as if we were at Simla; and it is very nice and cool at present—but plenty of flies. Thanks for the jams, &c., you are sending; but don't send too many. A tin or two of herrings, Mactier says, will be acceptable.

(*Diary*) 24*th July.*—Very cool morning, and drizzling rain all day. Go and pay a morning visit to Greathed; nothing doing in camp. Curious case of settling law—a European soldier is to be tried for murder; the General, having no warrant, decides to proceed under Article 144—martial law, in fact. Dine at the Artillery mess as usual.

CAMP, DELHI CANTONMENTS, *Saturday, 25th July.*

There has been nothing at all going on in camp since my last letter, the city scoundrels being as quiet as possible; and we shall trouble them very little, unless they trouble us, until our reinforcements arrive.

We are still without any authentic accounts of General Wheeler, but reports have come in from so many quarters of his having met with disaster that I fear it must be the case; but not, I think and hope, to the extent that some anticipate. Whatever has, however, happened to him, there seems no doubt that Cawnpore is in our hands again, and that Futtyghur also is safe.

What seems thought here as not improbable is that Sir Henry Lawrence will abandon Lucknow, and that we shall confine ourselves altogether to the right bank of the Ganges, holding Cawnpore, and pushing up as many troops as can be spared to Delhi; and then when that is taken the whole army will be available to settle all the disturbed districts, and reconquer Oude and Rohilkund. Should, however, unforeseen circumstances arise to delay the troops down below, there is a large force coming down from the Punjab, so that we shall be quite strong enough with the troops we have here to set to work to take Delhi properly.

The reinforcements that are coming from the Punjab must be close upon five thousand men,* including a regiment and a half of Europeans (Her Majesty's 52nd, and wing 61st), equal altogether very nearly to what we have here now. Nicholson was to leave Umritsur yesterday, and we cannot expect to have all here much before the middle of next month—a long time to look forward; but it is as well to wait, rather than run any risk.

Arthur Becher's arm is getting on very well, but it will be some weeks yet, I should think, before he will be able to get on horseback again.

* This estimate is nearly two thousand in excess of all the reinforcements that came.—H. W. NORMAN.

Yes, I must make an effort to come up to Simla in October, and I look forward to be able to manage it somehow or other. As the time approaches I shall be able to see my way better. We ought soon to hear something of General Grant, who must, I should think, decide upon coming up country when he hears how matters are progressing.

I see Dr Mackinnon nearly every day now; he assists Mactier in attending upon Chamberlain, and generally comes at least once a day. He is looking very well, though not quite so spruce as he used to do at Meerut. He rides on horseback now instead of in a buggy; but there are plenty of buggies in camp, and Dr Tritton, who is acting as Superintending Surgeon, always drives about in one to pay his visits to the hospitals.

Why didn't you tell the old *khansamah* that I would send his letter enclosed with mine to Harriott when writing to him? This is the only way to ensure any Native letter reaching its destination. His last one I merely addressed to Harriott's care, and hence, probably, the cause of no reply coming.

(*Diary*) 25*th July*.—Commenced raining soon after daybreak, and scarcely left off all day. Nothing stirring in camp again to-day, and the enemy uncommonly quiet—plotting some mischief, I suppose, the scoundrels! They talk of attacking us in rear again. The dâk in earlier to-day.

CAMP, DELHI CANTONMENTS, *Sunday, 26th July.*

Nothing going on here since I wrote yesterday—the enemy perfectly quiet, and we the same, attributable in some measure, perhaps, to there having been drizzling rain all day. The sun has now come out (2 P.M.); but there is no appearance or talk of the mutineers showing themselves. The newsletter of this morning says they talk of postponing their attack till the Eed (the 2nd or 3rd of August); and I am sure I hope they may, as they are just as likely on that day to have a row amongst themselves—the Mahomedans and Hindoos—as to which party shall come and attack us.

No authentic news yet of Havelock's movements; but I fear we must give up the idea of his joining us in any reasonable time, if there is any truth in the reports of the Cawnpore and Futtyghur disasters—for the same story is now told of Futtyghur as of Cawnpore, that after holding out for some time our people took to boats, and were nearly all murdered. We can only pray that in both cases the rumours may prove incorrect: a very few days must relieve us from all uncertainty. It is fortunate that they are able to spare so large a force for us from the Punjab; it will nearly double our strength.

Who was it told you that Sir John Lawrence could not afford to send any more men to our assistance? I am afraid there are some croakers who write from camp.

Not a word of the Saugar brigade for some time, but by the latest accounts they were said to be all right, and showing no signs of mutiny; I trust they may continue so, but it is hardly to be expected. I hope at any rate, if there is any rising, that 'long Jack' (a Sepoy) will give the Hamptons good warning, and take care of them.

The King will be rather astonished when he hears the result of the Jhelum and Sealkote mutinies. The newsletter to-day says he was expecting several regiments from the Punjab, and had given orders that they were to destroy all Europeans on their way to Delhi.

Tell Mrs Hall I have mentioned her proposal to provide the troops with cherry-coloured ribbons for the day of the assault. It is agreed that it would be a very pretty device; and some one remarked that it would make them very 'cheery'! I doubt your getting sufficient of the material, so some might wear a red geranium, or you might cut up the velvet archery jackets for the occasion; but, in fact, it is only the Cavalry that will require any distinguishing mark, the Sikhs and Goorkhas (we have no other Native Infantry) being an entirely different-looking set of people from the *Poorbeahs* or the *Pandies*, as they are always called here.

Saunders, of the Civil Service, left here this morning; he was asking me about you. He goes first to Kurnaul, and is to have a kind of charge of all the Cavalry between this and there, and to look after the Jheend Raja's troops. Captain McAndrew, who had charge of them, has been superseded, chiefly, I believe, on account of that Bhagput bridge affair, and he is succeeded by Lieutenant-Colonel Dunsford, 59th Native Infantry.

Telegraphic Message from Captain NORMAN *to* E. C. BARNES.

26th July.

Accounts received from Agra of the total defeat of insurgents under the Nana Sahib at Futtehpore, on the 12th instant. Our troops are said to have taken his twelve guns and seven lacs of treasure.

Colonel KEITH YOUNG *to his wife.*

CAMP, DELHI CANTONMENTS, *Monday, 27th July.*

Thank Major Goad for the offer of his revolver, but I do not want it. I have a brace of double-barrelled pistols, which, I think, are preferable to a revolver, for these latter have rather a trick of going off when you don't want them and of not going off when you do. Barchard, here on General Wilson's staff, shot his horse three or four days ago by his revolver accidentally going off—the horse, rather a valuable one, the veterinary-surgeon said could not live.

All quiet here, and no symptoms of the mutineers venturing another attack.

I suppose you have heard of Sir J. Lawrence's news of General Grant being at Cawnpore on the 11th July with six regiments; but this must be a mistake. There is news, however, in from Agra, of the 20th, that a battle was fought some forty miles from Cawnpore by the force coming up, probably under Havelock, on the 11th, and that he had gained a complete victory over the chief (Nana) opposed to him, taking eleven guns, seven lacs of treasure, and all the camp equipage of the enemy, whom he was pursuing towards Cawnpore. They seem to have no doubt at Agra of the truth of the accounts that have reached them; and what confirmed them in it was that the Gwalior Raja had written to congratulate the Lieutenant-Governor on the victory, and to assure him that he was keeping the contingent of mutineers all safe at Gwalior. Probably we shall get further intelligence on the matter in the course of the day, but the news of the victory is fully believed here, though it may not be accurate in details; and it tallies, too, with what we hear from the city, where it has been strongly reported for some days that the Nana had been beaten. This

Nana is the man that was opposed to Sir Hugh Wheeler at Cawnpore. We are still without authentic accounts from there, and of course the most contradictory stories are in circulation about him and his little band. For my part, I am quite prepared to learn that matters are not so bad as represented, either regarding him or the Futtyghur party.

What will Mrs Martin and Mrs Hall say when they hear of the 4th Irregulars having been disarmed? I knew nothing of it till I went to mess yesterday evening, when I was told that this measure had been considered necessary, and that they had been quietly disarmed about an hour before. The immediate cause of it, I believe, was some thirty of them who were on outpost duty about forty miles from here, at a place called Sonput, having deserted. I have not seen either George Hall or Martin since the occurrence, but of course their letters, which I have sent to-day to the post, will contain all particulars. The only mistake in the matter is the regiment not having been disbanded long ago; and other regiments ought to have been disbanded also, particularly the 9th Irregulars—the one that Fenwick commanded—and it was only the interests of Chamberlain, who had formerly commanded the corps, that prevented its being done. These 4th are the last of the Hindoostanees in camp except the Sappers, and they have behaved well, and are too useful, besides, to get rid of.

A large convoy of stores and ammunition came in this morning, and I believe George Ward was with it, but I haven't seen him. Mr Briscoe also came in, to Mactier's great delight. You never saw such a warlike individual in your life—riding an unusually tall horse, and armed to the teeth with pistols and what not.

(*Diary*) *27th July.*—Began to rain heavily about daybreak, and continued more or less till 2 P.M.; since then, fine. News of a victory over the Nana (by Havelock, probably) on the 11th came in last night. Large convoy in this morning.

CAMP, DELHI CANTONMENTS, *Tuesday*, *28th July* 1857.

We know nothing yet that can be relied upon regarding Cawnpore and Futtyghur. That disasters of some kind have happened at both places there can, I fear, be no question, but not, I think and trust, to the extent supposed by the desponding at Simla. You may imagine how anxiously we are looking out for the arrival of a *cossid* direct from Havelock. The news of the city is that he had reached Futtyghur, where the Nawab had come out to meet him and make his submission. All is quiet in the city—at least, they are leaving us alone; but it is said they are all quarrelling amongst themselves, and that there is a scarcity of powder, caps, and money, and no leader to keep matters straight.

The Neemuch mutineers came in yesterday, but, under present circumstances, they can only add to the inconvenience and discord.

I had a few lines from Arthur last night of the 17th instant. He was at Erinpoorah, and all well; he does not even allude to there being anything like disturbances going on in that part of the country. He says he has often written; but this is the first letter I have received since the outbreak. If you write to him, write *viâ* Lahore.

I also got a very kind letter from Mr Frere,* dated the 19th instant, stating all were well at Kurrachee. He writes to offer to do anything for you there; so if you have to run away home from Simla, you can go down that way and get him to take care of you and the children, and put you on board ship.

I must get you to call in at Mr Walker's some day that you are passing his shop, and order a new waterproof for me. That one of mine is completely spoilt by the heat. It got all stuck together; I managed to pull it out with some difficulty, but when I put it on the first rainy day found it quite useless. The gaiters, &c., are all right. The waterproof I wish Mr Walker to make for me is of a different material—light waterproof cloth, and exactly like the one he sent Hodson, tell him—the one that has a light cape, so that your arms are protected when you ride.. As to the colour, perhaps he has only the material of the same colour that Hodson's is made of; but you will see, and if he has a variety, choose which you like best. This light waterproof cloth is said to be much better and more wholesome than that mackintosh stuff that mine is made of.

I have not seen George Hall since his regiment was disarmed, nor do I know what he is going to do. They ought to

* The late Sir Bartle Frere.

post him to the 9th Lancers, or give him the command of the Guide Cavalry, which are said to be the best Cavalry in camp—the 9th Lancers hardly excepted. I met George Ward yesterday, looking well.

Arthur Becher, Mactier, and Norman send their kindest regards to you. They are all well, particularly Norman, who is getting stouter with his extra work and excitement.

3.30 P.M., and all quiet.

Mr BARTLE FRERE, *Governor of Sind, to Colonel* KEITH YOUNG.

KURRACHEE, 19*th July.*

MY DEAR KEITH YOUNG,—I only write a line to ask you where and how you are, and whether I can be of any use to you or Mrs Keith Young. I have received nothing from you since the two first letters, dated one from Simla, the other from Kurnaul; I mention this lest you should have sent others. The enclosures in those two were brought safe by the overland mail.

We are all looking anxiously towards Delhi; but when I consider the smallness of the force, and the immense size of the place and the numbers of its defenders, I am not sanguine of success till you get largely reinforced. Here we are all quiet, feeling the swell of the storm, but as yet have not been visited by any portion of the hurricane. We are as badly off for troops and leaders as the rest of the world, but doing what we can to make provision for the future by local levies and such temporary expedients, and by no means living in idleness. Good accounts, thank God, from home. When you have a spare moment, let me have a line just to say you are all well.—Believe me, ever sincerely yours, B. W. FRERE.

Colonel KEITH YOUNG *to his wife.*

CAMP, DELHI CANTONMENTS, *Wednesday,* 29*th July.*

The mutineers still remain quiet, and we know of no reason why they should be so, unless those that I gave you yesterday—viz., want of a leader, internal dissensions, and scarcity of caps and powder.

Hodson just now came into our tent and interrupted my

writing this. I took him to task for not writing to his wife, but he declares he does regularly except when he is obliged to go out. He tells me that a letter has just come in from the city confirming what we had before heard of the dissensions going on, and they seem likely to terminate in something serious at the Festival of the Eed, as some of the Mahomedan fanatics have declared their fixed intention of killing a cow as customary on that day at the Jumma Musjid. It is hoped that they will religiously adhere to their determination, and there is then sure to be a row between the Mahomedans and Hindoos. The letter also mentions the scarcity of powder and caps, and the latter they are quite unable to make, while they are at a loss for sulphur to manufacture the powder. Accounts are likewise contained in the letter of the march of the European troops upwards, some of which are said to have gone to Futtyghur, others remaining at Cawnpore and Lucknow. It is, indeed, annoying that we can get no authentic accounts direct from this force; but Daly, who got the men that were first sent with letters from here, says they are not due with their replies till the day after to-morrow, and only then provided they met with no interruption on the road and had a reply been given them immediately. At Agra, too, from which place there is a letter of the 24th (all well there), they have nothing but Native intelligence yet of the victory gained over the rebels and of the European troops moving up. The Agra accounts tally very much with what we hear from the city. Gwalior still all right, and the mutineers remaining there; and no more mutineers or deserters, so far as they know, at Agra in any direction.

Is Lord William Hay very irate at being called upon by Mr Montgomery to state what measures he has taken for effectually disarming the people of the bazaar, as also for forming a party of special constables? A copy of Sir John Lawrence's order to the above effect, as given to Mr Montgomery to carry out, was sent to Arthur Becher in reply to the letter I told you of, saying it was the general opinion that the bazaar people had not been properly disarmed. I hope the inquiry will have the effect of making Lord William Hay set to work in earnest to collect the arms of the bazaar scoundrels.

It is not pleasant for Congreve to be superseded by Colonel

(DELHI.) JUMMA MUSJID,
or Great Mosque, built of red sandstone and white Marble.

Lugard, who may very likely now get the *pucka* appointment from home if Havelock is made Major-General, which I have no doubt he will be. I shouldn't think it likely, however, that Captain Seymour will go to Bombay after all, for before he can get there the new Commander-in-Chief will probably be nominated at home, and if the choice fall on Sir P. Grant, Seymour will have all his journey for nothing; and unless it happens to be Sir Henry Somerset himself, there can be little use in his going to Bombay. In our camp it is thought that the new Chief will be either Sir Patrick Grant or Sir Colin Campbell —the former, *our* Company's officers all hope.

Brigadier Wilson was taken unwell last night, and was obliged to leave the mess, and we were all afraid it was going to be something serious; but it seems nothing at all of consequence, and Mackinnon and Mactier both expect him to be quite well to-morrow. I don't know really what we should do if anything were to happen to the Brigadier, for there is no man likely to assume the command in whom we have any confidence.

Yes, I saw the *kotwal* (policeman) you speak of that came from the city. He was the *kotwal* of the *sudder* (chief) bazaar here, but he told too many wonderful stories for them all to be true; and I don't see why he didn't leave the city and come and join us long ago.

Captain EDEN to Colonel KEITH YOUNG.

HODUL, *29th July.*

MY DEAR COLONEL KEITH YOUNG,—The two accompanying packets for the Commander-in-Chief I could not send earlier with safety. Captain Stewart will explain the reasons as regards my chivalrous Rajput Horse. As Mr Ford is going with him, we have been able to make up a mixed escort of men picked up from villages, where they were enjoying their leave of absence from their regiment.

We have no further tidings from the east and south—all surmise; but on 19th the Mynpoorie collector telegraphed to say there must have been a severe fight at Cawnpore, as the mutineers are marching up carrying numerous wounded with them from that place. They do not speak to any one, and nothing can be learnt of what has happened. This morning's account from Jeypore states that the Neemuch mutineers had taken up a position at Khooshalgurh, in the Jeypore district—the effect of Captain Hardcastle's approach with some three thousand Rajput troops, or the heavy rain; but others say that the regiment should be at Bhurtpore to-morrow! Three and a half companies of the jail guard bolted a week ago, with their arms and ammunition, from Agra.

I send a couple of papers on the chance of their being new to you. Two of my men are gone to you for news. The capture of Delhi you can't send in too soon. Pray give my kind regards to Becher, and wishes for his rapid recovery.—I am, yours very truly,   Wm. F. Eden.

Colonel KEITH YOUNG *to his wife.*

CAMP, DELHI CANTONMENTS, *Thursday, 30th July.*

All is quiet in camp, and the mutineers must, I should hope—as we all believe—be quarrelling amongst themselves, and unable to agree to come out and attack us again. The Eed, we trust, will bring matters to a crisis with them, and be the day for a grand row between the Hindoos and Mahomedans. I don't know whether I told you that in addition to their other difficulties there is now known to be a great want of money, and the troops have told the King that if he doesn't give them pay in four days, they must plunder the town and help themselves. This was two days ago, so we shall soon know if such is their intention.

Did Mr Philipe give you the newsletter to read that I sent yesterday? I did not put in the concluding portion that was in the original: it related to a proposal that was made to the King to make his peace with the British by giving up the city, and to which he is said to have agreed. Very likely he would wish to do so, but he would find it a most difficult matter to effect it.

No certain intelligence yet from Cawnpore or elsewhere below, but Native letters continue to confirm what we have heard. The first fight was near Futtehpore (not Futtyghur), and then there was another, it is said, at Cawnpore, after which our victorious little Army relieved Lucknow, and then went on to Futtyghur, where all was quietly settled. We must have one of our *cossids* back to-morrow or next day, and then the mystery will be cleared up; but we are fully prepared to find that a couple of European regiments or more are soon to be with us. Mr Philipe is not much out of his calculations, I fancy, when he talks of Nicholson's force not being here till the 18th or 20th; but Nicholson himself says the 15th, and, depend upon it, he will not loiter on the road. The Kemaon battalion are expected here the day after to-morrow.

I enclose a letter I got from Harriott last night. You will see what he says about the Cawnpore business, and you may be sure matters will not turn out so bad as some think. Why do you trouble yourself to read all these atrocities in the papers? Many of them are much exaggerated; and I don't believe that story about putting children in a box and burning them. The ill-treatment of women and children is not very general. At Sealkote, for instance, Bishop, of the Artillery, whose brother was killed there, told me that the mutineers did not attempt to injure Mrs Bishop, though she was in the buggy with her husband; and our friend Mrs Graham was not touched, though they shot her husband by her side and he died in her arms.

I think I told you Brigadier Wilson had not been well, and people began to shake their heads as if it were something serious. I was glad to see him out to-day, and Mactier says he hopes he will be quite well to-morrow. I expect we shall be here for another three weeks at the very least; but, as we were saying last night at the mess, there is really nothing as yet in the least to complain of, and I assure you we are suffering no real discomfort beyond that of sticking so long in the same place, and *outside* the walls of Delhi, too. The poor fellows who are marching to join us must be very uncomfortable, as they can never hope for a dry place to lie down on.

What nonsense ——— talks about Head-Quarters going to join General Gowan! There is not a shadow of foundation for the report. The story, too, about the Gwalior contingent having arrived here is all stuff.

Greathed (Colonel) told me this morning that the Goorkhas had been ordered from Jutogh to join the Head-Quarters of their corps.

Is this true? If it is, fifty Europeans ought to be sent to Simla. Who is to command the Volunteers when Seymour goes?

(*Diary*) 30*th July*.—Nothing doing to-day. Strange that we get no report direct from the officer commanding the force coming up.

Major HARRIOTT *to* Colonel KEITH YOUNG.

MEERUT, 28*th July*.

MY DEAR COLONEL,—I had been intending to write to you for some days, relative to ———, when your letter of the 25th came to hand yesterday and determined me upon delaying no longer. You remember ——— was put under arrest for omitting to obey the order relative to reading to his men the disbandment of the 19th Native Infantry. I don't know what decision has been come to at Army Head-Quarters relative to his case. Has it escaped attention in the Adjutant-General's department, consequent upon poor Chester's death and the change of Commander-in-Chief, or has it been decided? If any papers were despatched to Meerut with instructions upon the point, they have probably been *goojured;* at any rate they have not come to hand, and ——— is consequently still kept in limbo. This may not be of much detriment to the State, for as an officer he is less than valueless, but it is a hardship on the individual. Will you speak about it?

General Penny arrived last Sunday. He seems a sensible, shrewd man, though rather ancient-looking, and is a great improvement upon old Hewitt, who could do nothing, and generally followed the advice of any person who had the last word with him.

I should certainly much like to get over to Delhi about the 10th of next month; but unless you procure for me some kind of demi-official message from Chamberlain, as Adjutant-General, I do not think it is very likely that I shall be able to get leave. If he would only say that there could be no objection to my coming over, provided the General could spare me, I dare say I might succeed, but without some sort of sanction I do not think the General here will let me move. I have never seen any active service, and, as I positively leave India next year, it is not probable I ever shall see service if the present opportunity passes by.

The Movable Column under Nicholson, according to letters received here, had not left Umritsur on the 25th; nor up to the present moment has anything authentic been heard of the movements of European troops from Calcutta beyond the fact that three regiments left Allahabad on the 30th June, and were expected to be at Agra about the 23rd of this month : they surely must be near at hand, though reports say they have dwindled to one brigade and a half from leaving reinforcements at different places—Lucknow and Agra, it is presumed. Here all is quiet, and were it not for the stoppage of the dâks and the impossibility of communicating with any place down country, we should hardly be aware that such important and critical operations were going on round us.

We are very anxious for the fate of Wheeler and those with him at Cawnpore. Several Natives, describing themselves as eye-witnesses of the scene, declare he was obliged to capitulate, leaving the women and children prisoners, and that on his way to the boats, which he had bound the Bithoor Raja to furnish, he was treacherously fired upon and almost every man destroyed —a very few who managed to reach the boats being the exception. The man, a Mussulman, whom I myself examined was most positive about it, declaring most solemnly that he had seen the whole business, and that it occurred on the 28th or 29th of June; but Natives are such liars, and there may have been an object in fabricating misfortunes for us, that we do not give implicit credence to their tales, though confirmed in some manner from other sources. This man said that none of the ladies or children had been killed since they surrendered, but that they were kept in prison.

Get me over to Delhi if you can; and believe me, very sincerely yours, FRED. HARRIOTT.

Colonel KEITH YOUNG *to his wife.*

CAMP, DELHI CANTONMENTS, *Friday,* 31*st July.*

The enemy have been trying their long-talked-of attack to-day, but have done nothing. They were to attack us, it was said, on all sides, but on the front and right they have not ventured within many hundred yards of our batteries, and I have heard of no casualties on either side—certainly none on ours; and their attack in the rear—if really intended, which I much doubt—has been altogether frustrated by the heavy rain rendering the ground they would have to go over impassable for guns. A force of the enemy had moved out towards the rear, but it seems more probable that their intention was to try and intercept our convoy coming in with the Kemaon battalion. But whatever their object, the rain has frustrated it; but it has unfortunately also prevented our attacking them as was intended after they had crossed the canal, should they have succeeded in doing so. Hodson, who has been out watching their proceedings, returned a little while ago, drenched to the skin, and he said the whole country was impassable except along the high road, and this the mutineers would have a circuit of many miles to get to; and our troops who are out there are ready to receive them with guns and Cavalry and Infantry on their arrival. Some of the poor men have had a hard day's work of it, but an extra dram, which is always given them on such a day as this, goes a long way to reconcile them to its discomforts.

Still without any letter from the force advancing upwards; but Native accounts from the city again to-day corroborate all we have heard of the Nana having been well thrashed twice, and what they say is that 'the *raj* of the English is re-established from Cawnpore to Calcutta.' Unhappily the Natives continue to tell fearful stories of the fate of Sir Hugh Wheeler and his little band, and they now talk of all the women and children who were left behind at Cawnpore having been cruelly murdered. I cannot myself believe in anything so very atrocious—things must be exaggerated; but we shall very soon know the worst now. What dreadful vengeance our men will take should the Cawnpore story be true: they will hardly leave a person alive in Delhi!

Pyloo Das and Company had better tell their families to remove to Meerut or elsewhere; tell him and his friend—Luchman Das, isn't it ?—that I received their letter.

Don't mention what I am going to tell you now—the Jhujhur Nawab has written expressing his wish to come in and make his *salaam*. I saw the letter this morning. He is a man with a large territory not far from here, who has been hitherto assisting the King; and I suppose the news from below has induced him at last to see that ours is the stronger side.

I forgot to answer your question as to who the 'Nana' is. He is a relation, but what exactly I do not know, of the late ex-Peishwa, who lived at a place called Bithoor, about fifteen miles above Cawnpore, on the bank of the Ganges. Ask Mr Philipe: I dare say he will give you the scoundrel's correct pedigree.

It is so dreadfully dark in the tent I can scarcely see to write; but fortunately it does not leak—at least only a very little, and that is on Mactier's side! Do you remember what a pond we had in our large tent when we were returning from Peshawar? It is first-rate ground where we are encamped now, and with a nice slope to the canal, so that we are dry again immediately after the heaviest rain.

Harriott will not be allowed to come over here—at least Chamberlain will hold out no encouragement to General Penny to give him leave. He says, and very truly, that these are times when every man ought to remain at his post, and it would not be fair to others to allow Harriott to leave Meerut at this juncture. He will be much annoyed, I fear.

George Hall was here this morning, looking very well. I do not think that he disapproves of the disarming of the 4th Irregulars. The Brigadier (Wilson) is pretty well again.

(*Diary*) 31*st July*.—Alarm early this morning, and attack going to be made, it is said, all round. A force of some thousands, with guns, making for the rear, either to attack or to pounce on a large convoy coming in; whatever their intention, frustrated by very heavy rain coming on.

Colonel H. B. HENDERSON *to Colonel* KEITH YOUNG.

LONDON, 9*th July*.

Wherever we go this Mutiny, the dreadful occurrences at Meerut and Delhi, are the all-engrossing topics; and many fear that we are to hear of further disasters and worse intelligence by the mail yet to come. Never was India so much thought of in England—so much talked of as at this moment; and I believe if half our Queen's forces were required, or more than half, all here would long to see them sent out to put down this disaffection and avenge this outbreak.

I try to persuade myself and those around me that the Commander-in-Chief, before leaving Simla, would have taken ample precautions for the safety of those left behind. But on whom are we to rely at this juncture, with so few European troops available? How we watch daily for fresh tidings!—and unless an intermediate steamer shall have left Ceylon for Suez, it may be days yet ere we learn more.

There is no fear for our Empire in India. If every place in it were in the possession of rebels, in two years we should reconquer the whole with the means at our disposal; but it is the insecurity of those dear to us out there in the meantime that makes so many hearts anxious and apprehensive. Eventually we may, and must, establish greater security and more assured dominion; but it is the present danger to those we love that causes so much pain and suspense.

At the India House they are *now* taking information and advice from old Indians. A Board is to be appointed to take evidence and receive suggestions from retired officers and others—such a thing never heard of before at Leadenhall Street!

You will see our friend Tucker's letters to the *Times;* but I much regret to hear that Tucker himself in many quarters is held forth as one of the main causes of the continual lowering of Commanding officers with regiments, and of making them cheap and impotent in the eyes of the men. I heard an influential Director of the High Court assert this in strong language. Tucker will be able to fight his own battles; but I am sorry to hear this now quite general rumour. The Sepoys are much altered evidently from my time in 1815-19, when I was Adjutant of the old 9th (8th at present). But our corps was a very *Native* one; not a thing occurred in our lines that we did not learn, and the Native officers and men were really all known to us.

LONDON, SUSSEX GARDENS, HYDE PARK, 26*th July.*

MY DEAR KEITH,—We are in *intense,* and I need not say most painful, expectation of the arrival of the telegraph intelligence *viâ* Trieste, of the June mail—not we only, but England, I may say, waiting to hear what will be the result at Delhi, with its wretched, mutinous garrison. There are such conflicting and varying reports in letters from India by the last mail, such accounts of your

Army's want of carriage (even of ammunition for the men), of inability to reach or assault Delhi, that it is feared that not only has that city failed to have been carried, but it is dreaded that the insurrection will be announced to have spread on all sides—Native states and outbreaks in our own provinces all adding to the anarchy and turmoil.

Yesterday the mail was due: how we pray that it may tell us that Delhi has fallen, and that its mad contents have risen among themselves and the rebellion so far suppressed and self-crushed in its main stronghold! But all this is mere agony of conjecture, and a day or two more of its intensity will settle one way or other what we are so painfully waiting to hear. Meantime troops are pouring into screw-steamers and hired transports from every available port to the rescue of India, and, come what may, England is determined, under God's blessing, to save or conquer its Empire in the East. You will probably have from twenty to twenty-five thousand men from here at hand in three months after this reaches you, and some, it is hoped, sooner.

British bayonets will be pushing up in all haste to the rescue. Men of all arms, for the first time, will embark for India—Engineers, Her Majesty's Artillery, Sappers, transport-train, Dragoons, and Infantry; in fact, enough with your other resources to take all the principal places in Upper India, if in the hands of rebels and enemies from without. But meantime, what fearful sacrifice of life, health, and means to those who have to carry out all this work of retribution! So many also, here and elsewhere, will take advantage of our troubles. Even now we cannot send out our war-steamers with the troops—we cannot spare them, or, rather, man them with our small body of naval seamen; while France and Russia are working wonders, to train and have in readiness three or four times our number of men-of-war sailors—and France alone can now, from her system of making all her maritime able-bodied men serve two years each in her Navy, command upwards of one hundred and twenty thousand seamen used to guns and naval tactics, while we have about forty thousand only that we can depend on. True, we have thousands of fishermen and coastmen we can press in on emergency—but useless for three months. Meantime, with Russia at hand, and France—with *one* man, Napoleon, between us and its probable outbreak against us—

you can understand why war-steamers were not sent out by our Government with the troops for India.

Your two last letters are a great comfort to us, and from my heart I thank you for writing them, in all your trouble and confusion. They both came together: one dated 17th May, from Simla, and the other 27th May, from Kurnaul—which you had reached after so hot an express ride in a mail-cart. We pray you may not feel bad effects from the exposure; and deeply, most deeply, do we pray and hope you may be preserved by a merciful God with your dear ones in all the dangers now rife around you all.

Tell Charles Chester, with my love, that I wrote to Lady Eardly Wilmot and told her of his message through you, and have received a thankful reply. I was very glad to hear that he was so active, and that he was your best leader in camp; I always thought he would prove this, and only hope his health will stand by him.

We are longing to have F. and the *Babas* home, and away from such scenes. A letter to a friend of ours, from one of the Simla party, states that the families there were contriving plans to get to Kurrachee and thus home by steamer. Oh, how I hope that some such arrangement may be feasible, and that F. and your children are now on their way to us! India for the next two or three years, whatever the present result, is no place for European ladies with children, and in many places for ladies at all. May God in His goodness preserve and bless you all, and keep you all safe and well.

CHAPTER VIII.

SIEGE OF DELHI—*continued*.

Colonel KEITH YOUNG *to his wife*.

CAMP, DELHI CANTONMENTS, *Saturday, 1st August*.

We have had very heavy rain, and for about four hours or more this morning it came down in torrents, quite inundating the country. It has now left off, and the air is delightfully cool—so much so that I am wearing one of the nice flannel shirts you sent me, and find it very comfortable: almost every one in camp wears these flannel shirts—I mean the officers, and you see them of all hues and patterns.

There is nothing much to tell you since yesterday. To-day is the grand Festival of the Eed, and the gentlemen in the city commenced early in the morning, and have been amusing themselves all day, firing off their guns and making a great noise. I was told just now that they had also made an attempt to attack us on the left; but it must have been a very slight one, as no one in our camp heard of it till it was over. The whole of the convoy, with the Kemaon battalion, came in this morning; they must have had a sadly wet march for the last two days.

Still no *cossid* or letter direct from the force coming up; but there was a very good account received to-day from Meerut, from Toony Simpson, about this fight near Futtehpore and the advance of our troops, under Havelock, I fancy, as I see he was at Allahabad on the 1st. It would seem now that there was only one fight after all, according to Simpson's informant, a Native, who says he was present when the rebels ran into Cawnpore chased by our troops, who, after settling matters at Cawnpore and at Lucknow, had gone on to Futtyghur—which by some change of fortune, after having been lost once, had come into our possession again in some unexplained way. From Futtyghur, it was said, the troops were coming straight here; but really nothing seems known for certain about this. Perhaps they may go *viâ* Agra, and this is not unlikely; but we must soon know.

The massacres at Cawnpore and Futtyghur are still not cleared up; but they are believed to a certain extent. Simpson says that at Allyghur all is quiet, and that the revenue is being collected for us in the districts at the rate of from fifteen to twenty thousand rupees a day; this speaks more in our favour than almost anything else. It is mentioned that some of the Cawnpore rebels who have arrived in Delhi gave out that the army of Europeans opposed to them was twenty thousand strong; and they describe the regiment that wears petticoats (78th Highlanders) as perfect fiends to fight; while there is another regiment, they say, which has come from Lunka (Ceylon), who are cannibals! This is the 37th. Possibly enough this nonsense is believed by half the people in the city.

You would have noticed that one of the late papers in mentioning Oude said that all at Salone were safe, having gone to Allahabad. George Hall tells me that this is the station where his wife's sister was, so I trust to find that no harm has befallen her. Mrs Goldney, too, has escaped; but no tidings of her husband.

Mactier and I are just going to have our frugal *tiffin*—a bit of toast and a glass of wine and water. We sometimes, but very seldom, treat ourselves to a sandwich; but I never go to the mess now to have a regular *tiffin*, as some do. We have at last left the Artillery mess and joined the Staff one. I was sorry to leave the Artillery, but it is a long way to go these dark, rainy nights; and the Staff mess is not a stone's-throw off. It seems a very fair one, but rather too many members—some twenty and more sit down to dinner.

Tiffin over, and nearly half-past three, so I must think of finishing this, as there is no chance of the dâk coming in. Mactier sends his kindest regards, and says, 'It's a weary, weary world,' and wishes to know what your opinion is on this point!

(*Diary*) 1*st August.*—The large convoy and Kemaon battalion came in this morning, and a precious row they made, commencing at about three. They had a terrible drenching, poor fellows;

it rained bitterly till nearly twelve o'clock, and the camp must be quite flooded in many parts. The enemy still at the canal with their guns, and threaten our rear if they can cross. At five, word brought that their bridge is broken and they have retired. Grand attack on Hindoo Rao's in force after Eed.

CAMP, DELHI CANTONMENTS, *Sunday, 2nd August.*

Our hopes of a grand row in the city yesterday at the Eed Festival have not, apparently, been fulfilled—at least the only newsletter received from the city alludes to nothing of the kind. The King had issued strict orders against killing cows, or even goats, in the city, and this, if acted upon, must have satisfied the Hindoos; and instead of fighting amongst themselves they all joined together to make a vigorous attack to destroy us and utterly sweep us from the face of the earth, when it was arranged that the King should perform his evening prayers in our camp!

I told you that a large party of them had tried to get to our rear; but their attempt at a bridge over the canal entirely failing, they went back and joined in the attack with the people from the city, from which the whole force was said to have come out. Our right front, in the direction of Hindoo Rao's, was their grand point of attack, and at about six o'clock in the evening all Delhi nearly must have been out, judging by the noise they made. We all went soon after five o'clock, when the enemy were said to be in great force, to the Mound battery, and there we stayed with the Brigadier-General till between eight and nine, when, things getting a little quieter, and it being reported that the enemy could make no impression on our posts, we were not sorry to get back to dinner. Such a yelling and bugling as the scoundrels made! But though they had sworn to take our batteries, they never came nearer than four or five hundred yards, and then a volley or two of grape sent them back again; they kept at it, however, more or less the whole night long, and even at twelve o'clock to-day the firing had not wholly ceased. We do not know what their loss has been, but it is reported to be great. Our men for once, fortunately, remained in their entrenchments, and we have lost very few—only ten killed and wounded Major Reid reported this morning; but amongst the killed, unfortunately, is Captain Travers of Coke's regiment, who was shot through the forehead.

I send you rather an amusing account of the fight, given by a man who came in from the city this morning. The men who fought us are said to be principally the Neemuch mutineers, this being their first meeting with us. I hope it is true that they are badly off for caps, for they must have fired off an immense number of them in this attack. I hope the scoundrels will profit by this lesson and leave us alone now until our reinforcements arrive, and then we shall be able to smash them effectually.

No intelligence direct from Havelock yet, but a letter from Agra, of the 27th, says that he had gone against Bithoor, the Nana's place, and utterly destroyed it. I have just been writing a letter to Havelock giving him the news here, and telling him how anxious we are to hear of his doings. To-day or to-morrow the messengers that were first sent to him are expected to return here.

This morning we had Divine Service at 6 A.M., but there were very few present, only eight or ten of us. The firing was going on at the time, and most of the troops were either out or in readiness to go if required; so at my recommendation Mr Rotton dispensed with a sermon. There was to have been the Sacrament also, but this was postponed on account of the small attendance.

All the wounded are getting on well—Chamberlain, Daly, Money, and Seaton. Arthur Becher is progressing fast towards recovery.

We hear that the 26th Native Infantry have bolted from Lahore, but without arms.

*Translation of a Letter from the City, dated night of the 2nd instant.**

The King reproached the troops for not carrying the Ridge. They replied that neither Artillery nor Cavalry could mount the Ridge, and that they were consequently helpless and could not take it. The mutineers allow that they lost two thousand men killed and one thousand wounded in the last fight; and they are much discomfited. Both Cavalry and Infantry are asking for leave

* This was one of many letters received during the siege, from Natives inside the city and who were in our pay, coloured in a high degree to please us.— H. W. NORMAN.

to return to their homes on the plea that the English are threatening danger to their families; they say that people have come to warn them of this, and that they must go home. About six hundred Sowars have left, and in a day or two, two thousand more Horse and Foot will leave. Your fortune is such that the Nimukharams will disperse of themselves. Only one hundred and fifty are left of the Jhansi Rissalah. The report is that ten thousand English troops have arrived at Haupper and will be here in five days, and this has distressed the King.

The regiments in the city do not muster more than four hundred each. A large number are skulking, and trying to save their money. Many are wounded, and all disheartened. Their faces are turned yellow, and they have no longer any hope of success. To-day the King caused a proclamation to be made that fourteen thousand fanatics and eight regiments are on their way from Peshawar and will arrive in two days, and it enjoins all who wish to take part in a holy war to join this body.

The supply of powder is failing rapidly, and what is now manufactured cannot be dried, and materials are now not forthcoming; caps are also deficient. The Sowars who arrived from Cawnpore state that the Bithoor Nana fled to Lucknow, and returned with reinforcements and fought another action.

There are reports of disasters at Furruckabad which distress me. The mutineers seem disposed to go to Lucknow and Nepaul.

H. H. GREATHED.

Colonel KEITH YOUNG *to his wife*.

CAMP, DELHI CANTONMENTS, *Monday*, 3rd *August*.

We have been very quiet since the enemy retired yesterday, and they have hardly fired a gun, from which we augur that they are considerably down-hearted—and they can't well be otherwise; their loss is variously stated in the city at from five hundred to three thousand. The Sepoys themselves, I understand, fix it at the latter number, but probably a thousand or twelve hundred will be about the mark; and our loss now turns out to be four killed and twenty wounded, the greater part in Coke's corps of Sikhs. Altogether we have good reason to be satisfied; and I trust that if any future attack is made our men will see the advantage of remaining in cover instead of rushing out and following the wretched mutineers, and then getting themselves mowed down by grape from the walls of the city. Daly, who came over and paid us a long visit just now, says he thinks it is the very best fight for us there has been yet, as serving to show the enemy how utterly powerless they are to injure us if we only remain behind our defences, and what a terrible loss we can inflict upon them.

Hodson was mentioning this morning at breakfast that Lord William Hay was not at all pleased at having been written to from Lahore about not disarming the bazaar people; but never mind, so long as he effectually disarms the scoundrels.

News in at last direct from Havelock, who writes by one of the *cossids* who took a letter to him from here on the 16th of last month. His letter * is dated Nawaubgunge, 25th July. He had beaten the Nana on three several occasions, taking all his guns each time, and was then on his way to relieve Lucknow, where Sir Henry Lawrence was all safe.†

Sir Hugh Wheeler was, as we have heard, treacherously murdered with all his little band; but nothing was said about the rumoured murder of the ladies, women, and children of the 32nd, so, as Havelock has not alluded to it, it may not be true. He has sent on a copy of the letter from here to the Governor-General, and will be unable to move in this direction till he gets a reply—and perhaps not then; but he says that large reinforcements will soon be on their way up the country—those for China and those direct from England—and that Sir Patrick Grant will soon be on his way, too. This is excellent news, and will have the best effect in our camp and everywhere else. I think I have given you pretty well the whole contents of the letter; he says nothing in it about Bithoor.

I had heard before from some one that George Hall had applied for a Sikh corps. He is a good officer, and well deserves one; and I have said a good word in his favour to Chamberlain without being asked. George Hall is to do duty with Hodson's new corps; he is coming to dine with me at the Staff mess to-morrow night.

* See page 175.

† I do not think that any letter from Sir Henry Havelock at this time said that Sir Henry Lawrence was safe. We were surprised that Havelock did not refer at all to Sir Henry Lawrence.—H. W. NORMAN.

(*Diary*) *3rd August.*—The result of the fighting on Saturday night and Sunday morning seems to have been very satisfactory: from five hundred to three thousand said to have been lost by the enemy—killed, wounded, and missing; and ours twenty-five altogether. It turns out to have been forty-six.* Very quiet all day, and nice cool weather; rode in the evening towards 75th lines.

Copy of a Letter received at Meerut.

CAWNPORE, 26*th July.*

MY DEAR SIR,—General Havelock has crossed the river to relieve Lucknow, which will be effected four days hence. He has a strong force with him, and he has already thrashed the Nana and completely dispersed his force.

We shall probably march to Delhi with four or five thousand Europeans and a heavy Artillery—in numbers, not in weight. The China force is in Calcutta, five thousand men; more troops expected immediately. We shall soon be with you.—Yours truly,

TYTLER (*Lieutenant-Colonel*),
Acting Quartermaster-General, Movable Column.

CAPTAIN EARLE,
Assistant Quartermaster-General, Meerut.

General HAVELOCK *to Major-General* REED, C.B.

NAWAUBGUNGE, 25*th July.*

MY DEAR GENERAL,—Yesterday I received Captain Norman's letter of the 15th instant from Delhi, addressed to Sir Hugh Wheeler. That gallant officer and the whole of his force were destroyed, on the 27th June, by a base act of treachery. Sir H. Somerset is Commander-in-Chief in India, and Sir Patrick Grant in Bengal. Under the orders of the Supreme Government, I have been sent to retrieve affairs here. I have specific instructions, from which I cannot depart. I have sent a duplicate of your letter to Sir Patrick Grant. In truth, though most anxious to march on Delhi, I have peremptory orders to relieve Lucknow. I have, thank God, been very successful; I defeated the enemy at Futtehpore on the 12th, at Oung and Pandoo Nuddee on the

---

* One officer and nine men were killed, and thirty-six men wounded.—H. W. NORMAN.

15th, and at this place, which I recaptured, on the 16th. On each occasion I took all the enemy's guns.

Immense reinforcements are coming up from England and China. Sir Patrick Grant will soon be in the field himself. Lucknow holds out. Agra is free for the present. I am sorry to hear you are not well. I beg you will let me hear from you continually.—Believe me, yours very sincerely,

H. HAVELOCK (*Brigadier-General*).

MAJOR-GENERAL REED, C.B.,
    Commanding before Delhi.

Colonel KEITH YOUNG *to his wife.*

CAMP, DELHI CANTONMENTS, *Tuesday, 4th August.*

What strange stories you appear to hear at Simla about the movements of troops up here! Of course there is no truth whatever in the report of two European regiments being at Muttra, and Brigadier Wilson could never have written so to his wife. The only European regiments that we have positively heard of are those with Havelock, and I fear he had not, when he wrote on the 25th, more than two strong regiments with him, say sixteen hundred men, besides the Sikhs and Artillery; but there must be lots on their way up country, and probably some two or three regiments more have reached him ere this.

The *cossid*—a Sikh in Daly's Corps of Guides, and a fine intelligent fellow—says that there was a steamer also at Cawnpore, with two guns in it. So perhaps they may send some of the new corps up the whole way to Cawnpore, or even farther, in steamers.

After my letter was sent off yesterday, another *cossid* came in from Agra bringing a copy of a previous letter from Havelock, of the 16th, in which he speaks of his three victories, capturing twenty-three guns, and then mentions the sad news of the death of Sir Henry Lawrence, who, he says, died on the 4th July from the effects of a wound received by him on the 2nd. It is most strange Havelock's not mentioning this in his subsequent letter of the 25th, which is the first that has been received from him in this camp, and his only allusion in it to Lucknow was that all was well there. We are all strongly inclined to believe that his first announcement was premature, and we are the more inclined to think so

as the *cossid*, who stayed three days in Havelock's camp, declares that he heard nothing of Sir Henry's death—which he should certainly have done had it been the case, as many of the Sikhs knew him and would have been sure to mention it. I trust that Sir Henry may be safe; his death would indeed be a serious loss in every way.

The scoundrels in the city are quiet again to-day, and I have heard no news of any great importance. The report of many of the mutineers leaving Delhi is confirmed; they have heard how matters are going against them down below, and are beginning now to feel anxious about their families, who I dare say they fancy will meet the same fate from our hands that ours would receive from them if our places were changed. I fear it is all too true about the massacres of the women and children at Cawnpore and Futtyghur; it is very horrible to think of.

You would be glad to hear (for I suppose accounts have reached you by this time) of the almost entire destruction of the runaway 26th Native Infantry. Sir John Lawrence telegraphed down here to say that five hundred of them had been cut up by some Sikhs sent in pursuit. I don't know which is greatest—the folly or the villainy of these mutineering Sepoys.

George Hall was in our camp this morning, looking very well. There is no intention whatever, depend upon it, to give the 4th Irregulars back their arms.

Young Anson has just paid us a visit. He arrived this morning. He tells us that Congreve is very irate at being superseded by little Lugard. His (Congreve's) great occupation down here was killing flies! He used to catch them in a large cup, and then pour boiling water on them, and you may suppose he was never at a loss for sport here. Ask him if he ever found the flies troublesome in camp, and he will no doubt tell you how he hunted them down!

Past 3 P.M. Box just arrived with port wine, &c. Salaam to Gowroo and the servants.

(*Diary*) *4th August.*—Very quiet again to-day—the enemy said to be deserting in great numbers. Cool, pleasant weather. Letter in yesterday from Havelock at last 25th July, and another of previous date from Agra, giving the sad news of Sir Henry

Lawrence's death on the 4th July of a wound received on the 2nd; but the *cossid* says it is not the case, and we truly hope so.

CAMP, DELHI CANTONMENTS, *Wednesday, 5th August.*

Your letter of the 2nd only reached me this morning. I was *very* glad indeed to get it, as there were rumours in camp—though you had not alluded to them—that there might probably be a row at Simla on the evening of the Eed Saturday, and I now hear that the Volunteers were collected at the Library and one or two other places all ready in case of anything going wrong. I hope and think that this is the last time there is likely to be anything in the shape of an alarm at Simla.

Enclosed I send you a copy of a letter* from Cawnpore that reached me this morning from Meerut: the contents are very satisfactory, and the letter gives us authentic intelligence regarding the European troops coming up, which we have in vain been looking to receive from elsewhere. One of the copies of the letter received in camp says, 'We leave Cawnpore *to-morrow;*' but this is not in the official copy of the letter sent to the Brigadier-General here, and could not, in fact, be the case, as the force would of course wait for the return of Havelock from Lucknow, and he could not well be back at Cawnpore until the 2nd or 3rd. But we may be sure that they will lose no time in coming here, and I dare say will join us nearly as soon as Nicholson's Column: but if this arrives much before Havelock's force, it is very likely we shall not wait for the latter; and indeed it is not improbable, from the accounts that reach us of the state of affairs in the city, that there will be very few of the mutineering Sepoys left there before long—they are said to be leaving in great numbers. I enclose you two sketches of their General, Buktawa Khan. He is the Soubahdar of the Bareilly battery, and was appointed Commander-in-Chief by the King. His return after the fight is very good; and the sketch of the Ridge on the other one gives you really a very good bird's-eye view of it—on the left is the Flagstaff, and on the extreme right is Hindoo Rao's, with a mosque and another building between.

The scoundrels in the city are very quiet to-day, and we have been trying to destroy their bridge of boats by fire-rafts. Two have been sent down, but the Engineers have not been successful:

* See page 175.

A.L. Dickinson Mass. Commder. chief of the Royal army took a discreet view of his invincible Legions advancing to attack the Kafir position — His Charger lays hors de and himself the battle afar off — Come well supposedly be retreating to the byer

FACSIMILES OF TWO SKETCHES BY CAPTAIN MAISEY. SEE PAGE 178.

one drifted on an island, and then exploded, and the other the enemy got hold of and towed on shore. I should have thought the night would have answered better for our attempts. These will at least, however, have the effect of frightening the people, and make them think we are going to attack the city at once.

More boxes have arrived—four, I think they say, for me; but I have not yet seen them. I have just seen the boxes. There are only two for me, containing the things sent down by Goad. What made him send ladies' dresses and things! They are *no* use here. We have just been having a glass of the curaçoa at Becher's tent; he much approves of it!

(*Diary*) 5*th August.*—Nothing much stirring all day, and glad to be able to finish my report as to Brigadier Johnston's explanation. There is no doubt of his having blundered. Two fire-rafts tried on the large bridge to-day, but both failures—the first stuck against an island and exploded, and the second ran on shore and was taken possession of by the mutineers. Another raft of some kind was to have been started off at five in the evening, and I went with Mactier to see it; but it didn't come off, so had a ride with George Hall.

Lord WILLIAM HAY *to* Mrs KEITH YOUNG.

SIMLA, 5*th August* (5 A.M.).

MY DEAR MRS YOUNG,—I have just received the following telegraphic news from camp by express, dated 4th: 'A reply has been received by *cossid* at Delhi to a letter sent to General Havelock; he was on the left bank of the Ganges at Cawnpore on the 25th July, and going to relieve Lucknow. He had on three different occasions—on the 12th, 13th (15th?), and 16th—totally defeated the enemy, and on each occasion captured all their guns.'—Yours sincerely, WILLIAM HAY.

Colonel KEITH YOUNG *to his wife.*

CAMP, DELHI CANTONMENTS, *Thursday,* 6*th August.*

We all got our letters at the mess table just after finishing dinner, and such a reading as there was and telling of news to each other. All the Simla ladies appear to behave very well in writing to their husbands! Shute and Arthur Becher both had letters, and, I dare say, so had Hodson; but he was dining out. Mrs Becher seems always to write her letters on very thin paper, and crosses them—inexcusable act at any time, particularly now in these days of no postage. You will say I am severe; but I do hate to get letters out of which you can only make two or three words, and this with difficulty.

The enemy have been trying another attack this morning, but a very feeble one; and they have been keeping at a most respectable distance, scarcely venturing within a thousand yards of our batteries. A small party of about three hundred Cavalry made a show of charging up to camp by the Flagstaff road, but when they came within range of our guns, a shot or two soon sent them to the right-about—the scoundrels! I don't know if any of them were hit, but it is thought that they must have been.

Yesterday the Engineers—did I tell you?—made two unsuccessful attempts to destroy the bridge over the Jumna with fire-rafts; they neither of them reached their destination, one having got foul of some trees, and the other ran aground and fell to the lot of the mutineers, but couldn't have been of much value to them. A third raft of a different description was to have been sent off at five in the evening, and Mactier and I and many others went to see the fun; but it didn't come off, the attempt being postponed to another day, so I took a ride instead with George Hall, whom I met amongst the spectators. He said nothing to me about the Sikh corps, but he mentioned that he should have liked much to get the command of the Cavalry of the Guides. I dare say he would have got it had he applied when it fell vacant; he is an excellent officer, and will be sure to get some good appointment.

I have just seen Hamilton, the Pension Paymaster; he leaves here to-morrow morning for Umballa with the intention of remaining there till he gets better, and then going to Mussoorie. Major Olpherts goes with him on sick leave; he, I believe, will go on direct to Simla.

I am sending to-day by dâk a package of *pawn* leaves for Colonel ———; he wrote to me for them. How nice it must be to have a wife that chews *pawn!*

You never saw such an exhibition as there is to the rear of our tent—every kind of female garment hung up to dry! What could have induced Major Goad to send such things down here? There are no women refugees in camp, and none, so far as we know, in the city or adjacent villages. It is very kind of the people at Simla to send them; but after everything is dried—for they are soaking wet at present, and many spoilt—the only thing to do will be to pack them in boxes and send them to Umballa: they may be useful to the soldiers' wives at Kussowlie. The coats, shirts, boots, &c. will, of course, be useful here.

A brother of Mrs Wyld's left here for Simla about ten days ago. Have you seen him—Kennedy of the Guide Corps? He was wounded soon after he came down here.

We have heard nothing more yet regarding the force from Cawnpore, and not a word to clear up the doubt regarding Sir Henry Lawrence's fate. The Natives who came up all declare he was not dead on the 25th of July, though they allow that they heard of his having been wounded in the shoulder. We still are in great hopes that Havelock, when writing, had merely gone on some Native report of his death; and his not alluding to it afterwards in his letter here looks very much like his having subsequently found out his mistake.

3.30 P.M., and all quiet.

(*Diary*) 6*th August.*—About 8 A.M. alarm sounded; the enemy said to be coming out in great force; early breakfast in consequence. Not much has been done by them up to the present time, now 1 P.M., and the firing has nearly ceased. A party of three hundred Cavalry are said to have made a show of charging up the road by Metcalfe's, but they fled on receiving a shell or two amongst them.

CAMP, DELHI CANTONMENTS, *Friday, 7th August.*

The dâk came in yesterday afternoon with your letter of the 4th, in time to read it by daylight. To-day's dâk will, I hope, reach me in equally good time; but I am afraid not, as Brigadier-General Nicholson came in this morning in the mail-cart with two horses, and we are rather afraid there will be no good horses on the road for the regular mail when it does come! He is an active man, and with a good head, too. He hadn't been here more than two or three hours before he got on horseback and galloped away with Brigadier Wilson * to inspect our works—rather different from our former Commander, General Reed, who had hardly strength to get out of his carriage on arrival here, and could scarcely move from his bed for several days after.

Nicholson's Column was to be at Kurnaul this morning, and may be expected here about the 12th; they have come on at a good pace. I fancy when this force arrives we shall be thought strong enough to set to work at the city in good earnest, without waiting for Havelock's force; but I believe nothing is positively settled yet on this point. Havelock cannot well be here until the 23rd instant at earliest; we have heard nothing from him since his last that I told you of, of the 25th July, but Native reports from the city this morning say that he had succeeded in dispersing the rebel troops at Lucknow, which were commanded by one Nana Sing. So, suppose after this he stayed two or three days at Lucknow to settle matters, he might be back at Cawnpore on the 4th or 5th August and march up here with all the troops that could be spared—this would probably be some three or four regiments of Europeans and a Sikh corps—leaving the rest of his force for Lucknow and Cawnpore. However, there is really no use in speculating on the matter, as we shall probably hear in three or four days from himself direct as to what his intentions are.

I forgot to tell you that the Native who brought up that letter from Tytler (the red-haired man—do you remember him at Simla?) said that there were several steamers at Cawnpore, in which I suppose the additional regiments had come up from Calcutta.

We have heard nothing more about Sir Henry Lawrence except from the Natives, and all appear to agree in their story that he had only been wounded and was not dead on the 25th of last month. We therefore still think there is a great probability of Havelock having been misinformed in the matter, and I pray, as many will do, that it may be so.

* This is a mistake. I took him for the first time round all our right works on the afternoon of this day, and round our left posts early on the following morning.—H. W. NORMAN.

You tell me that I never mention to you half of what is going on like others do. It is great nonsense this writing about 'the enemy being in the rear,' 'an attack just about to take place,' and all that sort of thing; and if I were to tell you half of the reports in camp I must entirely omit to tell you what actually does occur. Yesterday there was a strong report of six thousand men and twelve guns having gone to get round our rear, and it was fully believed for some hours; the number gradually diminished, and they have now dwindled down to one thousand, their object not being to get to our rear, but to go to some Nawab's in the neighbourhood. Again last night the alarm was sounded, and the enemy said to be in great force; this was about midnight, but it ended in all going to bed quietly, the mutineers apparently being as sleepily inclined as ourselves. Scarcely a day passes without some absurd rumours and alarms.

Three officers were wounded in the batteries yesterday: Lieutenant Browne, 33rd Native Infantry, mortally—since dead; Lieutenant Temple, 49th Native Infantry, slightly; and Captain Kennion, Artillery, rather severely. Lieutenant Browne, poor fellow, they say brought his death entirely on himself; he would expose himself to the fire of the enemy by standing on the parapet, though continually requested to come down.

Half-past three, and no dâk in. Lots of firing from the batteries, but otherwise all quiet. The earthquake was felt slightly here.

(*Diary*) *7th August.*—Intelligence this morning of the enemy having erected a battery during the night with heavy guns that is totally to smash Hindoo Rao's; but nothing came of it. A good deal of firing all day on both sides. Nicholson came in to-day ahead of his column.

CAMP, DELHI CANTONMENTS, *Saturday, 8th August.*

Nothing of any importance going on since I wrote to you yesterday. Lots of firing from the batteries on both sides; but to-day we appear to have most of the firing to ourselves. We have had only two or three casualties by stray shots; but Major Reid reports that lots of the enemy were killed—and probably enough, for they are generally in such large numbers that a shot falling in amongst them is sure to kill some of them. In the afternoon yesterday their powder manufactory in the city blew up with a grand explosion, but unfortunately there were only some forty *maunds* of powder. It is not known how it took place—possibly from one of our shells; but most likely some of the people employed in the work were smoking hookahs and accidentally ignited the powder. The newsletter says that about four hundred people of all kinds were blown up; but, what is better still, the Sepoys attribute the accident to one of the King's principal advisers, whom they believe to be treacherous, and they forthwith went and plundered his house. It is stated that a nice little quarrel may arise out of this.

Becher got a letter yesterday from Agra, of the 3rd. It contains little of interest beyond what we have already heard, and nothing of more recent date than we have had of Havelock's movements. How very glad we shall be to get a letter from Havelock himself; but I hope it will be a letter fuller in particulars than his last.

Yes, the two cases that Mrs Hodson says ——— was written to about were alluded to by Becher in his letter about Simla not having been properly disarmed. One was the case of the man who twirled his moustache at Mrs Greathed—Greathed himself told me also of this; the other was of the milkwoman who told Miss Philipe, when spoken to about water having been added to the milk, that it didn't signify: she would soon have her throat cut. Mr Philipe sent the woman to Lord William Hay, who fined her five rupees. These instances were mentioned by Becher as showing the bad feeling that existed at Simla towards us amongst the Natives.

I fear it is too true that the 50th have mutinied, after having kept faithful so long. A letter that Greathed got says: 'The 50th Native Infantry from Nagode had crossed the river at Kalpi, but it is not known whether they are going to Lucknow or Delhi.' Poor old Hampton and Mrs Hampton: we know nothing yet of their fate, or of any of the other officers and their wives. I hope the 'long' Sepoy was faithful.

That Nana was the man who used to drive up and down the Mall at Meerut, when we were there, with a European coachman.

The ladies at Nynee Tal have been ordered up to Almorah, only thirty miles off.

(*Diary*) 8*th August*.—Lots of firing last night—big guns principally, and a little musketry. To-day comparatively quiet, most of the firing being on our side. Very hot and steamy to-day. An explosion is said to have caused considerable commotion in the city, and the Sepoys have plundered the house of Hakeem Hassen Oollah, the Prime-Minister, whom they accuse of having caused the explosion; something, it is hoped, may come out of this.

CAMP, DELHI CANTONMENTS, *Sunday*, 9*th August*.

I got your letter of the 6th early this morning; but as I was just going to church—and you may imagine that I was not much too early, when you hear that 6 A.M. was the hour for service—I had only time to open the letter to see that all was well with you, postponing the reading of it till my return. This was not for a long while, as it was Sacrament Sunday, and I stayed to take the Sacrament, though I don't know that I was fit to do so; nor, perhaps, were many of us who were there. The roar of cannon which was continually going on during service, and the aspirations of all of us that each discharge from our guns would send some of the wretched mutineers to perdition, seemed hardly in unison with the peaceful and sacred duties in which we were engaged. But God could not allow such miscreants to go unpunished, and we are merely the instruments employed by the Almighty to carry out His Holy Will. Still, it is dreadful to think of the horrible scenes that are enacting, and will be enacted, before this business is terminated.

There is nothing going on again to-day but cannonading, and this, I suppose, we shall have every day now until Nicholson's column arrives; it was to be at Paniput to-day, so may soon be expected. We shall then be strong enough to occupy all the suburbs from which their guns now annoy us, if not to take the city; but the impression still is that the city will be ours before many days, and that the Sepoys are all ready to desert. The story of the great deficiency of caps is revived more strongly than ever; they are said to have very few indeed left now, and these they are keeping for the last.

I told you yesterday that the Sepoys in the city had seized a man of rank and plundered his house when the powder manufactory was blown up. It seems that the individual was the old King's Prime-

Minister, Hakeem Hassen Oollah, whom the Sepoys suspect of being in treacherous correspondence with us; and, between ourselves, I believe they are not far wrong. However, be this as it may, they have taken him prisoner, and will probably take his life and perhaps that of the King too, for they appear to little respect his orders now. Some twenty other houses near the Hakeem's were also plundered, and as it is said that most of the Sepoys got a small share, it will very likely only serve as a whet to their appetite for more, and perhaps will terminate in their plundering the city altogether and then taking themselves off.

We have no further news from Cawnpore, but we begin to fear now that the report of Sir Henry Lawrence's death must be true after all, from the positive way in which it is stated in the *Lahore Chronicle;* and his brother, Sir John, also writes to camp of it as if it were confirmed by intelligence from Calcutta.

Arthur Becher showed me a letter for Mrs Arthur from Mrs Gough, who was campaigning it with John at the Curragh of Kildare, living, apparently, in a very small hut at the Camp of Exercise. I shouldn't wonder to see him sent out here as a Major-General on the Staff; his Indian experience will be thought of great value at home now. You should ask Mrs Becher to show you the letter. Lila (Mrs Gough) says she has taken to archery again; she has seen none of her old Indian friends except Vyse, whose regiment was at Newbridge, a few miles only from them.

I had a letter from Jeypore to-day of the 4th, where all was well; it contained lots of news, but nothing of importance that we had not heard before. It was from Captain Eden, to whom I have been in the habit of writing for Arthur Becher.

You do not seem to be so well pleased at Simla with the news of Havelock's movements as we are here. We are quite satisfied; but think, with you, that he might have told us something more than he did about Cawnpore.

Captain EDEN *to Colonel* KEITH YOUNG.

JEYPORE, *4th August.*

MY DEAR COLONEL KEITH YOUNG,—I send my friend once more, but this time to bring me a letter dated from the Chandee

Chouk, or the Imperial Residence! You might send off Oodeyram's brother with such intelligence as you may be able to give me, and keep Oodeyram and the Sikh for the final assault!—or one of them, please. You may be glad to see the papers I send by the bearer. I am not quite happy here in Jeypore; there is a strong party, and oh, *mon Dieu!* what lies they tell! The Pathans, or most of them, are discontented, and dictating to their government already; but quiet enough as yet.

They have it in the city that we have been driven from our position on the hill and have gone back some sixteen miles. The Agra news I enclose. It is said here that the Hyderabad contingent at four stations have mutinied and are coming towards Berhampore.

We have not any particulars of the reported fight between Havelock's force and the ruffians of Bithoor. Intelligence of the Delhi massacre and of affairs up to 28th May reached London 27th June. The following is an extract from Secretary to Government at Bombay to John Lawrence: 'English mail arrived yesterday afternoon.' By some mischance this mail, the letters of which should have been answered by this present opportunity, had not been received; but a telegram seems to have reached the Ministry, for Lord Clarendon at 5.30 P.M., 27th June, telegraphs to the Consul at Marseilles: 'Please to send a message to the Governor-General that reinforcements will be sent to India immediately.'

Please tell Mr Greathed what I have written likely to interest him. I have written to him twice lately in French. Best regards to Becher, if you please; and to Chamberlain, if you find opportunity. I want to hear of the fall of Delhi to stuff down the throats of the villains here.—Yours very sincerely,

W. F. EDEN.

Colonel KEITH YOUNG *to his wife.*

CAMP, DELHI CANTONMENTS, *Monday,* 10*th August.*

Nothing of any consequence stirring in camp, and only the usual cannonading going on, and that is not very lively to-day. In the city matters are reported as progressing favourably towards a general split; and yesterday evening it was said that the King had shut himself up in the Palace with the Hakeem and was in a manner besieged by the troops in the city, those in the Palace taking his side. I think it may turn out to be true.

We are still without any further news from Havelock or Cawnpore, but any day or hour now may bring us tidings of the advance of troops in this direction. We expect Nicholson's Column in the day after to-morrow; he (Nicholson) was in our tent just now, and said they ought to be at Lussowlie to-day, and he was going there to meet them and bring them in. It will be a grand thing having his Column here, and we shall soon know after their arrival whether it is intended to go in at Delhi at once or wait until Havelock or Grant come up with the terrific Highlanders, &c. The natives have received most fearful accounts of the appearance and doings of the Highlanders, and the following is an extract from a letter written by a *baboo* below to a *baboo* in camp: 'I give you another piece of intelligence, that from *some place* to *some place* a regiment of women have arrived, and play old Harry with everybody, and have an awful savage appearance, and no chance of escape for any one seems left. I only tell you this as I am your greatest friend.' I saw the original letter this morning, and I dare say the Natives, many of them, believe what is written.

I was amused to hear of Gowroo's story of there being three regiments of Sepoys at Bussee. There seems no prospect whatever of any of the mutineers that have left Sealkote or Lahore finding their way across the Sutlej, and I should doubt very much, notwithstanding what Arthur Butter writes, whether the men of the regiments still at Lahore will venture on a deserting expedition on hearing, as they must have done by this time, of the fate of the 26th; but, whatever may be their attempts and schemes, we understand by letters to this place from the authorities at Lahore that all possible precautions have been taken to guard against any rising and to provide for every possible emergency.

I had a letter from Major Goad this morning telling me of the things he sent down. The ladies' habiliments shall be packed up and kept for the present. Some women refugees may turn up after Delhi is taken, though I much doubt it; and, if not, the boxes can be sent up to Simla again.

I am amused at Colonel Congreve saying that Colonel Becher and I ought to return to Simla. There is no doubt that Colonel

Congreve himself ought *not* to have gone there, and I dare say he would like to get others to follow his example. I may not be of much use here, but it would never do for me or any other officer to leave unless compelled by ill-health.

3.30 P.M., and all quiet.

(*Diary*) 10*th August.*—Quiet to-day except cannonading, and principally down at the Metcalfe pickets. Rather hot and steamy. In the tent all day writing, and in the evening take a short ride across the bridge through the Garden. The story of the row with the Sepoys and the Prime-Minister gains ground.

Colonel KEITH YOUNG *to Colonel* H. B. HENDERSON.

CAMP BEFORE DELHI, 10*th August.*

My last letter will have led you to believe that we should be in Delhi long ere this; but time wears on, and we still occupy our old position, the same that we took up more than two months ago. But matters are certainly looking up now, and perhaps when Nicholson's Column joins we may be thought strong enough to move on to the attack, but if not, we must wait for Havelock or Pat Grant; and one or the other of them ought to be with us by the last week of this month at latest.

We have nothing whatever to fear from the enemy in the interim; they have tried again and again to force our position, and in some of their attacks they have come on with tolerable spirit, but they have latterly confined themselves very much to cannonading us as best they can, and sniping at our pickets behind cover, and they seem themselves now to have given up all hope of carrying our entrenchments. Their last grand attempt was on the evening and night of the 1st, at the Festival of the Eed, and it was fearful the yelling and firing that went on all night; they commenced, in fact, about five o'clock on the evening of Saturday the 1st August, and did not withdraw altogether till about twelve the next day. For the first time, I think, since these attacks have been made our men were induced to keep behind the breastworks, and the consequence was we had a very trifling loss, some thirty or forty only killed and wounded; while that of the enemy was said to be about five hundred killed and a thousand wounded, and the people in the city put it down as three thousand altogether. Many of the Sepoys who were engaged, instead of returning to the city, made off to their homes. This affair must have discouraged the mutineers a good deal, as ever since the 2nd we have had continual rumours from the city of disunion prevailing there and of the men leaving to go to their homes.

The explosion of their powder manufactory a few days ago has had a very good effect. It is not known how it occurred, whether from one of our shells or how, but the Sepoys took it into their head that it was the act of the Prime-Minister, Hakeem Hassen Oollah, who is suspected, and not without reason, of being in correspondence with us. They therefore plundered his house, murdered, I believe, some of his family, and made him a prisoner. The King is said to be in great distress at what has occurred, and wants to leave the city, but the Sepoys won't let him; and altogether matters are supposed not to be in at all a flourishing state. I dare say exaggerated rumours of the difficulties of the enemy are concocted to please us; but there can be no doubt that affairs must be somewhat in a fix with them.

We are told they are short of powder, and that their caps are running short. Most likely it is so, but judging from their firing they have not come to the end of either one or the other, and their stock of shot and shell must be inexhaustible; and they have lately found a store of rockets, which they have used with tolerably good effect. We have a few rockets, but, if one may judge from the practice, they are of inferior make to those in the city, which occasionally they throw right into our camp—at least into the Artillery camp, which is nearly as far from the city as the Head-Quarters Camp is.

Their Artillery practice on the whole is very good; but they have a great advantage over us in their command of heavy guns, having 24-pounders without number, and if one is damaged by our fire it can be immediately replaced by another. We have no 24's except what we took from the enemy on the 8th of June, and these are now very much the worse for wear; and the Artillery officers will be very glad to get some new ones that are with Nicholson's Column and are expected in to-morrow or next day. When Nicholson's Column arrives we shall have four brigades of Infantry, numbering altogether, I should think, about three thousand Europeans and nearly the same number of Native Infantry (Sikhs and Goorkhas): say after deducting sick, of which there are a good number amongst the Europeans, five thousand bayonets. Our Cavalry is probably about fourteen hundred, half Native (reliable men) and half European; and our Artillery must number about six hundred, all Europeans. The besieged party outnumber us, perhaps, six to one; so, considering they have a well-stocked arsenal at their disposal, which no enemy we have ever yet had to deal with in India has had, our not walking into Delhi at once, as was anticipated, may not be considered so surprising after all.

Our present Commandant, Wilson of the Artillery, gets on wonderfully better than any of his predecessors, and seems to have gained the confidence of the army, which they never possessed. He knows what he is about, and though he may be over careful, he is evidently a good man for the occasion.

Nicholson I dare say you have heard of; he has a great reputation, and did well in the Punjab. His appointment to be Brigadier-General has given great umbrage in Her Majesty's service, and it is declared that it is unauthorised by the terms of the Queen's warrant. To avoid all heart-burning as much as possible, it has been decided that when his Column comes into camp Her Majesty's 52nd, now under his command, and in which there are two full Colonels senior to him, shall be removed to another brigade, and he is to have a brigade consisting of the 1st Fusiliers, Coke's corps, and Green's corps. The other brigades of Infantry are commanded by Colonel Longfield, Her Majesty's 8th; Jones, Her Majesty's 61st; and Showers, 2nd Fusiliers. Hope Grant commands the Cavalry, Colonel Garbett the Artillery, and Colonel Baird Smith is Chief Engineer.

If we have to wait for the assault on Delhi until Havelock comes, or Pat Grant joins us with the troops from below, we shall probably be here nearly another month. At least I reckon that it will be at least a fortnight from to-day before either of them can be with us; but you will have much later accounts of their movements from the public prints than I can give you. We have nothing later than the 26th of last month from Cawnpore. By the time their force reaches here we ought to have also a large siege-train, which is on its way from Ferozepore to this place; we have now only a third-class one.

I can imagine the feverish anxiety with which the arrival of the Indian mail is looked for at home. What horrors after horrors you will have to read at home! We have become a little accustomed to them now, but it is truly dreadful to think of some of the atrocities that have been committed.

We are all very much disgusted in camp to read some of the late articles in the papers, and speeches made by arrogant civilians or purse-proud mercantile men, all totally ignorant of everything connected with the Army, and more particularly of the causes of the outbreak, who, without a show of reason, attribute the Mutiny to the misbehaviour and inattention to their duty of regimental officers. Nothing is further from the truth, and if the blame is to rest anywhere it must be on Government and on the home authorities who have supported them: but assuredly there is none to be with justice attached to the regimental officers as a body, though of course there are individual instances of misconduct; but the way in which the European officers generally have behaved throughout the late mutinies ought to secure them from such attacks as have lately appeared in the public papers, either as editorials or as speeches made at public meetings. These fault-finding gentlemen would do much better to confine their reviews in future to the acts of the members of the Civil Service during the present trying time. With a few rare but bright exceptions, and ———, the Lieutenant-Governor, is not one of them, they have shown off most lamentably; and I begin to think that Lord Ellenborough was right when he talked of its being the correct thing to abolish the Civil Service and fill up all civil appointments from the Army, as was done in Sind in former days.

But I must think of drawing to a close or I shall be wearying you with my blotted writing; it is difficult to write at all on this thick paper with the *punkah* going, and besides the air is so very damp that it is with difficulty I can get the ink to dry. Although we have a *punkah*, the weather is tolerably cool for this season of the year, and there is not any very great amount of sickness considering the exposure the men are subject to.

We are fortunate in having a very well-supplied bazaar, and all the necessaries of life are cheaper than at most stations in India. This shows the extreme confidence that the Natives have in us, bringing their things so readily for sale, and I have no doubt they are quite as confident of our eventual success as we are ourselves. There was one time, perhaps, when their faith was a little shaken in us—this was on the 19th and 20th June, when the enemy were allowed to get in our rear and pour shot into our very camp; and when I come to look back on what took place then I am not much surprised at the alarm created, for, with the small force we then had, a little more activity and daring on the part of the enemy and it would have gone hard with us, perhaps, for our defences were then in a very unfinished state.

Colonel KEITH YOUNG *to his wife.*

CAMP, DELHI CANTONMENTS, *Tuesday,* 11*th August.*

The dâk was delivered to us at the mess table yesterday evening just after dinner. It is an interesting affair the distribution of the dâk when it arrives during the time we are at dinner. All the Head-Quarters' letters are brought in together in a large bag, and the contents being emptied on the table, one or two of the party—generally Maisey, and Stewart of the 9th (an old postmaster you may remember at Peshawar)—sort and throw them across to the different proprietors. Poor Arthur Becher was much distressed last night at not getting his usual letter, and sent and had the whole post-office ransacked for it, but without success. The reason most likely is that Mrs Arthur was too late in sending to the post-office. Here the postal arrangements are under Becher, and the post is never closed until he gives the order—and I fancy it is very often delayed a little.

The curaçoa is quite appreciated by Becher and myself; but he told me to-day that he has got a supply of cherry-brandy, and we are to attack it when we have finished the first bottle of curaçoa. The box you sent me with the jams came in this morning; they will be very acceptable. I always now breakfast at the mess, and have been indenting there on Becher's stock of jams.

Nothing of any importance going on since I last wrote. Very

little firing except from the batteries, and there seems less of this even to-day. I was sorry to hear that there were two officers wounded yesterday, but neither of them badly—Sandilands, Her Majesty's 8th, and Baillie of the Artillery.

We hear the same stories about the dissensions in the city, the imprisonment of the Hakeem, and want of unanimity amongst the mutineers; and to-day we are told that the King and some of the Princes are most anxious to go with their families to the Kootub, but the Sepoys will not consent. There must be a great deal of truth in all this, but how much it is difficult to say; a few days will show, however.

No further word from Havelock or Colonel Tytler, but letters from Meerut of the 9th say that the troops were reported by a Native to be at Meerun-ka-Serai some days ago; this is several marches on this side of Cawnpore. When we see in Havelock's handwriting that he is on his way here, I shall believe it, but not before. The copy I sent of Colonel Tytler's * letter in which the word 'to-morrow' was omitted was the correct one. I had first put these words in, but found out my mistake. Becher got Colonel Tytler's original letter over from Meerut yesterday in order that it might be ascertained what really was written. Colonel Tytler is not very happy in his style of writing, but perhaps it was intended to mystify. The opinion here is that if five thousand men are to march up here Havelock's force must be included in the number. Very probably some had come up in steamers just as he was leaving for Lucknow, and there was a report to this effect; but at the time of Colonel Tytler's writing there could not have been more than five European regiments up there exclusive of the 32nd at Lucknow. When they once leave Cawnpore they won't be long in getting here even should they go round by Agra to pick up another siege-train, which it is not at all improbable they will do.

There has been obliged to be a grand move amongst the regiments in the different brigades so as to allow of Nicholson having a brigade in which there shall be no officers of senior rank to himself. Greathed was over here yesterday, and there seems to be a very unpleasant feeling in camp amongst the officers who are senior to Nicholson; Greathed himself is one of them. There are two senior to him in Her Majesty's 52nd, Dennis and Campbell; and

* See page 175.

(NEAR DELHI.) RUINS OF KUTUB MINAR.
The pillar is about 240 feet high and said to be the highest in the world.

though they have been acting under his orders hitherto, it was thought best to remove them from under his command here. The 52nd is therefore posted to Colonel Longfield's brigade, and the 1st Fusiliers is to be under Nicholson, whose brigade will consist of this regiment, Coke's corps, and Green's; while to keep Showers in command of a brigade, he being also junior to the two 52nd Colonels, another change has to be made involving a good deal of trouble in the unpitching and repitching of tents, many of which have become so rotten from the constant damp that the latter operation (repitching) will be a very difficult one. In the changes, the 9th Lancers had to move their camp yesterday, and they say the upper part of the mess tent came away bodily when they tried to repitch it.

It is past three o'clock, so I must think of closing this. The only news from the city is that several of the Princes (the wretched curs!) have already left the Palace with their wives, and gone out to the Kootub.

(*Diary*) 11*th August.*—A coolish morning. Walk down to look at the 9th Lancers' lines being got ready for the 1st Fusiliers and Nicholson's brigade, of which they are to form part, Her Majesty's 52nd being made over to another brigade. Dine with Greathed at the 8th mess this evening.

CHAPTER IX.

SIEGE OF DELHI (*continued*)—CAPTURE OF ENEMY'S GUNS, AND ARRIVAL OF NICHOLSON'S COLUMN.

Colonel KEITH YOUNG *to his wife.*

CAMP, DELHI CANTONMENTS, *Wednesday, 12th August.*

I was dining with Greathed last night at the 8th mess, and on my return, seeing a light in our own mess tent, I went in and found these home letters (which I enclose) and your letter of the 9th instant. I had just finished a letter to your father yesterday, but was glad it wasn't sent off, as I can now add a few lines and tell of the arrival of these. How strange it seems to us out here, in the midst of all our trouble and turmoil, to read of everything being so quiet and peaceful at home! I wish we were there with the little boys, and not obliged to come out again to this murderous country.

There have been grand doings here this morning, an attack on the enemy's outposts on our left front resulting in the capture of four of their guns, which were brought triumphantly into camp; one of them belonged to Murray-Mackenzie's troop. A great many of the mutineers were killed—probably two hundred of them, including three Native officers. Our loss, I am sorry to say, has not been small, about fifty killed and wounded, and six officers wounded—one Sheriff, a brother of the Miss Sheriff who was at Simla, it is feared mortally: the others not any of them very badly—Brigadier Showers; Major Coke; Greville; Lieutenant Innes, 60th Native Infantry; and Owen, 1st Fusiliers. The enemy, it seems, had been annoying our Metcalfe pickets for some days with guns they had brought out, and it was determined to make a dash for them; the attack was planned last night to come off at early dawn this morning, and everything was very well managed by Brigadier Showers, who commanded the attacking party. It was a complete surprise to the enemy, who were mostly posted in and about Ludlow Castle—the house, you may remember, just before you come to the North-Western Dâk Company's Office.

Our men, both European and Natives, are highly delighted at the success of the expedition; and the first two guns were brought in by men of the 1st Fusiliers, mounted on the horses, which were also taken, and stopping occasionally to give a cheer for Brigadier Showers. By six o'clock the guns were in camp, so the affair, important as it was, didn't last very long. Having taken the guns, our people returned as quickly as possible, as they were within the range of the city guns, and it was by a piece of shell from one of these that the poor young fellow Sheriff was wounded : his wound is in the head. The 1st Fusiliers and Coke's were the corps principally engaged. The men of the latter regiment—Sikhs and Afghans—were highly elated at taking the guns, the first they had ever taken ; and one of them in speaking to me spoke of the number of *Matadeens* his regiment had killed. This, it appears, is the name that the mutineers always go by amongst the Sikhs. It is to be hoped that this morning's business will keep the scoundrels quiet for some time to come : they are very much so just now.

I enclose with this a copy of a letter of the 31st July from Cawnpore that reached our camp last night.* This will show you the absurdity of entering the word 'to-morrow' in that letter from Major Tytler.

I was speaking to Chamberlain just now, and it is his opinion that no troops will march from Cawnpore to here until after Havelock has returned there from Lucknow, when with the reinforcements now pouring up country he would probably have four or five thousand men after leaving sufficient garrisons at Lucknow and Cawnpore. This is much what I think myself; and under this arrangement he will probably be up here some time during the last week in this month. It is dreadful to find that the sad tale of the double massacre at Cawnpore is confirmed : no wonder our men slay all the Natives there they come across.

We have just begun to use the tin of tea you sent with the

---

* See page 198.

port wine, and we want to know if there is any of the Kangra tea in it. It is a very nice mixture whatever it is.

Becher told me just now that Lord William had sent him a pistol, showing, as he said in his note about it, that he bore no malice to him for his letter, but that he considered Simla quite safe, or he wouldn't part with his pistol.

Let Mr Philipe see the letter from Cawnpore, and tell him particulars of the fight. 3.30 P.M., and all quiet.

(*Diary*) 12*th August*.—Woke up early this morning before daybreak by very heavy musketry firing, and by Becher coming into my tent in a state of great excitement and telling me it was our attack and not the enemy, and the result very satisfactory. We took four guns near Ludlow Castle, and killed and wounded some five hundred of the enemy. Very amusing to see the Fusilier men bringing in the guns in triumph. Coke's corps was very good too. One man told me they had killed lots of *Matadeens* (Sepoys). The band of the 8th playing in the Head-Quarters' street this evening.

Captain SPURGIN *to Captain* SIMPSON.

CAWNPORE, 31*st July*.

MY DEAR SIR,—Sir Hugh Wheeler and his garrison have ceased to exist. The Nana promised them a safe passage by the river to Allahabad and Calcutta; but when he got them into boats he treacherously murdered them by bringing guns to fire upon the boats. The women and children appear to have been spared that day, for they were brutally and cruelly murdered (two hundred and ten in number) the day the British troops retook Cawnpore. It is reported that there are two who escaped from the boats; from them an account of the sufferings of the garrison may be gathered. General Neill, of the Madras Fusiliers, now commands at Cawnpore; General Havelock the advancing column to Lucknow: their success has already been great, taking twenty guns the first day. In all probability the column would be at Lucknow to-day.

Fifty-six guns were taken from the rebels between Allahabad and Cawnpore. They blew up the magazine, but heaps of everything have been dug from the ruins—even to gunpowder. All is well here, and a flow of European troops still continues from Calcutta, and regiments coming overland from England.

(Delhi.) Cashmere Gate.

General Neill is too much occupied to reply to your note of the 18th, which arrived only this morning, the 31st, and the bearer is despatched again at noon to-day.—Yours truly,

J. B. SPURGIN (*Captain*),
Staff Officer to General Neill.

CAPTAIN SIMPSON, D.A.A.G., Meerut.

Lord WILLIAM HAY *to Mrs* KEITH YOUNG.

SIMLA, 14*th August.*

MY DEAR MRS YOUNG,—I have just received the following: 'Camp, Delhi, 12th August (8 A.M.)—The mutineers having annoyed our pickets with guns placed near the Cashmere Gate, a force under Brigadier Showers surprised them at daybreak. The affair was most successful. The guns captured were one 24-pounder howitzer, two 9-pounders, and one 6-pounder; all brought off.' Our loss small. Lieutenant Sheriff, 2nd Fusiliers, mortally wounded; Showers, Coke, and Greville wounded slightly. Kindly send to Mrs Norman.—Yours sincerely,

WILLIAM HAY.

Colonel KEITH YOUNG *to his wife.*

CAMP, DELHI CANTONMENTS, 13*th August.*

I am very sorry to find that you are still fancying massacres and disasters at Simla, for which there really seems no good cause whatever now; but I was told by Greathed that ——— had given a sermon in the evening bringing in all kinds of horrors, just as it was becoming dusk, and frightening every one out of his or her senses. I suppose Greathed had received a letter from his wife on the subject.

All is quiet in camp now; but there was a tremendous deal of firing last night, both cannonading and musketry, and yet it seems there was not a single man hit on our side during the whole night, and perhaps very few on the side of the enemy either, as our men were probably firing away at a long distance just to show the enemy that they were awake, and prevent them coming nearer.

As usual I underrated our casualties yesterday, for it appears that when the total was totted up our loss was found to amount to one hundred and thirteen; of these, however, I know a great many were very slightly wounded. I saw myself an officer who was returned as wounded driving about in a buggy in the evening. That poor lad Sheriff is still alive, but in an almost hopeless state; the wound is in the head, and part of the brain has been carried away. Instances are known of men recovering even from such injuries, but they are very rare.

I am amused at Mrs Hall's account of cases of Lieutenant Browne and Lieutenant Temple, as given by her husband. My version was the correct one, and could not be wrong, as I had heard all particulars from Dr Tritton, who had been up to see the wounded men. I met George Hall this morning, and asked him how he came to write as he did—that one man had had his head taken off and the other his leg by the same roundshot! George said it was very stupid of him, as he was told they were walking together at the time, and if he had thought of it for an instant he would have seen the absurdity of the same shot hitting one in the head and the other in the leg! The truth, I believe, was, as regards the unfortunate man Browne, that he brought his death entirely on himself by standing in one of the embrasures, against the frequent remonstrances of those in the battery with him.

The newsletter from the city mentions the loss of the enemy yesterday morning at five hundred killed, and lots of wounded also; the sight of the latter limping into the city must have a very disheartening effect upon the other scoundrels there.

I was glad to hear that a *bheestie* yesterday got a purse from one of the men who was killed containing fifty-five gold mohurs (nearly nine hundred rupees, or, according to the present value of gold mohurs, much more). They are excellent servants the *bheesties*, and several of them have been killed and wounded taking up water to our men in the batteries and at the pickets.

We are certainly very fortunate in our weather. It has been threatening rain for some days, but none has come down; and though the sun is rather hot, there is a nice cool breeze blowing. I went over this morning to see Waters of the Rifles, who wrote a curious note to me a little while ago to say that he had been wounded (a slight wound in the foot, two or three days ago), that he was engaged to be married, and was anxious for a Brigade

Majorship, which he trusted to me to get for him! From Waters' tent, after explaining to him that he must not look to me for a Brigade Majorship, I went and paid Sir Edward Campbell a visit; he seems more cheerful and jolly than he used to be up at Simla.

Mr Greathed has had letters from Agra, of the 7th, where all was well, and no mention of the mutineers from Gwalior leaving that place. They had news from Cawnpore, of the 1st August, confirming the account of Havelock's victory and of his taking twenty guns; and reinforcements had been sent out to him, and on their reaching he was to move on to Lucknow. As I told you, the Native news is that he did move on, and that Lucknow had been sacked by our troops. There is a rumour, too, that the three Native regiments at Dinapore had decamped with their arms; General Lloyd was after them.

The 8th band played in the Head-Quarters' Camp yesterday evening, and the street was crowded with 'fashionables!'

(*Diary*) 13*th August*.—Firing going on during the night, and heavy cannonading all day, but no damage done, or very little. Paid a visit or two in the Rifle lines to-day, and then do writing. Write to Frere.

CAMP, DELHI CANTONMENTS, *Friday*, 14*th August*.

I was speaking to Hodson yesterday on the subject of Goolab Sing's death, and it is his opinion that no bad effect to us is likely to arise from it. Formerly the son and heir, by name Runbar Sing, was known to be inimical to our rule, but it is said he has grown wiser now; but, whether or not, he will have more than sufficient to employ him in his own country to think of making any attempt to trouble us.

I don't think you need be under any apprehension of matters going wrong amongst the hill tribes about Simla in consequence of anything that may occur at Cashmere, and when we are once inside Delhi all will soon quiet down. But you say, When will this be? I am not in the secret, and I fancy, indeed, that the General himself and those he consults have not yet positively settled whether we are to attack the place at once, now that Nicholson's Column has arrived, or wait for Havelock. I dare say the question will most likely be decided by circumstances, and by the intelligence we may receive from the city after it is known that they have heard of our reinforcements having come in; they appear last night to have been in a state of great alarm that we were going to attack the city.

There was a tremendous fire of musketry from the walls twice: first about ten o'clock, just as I was reading your letter; and then again at one o'clock this morning, when I was awoke by it and by Becher calling out to his servants to know what o'clock it was. They fired away their ammunition to very little purpose, as, of course, none of our men were within shot.

I went out to see the troops come in this morning, and a very pretty cheering sight it was—about twelve hundred European Infantry (Her Majesty's 52nd, and wing 61st), and the same of Sikhs (Green's corps, a very fine regiment), and a wing of the new levies, with some Cavalry and a Horse battery. There was a large convoy, too, with five heavy guns, lots of ammunition and powder, and several lacs of treasure. It cannot be very consoling to the people in the city to hear of these fresh arrivals for us, especially as they had been expecting troops themselves from the Punjab, which they are certainly not very likely to get now.

Do you know I am very much inclined to think after all that the old 50th has remained staunch, for I see that a Calcutta government notification of the 9th July says that all was well at Nagode on that date, and the regiment that was said to have crossed at Kalpi was the 42nd Native Infantry, which is reported to have gone to Futtyghur. How proud old Joe Hampton will be if the regiment does actually prove faithful! Norman, too, is delighted to find that his regiment, the 31st, at Saugar, so far as we know, is behaving well, except a small detachment of it.

Nothing to-day of Havelock; but I forgot to tell you that the letter yesterday said that when he had relieved Lucknow he was to be joined by two thousand five hundred Goorkhas that were on the other side of the Gagra River waiting for him. Their joining him, however, would be the work of some days, and I fear we must not expect to see Havelock here before the end of the month, if we are to wait for him.

We could not be more fortunate than we are in our weather to-day: it is most pleasant—cloudy, with a cool breeze; and, now that Nicholson's force is comfortably housed in camp, a good fall of rain—which we seem very likely to have—will not be unwelcome.

I forgot to notice Mrs Nicoll's amusing account of the sketch of Delhi that Arthur did 'with his left hand,' which of course was not the case. I thought it had been done by Maisey, but I asked Becher, who was much amused to hear what Mrs Nicoll said, and told me the plan was drawn in the office.

I have just seen the city newsletter of to-day; it contains, amongst other items, an account of the number of mutineers there are in the city, and the whole do not amount to more than about seventeen thousand, of which between three and four thousand are Cavalry. I dare say that this is somewhat near the mark, as the number of light guns is also given, and this is correct. The letter says the King wants the Sepoys to try and make their peace with the British, but they reply that there is no hope for them, and that they must either conquer or die; and the letter goes on to say that the King ordered his elephants with the intention of going into the British camp himself, but the Sepoys would not let him.

Some of the new percussion-caps that they have been making in the city were brought into our camp this morning. They are very well made indeed, but the detonating powder is wanting in them, and this, the letter says, they have in vain tried to manufacture.

I forgot to tell you that we tried some of the apricot jelly yesterday, and again this morning at breakfast, and it is most highly approved of by my next neighbours as well as myself. Becher, Hodson, and others also have had some of it. It is indeed particularly nice, and so all say. As large as the stock is, we shall get through it in time.

3.30 P.M., and all has been quiet to-day except a little firing from big guns. That poor young Sheriff is still alive. Mactier, who is lying down reading a novel, sends his kindest regards.

Here is a copy of Havelock's order to his men after his first victory:

Movable Column—Morning Order.

FUTTEHPORE, 13*th July*.

Brigadier-General Havelock, C.B., thanks his soldiers for their arduous exertions of yesterday, which produced in four hours the strange result of a whole army driven from a strong position, eleven guns captured, and their whole force scattered to the winds without the loss of a British soldier!

To what is this astonishing effect to be attributed? To the fire of the British Artillery exceeding in rapidity and precision all that the Brigadier-General has ever witnessed in his not short career; to the force of the Enfield rifles in British hands; to British pluck, that good quality which has survived the revolution of the hour; and to the blessing of Almighty God in a most righteous cause, the cause of justice, humanity, truth, and good government in India.

(*Diary*) 14*th August.*—Heavy musketry firing last night about eleven, and again at one this morning. It seems it was principally from the walls of the city, and they must have fancied themselves attacked. Nicholson's Column came in this morning—about two thousand four hundred Infantry, six guns, and some Cavalry; went to see them march in. Green's Sikh corps very fine men. Quiet to-day. In the evening rode to see Coke, who was slightly wounded on the 13th.

Captain EDEN *to* Colonel KEITH YOUNG.

CAMP, GOVINDGHUR, 14*th August.*

MY DEAR COLONEL KEITH YOUNG,—I have been compelled to relinquish my position on the road between Delhi and Agra, and am *en route* to Jeypore with this chivalrous army. I have done my best, and held together under many difficulties, and indeed the force is still entire; but this approach of the Neemuch mutineers who are at Muttra (?) was the signal for an ignominious retreat, or flank march, and my pusillanimous Commander-in-Chief took care it should be in this direction, wherever it was. I had no hope of ever getting back to Gwalior; and as the temper of the men is by no means improved, and they were exposed to this severe weather, attacked by cholera, and I had no money, my best plan manifestly was to take them back to their own place. Howbeit, I believe the want of pluck is more with the officers than men; but with regard to the latter also it was very necessary to be on the *qui vive*, and, all things considered, it was better to take them back still a force than run the risk of utter disorganisation by collision or collusion.

For myself this move is most painful. I had fondly hoped to hold on till Delhi fell—*mais que faire?* I am utterly helpless. I can get no news of, or from, Agra.

I send you a note from Morrieson; the reports we have are unsatisfactory, though on imperfect information. The dâks are quite cut off in Muttra and towards Jeypore. Yesterday I heard that Morrieson had been obliged to leave Bhurtpore on the 10th, and has gone to Ajmere. Colonel Lawrence * refers to the China troops as having arrived in Calcutta—four thousand Infantry, two thousand Marines, two French (?) regiments, and Artillerymen. I have no news from Cawnpore. Brigadier Havelock was appointed to the Movable Column forming at Allahabad, so surely a force must be soon up. Reports of the Mutiny at Mhow received in Jeypore on 3rd: treasury plundered. One report wounds Colonel Durand, another kills him and other officers; the worst feature is that Holkar's troops are said to have joined the insurgents.

Colonel Lawrence has sent one hundred Europeans of 83rd, two 9-pounders, and two hundred Bombay Native Infantry to Neemuch; but *cui bono?*—pity to break up his little force at Nussereebad.

I have tried to get notes into Agra on two sides, but without success as yet. Morrieson's fractious strictures on this force you must receive with caution; the men are no worse than their neighbours, and have on the whole behaved better.

At Koeg (?) nearly the whole of Harvey's escort, chiefly of the 8th Indian Cavalry,† and some few others of different regiments, deserted and went to join the mutineers at Muttra. I much fear the Mhow men will take Mahidpore *en route*, and possess themselves of the six guns. On the 8th I despatched a party of one hundred and twenty-five Horse to your camp with some packets for the Commander-in-Chief, some for the Postmaster, and a batch of newspapers for you. You may imagine my disgust when I found this party here this morning! The fact is, the Ulwar Raja

---

* Colonel George Lawrence, commanding at Nussereebad, a brother of Sir John and Sir Henry Lawrence.
† This is a mistake—the 8th were in Delhi. I do not know what corps Eden meant.—H. W. NORMAN.

died four days ago, and the officer in command received his orders not to go. I'll make another effort to send some men. Captain Stewart will explain how these fellows work. Kindly show him this, and give him my regards; his note and Ford's, of 1st, I got on 10th.

Please thank Mr Greathed for his note. I shall be thankful for any news. I hope all will go on well at Jeypore—it will, so far as the Chief is concerned; but some villains are unfurling the green flag and trying to get up a row. I should be there (at Jeypore) this, 20th, and you doubtless in Delhi. Kind regards to Becher.—Sincerely yours, W. F. EDEN.

Major MORRIESON *to Captain* EDEN.

BHURTPORE, 6*th July.*

MY DEAR SIR,—In case you may not have heard of the mutineers at Agra, I write you on the imperfect information current in the place that the Kotah Cavalry, whose fidelity had been assured to us by their own protestations and by our liberal promises, turned upon us at the critical moment, dispersed the Kerowlie levies of Nawab Syfuola Khan, released the few prisoners left in the jail, joined the insurgents, and attacked our batteries, which, after a severe contest, we had to withdraw. The Government House and various bungalows have been destroyed; but the city has not been plundered or injured so far as I have heard, and the mutineers, according to the plan they have all along proposed, will pass on to Delhi. The injury that has been done is insignificant compared to the insult; this has been so grievous that we cannot show our faces, and you will feel it in your own camp, and all over Rajpootana. I write to let you know the movements of the mutineers, and expect they will pass you with as perfect impunity as the Muttra company passed the Bhurtpore troops.

You have been alarming our authorities by threatening to make Kama your Head-Quarters. I shall have to protest against this, as Kama was formerly a Jeypore district, wrested from us by Bhurtpore, and the memory of the capture still rankles in the minds of the Jeypore people. Your force, besides, is a perfect calamity to the country through which they move or in which they remain, by all accounts ; and, if you come for punishment, pray take up your residence in the Poonahana Pergunah, and *loot* the mess there *ad libitum*.

My position at this place is very precarious. The common people and soldiery are delighted at the progress of sedition, and so perhaps are a good many of the Sirdars. They would fall to pieces among themselves if I were to leave—it is the best punishment that could be inflicted upon them: but it would occasion great embarrassment by interrupting our communications, and I remain; but had the mutineers only been joined by the Gwalior contingent or other force, so as to be able to invest Agra or shut up the garrison, I should have been obliged to leave here. This delay at Delhi is ruinous to our credit, and it is clear we have made a great mistake in attempting to besiege before providing for the security of all.—Believe me, yours sincerely, MORRIESON.

Colonel KEITH YOUNG *to his wife.*

CAMP, DELHI CANTONMENTS, *Saturday, 15th August.*

All is very quiet here to-day, and so it was all last night, the enemy scarcely firing a shot. I fancy they have given up all hope of driving us out of this, and are perhaps going to remain quietly where they are till we go to attack them. Mr Philipe, in his letter received yesterday, tells me it is rumoured at Simla that the city was to be assaulted on the 16th (to-morrow). I don't think there is the slightest chance of this, indeed I may say certainly not; and, in fact, unless the mutineers take to bolting in a body from Delhi there is little prospect of our doing anything preparatory to the arrival of the siege-train, now on its way from Ferozepore. I suppose it will be here about the 26th, and then if Havelock is not likely to come here soon they will probably advance our batteries, blaze away at the city for two or three days with all available guns and mortars, and then assault the place, which, no doubt, would be carried at once. However, there is plenty of time between this and then to write to you how matters are progressing.

You will perhaps have heard that there is a force out from the city trying to get to our rear, and, if you hear it from ———, the number may be given at six or seven thousand men, with thirteen guns, for this is what some of the Native spies say; the real number is probably about a thousand of all kinds, with a couple of guns, and their object is said to be to plunder Paniput, from which place most of our supplies are derived. Hodson went out last night with some three hundred Cavalry to dodge them and find out what they were doing; George Ward and several other officers are with him. No accounts have come in from him yet; but Colonel Dunsford, who went out last night with a party also from Lussowlie to Paniput, has just reported that he has reached the latter place and can hear nothing of the mutineers being in that direction. By to-morrow we shall hear, I hope, from Hodson if he can learn where they are; perhaps a small column may go out under Nicholson to attack them.

There is nothing that I have heard from the city to-day, and no more news from Cawnpore; but a letter from Agra of the 6th (rather old, for one of the 8th had been received two days ago) says that the Governor-General had written that he expected something more from General Barnard than merely repelling the enemy's sallies. What will he say when he finds our present force, which is nearly treble the number, equally inactive?

Cotton, of the 67th, is appointed to command at Agra, superseding Brigadier Polwhele and several others. He is said to be the very best man, and he writes that he is already beginning to reoccupy the cantonments.

Did you hear that Colonel Graham's daughter is going to be married to Mr Colvin, of the Civil Service at Nynee Tal, a son of the Lieutenant-Governor? I have heard nothing more of the ladies at Nynee Tal going to Almorah, but I believe it has been done, and all those up there say it was a very foolish move.

Tell Major Goad, please, when you see him, that most of the things sent, except the ladies' habiliments, have been disposed of, and these will be more useful at Kussowlie, where we will send them soon.

(*Diary*) 15*th August.*—Took a ride up to the Mound battery this morning. What a change in the appearance of the country since our first arrival!—all the trees in front cut down, and everything looking cheerful and green. Nothing doing all day but the usual quiet and writing, except cannonading. In the evening the band played in the Head-Quarters' street—an immense concourse of people assembled. Lovely weather; rather warm, perhaps, but very pleasant on the whole.

CAMP, DELHI CANTONMENTS, *Sunday*, 16*th August.*

You would have heard on the 14th that there was no truth in the report of Sir John Lawrence having been stabbed; at least no rumour of it has reached here, and there was a telegraphic message from himself yesterday. It is a mischievous kind of report to set about, and the person with whom it originated ought to be turned out of Simla.

So it was expected at Simla that Delhi was to be attacked on the 16th! The day is nearly over, and there are no signs of it. In my opinion, if we are inside Delhi by the end of this month we shall be almost more fortunate than I expect. It will depend in some measure upon the arrival of the siege-train, and this at the earliest can scarcely be here until the 26th.

So George Hall has been writing to his wife about the enemy's batteries outside the walls. Was it the guns that were taken the other day that he alluded to?—for there are still guns outside the walls that we have not taken, nor are likely to attempt to take so long as they do us no particular mischief. Were I to write you half the stories I hear about guns and batteries and troops marching to our rear, and other *shaves*, as they are technically called in camp, you would be more tired of reading than I of writing them, perhaps. Scarcely an hour passes but there is some strange story narrated, altogether without foundation. There was rather a serious one this morning, however, that is too true. An attempt was discovered this morning in two of the batteries near Hindoo Rao's to spoil the priming powder of the guns by putting little stones in it; the effect might have been to prevent the guns going off at a most critical moment, though the number of troops we now have up there would have been quite sufficient to repel any attack that might have been made at the time. An inquiry is going on, and as no Natives are admitted into our magazines here, it is strongly suspected that some of the Native lascars in the batteries are the culprits. It is just possible that the mischief may have been done before the powder was sent here; but whoever done by, the discovery will have the good effect of leaving nothing that can possibly be avoided in the hands of any of the natives, and as it is, very few of them are trusted except in very small matters. Brigadier Wilson has always been very suspicious of the Natives who have anything to say about the guns, and this business will make him doubly so. These men are all *Poorbeahs*, and we have not as yet had the least reason to suspect anything wrong either in the Punjabee or Goorkha regiments, from which I believe there has not been a single desertion since they joined us.

You will be sorry to hear that that poor young fellow Sheriff is dead. All the rest of the wounded are getting on well, and Brigadier Showers is able to sit outside his tent. Several wounded officers came into our camp yesterday evening to hear the band, which played again; the big street was perfectly crowded. Now that the 52nd have arrived I dare say their band will play also. Our present band is composed of men from the 8th and 61st. Young Clive, the Aide-de-Camp that was, is here; he is looking rather thin, but well.

Both packets of paper arrived this morning in excellent order. Mactier was highly amused at the careful way yours was packed. He sends his kindest regards to you, as do also Becher and Norman; they are all well.

Nothing in yet from Hodson's party; they have probably gone in the direction of Rohtuck, to which quarter it is said the rebels were bound. This party consists principally of men of the Hurrian Light Infantry, so there can't be many of them; and with Hodson, the Jheend troops under Colonel Dunsford, and General Van Cortlandt's force, they ought not to escape.

No further news from Agra or Cawnpore. It is thundering heavily, and looks as if it were going to rain cats and dogs. Word has just come in from Hodson of his having fallen in with a small party of the enemy and cut them up, and he has sent in several horses; only one or two slightly wounded on his side.

Half-past three, and all quiet in camp. No rain yet; it must be with us soon.

(*Diary*) 16*th August.*—Special Service of Humiliation: Mr Ellis preached. Quiet all day; rain in evening.

Camp, Delhi Cantonments, *Monday, 17th August.*

Your letter—No. 82, of the 14th—reached me early this morning, and after reading it I went out and had a short ride. I intended going farther than I did, but it came on to rain, and I was only just home in time. For some hours it came down very heavily, but it is now clear and bright again, but still cool and pleasant, though nothing, of course, like the lovely weather you must be having occasionally at Simla. I do indeed wish that I was up there to enjoy it with you.

I am much afraid your prognostication that the 19th is to be the happy day of our entry into Delhi is not likely to be fulfilled : and, as I mentioned before, I don't think there is any chance of an onward move till the arrival of the siege-train, if then. Nothing from Havelock yet : I suspect he must be forming a junction with the Nepaul force; but whatever the cause of his silence, it must be soon cleared up. There are letters from Agra, of the 11th, received to-day, I understand, but I have not seen any of them; I believe they contain no news beyond all being well at Agra.

I was much amused to hear how the 4th Irregulars should have been treated so as to have induced them to preserve their fidelity. Did it never enter into the wise heads of ——— and ——— that if the regiment had remained at Hansi, and all other doubtful regiments had been kept at their stations, too, it would have been rather difficult to have brought an army before Delhi? The truth is, the 4th was no worse than other regiments, but it was fully as bad, and it is only a pity it was not disarmed a month or two sooner, which it would have been had not Major Martin so strenuously objected to the measure.

Nothing further from Hodson. He wrote a few lines yesterday giving an account of his cutting up this party of the Light Cavalry; there were twenty-four, I think he said, of whom two only escaped. One of those shot was a Ressaldar of Chamberlain's corps at Mooltan (the 1st), Busarat Khan by name; he wanted to make out that he was recruiting, but it was well known that he had been in Delhi for a long time, and he was perhaps out now on a looting excursion, or, it may be, returning to his home, finding matters going wrong here. There are several officers out with Hodson, amongst them young Gough; also George Ward, who, though senior to Hodson, is very glad to serve under him.

None of the Saugar mutineers, as far as we know, have come into Delhi, and from what I can learn I think it is more than doubtful after all if the 50th has mutinied; and Norman's corps, the 31st, is said also to be right at Saugar.

What account does ——— give of the attempt to spoil the priming powder? This could not be brought home to any one; but a fresh business came to light yesterday, the *classees* tampering with the charges of powder after they were made up, with the intention of rendering it impossible to throw the shot and shell to the proper distances: two men were tried for this offence, found guilty, and hanged this morning. It is to be hoped that it will not only have a good effect upon the rest of the Natives, but will make the European officers of Artillery rather more careful how they trust to Natives in future.

We had special service here yesterday, and Mr Ellis gave us a sermon; he arrived a few days ago. Mr Levien and Lord Frederick Hay leave by mail-cart this evening.

No word of Major Goad's arrival here. I have sent Mr Philipe a list of the Force here—Staff Officers, &c.: ask him to show it you; it is for publication in the Simla paper.*

All quiet here, not a gun firing. 3.30 P.M.

(*Diary*) 17*th August*.—Took a ride this morning, but was glad to gallop home to escape the rain. After breakfast it came down in torrents for an hour or two, and then fine. Hodson out on an expedition with three hundred Sowars; promises to be very successful—has cut up twenty-two of the enemy, and taken several horses.

* It is not known whether the list of the Force here printed is the original one sent by Colonel Keith Young for publication. The following list is taken from the *Weekly News* 'General Intelligence,' published at Calcutta, but may have been a reprint from the Simla paper.

Detail of the Troops, &c., forming the FORCE *before* DELHI,
August 1857.

COMMANDING.
 Brigadier-General Archdale Wilson, Artillery.

AIDES-DE-CAMP.
 Capt. Barchard, 20th N. I.
 Lieut. Turnbull, 75th Foot.
 Lieut. Lowe, 74th Foot (extra).
 Lieut. Low, 9th Light Cavalry (extra).

STAFF OF HEAD-QUARTERS, &C., IN CAMP.
 Brigadier Chamberlain, Actg. Adjt.-General.
 Lieut. Norman, Asst. Adjt.-General.
 Lieut.-Col. Keith Young, Judge-Advocate General.
 Col. Becher, Qr.-Master-General.
 Capt. Garstin, D. Asst. Qr.-Master-General.
 Capt. Johnson, Asst. Adjt.-General, Artillery.

ADJUTANT-GENERAL'S DEPARTMENT.
 Major Ewart, Asst. Adjt.-General.
 Capt. Stewart, 9th N. I., D. A. Adjt.-General.

QUARTERMASTER-GENERAL'S DEPARTMENT.
 Capt. Shute, D. Asst. Qr.-Master-General.
 Lieut. Roberts,* Artillery, D. Asst. Qr.-Master-General.
 Lieut. Jones, 9th Lancers, D. Asst. Qr.-Master-General.

JUDGE-ADVOCATE GENERAL'S DEPARTMENT.
 Capt. Maisey, D. J.-A. General.
 Capt. Wilson, D. J.-A. General.

COMMISSARIAT DEPARTMENT.
 Lieut.-Col. Thomson, D. Com. General.
 Capt. Sibley, Asst. Com. General.
 Capt. Briggs, 71st N. I., S. A. Com. General.
 Lieut. Waterfield, 23rd N. I., S. A. Com. General.
 Capt. Grindall, 8th N. I., S. A. Com. General.

* Now Field-Marshal Earl Roberts.

MEDICAL DEPARTMENT.
  Surgeon Tritton, Supg. Surgeon.
  Surgeon Batson, Field Surgeon.
  Asst.-Surgeon Mactier, Surgeon to Staff.

ORDNANCE DEPARTMENT.
  Capt. J. Young, Commissary of Ordnance.

PAY DEPARTMENT.
  Capt. Tytler, 38th N. I.   (In charge of Military Chest.)

BAGGAGE MASTER.
  Lieut. Douglas, Horse Artillery.

ECCLESIASTICAL DEPARTMENT.
  The Rev. J. E. Rotton, Epis. Chaplain.
  The Rev. Fred. Bertrand, R.C. Chaplain.

PROVOST MARSHAL.
  Sergeant-Major Stroud, Horse Artillery.

ARTILLERY.
  Brigadier Garbett, Commanding.
  Capt. Frith, Brigade-Major.

HORSE ARTILLERY.
  Lieut.-Col. Mackenzie, Commanding.
    Troops—1st Troop, 1st Brigade.
            2nd   ,,   ,,   ,,   (Four Guns).
            5th   ,,   ,,   ,,   (Without Guns).
            2nd   ,,   3rd   ,,
            3rd   ,,   ,,   ,,

FOOT ARTILLERY.
  Major Brind, Commanding.
    Troops—3rd Co. 1st Batn., No. 17 Battery.
            3rd Co. 3rd Batn., No. 14 Battery.
            1st Co. 4th Batn.
            Details of other Corps 4th Batn.
            4th Co. 6th Batn.
            Detachment of European Recruits.
            Two Companies new Sikh Artillery.

DETAIL OF DELHI FIELD FORCE.

ENGINEERS.
    Lieut.-Col. Baird Smith, Chief Engineer.
    Capt. Chesney, Brigade-Major.
        Troops—Three Companies (or thereabouts) Sappers.
            Three hundred Sikh Sappers.
            One thousand Pioneers (not armed or disciplined).

CAVALRY BRIGADE.
    Brigadier Hope Grant, 9th Lancers, Commanding.
    Capt. Hamilton, 9th Lancers, Brigade-Major.
        Troops—Four Troops Dn. Guards.
            9th Lancers.
            Two Troops 1st Punjab Cavalry.
            Two Troops 2nd Punjab Cavalry.
            Two Troops 5th Punjab Cavalry.
            Lind's 'Mooltan Horse.'
            Hodson's 'Sikh Horse.'

1ST INFANTRY BRIGADE.
    Brigadier Showers, 2nd Fusiliers, Commanding.
    Capt. Simpson, 8th N. I., Brigade-Major.
        Troops—75th Foot.
            2nd Fusiliers.
            Kemaon Battalion.

2ND INFANTRY BRIGADE.
    Brigadier Longfield, 8th Foot, Commanding
    Capt. Nicolls, 50th N. I., Brigade-Major.
        Troops—52nd Light Infantry.
            60th Rifles (Six Companies).
            Sirmoor Battalion.

3RD INFANTRY BRIGADE.
    Brigadier Jones, 61st Foot, Commanding.
    Capt. Burnside, 61st Foot, Brigade-Major.
        Troops—8th Foot (Five Companies).
            61st Foot.
            Rothney's Sikhs.

4TH INFANTRY BRIGADE.
  Brigadier Nicholson, 27th N. I., Commanding.
  Capt. Blane, 52nd Light Infantry, Brigade-Major.
    Troops—1st Fusiliers.
        Coke's Sikhs.
        Green's Sikhs.
Not Brigaded.
        Corps of Guides.

Colonel KEITH YOUNG *to his wife.*

CAMP, DELHI CANTONMENTS, *Tuesday,* 18*th August.*

The Queen's officers are the only people in camp who are irate, I fancy, at Nicholson's being appointed Brigadier. The general opinion is that it would have been hard to pass him over after the service he had done in the Punjab, and even Greathed, who is a great stickler for his order, spoke very sensibly to me about it, and seemed to think it was all right now that the 52nd has been removed from Nicholson's command; and I believe there is some arrangement by which Colonels Dennis and Campbell of the 52nd are made Brigadiers, but without brigades, so as to prevent their coming under Nicholson's command.*

Not a word of news in camp to-day from any quarter, and all is as quiet as possible, scarcely a gun firing except at very long intervals. Young Harry Chester was here just now, and spoke of a battery that was being commenced by the enemy on the right flank; it cannot, however, be of much importance, or we should have heard of it here long ago. But no apprehensions appear to be entertained in camp now of the scoundrels attempting to do much again in the way of attacking our position, and we shall do nothing, I think, in the way of attacking them either until the siege-train reaches us.

There was a letter from Hodson again last night; he was all right, near Rohtuck, and had fallen in with no more of the insurgents. It seems that the party he was after had gone on towards Hansi, where they would most likely fall in with Van Cortlandt's force. It appears that both the Goughs are out with

* Campbell and Dennis were not made Brigadiers; the report must have been a camp *canard.*—H. W. NORMAN.

the expedition, one with a party of the Guides and the other with Hodson's own Cavalry.

You will be glad to hear that Goolab Sing's son and heir, Runbar Sing, has decided on following in the steps of his father and proving our faithful ally and friend. I send you a letter that I received this morning from Drake on the subject; and the Brigadier (Wilson) told me at breakfast that he had heard from John Lawrence to the same effect. This is very satisfactory, and, I hope, ensures the entire peace and safety of the Punjab.

Did I tell you that Peake & Allen have sent down their representative here with lots of stores? There are two Parsee merchants also in camp, Jehangeer and Cowasjee, with lots of supplies, particularly beer, brandy, and soda-water. Beer they wanted twenty-four rupees a dozen for at first; but they came down to fifteen rupees for their best English bottled, and the Head-Quarters' mess took a hundred dozen from them at this price. They will get a good profit on it, and I believe they have some two thousand dozen altogether, which is pretty sure to be all sold. The mess have also got a barrel of commissariat beer, which is said to be first rate, and it is to be tapped in a day or two; so you see we are not badly off.

Mactier sends kindest regards to you. We have been talking of Loch Katrine and other pretty places that we are to visit when we go home!

More than half-past three o'clock, and no more news to give you. Our not hearing direct from Cawnpore is accounted for, it is said, by a small rebel force being on the road that prevents the *cossids* coming that way.

Major DRAKE *to Colonel* KEITH YOUNG.

SEALKOTE, 14*th August.*

MY DEAR COLONEL,—The Jummoo man, Runbar Sing, appears inclined to follow his father's steps. It is said that Goolab Sing impressed upon him strongly the necessity of continuing his alliance with us if he wished to retain his rule. His troops are steadily advancing towards you; but the General was obliged to have recourse to a ruse to get his men on. He heard of Goolab's death while his force still was in the Jummoo territory. On reaching his ground a messenger ran up breathless; the letter he brought was opened, and the news of the Maharajah's death made known. Many were for going back; it was too late—the force was in the Company's territory, its faith pledged to advance, and so they went on a march or two more slowly. When the General gave out that John Lawrence was highly irate at their tardy movements, and had in consequence imprisoned his (the General's) brother, it had the desired effect of increasing their pace. This is the story sent in from their camp. An express arrived from Jummoo on the night of the 12th saying that they required fifty camels, as fifty camel-loads of treasure were ready for our acceptance. The camels went off last night. This is considered only the first instalment of the Jummoo loan.

It is rumoured at Lahore that Sir Henry Lawrence is not dead, only wounded: that his brother, Sir John, has received this news. I wish I could believe it. I heard from Macpherson yesterday; had any such good news been received he would not have omitted to mention it. We are to have two Rissalahs of 2nd Irregular Cavalry from Gondeepore here soon; we would much rather be without them, but the regiment is suspected. John Lawrence wants to disperse the men, and he therefore sends us a batch. To give the fellows their due they behaved well in keeping the 46th from a ford, and afterwards aided in cutting up some of the 26th, in which last business they suffered.—Yours sincerely, J. DRAKE.

(*Diary*) 18*th August.*—Took a ride this morning towards the powder magazine, on the bank of the river; very steamy and warm. At work all day writing. Very strange no news direct from Cawnpore; have heard of date 3rd, *viâ* Agra, but no word of any further fight. The band of Green's Sikh corps plays in the evening. Ride down in the evening to see Showers, and find him sitting outside his tent.

CHAPTER X.

SIEGE OF DELHI—*continued*.

Colonel KEITH YOUNG *to his wife.*

CAMP, DELHI CANTONMENTS, *Wednesday*, 19*th August.*

The dâk came in, as it usually does now, during the night, and I received your letter of the 16th in time to read it over my tea. Dr Scott brought it from the post-office for me; he always comes over here, sometimes as early as five o'clock, for his cup of tea, and when the dâk has not been delivered goes to the post-office for our letters while the tea is being made. That is very nice tea you sent down to me, only the servant used to put too much into the teapot. We have now limited him to two teaspoonfuls, which is quite enough, we find. I shall not require any more, for when mine is done, which it will not be for some time yet, Mactier has a large box of the same kind of tea which we are to commence upon.

There is another letter from Havelock, a copy of which has been sent down by Mr Colvin to Greathed. Mr Colvin's letter is dated the 13th, but, strangely enough, Havelock's is not only not dated but contains no date in it whatever. It is mainly a recapitulation of what had reached us before of his having beaten the enemy between Cawnpore and Lucknow at a place called Oonao, and also at Busharuttgunge, some twelve miles from Cawnpore; he mentions taking nineteen guns on this occasion, and says he had taken forty-four from the Nana before. He had run short of ammunition, and, having got a supply from Cawnpore, was then advancing to Lucknow, after relieving which place he was to march here *viâ* Agra, perhaps taking Futtyghur on his way. Under these circumstances we cannot expect to see him for a pretty long time, but from what we hear of affairs in the city there seems very little chance of our waiting till he arrives; and, in fact, if we wait much longer there won't be many of the mutineers left here. All the letters— and there were several received last night and this morning— seem to say that the Sepoys are deserting in great numbers; and a great change has certainly come over them of late.

To-day, again, hardly a shot has been fired, and all has been as quiet in camp as possible—for we have no object to gain in firing at them, and remain equally quiet, patiently awaiting the arrival of the siege-train, which is being hurried down as quickly as possible, but cannot be here under the most favourable circumstances for another week or ten days. One day early in September will probably see us inside Delhi, and it is terrible to think, but I fear it will be so, that no human being found within its accursed walls who has taken up arms against us will be spared.

This morning a female European captive came into camp, a Mrs Leeson, the wife of a clerk or patrol of that name; her maiden name was Collins. She was wounded on the day of the outbreak, and some friendly Afghan took her away, and has concealed her ever since, treating her, we understand, with all proper kindness and respect. She is now with Mrs Tytler,* the only lady there is in our camp. Captain Tytler has been offered the run of the female wardrobe that Major Goad sent down, for the use of the young lady.

No further word from Hodson direct, but we hear from Lussowlie that he is still close to Rohtuck, where Colonel Dunsford, with some of the Raja of Jheend's troops, is, I believe, going to join him.

I hear the band of Her Majesty's 52nd practising, so suppose it is going to play in the main street this evening. Yesterday we had the band of Green's corps—regular snake-charmers. Green is an old friend of mine, and, meeting him this morning, I was rather put to it when he asked me how his band played last night!

---

* Mrs Tytler, the wife of Captain Tytler of the 38th Native Infantry. Her baby, born in camp on the 21st of June, was christened ' Stanley Delhi Force.'

Norman has been making out a list of the casualties; including those in Brigadier Wilson's first engagements we have had twenty-six officers killed and eighty-one wounded. I trust there are to be no more.

Half-past three o'clock, and all quiet.

CAMP, DELHI CANTONMENTS, *Thursday, 20th August* 1857.

Yours of the 17th reached me last night just after I had returned from mess, and before going to sleep I was able to read it and know that you and the dear little boys were all well at Simla. The lanthorn I got from Anderson is our only light, and you would be amused to see our arrangements for reading in the evening; but our amusement in this way is merely confined to reading the letters we get.

You need not be under any alarm at Simla about probable disturbances in the Mohurram. You may be sure that the Mahomedans up there, however much inclined they might be for a row, are by far too much cowed by this time to think of getting up any; and before the Mohurram is over I think it will be odd if we are not inside the walls of Delhi.

You will have heard ere this reaches you, I hope, of the siege-train having passed through Umballa; and a week or so from this ought to see it safe in our camp.

There has been another letter from Hodson, who reports having had a second brush with some of the enemy and cut up a good many of them; but I believe instructions have gone out to him to return to camp, as it is not wished that he should go farther away in pursuit of the enemy, as he seems inclined to do. A Movable Column under Nicholson went out last night with the intention of marching somewhere in the direction of where Hodson is, but the intervening country was found so wet and impracticable for guns and camels that after getting little farther than Alleepore the party came back again this morning, having all had a few hours' complete drenching. It is curious that we had hardly any rain—and they were not more than six or eight miles from here.

There are other letters from Agra of the 14th, with just the same news from Havelock as before; no word of his having entered Lucknow, though Native report at Agra states such to have been the case. It is also mentioned that another steamer was close to Cawnpore. I suppose this is the one with the 5th Fusiliers on board; and I suppose we shall soon hear of the troops that arrived by the *Himalaya*, fifteen hundred in number, having been pushed up country. The mail of 26th June, too, which has probably reached you by this time, ought to give us some certain intimation of the regiments coming out by Suez.

Norman got an official letter to-day from Birch, containing the first acknowledgment that has come of the receipt of the despatch with the account of the business at Budlee-ka-Serai on the 8th June; the whole burden of the letter is impressing on General Reed the necessity of taking Delhi *at once*. 'Government was sorry to learn from private sources that up to the 19th June the city was still in the possession of the mutineers!' What will they say in Calcutta when they hear that more than two months afterwards we are still in our old position?

I told you yesterday of Mrs Leeson having come in from the city. I have since seen her statement as taken down by Captain Tytler. She gives a horrible account of the massacre on the first day, and it is almost a miracle her escaping. After having been wounded and her children killed, she was left for dead on the ground, where a friendly Afghan found her, and in the evening came and put her on a *charpoy* and took her away to a *moulvie's* house, with whose family she has been residing ever since, being treated by them with the greatest kindness and respect. She never went out; so beyond what occurred on the first day in the city she knows nothing. She says, however, that it is reported that there are still some thirty Europeans concealed in the city, but cannot say whether this is true or not; and that those who have Europeans in concealment wouldn't dare to acknowledge it, or to talk about it to their dearest friends, as they would be certain to be murdered if the Sepoys found it out. She leaves to-morrow, I believe, for Umballa, where she has some friends.

I fancy Mrs Montgomery's news of the row in Rohilkund must be true, as we have heard here to the same effect, and that the Hindoos had got the upper hand.

Becher had his arm cut open yesterday, or the day before, and a large piece of loose bone taken out. The arm is getting on very well, and it must be a relief getting rid of this bone ; but he cannot use the arm yet.

Cannonading going on ; otherwise all quiet. Nearly 4 P.M. ; no firing, and no news.

(*Diary*) 20*th August.*—Nicholson's Movable Column started about twelve last night to join Hodson ; but, after going little farther than Alleepore, they were obliged to return on account of the country being flooded. I should have thought that a small force might have pushed on anywhere—Europeans on elephants, and guns with double teams. Take a ride in the evening through the bazaar, and call on Frank Turner on my way home ; he is laid up with fever.

CAMP, DELHI CANTONMENTS, *Friday*, 21*st August* 1857.

How grandly the Simla paper appears to be getting on—an extra in this morning! With Miss H—— and a few other such as she at Simla, the ladies need never be in want of news ; her account of the Hindoos massacring the Mahomedans at Benares is the first we have heard of this pleasurable little event. I hope her rumour of the intended rising at Simla during the Mohurram will turn out to be equally unfounded, as there is no doubt it will be. There is, however, some foundation, I fancy, for the story of the feuds in Rohilkund. We also had heard here from other sources that they—the Mahomedans and Hindoos—had been fighting together, and that the former were victorious.

After I wrote to you yesterday—but too late to write again, the post having left—a letter came in from Brigadier-General Neill to *Major*-General Wilson, dated Cawnpore, 4th August. It gave extracts of General Orders from Calcutta, 29th July, appointing Wilson a Major-General, and removing General Reed from the Peshawar to the Sirhind division. It then gave some further particulars of Havelock's fight—he has been reinforced with three guns and some Highlanders, and was then marching on Lucknow—but there was a report that the Goorkhas were beforehand with him and had already joined our troops at Lucknow, themselves dispersing the mutineers. The intention, so far as one can judge from General Neill's letter, is to abandon Lucknow for the present, bringing away all the troops and people we have there—keeping a force at Cawnpore only, and sending all the rest up here *viâ* Agra. The 5th and 90th regiments were on their way up to Cawnpore, but might, General Neill says, have been detained on the road owing to the Dinapore mutiny. It seems that, of the Sepoys who deserted there, many had not their arms, and none had more than four rounds of ammunition in their pouches; so if General Lloyd comes up with them they won't be able to do much in the way of fighting. I think I have given you pretty well the substance of the whole letter; nothing is said in it of Sir Henry Lawrence, but I fear there can be no hope of his being alive. It does not, however, name in any way the officer who is now commanding at Lucknow.

Except a little cannonading, all is quiet here. The enemy have been erecting a heavy battery on the other side of the river, opposite Metcalfe's House, and have been firing rockets also. I believe their shot have just reached, but they are not likely to do much harm as we have merely pickets in the compound, and nobody in the house, which is what they are apparently firing at; but if they get troublesome we could soon put up a battery to silence them, as we have plenty of heavy guns now.

We were sorry to find, by a telegraphic message this morning, that the 10th Cavalry at Ferozepore have mutinied and deserted after an ineffectual attempt to seize the guns; but they killed and wounded some of the Artillerymen. There must have been some grave mismanagement, I fear, on the part of the Brigadier to have allowed this, and if it should prove to be so, I dare say Government will remove him from the command. I shall be very sorry for this, for he is a very good fellow—and a good officer, too, I always thought till lately.

There was a letter from Hodson this morning giving a grand account of his doings; and I believe he is to be back again to-morrow. All say that his men will return loaded with plunder of all kinds, from camels and horses downwards.

Not a word of Sir Patrick Grant coming up the country; perhaps he is waiting until he can learn whether he is to be appointed *pucka* Commander-in-Chief in India or not—though some appear to think that he won't come up country under any circumstances, but will remain in Calcutta with the Governor-General to settle the remodelling of the Army. In this case we should have to join him; but it will be time to think of this when we know that it is to be so.

General Wilson intends retaining the command of the Artillery till he hears from the Commander-in-Chief to the contrary. I believe this is done to keep Colonel Garbett out of the command—I mean the command of the regiment of Artillery, not of the Artillery now here.

Nearly 4 P.M., and no news in from anywhere. All quiet now.

(*Diary*) 21*st August*.—The enemy, it seems, have got heavy guns and rockets across the river, and are firing into Metcalfe's compound and Coke's camp, but they don't appear to do much harm. We tried some rockets at them, but they were a failure. In the evening took a ride up to the Ridge to look at the enemy's batteries; many other would-be spectators, but no firing going on from the other side or from ours, so had a short ride and home to mess.

CAMP, DELHI CANTONMENTS, *Saturday, 22nd August* 1857.

The Meerut dâk has come in, but no news of any interest from there. They can't get any intelligence at all from Cawnpore owing to a scoundrel near Bolandshur, the Nawab of Malaghur, who had possession of the road in that direction, and had caught three of our *cossids* and hanged them—the villain! His turn will come soon, I trust.

I will send on the old *khansamah's* letter to Harriott, and stand the risk of incurring the penalty of fifty rupees, to which, Mr Philipe says, I shall render myself liable!

I believe Hodson is not to return at present, but was to go first to Sonput and then to Jheend; he may possibly be fortunate enough to fall in with some of the 10th Cavalry mutineers. It seems that only about one hundred of them got away, and only some of these were armed. They mounted themselves on horses belonging to officers and to the Artillery; but I dare say you have detailed accounts of their proceedings by this time. There is a great cry in camp against George Hall for having allowed the men to go off, and it certainly is a pity. Not many of them, I should think, will escape to reach here, if they attempt it; but very likely they will try at once to make for their homes.

I have just seen a long statement of the sad Cawnpore business by Lieutenant Delafosse of the 53rd Native Infantry, one of four (the names of the other three he does not give) who escaped from the boats after they had been fired upon by the mutineers. It seems that the whole of the European inhabitants went into the entrenchments that had been made on the 5th of June, and that they were attacked immediately afterwards by the mutineering regiments and the Nana's people. Sir Hugh Wheeler held on till the 27th, when the Nana sent a European half-caste woman with a letter offering terms to '*all who had not assisted Lord Dalhousie's Government.*' (It was Lord Dalhousie's Government that refused to continue the Peishwa's pension to him.) Boats were provided, and all went on board without molestation; but after the arms were given up guns were opened upon the boats, and all appear to have been destroyed except the one that Lieutenant Delafosse was in. This was, however, eventually abandoned—at least Lieutenant Delafosse and a party of thirteen others left it, when hard upon a sand-bank and unable to get off, to drive away a party that were firing at them from the shore. The narrative is not very clear here; but it seems that, though successful at first, they were eventually overpowered, and saw nothing more of the boat, but, rushing into the river, swam for their lives, only four escaping, who landed on the left bank of the river and were concealed by a friendly Raja for nearly a month, when they were sent towards Allahabad and joined the Advancing Column. He says nothing about the after massacre of the women and children at Cawnpore; but I suppose this must be the case. He gives a long list of all the Europeans that were at Cawnpore in the entrenchments, and mentions the names of all who were killed there by the guns of the mutineers or died of heat and fever. Colonel Wiggens, I am sorry to say, was killed in the boat; Mrs Wiggens and the children, he says, were there, but he does not mention their death. Major and Mrs Vibart and children killed. Captain Moore, Her Majesty's 32nd, killed; Mrs Moore was there, but no word of her death, or of that of Mr and Mrs Hillersden, who were also there. Lieutenant Quin supposed to be killed. Major and Mrs Lindsay died of fever; Colonel Williams also died of fever. But the narrative, as I said before, is very imperfect, and the list of names very roughly given from memory. I dare

(CAWNPORE.) MEMORIAL MONUMENT,
by Marochetti, erected over the well.

say there will be a very complete account in a day or two in the papers, so I will not dwell more on this very painful subject.

A letter has also just come in from Agra, where all was well, with news from Cawnpore of the 12th. General Havelock had fought another successful action, but had not, up to the time of writing, reached Lucknow, from which place the most cheerful accounts were received, and no fears are entertained of their not being able to hold their own till relieved. The letter says that Sir James Outram was expected soon at Allahabad, in what capacity was not exactly known—perhaps as Commander-in-Chief in the Upper Provinces—with Mr John Peter Grant, the Member of Council, I suppose, as his civil adviser. The troops, it said, that were coming up—the 5th Fusiliers and 90th Regiment, and some other regiment—also had been delayed by the Dinapore affair. The regiments that mutinied there had been followed up and dispersed; but no particulars were given.

Mactier and I have just finished our *tiffin;* we have become great gourmands of late, having discarded the biscuits and taken to sandwiches, which they manufacture very well at the mess—and with a glass of sherry we fare very luxuriantly. The only objection that I have against this is that it rather spoils one's dinner. I have still a whole bottle of curaçoa left; and I don't think Arthur Becher has yet touched the one you gave him at Simla, and which Mrs Becher sent down to him. It is rather too hot just now to touch curaçoa. No appearance of the beer yet, but it may be expected in a day or two; I only want it for the Artillery mess, as we have plenty.

You will be sorry to hear that I have had to have the poor old pony shot. He was under cover in the bazaar, and every care taken of him, his food being changed, and what not; but it was of no use—the poor brute got covered with sores, and it seemed a mercy to have him shot; the sad operation was performed this morning by one of the Sowars under the superintendence of Soobhan and Gowroo. Poor old pony! I was very sorry at parting with him thus.

The enemy fired away a good deal this morning from their batteries on the other side of the river, but I have not heard of their doing any damage; they are now (3.30 P.M.) quite silent. We are going, I believe, to have a heavy battery got ready to-night down in Metcalfe's garden, which it is expected will throw shell into the Palace. A vast quantity of large shells came in this morning, and they could not be better employed. The siege-train you will hear of as it passes Umballa; it may be here in about six days, but is hardly expected until the 1st of September, about which time, too, we look for a party of Artillerymen from Meerut. Some Rifles (60th) are also coming.

(*Diary*) *22nd August.*—Up late this morning—dark and cloudy, and an attempt at rain; but it soon stopped, and is now rather hot and steamy. Dine in the evening with Greathed at the 8th mess, and walk home with young Greathed to our mess in the hope of finding the dâk—but disappointed. Talk of breaching the walls at four hundred yards when the siege-train comes, and then going in.

CAMP, DELHI CANTONMENTS, *Sunday, 23rd August.*

I have no news to give you to-day. All is quiet as possible, and there has not been a letter in from any direction that I have heard of except from Hissar, where General Van Cortlandt has been thrashing some of the rebels well; but as he corresponds direct with Lahore, you will, I have no doubt, see an account of the business in the *Chronicle* ere this reaches you. I know little more than that a large party of the scoundrels, both horse and foot, have been well punished.

I met George Hall when out walking this morning. We were watching the elephants in the Sepoys' old lines knocking down the walls; it was very curious to see them putting their heads against the large, thick mud walls and pushing them down. A poor elephant belonging to the rebels was knocked over yesterday by a round-shot from our batteries; they were employing it to drag a large tree across a road where it was thought likely our troops might move to attack the city, and our guns commenced firing, and the second shot from a 24-pounder knocked the poor animal over—the distance was about six hundred yards.

We have only heard to-day of the arrival of the siege-train at Umballa, which it reached yesterday. Supposing it leaves again to-day, we may expect it here about this day week; and at the same time, or probably a day or two later, we shall have some hundred more Artillerymen and about two hundred Riflemen from Meerut. They were to leave Meerut to-morrow and march to this place *viâ* Kurnaul. In their place they are to have a Sikh regiment at Meerut, and a wing of the Belooch corps and some Punjab Cavalry, so they will not have made a bad exchange.

I said to you the other day that the 2nd September would perhaps see us inside the city, but I think now that I rather anticipated events, and that we can hardly expect to attack the place before the 8th or so; for I gather from what I hear that it will not be a mere assault of the place, but that we shall gradually advance our approaches when the siege-train comes and breach the walls. We are already within some six hundred yards' distance of them, and it is calculated that ten days will allow of our making safe approaches within easy breaching distance. By this plan there will be no risk of failure and much less chance of loss of life.

We are anxious to hear again from Havelock, but I fear we can't expect another letter for some days now. It is quite clear that we need expect no reinforcements from below for a long time to come, but when the train comes I don't think we shall need them.

Hodson is now at Lussowlie, I believe. The telegraph wire is being laid down to this place again, and has already reached Raie; it will be very convenient when the office is in our camp.

Half-past three, and everything very quiet. The enemy are apparently taking their guns away from the opposite side of the river, seeing they can make nothing of them.

Such a nice, cool, cloudy day.

Captain EDEN *to Colonel* BECHER, *at Delhi.*

HODUL, 23rd *August.*

MY DEAR BECHER,—I'm heart-broken at having been obliged to relinquish Pulwal, but will stick to this as long as I can. My men are quiet enough now; many came back again (some thirty deserted), and several Irregulars in our camp. Troops of Native states are not able or willing to come into collision with Regulars. Bhopal Sing came away in a hurry! *Verb. sap.!*—Yours truly, W. F. EDEN.

Colonel KEITH YOUNG *to his wife.*

CAMP, DELHI CANTONMENTS, *Monday,* 24*th August.*

Mrs Leeson has now gone to Umballa; but Mrs Tytler, with her children, is still here—the only lady in camp. We have not heard Mrs Leeson's story confirmed about there being thirty other Europeans concealed in the city.* I hope if it is so that when we enter the place none of them may be killed in the confusion.

Hodson came back last night with all his party; he is rather sunburnt, but looking very well. He appears to have been most successful in his expedition, having cut up altogether some eighty-eight of the rebel Sowars, including three Native officers, one of whom belonged to the regiment that was at Jhansi—the 14th, I think. None of Hodson's men were killed, only a few wounded —amongst them Hugh Gough, slightly in the wrist. George Ward has returned with a slight attack of fever; Mactier has just been over to see him, and I hope a few doses of quinine will soon put him to rights again.

Yes, there is a little fever in camp, but nothing of any great consequence, and the Natives, fortunately, are much more subject to it than Europeans, particularly the poor little Goorkhas. However, we have not much longer to wait now, I hope. The siege-train ought to be at Kurnaul to-morrow or next day, and it won't take more than four days or so from there. Then there are the Artillerymen and Rifles coming from Meerut, who ought to reach here about the same time as the siege-train does.

Nicoll knows nothing whatever about the intention of the General with regard to the attack. It is, I am quite sure, settled to wait only for the siege-train and then set to work in earnest: and no one has a doubt about the result being altogether successful. The only doubt appears to be whether there will be many mutineers left in the city by the time the train arrives, for they are still said to be deserting in great numbers.

We are without any further news of Havelock's proceedings, but it seems clear that we cannot expect any aid from him for some time yet. We should like much to know if he has advanced on Lucknow; again, it may be that he is waiting until

* This report was apparently quite untrue.—H. W. NORMAN.

the Goorkhas join him, or until the European regiments join him, which they must have done by this time. I have heard nothing of a siege-train coming from Calcutta: it is probably gun-boats which I noticed had been sent up; but whatever it is it can't be for us, and there are plenty of guns of all kinds to be had at Agra. The Agra people are all well, and the mutineers at Gwalior still safe there.

We had telegraphic news of the mail last night; it said nothing of sending troops out overland, but it mentioned the arrival at Bombay of the steamer *Pottinger* from the Cape with troops, which is very good news, as other steamers have probably been sent to Calcutta from the Cape.

News from the city says the Sepoys are very much displeased with Prince Mirza Moghul, whom they accuse of treachery, and talk of trying him by Court-Martial. Tell Mr Philipe of the intended Court-Martial on the Prince of Delhi. I don't know whether the proofs are to be sent to me when they are finished!

Mungroo, the *syce* of the poor old pony, is going up to Simla to see his wife. I have paid him his wages.

3 P.M., and all quiet.

P.S.—I am glad this letter was not sent off, as Arthur Becher has just been in with a letter from Colonel Cotton from Agra, of the 20th, where all was well on that date, and all quiet at Gwalior. Colonel Cotton had felt himself strong enough to send out a detachment a short distance from Agra to keep things straight. The same *cossid* brought also a letter from General Neill to General Wilson, dated Cawnpore the 12th. He says that Havelock had fought the enemy again and thrashed them, with very little loss on our side, and taken two more guns; but he does not seem inclined to advance on Lucknow at present on account of his want of Cavalry, and hearing that Lucknow was not only all safe, but that the enemy had no chance of making any impression upon it. It seems there would have been three more European regiments at Cawnpore by this time if it had not been for the Dinapore mutiny. The mutineers had been severely punished and dispersed, but many were wandering about the Grand Trunk Road, and had stopped the dâks. The three regiments detained to follow them were the 5th, 37th, and 90th, and two batteries, but it was hoped all would soon be available again. General Lloyd has been removed from his command in consequence of his want of energy in the business. The letter goes on to say that three European regiments were to reach India by this mail from Malta—the 48th, 71st, and 57th—and that six other regiments were to follow by the same route. Two regiments from Madras were coming—one Infantry, and one Native Cavalry. All well at Nagode, Saugar, &c.

(*Diary*) 24*th August.*—At work to-day rather earlier than usual, and write home letters. The enemy are said to have marched out in force towards Nujufghurh, and a Movable Column under Nicholson is to march in the morning to look after them. The mail in after dinner. Speeches read out at mess table—Lord Ellenborough's good; Vernon Smith's received with shouts of derision.

CHAPTER XI.

SIEGE OF DELHI *(continued)*—VICTORY OF GENERAL NICHOLSON.

Colonel KEITH YOUNG *to his wife.*

CAMP, DELHI CANTONMENTS, *Tuesday, 25th August.*

Your letter of the 22nd reached me after dinner at the mess, and with it also came the letter herewith enclosed from your father and the home news, which I also send; but before I say anything of these, let me speak to you about your groundless apprehensions with reference to the cook. So long as all goes well here—and we all reckon that we cannot have to wait more than ten or twelve days or so longer, and perhaps less, for the fall of Delhi—there is no fear of any of the servants committing themselves, however much they might be inclined that way, and I should very much doubt the cook being traitorously disposed, or, in fact, any hardly of our Native servants; but still, if you have taken such a determined dislike to the man, and would wish to turn him off, the only way will be to have him turned out of Simla on the very day of his dismissal, and this might be done, I dare say, if you sent for Captain Seymour and spoke to him on the subject, telling him about the powder-flasks and the conversation about the letter from Meerut. But if you do turn him off, will you be able to get another cook you can depend upon ? —— is a donkey, and always sees a cause for alarm in everything, so don't be guided by him in the matter, but consult with Seymour if you have any doubt how to act. I will now leave the matter to you to do as you think best; but be sure of this, that you have nothing to fear from any of your servants. Ask Sergeant Larkin to sleep in the house again.

What do you think at Simla of the news from home? It seems that they are not sending troops out overland after all, but some of them that are coming round the Cape in screw-steamers will be out very soon; and I forgot to tell you yesterday that it has been decided that all the China troops were to come to Calcutta except the Marines.*

You will have intelligence ere this of the siege-train having passed Umballa; but there is a talk after all of its not being required, and of our being able to get into Delhi without it. A large party of the mutineers—it is said six thousand, with eight guns—left the city yesterday evening, and another party, though not so large, and with guns, left only this morning, and they gave out that it was with the intention of getting to our rear and attacking Alleepore or Sonput; but from what has since transpired it seems not unlikely that they are leaving Delhi altogether and are making for Goorgaon, with the intention, perhaps, of returning to Oude, or it may be of proceeding to Gwalior and joining the other mutineers there. A powerful Movable Column, however, under Nicholson has gone to look after them, and if he comes across them they will have little chance of escape: his Column consists of two European corps—the 1st Fusiliers and Her Majesty's 61st; and two Sikh corps—Coke's and Green's, with some of the 9th Lancers and Native Cavalry, and Horse Artillery (sixteen guns). His greatest difficulty will be the ground he has to get over. He started at daybreak, but about nine it came on to rain, so I fear Nicholson will not have a pleasant march of it; he will probably not fall in with the enemy under any circumstances for the next day or two. Shute has gone out with the Column as Quartermaster-General, and Sir Theophilus Metcalfe also, to show them the way.

The enemy, or what are left of them in the city, are very quiet to-day; they have fired a few shots from the batteries on the opposite side of the river into the Metcalfe compound, but they have done this every day for some days past, and I have not heard of their having hurt anybody.

What do people say at Simla to Sir Colin Campbell being Commander-in-Chief?—for this seems evidently the intention. This will stop Seymour's trip to Bombay. Congreve will be

* See note, page 249.

rather delighted at it, I fancy, as he seems to think he has been very ill-used by Sir Henry Somerset.

Tell me if all the jars you sent contain apricot jelly. I have given one to Daly, who thinks it delicious.

What a very sensible speech Lord Ellenborough's is, except that part about the canal and tank. We had all the speeches read out at mess last night, and we decided that the President of the Board of Control, Vernon Smith, is a *donkey and noodle!*

The total number of officers killed and wounded is, I believe, one hundred and twenty-four—namely, eighty-seven wounded, eleven died from diseases, and twenty-six killed. This includes the casualties with General Wilson at Ghazeeoodeen-Nugar.

Half-past three, and no news. The rain nearly over, and everything quiet.

(*Diary*) *25th August.*—Force under Nicholson (Her Majesty's 61st; 1st Fusiliers; Coke's and Green's corps; Money's, Tombs', and Remington's troops Horse Artillery; one hundred Her Majesty's 9th Lancers; Guides; and Mooltan Horse, &c.) left before daybreak this morning to march to Nujufghurh, where two columns of the enemy are said to have gone, another having started yesterday evening from the city. Heavy rain came on about 10 A.M., but fine later.

J. W. SHERER *to* R. NIXON.

CAWNPORE, *25th August.*

MY DEAR NIXON,—Nothing new from this place. Havelock encamped on this parade-ground. Cholera has been prevalent, but moving the men into the stables of the 2nd Cavalry has had the effect of stopping it. Brown, who escaped so wonderfully, has died of cholera; so have Grant of the Volunteer Cavalry, Kenny of the 84th, Chisholm of the Madras Fusiliers, and Young of the 4th Native Infantry. I think I mentioned this last death before.

We believe there is no enemy very near us now. The Oude fellows, indeed, come down every day to the *ghat*, but they cannot cross. We hear nothing of the Gwalior troops, and hope they may not have moved.

The Dinapore rebels, as you will hear, are in the Allahabad district, but they have no guns. The Baillie Guard is still holding out, and it is reported can do so for fifteen days longer; may God preserve these poor people, for I am afraid that it will be impossible to send relief from this quarter until reinforcements arrive. The best prospect of an augmentation is this—two thousand of the 78th Highlanders are, this day, half-way between Allahabad and here; and on the 24th three thousand of the 5th Fusiliers landed at Allahabad. Two hundred sick, wounded, and disabled start for Allahabad to-night; and I should say we had about eight thousand Europeans left fit for duty, including the garrison. Guns and ammunition in abundance. You must take a cipher off all these numbers, except the sick. There is a general impression in the bazaar that the rebel cause at Delhi is coming to grief. They are gloomy at Allahabad, but depression is chronic there.

With kind regards to all friends, believe me, yours sincerely,
(Signed) J. W. SHERER.

(True copy) R. NIXON.

Colonel KEITH YOUNG *to Colonel* H. B. HENDERSON.

CAMP BEFORE DELHI, 25*th August.*

'Still outside of Delhi!' you will exclaim in receiving this. Yes, we are on the same old spot, encamped on the parade-ground, with the canal to our rear and the high Ridge overlooking Delhi to our front; but though our position is the same, our approaches to our right front have been slowly but steadily advancing, and when the battering-train arrives—and it ought to be here in five or six days, or even less—we shall be able, I trust, without further loss of time, to bring our heavy mortars and guns to play at a reasonable distance from the city walls.

From what is going on, it seems likely that the intended plan of attack is to erect heavy batteries within about four hundred yards of the walls (and this, from the inequality of the ground, it is found can be done without subjecting our men to much exposure), and when the batteries are ready, to pound away with all our might for twenty-four hours or so. This will make a tolerable breach, but not a very perfect one, owing to the protection afforded to the wall by the glacis; but there seems no doubt that it will be perfectly practicable, and should there be much opposition—which is not anticipated—it will be easily overcome by our men, protected as they will be in their advance to the breach by all the available riflemen in camp. In addition to these we have two hundred more of the 60th Rifles coming over from Meerut to join; they will be a great assistance. It is a first-rate regiment Her Majesty's 60th Rifles, the best, perhaps, we have in camp.

I should tell you that I have no official information of the intended plan of attack, or of course I could say nothing about it; but I feel persuaded that it will be much as I think, unless circumstances occur to modify it—and there is no saying what may not happen any day. Indeed, this very day a large party of the enemy—the spies say some twelve thousand men, with fourteen guns, half of which left yesterday evening and half this morning—started with the avowed intention of getting to our rear, attacking Sonput, and cutting off our supplies; but there is reason to suppose that after all they have gone in the direction of Goorgaon with the intention of not returning at all to Delhi, and in this case their destination may be Gwalior, where the mutineering regiments of that place still remain, or, perhaps, they may wish to push on to Oude and join the disaffected there.

I don't think myself that there is a safer place than Simla, except, perhaps, the Presidency towns. Those living there are, however, troubled with frequent alarms from rumours set about by weak or mischievous people, and, on this account, I wish F. and the boys were at home. As to any real danger at Simla, I cannot think that there is any unless we meet with failure here, and this is a thing never contemplated or thought of by any one of our force from the lowest private upwards.

The mail reached us at the mess (the Staff mess) just after dinner last night, and when we had finished reading our private letters we got one of the party, Sir Theophilus Metcalfe, to read out the principal speeches about the Mutiny that were made on the first arrival of the sad news in both Houses. Lord Ellenborough's was universally applauded. He made a little mistake about the benefit that was to result to our force from cutting off the supply of water furnished to the city by the canal; but in every other point he took a correct view of our position, and his speech was that of a statesman and a soldier.

Mr Vernon Smith, again, showed an utter want of knowledge of the subject he was speaking about, and was received throughout the mess with shouts of derision. It is really lamentable to think that the destinies of this Empire should be in the hands of such a man—that is, if the speech I allude to is to be regarded as a fair specimen of his general knowledge of India. I fear from his style of speaking he could not be aware of the danger this country is in, and that the want of activity, as it strikes us, in not sending troops by Suez, is mainly owing to him. There was one part of his speech that particularly amused us, in which he talked of our being able at least to surround Delhi and storm the mutineers into submission. The truth really is, we are perched upon a ridge of rock about a mile or so from the city, and this we are glad to be able to hold, and keep the enemy from annoying our rear; while the enemy have possession of the bridge of boats, and all the country, consequently, on the left bank up to near Meerut and Allyghur, while on this side of the river they have undisputed control over the whole of the districts from Hansi up to Agra. As to surrounding Delhi, we have some six hundred European Lancers and Dragoons, and the same number of reliable Native Cavalry—a pretty force with which to surround a place like Delhi, a city seven miles round; but one cannot wonder at Mr Smith being so far abroad when it seems that a man like Mr Colvin, the Lieutenant-Governor of Agra, wrote deprecating the idea of General Anson waiting for a siege-train. It was thought, in fact, that we had nothing to do but appear before Delhi and the gates would be opened to us.*

Up to this day we have had one hundred and twenty-four casualties: that is, thirty-seven deaths in action, ten deaths from sickness, and eighty-seven wounded—I mean amongst the officers of this and General Wilson's force.

The enemy appear to have given up attacking us as a bad job; but we must expect to lose a few more when the assault takes place. I don't know the loss that there has been amongst the men, but it must have been very great in proportion to our small numbers.

* A description of Delhi and its fortifications is given in Appendix C.

I don't know whether I mentioned to you in my last that Mr Colvin's head was gone; and I believe he is not right yet. I wish they would send Frere from Sind to succeed him—out and out the best man in India for the appointment; but I see that Grant, the Member of Council in Calcutta, is coming up, so I fear he is to be the man.

You will have particulars probably by this mail of the Cawnpore massacres. We got an account of the Cawnpore one, a day or two ago, from Lieutenant Delafosse of the 53rd Native Infantry, who with three other officers had escaped; but who the three others were he doesn't say—they may, perhaps, have been privates, but he should have given their names. He gives a fearful account of the miseries endured by our poor suffering countrymen and countrywomen at Cawnpore before the compact was made with that treacherous brute, the Nana. For about twelve days all the ladies, and children as well, were exposed without any shelter whatever in the open entrenchment.

Those who are endeavouring at home to malign the officers of this army, and attribute the outbreak to their misbehaviour and want of proper treatment of the Sepoys (Mr Mangles, to wit), would have formed a different estimate on the subject had they, their wives and children, formed a part of this unhappy garrison.

Strange that as far as we know up to the latest accounts my corps (the 50th) has remained altogether staunch, and they are at Nagode, not very far from Jhansi, where they say hellish atrocities were committed. They were always a good corps, the old 50th: I only trust they will remain faithful.

A Movable Column under Nicholson, with two European and two Sikh regiments, some European Lancers and Sikh Horse, and three troops Horse Artillery, have gone to look after this force of the enemy that left Delhi last night and this morning, and will give a good account of them if they come up with them.

Colonel KEITH YOUNG *to his wife.*

CAMP, DELHI CANTONMENTS, *Wednesday, 26th August.*

Really you are very good not to be altogether inoculated by your painfully nervous guests. It is a good thing they are not in our camp, as they would be fancying everything a disaster.

You can cheer them up to-day by telling them that Nicholson has been quite victorious, having captured twelve of the enemy's guns, with all their tents and baggage, and completely routed them: young Low, 9th Cavalry, extra Aide-de-Camp to General Wilson, who was in the fight, returned this morning with the news. I am very sorry to say that two officers are killed—Lieutenant Lumsden of Coke's corps, and Dr Ireland* of the Artillery; and one officer only wounded †—Lieutenant Gabbett, Her Majesty's 61st; and about forty or fifty men on our side killed and wounded, Low says. The enemy's loss is not known yet, but some wounded men were seen being taken into the city this morning accompanied by a few stragglers. The greater number of those who have escaped will not, it is supposed, return to Delhi, but take themselves off to their homes or elsewhere; indeed, the newsletter from the city yesterday said that such was their intention in case they were beaten. The rebels engaged are said to have been principally the Bareilly mutineers commanded by Buktawa Khan Soubahdar, and amongst the things taken was a buggy in which he is supposed to have been conveyed, as he is too fat and heavy to ride.

I told you that Nicholson with his Column marched out very early yesterday morning, and they did not come up with the enemy until nearly four o'clock in the afternoon, whom they found posted in two villages near Nujufghurh; and in one of them, Low says, there was very great opposition—the fighting lasted from about 4 P.M. till near 8 P.M., when the scoundrels bolted in the greatest confusion, throwing away their arms and everything that could hinder their flight. It must have been very trying work to our men, who had had a twenty-mile march, and for three or four hours they must have been exposed to a pitiless, pelting rain; I hope none of them may get sick in consequence, poor fellows. Cattle have gone out to bring in the guns and other things, and probably Nicholson will not return until to-morrow.

Soon after breakfast this morning the wretches in the city, hearing, I suppose, from the fugitives that all our troops must be with Nicholson, came out to attack us on the right front; but

* See page 272.
† Lieutenant Elkington (61st) was also mortally wounded.—H. W. NORMAN.

our guns have soon sent them back again. There are lots of troops and guns, too, in camp to thrash them, in whatever numbers they may come; but they say only about a thousand came out this morning—perhaps they haven't many more left. I wish the siege-train were here, and then we might take advantage of the depression that they must be now suffering under, and go in with very little trouble. I trust there is no reason to think that the 10th Cavalry men have got hold of the train, as Mrs Martin fears: the confiding officers have now had a pretty lesson read them, and have, it would appear, many of them been personal sufferers on the late occasion, the troopers helping themselves to the officers' horses.

By a letter from a man in Her Majesty's 61st to his brother here, it seems that more of the troopers were killed than the *Lahore Chronicle* says. I dare say Mrs Burnside has a copy of the letter, and you should try to see it. It is a most excellent letter; Norman got hold of it for a minute, and came in here and read it to us. Talking of letters, how fortunate you and I are in always getting ours so regularly, and it is really wonderful considering the carelessness of the Post-office people. A letter came here the other day with 'Try Head-Quarters' Camp' written upon it. The address on it was to John Brown or *somebody*, 'Steamer *Simla*,' and it had gone actually to Simla instead of to Calcutta, where the steamer is!

No further word from Havelock or Agra since I last wrote to you. We are quite satisfied here, whatever they may be at Ferozepore, that all is well at both places.

Turnbull, another Aide-de-Camp, the man who used to send the plants, has just returned from Nicholson's camp. Thirteen guns have been taken, and the force returns this evening. The casualties are between fifty and sixty, and no other officers but those I have mentioned.

3.30 P.M., and all quiet.

(*Diary*) *26th August.*—Heard what struck me to be guns in Nicholson's direction, about 4 A.M.; it turned out afterwards to be tumbrels he was destroying. I rode out to the Peinbaree bridge, and on my return found that Low, Aide-de-Camp, had returned with an account of Nicholson having gained a complete victory, taking thirteen guns. The force returned in the evening while we were at dinner, bands playing them in, and cheering to a great extent. Must have been a well-managed business, and only succeeded by Nicholson's determination to advance. The distance about eighteen miles. Not feeling at all well to-day. The brutes from the city out to attack.

Telegram from Camp before Delhi to E. C. BARNES.

UMBALLA, 26*th August.*

It is now 9 A.M., 26th August.—Brigadier-General Nicholson attacked the enemy's force at Nujufghurh yesterday evening (25th) and completely routed them, capturing all their guns, twelve in number. Our loss small; but Lieutenant Lumsden, one of the best officers in the army, was unfortunately killed.

Nicholson left the camp with sixteen guns and two thousand men. The enemy's force was the Bareilly brigade, with the 8th, 13th, and 14th Irregulars.

CAMP, DELHI CANTONMENTS, *Thursday,* 27*th August.*

All Nicholson's Column returned yesterday evening. We went out to see the victorious army march in, bands having been sent just outside the camp to play them in; but they did not reach here until after dark, and we merely heard the music and the cheering at a distance when we were at dinner. The thirteen guns were all safely brought in, and are now in the park. Five of them belonged to Murray-Mackenzie's troop; one had been taken on a previous occasion, so all his guns are now here. Three or four of the guns are of Native manufacture, apparently 3- or 4-pounders, and very pretty ones they are; they would do to send home to put in St James's Park.

I am glad to tell you that we were misinformed yesterday about Dr Ireland, who was reported dead by everybody. It seems that he is only dangerously wounded; and when you hear what his wound is you won't be much surprised at word having come in that he was dead. A ball from a shrapnell struck him in the left eye, coming out at his right ear; but both Doctors Mackinnon and Mactier told me that they had seen him, and that there is no reason why he should not recover. The eye, of course, is gone.*

* See p. 272.

1. Impressions from the King of Delhi's Seals (The King was taken prisoner by Major W. S. R. Hodson).
2. Cossid or Secret Letter from Delhi. (see page 243 and appendix I. for translation).

I made another mistake yesterday in telling you that it was the Bareilly troops Nicholson was engaged with; it seems that it was with the Neemuch brigade, who had the Kotah contingent and some Oude troops with them. The Bareilly brigade were behind, and only came up at the close of the fight, and then ran away; they had left the city first, but had allowed the Neemuch people to go ahead of them. There seems no doubt now that word was taken back to the city by the fugitives that all our troops were out with Nicholson, and the city people were, I suppose, under the full impression that they had little more to do than to come up to camp and plunder it, after killing the few to be found there. In the first crowds from the city lots of women and unarmed men were seen coming out, and from what I hear there must have been a great slaughter amongst those who attempted to take the batteries; but there has been no newsletter that I have heard of from the city to-day. We had some thirty or forty casualties, too; no officers that I am aware of. Almost all the loss in Nicholson's fight the day before yesterday was in Coke's corps; and there was another officer wounded besides those I mentioned—Lieutenant Elkington,* Her Majesty's 61st, dangerously.

Touching the newsletters and the plan of Delhi you ask me for, I fear there is no chance of getting any of the former that come from the city, for they are, or ought to be, all filed, and in fact, with very few exceptions, they are Native letters, and there are not very many of them; the news is generally taken down by word of mouth from one of the spies. I can get you lots of letters, like the one I now send you, from Eden and others. Havelock's and General Neill's are written on little scraps of paper, but these there will be no chance of getting, as they will be considered strictly official documents. Who should come while I was writing but Hodson, and I mentioned to him your wish, when he said, 'Oh, I'll give you one;' and he went and brought the enclosed little Persian *chit*.† I have no translation of it, but I will make you one when I come up to Simla. Hodson says this was brought out in a very ingenious way: two pieces of cloth being stitched together so as to imitate tape, and then this wrapped up in them, the manufactured tape being used to fasten the buttons of a jacket. These letters from Eden, and others of a similar kind, are generally

* See note, page 240. † For translation, see Appendix I.

put in the hollow of a stick or sewn in the sole of a shoe. The map of Delhi and our position I am much afraid I can't get down here. Becher was to have one copied for me, but his only man that does them has so much work that I don't like to ask him; but if George Hall's is a good plan of our position, and his wife will lend it to you for a day or two, I have no doubt Becher will let Mr Lawrie copy it for you, and I am sure he will do it well. Let me know about this, and I dare say I shall be able to get a plan of some kind for you down here if there isn't one at Simla: I rather think Mrs Arthur Becher has one, which might be copied. When we go into Delhi I will get you some mementos of the place.

The *bheestie* was delighted to get his letter; he often asks me how *Toony Baba* is, and this morning after doing so he asked also after *Gooda* (as he calls Artie), hoping he was well. I enclose a letter from Soobhan.

No further word from Agra or Lucknow. Weather getting much cooler here. Colonel Pelham Burn has arrived in camp from Mussoorie; Mrs Burn, he says, is very well.

3.30 P.M., and all quiet; hardly a shot fired from the city to-day.

(*Diary*) 27*th August*.—It seems they were under the impression in the city that all our troops had left the camp with Nicholson, and out the wretches came in great numbers, expecting to take the right batteries; but they met with a warm reception, and must have lost a great many. Went and had a look at the captured guns this morning; five of them belong to Mackenzie's troop, and some are of Native make, 3- or 4-pounders.

CAMP, DELHI CANTONMENTS, *Friday, 28th August.*

The Markunda River has risen, I hear, which is the cause of the dâk having been late again. It has bothered the siege-train too, I understand, this rise in the river, and very likely the train may not be here after all until the 2nd September; but the General says he does not want it till then, or even later, as he can do nothing till the Artillerymen arrive from Meerut, and they will not be here until the 3rd or 4th. By the last accounts all the guns were over the Markunda, but there were still several *hackeries* to cross, but these there would be little difficulty about. When once across the Markunda the train ought to reach here in five days, there being lots of fresh bullocks here that will be sent out to assist them in if necessary.

I can scarcely tell you what I think of ——— and her sage opinion that we are all a *pâjee* (stupid) set here. I fear if some of our men heard of it they would give her a good ducking in the canal, and perhaps serve out her husband in the same way. We might perhaps have taken Delhi that time that Greathed wrote up to his wife the plan of assault, but it was rather a doubtful affair, and, at any rate, there is nothing to blame the Army for in not taking the city—if there is any blame at all it must rest with the late Generals; the Army has behaved as well as any Army possibly could have done.

After I wrote to you yesterday there was a letter from Mr Colvin to Mr Greathed saying that all was right at Agra, and the Gwalior mutineers still at Gwalior; and Havelock had gained another victory, but not finding himself strong enough to advance on Lucknow, he had returned to Cawnpore to await reinforcements. This is unfortunate; but Lucknow is said to be capable of holding out for some months, and their position was so good that they were almost secure from the enemy's guns. They will not, however, have long to wait, as the Dinapore mutineers had been disposed of, and the corps that had gone after them (three) were proceeding up to Cawnpore, Mr Colvin said. He also mentioned that Lord Elgin had come to Calcutta and brought with him some more of the China force, all of which was to come; and some gun-boats, one of which was probably up as far as Benares by this time. The Native regiments at Ghazeepore and some other station near had been disarmed. Altogether the news is considered by us in camp to be very good.

(*Diary*) 28*th August.*—Very cool, pleasant morning, and much the better of a good night's rest, but still not the thing. Hard at work writing; in the evening go out rather late to see Robertson, 8th, who has been very ill with fever, and is still suffering much from the effects of it. Hodson going out to-night to see if enemy are now at Nujufghurh.

CAMP, DELHI CANTONMENTS, *Saturday*, 29*th August.*

I am glad to hear this morning that the siege-train had got across the Markunda all right, and I suppose is by this time at Kurnaul. Some five hundred *hackeries* came in here this morning with shot and shell—such a string along the road! I was glad to see lots of 10-inch shells; and four mortars are coming for them with the train.

I have just seen a letter from Mr Colvin to Greathed, Agra the 22nd, when all was well there; and news from Cawnpore of 17th. Waiting for troops from below, which were shortly expected to advance on Lucknow; and no fears appear to be entertained for the safety of Lucknow, the previous advance on which has had the effect of withdrawing the enemy and enabling our people to lay in another month's supply of provisions.

I can imagine your having lovely weather in Simla now. This morning it was delightful here, quite like an October morning; the sun is hot, but it is bearable in tents.

We hear nothing of Sir Colin Campbell being Commander-in-Chief beyond what is in the *Bombay Extra*.

3.30 P.M., and all quiet. No news from the city except that they are terribly put out about their defeat by Nicholson.

We still hear reports of Sir Henry Lawrence being alive, and of one hundred and fifty ladies, &c., having escaped from Cawnpore to Calcutta. We must soon know the truth. The Gwalior people were quiet. General Outram appointed to command the Dinapore division. Lord Elgin had reached Calcutta on the 8th. This, I think, is all the Agra news of importance.

There is no doubt of Sir Colin Campbell coming out as Commander-in-Chief, for Norman has just had a letter from him written at Suez, and long ere this he must be in Calcutta. It seems that a telegraphic despatch reached London the day after the mail left with news from Delhi up to the 11th June, and other places of nearly similar dates. Sir Colin was asked to come out, which he did at a day's notice, and caught up the mail. Colonel Mansfield, formerly Her Majesty's 53rd, comes as Chief of the Staff; Captain Alison, Military Secretary; and Sir David Baird and another Captain Alison (son of the historian) as Aides-de-Camp. It is satisfactory to think that they had got intelligence of the state of affairs in

India as they actually were, and no doubt they will exert themselves now in good earnest to send out troops; and most likely some are by this time in Bombay, overland.

All is quiet here to-day; and I am glad to see that it is getting very cloudy again. We want more rain, or it will soon be very hot again.

Hodson has gone out. He left last night after mess with a party of Cavalry to reconnoitre and find out what had become of the Bareilly brigade, which some of the villagers said was still out near Nujufghurh, where Nicholson's fight took place the other day. Hodson writes in that they are not out there, or anywhere in the neighbourhood; and it seems not improbable that they have walked off altogether. Hodson still remains out, looking about him.

I send a letter for the old *khansamah*, which will rejoice his aged heart. Harriott sent it to me yesterday afternoon, having paid the twenty rupees as requested.

All was well at Meerut. The Rifles and Artillery only left on the morning of the 27th, but I believe they will be here on the 2nd or 3rd notwithstanding.

Daly, who is just now in our tent, is pretty well, but has not the use of his arm yet; I think he will go up to Simla after Delhi is taken. Young Walker of the Engineers, who married Brigadier Scott's daughter, has been very unwell, but is better to-day and out of all danger; he is living in the same tent with Daly, and is a particularly nice fellow. He was wounded about six weeks ago. That poor man, Dr Ireland, is getting on wonderfully well. Major Palmer has come down here from Mussoorie; I have not seen him yet.

Hodson has just returned, and reports the mutineers to have returned to Delhi; he has brought in a couple of ammunition wagons of the enemy's from Nujufghurh.

Near 4 P.M., and all quiet.

(*Diary*) 29*th August*.—Take a short ride, and meet lots of carts coming in with shells—some five hundred carts, they say. Glad to see 10-inch shells. The siege-train to be in on 2nd. Hodson returned. No signs of enemy; supposed to have returned to Delhi. Norman has a letter from Sir Colin Campbell—positively coming as Commander-in-Chief, and Mansfield as Chief of Staff. Short ride in the evening. The band playing in the lines. Firing as we were at dinner.

CAMP, DELHI CANTONMENTS, *Sunday, 30th August.*

There is little to tell you since yesterday. All is very quiet to-day; but last night there was a great deal of firing going on—it commenced about dinner-time. It seems the firing was our driving in one of the enemy's advanced posts to allow of our working parties going on with preparations for the batteries that are to be erected when the siege-train arrives. A good deal of opposition was expected, but they made very little, not being able to get the people from the city to come to their assistance; and our people made a very good night's work of it. I was, however, very sorry to hear that two of the 60th Rifles were killed, poor men; we can little afford to lose them, but it is a wonder we did not have more casualties, for the firing continued more or less all night. The enemy had some twenty killed.

The siege-train was to leave Kurnaul this morning, and will be here on the 2nd September if they make forced marches, otherwise not till the 4th, which is the day, I believe, that the Rifles and Artillerymen are expected from Meerut; and the General says he does not want the train till they come. A week after the arrival of the train will, I hope, see us safe inside Delhi.

We have very nice weather now, but the rain continues to keep off, which is, perhaps, just as well, for those who know Delhi, say, that the later the rains are, the less the sickness. Who was it said that there had been so many deaths from fever in Her Majesty's 8th or 61st—Nicoll, was it not? I haven't heard of a single death from fever; but there was a great deal of cholera in the 61st a short time ago. Since their return they have been encamped on a different piece of ground on the opposite side of the Nullah, and they have been comparatively healthy notwithstanding the fatigue and exposure they suffered when out with Nicholson. They were out two whole days exposed to the sun, and marching or fighting nearly the whole time in the intervening night; the only place they had to lie upon was the cold, damp ground, having themselves been exposed for some hours to heavy rain, to say nothing of having to wade occasionally through pools of water waist-deep. The fever here, fortunately, though very prevalent, is said to be of an extremely mild kind, and a little quinine generally sets a person up again.

Letters in from Agra of the 24th and 26th with accounts from Cawnpore of the 19th, and Allahabad 15th. As I told you, Lord Elgin had reached Calcutta with the Frigates (steam) *Shannon* and *Pearl:* one of them had one thousand Marines* on board, and the other soldiers. A Naval Brigade was coming up the country under Captain Peel, R.N. Havelock had fallen in with the 42nd Native Infantry, and nearly destroyed them; all well at Cawnpore, but no direct news from Lucknow. The expedition that went from Agra to Hatrass had been most successful; a large party of the enemy were attacked, after Hatrass had been settled, near Coel, and completely routed—four hundred were killed on the field, and our party then returned. We lost three or four killed, and a few wounded: of the former, Mr Tandy of the Volunteer Horse, I suppose; and of the latter, Longueville Clarke. Altogether the news seems very satisfactory; and if all continues well at Lucknow till the troops from below reach Cawnpore and enable Havelock to move out to their relief, we shall soon have matters on a different footing again.

Near 4 P.M., and all quiet, not a gun firing on our side or theirs.

Do you see Chamberlain in Orders as *pucka* Adjutant-General? But he does not intend to keep it.

CAMP, DELHI CANTONMENTS, *Monday, 31st August.*

I received your letter of the 28th yesterday evening at the mess. Arthur Becher got his also, and so did several others. You say that your letter was a very shabby and untidy one; but it didn't strike me to be so. I thought it just what it ought to be, except that I should have liked it to be a little longer; but, as Sam Weller says, 'the perfection of letter writing is to leave off always so as to make the person to whom you write wish for more!'—and this, I think, I should always do with yours, however long they were. I took Arthur Becher to task yesterday for allowing his wife to write to him crossed letters; the one he was reading was

* This story as to the 'thousand Marines' was untrue.—H. W. NORMAN.

so, and indeed they usually are. This letter, I fear, will be a very untidy production, for I can hardly see to write. It came on to rain about an hour ago, and is pouring down in torrents. We are obliged to keep the *chicks* down on account of the flies, and the consequence is that the darkness in the tent is something like what you describe and complain of when you have such cloudy and rough weather at Simla.

The rain here had been brewing up for some days past, and there is every prospect of our having a deluge of it now for several hours to come. We are rather glad of it in camp, and it will do a great deal of good, we hope, in driving off what sickness is still flying about; and it will effectually prevent the enemy from leaving the city for some days to come to try and bother our rear, should such be their intention. And now that the siege-train is well in the *pucka* road, the rain won't stop it; it was to have been at Paniput this morning, and will not reach here until the 4th or 5th September. The Rifles and Artillery are to be here about the same time. It is a pity we have had to wait so long for the train, and I don't know who is in fault. They say, I believe, that carriage couldn't be procured, and so, in fact, nobody is in fault; but it seems strange, for the siege-train was ordered to be got ready about two months ago.

There has been nothing further from Agra or Cawnpore since I wrote to you yesterday, but I hope in a day or two we shall hear of Havelock having got reinforcements moved on to Lucknow. Troops appear to be arriving fast in Calcutta and Bombay. I told you of the two steamers full at the former, and one at the latter place; and I see by a Bombay paper that reached here to-day, of the 12th August (it has come very quickly), that a vessel which left England in May for the Mauritius, with the 4th Regiment, was expected to come to Bombay—and she ought to be there by this time.

There is no particular news from the city, but the wretches inside are said to be in a sad plight, and there is a rumour in camp that they are anxious to obtain terms; of course no terms would be given but unconditional surrender. It is to be hoped, however, that there may be no surrender, as it would be a most puzzling thing in such a case to know how to deal with them. There are said to be now about ten thousand Infantry and four thousand

Cavalry in the city and the environs; at one time they are supposed to have numbered about forty thousand altogether.

What do you think of the Umballa business? It seems rather to have been sharp practice, that adopted with the mutineers; but with such brutes as they have shown themselves to be no treatment of them can be too bad.

There are some Government General Orders in the paper I spoke of the 12th August, and I see that Mackinnon is made an Acting Superintending Surgeon. Curzon's leave is also in Orders, and it does not read very well.

The box of books arrived all right; some have been made over to the sick and wounded, and some Mactier (who has taken charge of them) has kept for our edification. The letter you speak of from Mrs Carlyon must be a very interesting one. Poor Goldney, I hope he is safe; and with his knowledge of the language and of Natives he is very likely to have escaped.

(*Diary*) 31*st August*.—Take a ride early this morning up to the left flank—what a wretchedly dirty place it is! Came on to rain soon after breakfast, and poured down in torrents for three or four hours. Nothing going on. An attack was spoken of, but none came off.

Captain EDEN to Colonel KEITH YOUNG.

JEYPORE, 31*st August*.

MY DEAR COLONEL,—I am not in the way of giving you later intelligence than that conveyed to Delhi by Mr Colvin from the southward and eastward. We are all quiet here, and the Mohurram has passed off without disturbance in Jeypore; I was very apprehensive about it.

The Joudhpore Legion mutinied on 23rd, and have, it is said, the Adjutant, Sergeant, and families prisoners, having looted the cantonments. A company sent by Colonel Hall to check some *Goojurs*, went off to Aboo, stirred up forty others on duty there, and, in a dense fog, fired on the Erinpoorah barracks and Colonel Hall's house, but would seem to have been driven off the hill again. Lawrence's son was wounded in the hip slightly; all rest safe. One hundred and fifty of the Legion on duty at

Nussereebad disarmed; the two hundred men of the 12th Bombay Native Infantry, you have no doubt heard, were disarmed, or most of them, at last.—Yours, EDEN.

Colonel H. B. HENDERSON *to Colonel* KEITH YOUNG.

LONDON, GRESHAM HOUSE, 8*th August.*

By the time this reaches you, you will have proof of the anxiety here to preserve India. There will be, including those now in India or near at hand, between fifty and sixty thousand troops, all European; and more yet will follow if necessary. England is determined to assist you to the utmost; and if fresh outbreaks and defections do not arise, and the feeling against us does not break out into actual enmity on *every* hand in the East, we shall yet trust that you will hold your own till ample means reach you, not only to avenge the past, but to put things on firmer footing than before. But the loss and destruction meantime we dare not think of.

The fall of Delhi we hope to hear of by the coming mail, and that the inhuman wretches have been taught a fearful lesson. It is strange to hear the mildest here talk of what they would do to the monsters. One thing mentioned the other day will show the horror with which the cruelties are here thought of. 'The military authorities ought to flog every rebel, before blowing from a gun or shooting or hanging—nay, again to introduce the *knout*—not in cruel revenge, but to mark the sense entertained of the unheard-of atrocities committed on women and children, and to show that mere death by a soldier's hand is too good for such monsters.' This was from a man who is the meekest Christian I know. I say *Amen* to it; and if we are to hang or shoot all ringleaders and rebels, I say also, let them first be flogged and disgraced.

I hear that the Oude family here are loud in their protestations of innocence: but their feelings creep out. The young Prince not many evenings ago told one of our Army that the row was all right, and that he wished he were in India to share it! The police are watching them.

It is strange that up to the latest advices the 8th and 21st Native Infantry, which formed the 1st and 2nd battalions of the

9th—my old corps—had not broken out. True, they are both beside European regiments, and therefore probably quiet; but even their quietness is pleasing to me, though it is thirty years since I was with them.

I have some business letters to write, and must conclude this stupid and anxious one. Do not think I am fearful of the *result* for India; no one here is this, but we are thinking of you all.

LONDON, GRESHAM HOUSE, 21*st August.*

Most unexpectedly it has fallen to my lot to take the initiative in getting up a large public meeting at the Mansion House, which took place yesterday, and I am on the Committee sitting to-day to carry out the wishes of the meeting. I have no time to write to you except very hurriedly.

I have no letter by the last mail from any of you, but know how much you are occupied; and I see in the *Times* a short extract from a letter from you to an official at Sealkote, saying you were well before Delhi on the 24th June, and thought the city might be carried in a few hours were it not thought prudent to wait for reinforcements.

The hurried meeting at the Mansion House got up under so many difficulties—the Lord Mayor's friends and all public men being out of town—went off admirably, and to-day all the mayors throughout the United Kingdom are called on by the Lord Mayor to get up meetings. No doubt there will be a universal display of sympathy from home for the fearful calamity which has overtaken you all in India. The Lord Mayor has to-day written to Lord Canning announcing this, and sending as the first-fruits of subscriptions £2000, or some such sum, to begin with. The Governor-General is addressed for this purpose, that the people here may hope their contributions will be well applied. There are full accounts in the *Times* of to-day of yesterday's meeting; but I have cut out and enclose a short notice, abridged by the reporter of the *Daily Telegraph*, of the proceedings at the Mansion House. The Court of Directors, I may say, from what Sir James Melville has stated to me, will do their best. All the large firms have come forward handsomely.

You have had hard work and much fighting at Delhi. Your

army has behaved admirably. We hear of General Barnard's rumoured death, and are in dreadful anxiety for further intelligence.

Colonel H. B. HENDERSON *to Mrs* KEITH YOUNG, *Simla.*

LONDON, GRESHAM HOUSE, 21*st August.*

I must hastily write a few lines to tell you how anxiously we are thinking of you at this time of trouble and danger. All yesterday and the greater part of to-day I have been engaged at the Mansion House, and am going there again immediately, being one of the busiest in the general subscription which has been put on foot in London and throughout the United Kingdom for the sufferers by the late Mutiny in India. Never has an event for centuries aroused such feeling and sympathy in England. I have enclosed to your husband an abstract of the meeting which took place at the Mansion House yesterday for their relief, and to-day the Lord Mayor is sending out to Lord Canning £2000, the immediate first-fruits of the collection. It fell upon me to get up the meeting, which the Lord Mayor and Lady Mayoress most kindly took in hand, and managed the thing beautifully. It would show to India how much it is cared for by all at home.—Believe me ever, your most affectionate Father, H. B. H.

CHAPTER XII.

SIEGE OF DELHI (*continued*)—ARRIVAL OF SIEGE-TRAIN.

Colonel KEITH YOUNG *to his wife.*

CAMP, DELHI CANTONMENTS, *Tuesday, 1st September.*

The siege-train was to leave Paniput this morning, and say that it arrives on the 4th, a very few days ought to suffice to put the guns and mortars in battery, and then it will not take long to settle the wretched city. The troops—Rifles and Artillery—from Meerut should reach here the same day as the siege-train, as they are coming a short cut by Paniput, instead of by Kurnaul as originally intended. What lots of troops there will be here soon, for the Cashmere contingent is also on its way to this place, and will arrive, I believe, in a few days; and amongst other horrible implements of war there are two 13-inch mortars coming from Umritsur, with a great number of shells—immense, large things —sufficient to demolish the whole of the largest building they may fall upon, and these mortars carry an immense distance. We have nothing here now larger than 8-inch; there are, however, plenty of 10-inch with the siege-train, and these are most formidable in their effects.

There is another letter from Agra to-day of the 27th, but no fresh news, just a recapitulation of what I have told you already, except I do not think I mentioned that Captain Peel, with his Naval Brigade, was bringing up a 68-pounder. What a grand thing it would be if they could get it up to Cawnpore in time to be of use in destroying the wretched mutineers before Lucknow!

Arthur Becher told me to-day that ——— had got some other cause for alarm, having heard that some hill Raja or other had written down to the King of Delhi to ask what reward would be given for murdering all the Europeans in the hills; and ——— also writes, I believe, to Norman, for he told me that the Persians were in full march on Candahar. He is really a wretched alarmist, and it's Arthur Becher's opinion that he ought to be sent away from Simla. Of course the story of the Raja is some concoction of his own; and as to the Persians, accounts have been received of a directly contrary nature, and that they are evacuating Herat.

I am sorry to hear of Mrs Greathed being so unwell. I often see Greathed; he told me of his wife's illness. He and Sandie Robertson are living together; the latter has had a very smart attack of fever, but is recovering.

One of the Peshawar regiments has, you see, 'gone' at last; it must make Mrs P—— very anxious.

Mactier is much obliged for the letter you sent; he still calls this a 'weary, weary' world! I hope Sir Colin Campbell will make him his surgeon.

(*Diary*) 1*st September.*—Contented myself with walking up and down the street, and at work all day at that Ferozepore syce-driver's court-martial. Late in going out, but managed to get as far as the burial-ground to show the *mistry* the situation of poor Chester's grave; bricks are being collected to build a tomb. A lovely moonlight night.

From Mr BARTLE FRERE *to Colonel* KEITH YOUNG.

KURRACHEE, 1*st September.*

MY DEAR KEITH YOUNG,—It was only when I was reading over a second time this very interesting letter from Arthur, of which this is an extract, that I observed the message to you. I have sent the original to my wife, and give you the whole of what he says of the affair at Aboo, in case his letter to you should have miscarried. We have letters a day or two later from Ahmedabad and Deesa, which describe all quiet there and at Aboo; but the dâks from Neemuch and Nussereebad to Deesa had been plundered. Five men of our 12th Native Infantry have been hanged at Nussereebad. The 2nd Cavalry at Neemuch are in a very ticklish state.

You will see by the papers all is quiet again at Kolapoor, and in the south Mahratta country; but there has been partial disaffection and three executions in Maclean's 29th Native Infantry at Dharwar, and Jacob has executed a large number of the 27th at Kolapoor. You will not be surprised at Maughan's little failure. All quiet at Joudhpore on the 27th August, and no certain intelligence of the whereabouts of the mutineers.

Is it any use sending you or Mrs Keith Young the Sind papers for the sake of the extracts they give, or can I be of any other use to her or you?—Yours ever sincerely, B. H. FRERE.

Extract from a Letter from Mr ARTHUR YOUNG *to Mr* BARTLE FRERE, *dated Aboo, 22nd August.*

Yesterday morning the guard here, who had been joined by some men of the Company at the foot of the hill, commenced firing into Colonel Hall's (officer commanding) house, but luckily without hitting anybody; and Hall got his family out a back way to the Lawrence School, the compound of which adjoins his. I thought the firing was only the unloading of their damp muskets, till a servant of Hall's ran over to tell us to go to the Lawrence School; we found nearly all the residents there, and the whole had soon joined except Mrs Mildmay, and Dr Touch of the 83rd. It was a very foggy morning, and we could see nothing of them, so Hall and I went with six Europeans to try and find Mrs Mildmay, and on getting to her house found it quite empty; but she had been concealed in the Odeypoor Vakeel's house, and came to the School soon after we got back.

Near the Mildmays' house we came upon a party of the Sepoys at the Agency Office, where they were helping themselves to ammunition; but when they came out we could only fire at the place where we heard them. They fired a few harmless shots at us, and went off down the hill where we could not follow them, having left only about eight men to take care of all the families at the School. The men at the barracks could not help us then, as they were attacked by a much larger party, and had also a great number of women and children to protect.

General Lawrence's son was shot in the thigh, but is, I trust, in no danger; Hall's *moonshee* shot through the arm—and that is all the injury to any of our people, thank God. I don't know how the Europeans in the barracks escaped, for the walls are covered with bullet-marks, and the soldiers were in bed when the great volley was fired. They took one wounded prisoner, who will be hanged, I fancy, to-day. We found a dead *tattoo* by the office, but the rider escaped, I hear.

I have written to Keith (from whom I heard on the 20th, and enclose his letter) by Deesa and Omercote, as the Erinpoorah line is stopped. I left Erinpoorah on five days' leave on the 20th, and, up to the hour of the mutiny, we all had perfect faith in the loyalty of our men; and we hear for certainty that it all originated here, and at the foot of the hill, so I trust some of our men at Erinpoorah may keep true and save our adjutant and two European sergeants, with the families of the latter, who had, in our fancied security, been allowed to go to Erinpoorah.

There was a Havildar's party of the 17th Bombay Native Infantry over the Commissariat stores near the barracks; they did not join the mutineers, but rendered no assistance, and dressed and loaded without orders. They have been disarmed.

Colonel KEITH YOUNG *to his wife.*

CAMP, DELHI CANTONMENTS, *Wednesday, 2nd September.*

I haven't a word of news of any importance to give you from here. There are several letters from the city, all telling the same story of divided counsels, internal dissensions, and troops running away. No doubt there is some truth in these reports, but I am become rather sceptical of them; and I fear if we wait here till all the mutineers bolt, or the powder and caps are expended (for this is another cry), we shall have to wait a very long time. Our siege-train, when it is once in our batteries, will have more effect than anything else in changing the state of affairs in the city. I am glad to say it is to be here the day after to-morrow, and the Rifles and other troops come with it, so there will be little delay on its arrival in commencing the grand operations.

Colonel Hogge (do you remember poor Colonel Chester's jokes?) came in this morning, having left the train at Lussowlie, and an escort has been ordered to go out to-night to meet it. Hogge gives a very pleasant account of affairs at Meerut; he says their band plays as usual, and that ladies go out driving on the *mall* in their carriages.

Poor old General Hewitt! He had a valuable pair of carriage

horses that he gave upwards of two thousand rupees for, and his coachman walked off with the best of the two a short time ago and rode into Delhi on it.

I mentioned ——— setting about a report that the Persians were in full march to Candahar; by this post he will hear that Arthur Becher got a letter to-day from Captain Lumsden from Candahar, the 15th August, to say that the Persians had actually evacuated Herat, according to treaty. You might tell this to ———, as the news is interesting and very favourable.

Do you remember Mr Lane, the good archer? He is in our camp to-day, and came to call a little while ago on Mactier. His wife, he told me, is at Lahore, but is going home this cold weather. He is doing duty with the Jheend Raja's troops at Lussowlie, and came in here with a convoy of carts with stores.

——— came this morning to tell me that he was anxious to get posted to the Guide Cavalry, but at the same time he would not like to stop in the plains long as he was so subject to fever. Just the sort of person for the Guide Cavalry, who have sometimes to be in their saddles day and night in all weathers. I told Daly ——— was a candidate, and he laughed at the idea of such a man being foisted upon him.

Poor Mrs ———! How I laughed when I read what she said about no one of our party escaping from Delhi when once we went into it; the general expectation is that there will be little or no loss in taking the place.

What a fearful example appears to have been made of the 51st at Peshawar! I should think that this would have the effect of keeping the 64th and other corps there quiet. I think, from what I hear, that we did not behave very well at Umballa.

Near 4 P.M. Mactier has just got a letter from Agra of 28th August; all well there. No further news from Cawnpore or Lucknow, but all well at both places by the latest accounts.

CAMP, DELHI CANTONMENTS, *Thursday, 3rd September.*

I got your letter of the 31st August early this morning, and am so glad to find that the Mohurram has passed off without any disturbance; but it is not likely that the Mahomedan population would venture to kick up a row.

Nothing going on since I wrote to you yesterday. The scoundrels in the city are very quiet, contenting themselves with firing a few shots occasionally; but it is reported that they have no intention of coming out to attack us again.

I enclose rather an amusing letter of yesterday's date that Becher has had copied for me, and if the account given in it is to be depended upon, the state of those in the city cannot be a very enviable one. Although exaggerated, I have no doubt there is a considerable deal of truth in the story of their dissensions and of the rows about pay. A spy who came out of the city this morning tells me they have heard of the reinforcements and guns that are coming for us from up above, and are in consequence very much cast down; they make out our force now expected to be very much larger than it really is, but this is always the case with natives. They are expecting reinforcements also themselves, the city people say, both from the Punjab and from below, but there seems no chance of any reaching them from any quarter: the only troops they could have got were those from Gwalior, and were they to start at once they couldn't possibly reach them for another fortnight or more, before which Delhi must be ours; but by the latest accounts from Gwalior the mutineers had no immediate intention of leaving.

The siege-train is expected in to-morrow morning, and with it also the Meerut detachments; and I suppose it will take some three or four days after the train reaches to get the guns in position.

I am very sorry to say that there is a very sad report about Holmes and Mrs Holmes, and I much fear that it is true; they are said both to have been murdered, and the doctor of the regiment also, when they were at dinner. I only hope there may be some mistake; but we have heard it from more than one quarter. You will see the account probably in one of the next Bombay papers you get.*

The old 50th and Joe Hampton were all right on the 1st August.† Becher had a monthly present state of the regiment this morning of that date, signed by Colonel Hampton himself; it is very wonderful the regiment behaving so well—not a single desertion during the preceding month of July, and only one Sepoy

---

* Major Holmes was Commandant of the 12th Irregular Cavalry, and with his wife was murdered by mutineers at Segowlee.—H. W. NORMAN.
† See Appendix D.

in the return entered as 'absent without leave.' All the rest of the corps are satisfactorily accounted for, and about seven hundred were present with the Headquarters of the regiment at Nagode.

The 31st Native Infantry also (Norman's corps) appear to be all right at Saugar. You may have seen a story in the paper, of the regiment having behaved so very well in attacking the mutineers, and none of their European officers being with them. It seems they had been expressly ordered into the Fort at Saugar by Brigadier Sage, and he threatened to put them all in arrest when they made a request to be allowed to go and join their men. Norman got a letter from his regiment this morning about it; he is quite delighted at the good conduct of the corps.

You complain of your pens, but I think you cannot be so badly off as I am. I have been trying in vain to mend one to my satisfaction, and have been obliged at last to take to writing with the back of one, which I find answers about as well as the best pen I can make.

I have been reading Nicholson's despatch giving an account of his fight the other day; it is a very good one, and in plain language. He praises all commanding officers except Lieutenant-Colonel ———, who, it seems, said his men were tired and couldn't go on, and threw other impediments in the way of advancing. Nicholson speaks of the men in the highest terms.

Near 4 P.M., and all quiet.

Copy of a NEWSLETTER *from the City of* DELHI *by a paid* SPY.

2nd September.

Yesterday great tumult took place in the Palace on account of the pay of the troops not being distributed. Two companies of the rebels surrounded the King's house, and the King, being informed of this, came out before these troops. The Soubahdars requested His Majesty to distribute the pay of the army. His Majesty said, in reply, he had neither invited the rebel troops nor did he expect anything from them; and, after all, he had no money that he could pay them. This altercation continued for a long time, and at last Selemshah Ressaldar, who had returned from furlough, persuaded these Soubahdars to cease from making a tumult. The King then said to the Soubahdars that forty thousand rupees were ready—they might take them; but they replied that this sum of money was not sufficient. On this His Majesty offered to give one hundred and one gold mohurs which he had received from Bareilly as a *nurzur;* but the Soubahdars returned the same answer as before. At last His Majesty said to them that they might take the jewels of the Begum (or the King's wife of the highest rank); and, having said this, he took up a small embroidered carpet which was spread under his chair and threw it down before them. After this all the officers of rank —His Majesty's servants—shed tears, and took the Soubahdars away from his presence. The fact is, that great altercations and disputes are going on about the pay of the rebel troops; if this state of the pay-question continues, God alone can protect the city and the Palace.

Yesterday, the first half of the night, the Delhi rebel troops remained present in the Morcha as guards. For the last half of the night the Neemuch troops were sent to relieve them, but the Delhi troops said that they would not suffer the fugitives— that is, the Neemuch troops that had fled away from the battle-field near Nujufghurh—to relieve them. This altercation continued for about two hours, and at last they came from words to blows, and blood was shed on both sides. The Bareilly troops, having heard this, sent some regiments and Sowars from amongst themselves to the scene of quarrel; they stopped the contending parties from fighting any more, separated them from each other, and sent their own troops to the Morcha.

The Chief of Bullubghur has sent a petition to the King, stating that with His Majesty's favour he has established *Mohurram Sabells* (or shops in streets, wherein sherbet vessels are laid on benches for the use of all Mahomedans who may feel thirst on the way in the month of Mohurram) with great pomp; that he has embraced the Mahomedan religion, and has become a disciple of Mezamoodeen, son of Ralai Sahub, and that he will shortly arrive in Delhi and will eat the food remaining on the King's table after the dinner is over.

From a trustworthy letter it appears that the Maharajah of Gwalior has taken three regiments of Native Infantry, and some cavalry corps from the Moorar cantonments at Gwalior, into his own service.

In consequence of the inundation of the Chumbal, the intended

(DELHI.) MOTEE MUSJID,
or Pearl Mosque; inside the Palace.

bridge on the river could not be constructed. It is difficult for the rebel troops to cross the Chumbal.

(True translation.)

(Signed) {
W. S. R. HODSON (*Lieut.*), Asst. Qr.-Master-General.
A. BECHER, Qr.-Master-General of the Army.
}

Colonel KEITH YOUNG *to his wife.*

CAMP, DELHI CANTONMENTS, *Friday, 4th September.*

Another grand arrival this morning, or rather during the night, was the siege-train. I had intended to get up early to see it come in, but except a few carts all had reached camp long before daybreak. It would have been a pretty fine sight the large, heavy guns and mortars, each with a couple of elephants harnessed to them; and they walked along as if they had only a little child's small cart to pull, I'm told. The Rifles and Artillerymen are a march behind, it being thought desirable not to hurry them as they will not be required for a day or two, as a few preparations are necessary before the guns can be placed in battery.

The 11th is now the favourite day for the attack, and it is the anniversary of Lord Lake's successful assault some fifty years or more ago.* I fear the entry of our troops into the city will not be so bloodless a one as his was for the wretched inhabitants; and, if there is much opposition offered, few will stand much chance of their lives.

They are talking at last of appointing Prize Agents, but I do not know yet who they will be, or how many of them. I have written to-day to Mr Philipe to ask him if he can lay his hand upon anything in the office bearing on the question. There is no certainty of any prize-money being allowed, and at any rate I imagine it will only be such property of the King or the rest of the Royal Family that may be found in the Palace; and I dare say there will be lots of pickings to be found there.

George Hall was over here this morning, and he showed me a letter he had received through Arthur Butter from the old doctor. I am truly glad indeed to hear of the Carnegys being safe. Still

* See Appendix F.

good reports of the 50th. Poor old Colonel Hampton, I trust he may be able to get through safely; they ought to make him Aide-de-Camp to the Queen if he does succeed in keeping the regiment staunch.

Here for some two or three days past it has been very hot, with a cloudless sky; but, while I am writing, I am glad to say it is thundering in the distance, and with the sky awfully black, as if we were going to have a delightfully cool, rainy afternoon. I hope we may, for we much want a few heavy showers, and now that the siege-train is in it can do no harm on the road.

C—— has written an absurd letter to Mactier, begging him and others to certify that General Anson died of cholera and not of poison (as some have said), and by his own hand! We had never even heard of such a report.

3.30 P.M. No news of any kind. All quiet except the thunder —it is thundering away and raining all round apparently; but no rain has fallen here yet.

(*Diary*) 4*th September.*—Siege-train in this morning, or rather in the night. Warmish day until about twelve, when a very black thunder-storm commenced brewing; very little rain here after all, but a great deal must have fallen round about, and it made the air very cool. In the evening took a ride to the burial-ground; lots of bricks, &c., for poor Chester's grave. Take a look at the guns.

CAMP, DELHI CANTONMENTS, *Saturday, 5th September.*

Nothing going on of any kind since I wrote to you yesterday. There have been no letters in from Agra or Cawnpore that I have heard of, and no news of any interest from the city. A very large number of laden carts and *tattoos* were observed yesterday crossing the bridge to the other side of the river, which looks as if the people were taking the precaution of sending away their property to some place of greater safety than Delhi is likely soon to be.

The Artillery are hard at work getting the heavy guns ready to put into battery; they came down with elephants, and have to be altered for bullocks to drag them, it not being safe to send elephants where there is a chance of their coming under fire.

The Engineers must also be hard at work, and I fancy that in two or three days all will be ready to begin playing on the wretched city. I went to have a look at the guns yesterday evening, and a very formidable appearance they have. The Rifles are not expected to be in until to-morrow morning; and the Jheend Raja's troops are also coming, His Highness the Raja having made a particular request that they should be employed when the attack on the city took place; they are a very fine body of men, and will, I dare say, do very good service. Some of the Cashmere troops of Runbar Sing are to take their place at Lussowlie, the rest coming on here.

I see that the *Lahore Chronicle* has published Lieutenant Delafosse's narrative of the Cawnpore tragedy, so I will not send you the *Simla News* extra containing it. This 'extra' only reached me this morning, having 'too late' stamped on the cover. I suspect that the paper will very soon go to the wall if Mr Philipe withdraws his assistance from it, as he threatens to do.

I told you that Prize Agents were to be appointed. There are to be three—one appointed by the General and Field Officers of the whole force, one by Queen's officers under the rank of Field Officer, and one by Company's officers of the same rank. I believe Major Baynes, Her Majesty's 8th, will be one; and Stewart of the 9th, or Maisey, was spoken of (one of them), but they neither seem very anxious to act. It is certain to be a very troublesome duty, but it may perhaps be a very remunerative one, for there is certain to be lots of plunder if it can only be secured.

I met Burn in my walk this morning; he says Mrs Burn is very well now. There is a letter just in from Agra, I don't know the date—all well; but no further news from Cawnpore or Lucknow. The Gwalior mutineers still hesitating.

(*Diary*) 5*th September*.—A walk this morning up to the Ridge, and met Burn, who joined me. To-morrow talked of as the night to commence the batteries, and the morning of the 8th or 9th for the assault. Very hot to-day, and a great deal of sickness—nearly fifty per cent. of the Europeans in hospital; the sooner Delhi is taken the better. Bad news in from Agra of Cawnpore and Lucknow; only eight hundred Europeans apparently in the former, and the latter can only hold out fifteen days. A ride in evening.

CAMP, DELHI CANTONMENTS, *Sunday, 6th September.*

The Rifles and Artillery from Meerut marched in this morning very early, soon after daybreak, and such cheering and hurrahing as there was, with the band of the 52nd playing 'Auld Lang Syne' and 'Cheer Boys, Cheer.' Amongst them were several men who went away from here wounded. Wilde's corps of Sikhs are expected in this evening; they had telegraphed to say that they had reached Kurnaul, and would make Delhi in two marches if required here in a great hurry. They were told, I believe, that they need not hurry themselves, and that it would do if they came in three days. It is some seven regular marches, but not long ones. The Dogras are also close behind, and their General is to be here this afternoon to make his salaam to our General; so you see the net is now closing round the city at last, and I believe to-night has been fixed upon to commence our first battery that is destined, I hope, to smash them to atoms.

Greathed, the civilian, was here a little while ago, and he says that they appear to have no fixed plan of action in the city, and evidently don't know what exactly to be about. I only trust we shall not give them time to make up their minds for any fixed arrangements of defence. The impression now is that when we take the city, all who can will try to cross the bridge of boats and make their way, if possible, into Rohilkund; but I hope we shall be able to effectually prevent this by bringing guns to bear upon the bridge, which can easily be done when we have possession of the city, but is now impossible on account of the fire from the walls.

Some of the 10th Light Cavalry are reported to have arrived in the city, but in a state of great destitution; and the Sepoys of the 45th have objected to their being entertained in any way, on account of their having taken an active part in disarming the infantry regiments at Ferozepore.

The vote-papers for Prize Agents have just been circulated, and I have put my name down for Captain Fagan of the Artillery, who seems to be the favourite candidate of the Field Officers. The officers of the Queen's service will, I think, nominate either Sir

E. Campbell or Major Baynes; and those of the Company's, Captain Wriford, 1st Fusiliers, or Major Scott of the Artillery. They will have a troublesome duty, whoever are nominated; but if there is plenty of prize-money, which is not at all impossible, they will all be well paid.

There was a letter in last night of the 1st September from Agra. All was well there, as also at Cawnpore and Lucknow by the latest accounts; but I am sorry to say that they do not appear to be pushing up reinforcements to Cawnpore as fast as they ought to be able to do. They talked of assembling a large army at Benares, but I should think that they would push all the troops up to Cawnpore at once, when it was found that Lucknow had not been relieved. The Agra letter also contains an account of the Aboo business, making out that everybody there had been massacred; of course they had got the story through some Native agent, and hence its incorrectness. I am much afraid, however, for Erinpoorah, and poor Arthur will probably have his bungalow and property destroyed; but never mind since he and all his are safe.

I have heard nothing more of poor Holmes and Mrs Holmes, but I fear sadly that the account of their murder is only too true.

Near 4 P.M. Everything is quiet in camp, and it has been a comparatively cool day. We had church this morning in the 52nd mess tent; not a very large congregation.

CAMP, DELHI CANTONMENTS, *Monday, 7th September.*

Chamberlain will stay here, but Norman goes on with the first troops that move from this. There are very satisfactory accounts in to-day from Agra. The Cawnpore news was in a very nice long letter from General Neill to Colonel Cotton at Agra, who sent down the original letter here; he must be a fine old fellow, General Neill, he writes so cheerfully always, and he writes confidently of Lucknow being able to hold out well until relieved by the advancing force. There are also a few lines in original from Havelock to Mr Muir * at Agra, which the latter sent down here, but with no fresh or later news. Havelock's is written in quite his own style, beginning: 'For reasons which I cannot detail I was obliged, as a General, to abandon my intention of marching to Lucknow, while as a man I felt,' &c.

* Now Sir William Muir, K.C.S.I., Principal of Edinburgh University.

I have no doubt myself, from all I hear, that Havelock was quite right in not going on, though I dare say just the same clamour has been raised against him as there was apparently at home, and in this country too, against this force for not marching straight into Delhi. Matters are progressing most satisfactorily now towards this desirable end, and I hope, before this day week, I shall not require to date any more letters from 'Camp, Delhi Cantonments,' but from 'Delhi City.'

Major Goad's 'Man Friday' came in here a little while ago, and has been giving us an interesting account of his adventures. He was a prisoner at Delhi after he left here, but received no injury.

Saunders, with the Jheend Raja's troops, came in this morning and breakfasted with us. Bunny is here; what an escape Mrs Bunny had!

Near 4 P.M., and all quiet.

(*Diary*) 7*th September*.—It was said at first that the heavy advanced battery was to be made last night, but it is put off till to-night, and nothing has been done but to arm the light advance batteries. Go this morning to see the work at poor Chester's grave. Wilde's corps came in; fine, rough-looking fellows. English mail of 26th July in.

CAMP, DELHI CANTONMENTS, *Tuesday, 8th September.*

To-day's dâk was in early, but it has brought no Simla mail with it, so as everybody else in camp is as badly off as myself, I have nothing to complain of. I suppose you have had rain in the hills to detain the Simla dâk, or perhaps the Lahore dâk has taken to reaching Umballa at an earlier hour, and was despatched at once without waiting for the Simla packet; but whatever the cause, I wish they would remedy it. As Arthur Becher is equally interested with myself and others, I dare say he will write to Umballa on the subject; the post-office arrangements here are, in a manner, under his superintendence.

There has been a grand cannonading going on to-day. Last night the Engineers succeeded in getting ready our first advance battery of heavy guns—ten 18's and 24's, including one 8-inch howitzer, which were all got into the battery early this morning, and with only the loss of one native on our side. The enemy appear to have been quite ignorant of what was going on, as had they molested our working parties we must have lost many men; they were firing away in the night, but never apparently in the right direction. There were, for instance, fifteen hundred camels that went down with Engineers' stores, fascines, &c., and only one camel was struck by a stray shot. To-night the heavy breaching batteries are to be commenced upon and finished, if possible, but this will be a far easier and less dangerous task than that of last night, as our battery is now playing away on the enemy's walls and bastions, and has, we hear, already silenced most of their guns, and will do so altogether, it is expected, before evening. We have also a strong party of infantry that took possession last night, without opposition, of what is called the Koodsee Bagh—the garden, you may remember, quite close to the Cashmere Gate; the city wall is at one side of the garden, so you may suppose what an advance has been made in one night by us.

The enemy came out in great force this morning to attack the new battery, and to try and drive us out of the Koodsee Bagh, but they were repulsed on every side, and numbers of them killed and wounded, both Horse and Foot; but we, too, have had a few casualties, I am sorry to say—two officers killed, Lieutenant Hildebrand, Artillery, and Lieutenant Bannerman, Belooch Corps; and one officer, Lieutenant Budd, Artillery, wounded, and about twelve or fourteen men killed and wounded; and, I fear, the poor men in battery have all suffered very much from the heat, for it was very hot and sunny till about an hour ago, when we had a blinding dust-storm, with lots of rain in the distance. Hardly a drop fell here, but the air is now delightfully cool, and the sky quite cloudy. I only hope it will remain so for the next few days to come.

The Cashmere troops came in this morning, and we all went out to meet them. Such a picturesque-looking lot, dressed so gaily! There were between two and three thousand of them, apparently—artillery, four brass guns, with lots of small guns on camels; cavalry, with bright brass mambrino-looking helmets (*à la* Don Quixote!); and infantry, fine, strong, powerful-looking men, armed with long matchlocks fitted with flint locks. Altogether they made a most respectable appearance, and are a welcome addition to our Force.

There is no news from the city since our new battery began to open, but before that letters said that they had heard of the Cashmere troops coming, *ten* thousand in number, and that many of the mutineers, particularly the Sowars, were preparing to bolt. I dare say it is true to a certain extent, but to-morrow's letter will be interesting.

I was sorry to hear that Duncan Pemberton had fever, and I went to see him. He was sitting outside, and is now only complaining of weakness. Robert, his brother, has also come from Roorkee, but I have not seen him.

What think you of the Murree panic? Richard Lawrence is here; he thinks the attempt at plunder was of no consequence at all.

Near 4 P.M., and no further news; nor are there any *cossids* in to-day from anywhere.

(*Diary*) 8*th September.*—Ride to the park. Had little sleep last night; not very well, and anxious, I fancy, about the new heavy battery, and there was a good deal of firing at intervals all night. The battery of nine guns and an 8-inch howitzer was erected and armed last night, and only one native killed. The enemy must have been quite adrift as to our intentions. Firing all day, and we have lost two officers killed and one wounded. Very hot day. The Cashmere troops came in this morning—fine men. Go and see Coke in the evening.

CAMP, DELHI CANTONMENTS, *Wednesday,* 9*th September.*

All goes on well here, but they seem to have a rather more difficult job than was anticipated in making the heavy batteries. The work is certainly tremendous. In the first battery the earthwork and gabions together form a wall eighteen feet in thickness; and in the breaching batteries this is, I believe, to be increased to thirty feet—thick enough, we should think, to prevent any, even the largest, shot having any visible effect. The breaching batteries are to be ready, it is hoped, to-morrow morning, but this seems doubtful. The heavy mortar battery was completed and armed last night, but it is not to open till all the other batteries are ready or nearly so. In addition to the ten heavy mortars, there are also twelve smaller $5\frac{1}{2}$-inch ones, which are to be placed in position; and altogether, when everything is completely ready, there will be thirty-five heavy guns and howitzers and twenty-two mortars firing away at once on the city and Palace. On the 11th, most probably, the guns and mortars will all open; and by the time you receive this, Delhi will be by no means an enviable residence. An order has been issued by General Wilson, calling upon the soldiers to spare all women and children when the assault is made. It is a very good order, and, I have no doubt, will have a very beneficial effect, especially in preventing the men from separating to plunder.

It has not been settled yet who are to be the Prize Agents, but it will be amongst those whose names I mentioned to you. I rather think the agents will be Major Baynes, Her Majesty's 8th; Captain Wriford, and Captain Fagan.

What a dreadful loser Sir Theophilus Metcalfe has been by the mutiny! His house here was all plundered at the commencement, but the *kootub* house that we went to see was preserved all right till two or three days ago, when he received intelligence that, after being preserved till then by the influence of the King, it was plundered by a party of Sepoys. I am very sorry that he has suffered so much. His sisters have lost also, having a small share in the property.

We had rather an alarm in camp yesterday afternoon—an explosion—of which, perhaps, you may hear an exaggerated account. Some shells had been sent down to camp from a dismantled battery, and the powder in *one* of them got shaken out by the motion of the cart, and in tilting the cart up when it reached the park the shells knocked together, causing a spark which ignited the powder, and, as the consequence, blew up everything near. Four *classees* were reported killed, and four or five Europeans and Natives wounded. Becher and I, and one or two more, were standing outside our tents talking together when the explosion took place, and there was a terrible commotion, for the large magazine was not very far off. It is rather fortunate it happened, for it will make everybody more than usually careful in looking after their ammunition.

Letters have just come in from Cawnpore, the 30th August, and

Agra, the 4th instant; all well at both places, and Lucknow is reported all well too. Five hundred British troops had reached Cawnpore, and fifteen hundred were expected immediately; and when they arrived the force was to move on to Lucknow. The people there and the Oude Sirdars generally would have nothing to say to the Nana, who had been obliged to leave. The letter does not say why they have refused to fraternise with the Nana, but it may be on account of his brutal cruelties at Cawnpore. I misled you in a former letter about the Nana. It seems that the man who was at Meerut was another person altogether, the Nunda Sahib, and that he has always behaved well. The Nana never apparently came to Meerut.

The Gwalior mutineers are still at Gwalior, and I trust Delhi will be ours before they make up their minds to leave.

You ask me to send you a telegraphic message when Delhi falls. I don't think any private messages will be allowed to be sent, but if they are you shall certainly have one; but you may be sure that Lord William Hay will get a copy of the official message sent up, and will lose no time in circulating it.

Dr Mactier wants the enclosed about Dr Ireland given to Mr Philipe to put in the Simla paper, as the poor man was reported dead.*

Extract from LETTER *of 9th September.*

'Dr Ireland, who was severely wounded in Brigadier Nicholson's late action with the mutineers, is progressing most favourably, I am happy to say.'

(*Diary*) *9th September.*—Past 4 P.M., and all well. A letter has just come down from the batteries—no more casualties. Take a ride round by the burial-ground, and then to see the Cashmere troops; they have squeezed themselves into a very small space. Amused at their comical swivel guns (*sherbachas* or *gerbauchs*, as they are called); they have been put in battery to protect the right flank. At home all day. Very hot. Mortar battery up in Koodsee Bagh, but the breaching batteries not ready. Up at the Flagstaff in the evening; the rockets from the city the prettiest part of the entertainment.

* See pages 240 and 242.

Camp, Delhi Cantonments, *Thursday*, 10*th September.*

Your letter of the 7th instant reached me early this morning, and after reading it I went up to the usual place of rendezvous of all the idlers here—the Flagstaff—to see what was going on. It was a very foggy morning, and we could not see much, but sufficient to show that we have already done a great deal of damage to the walls and bastions with our one battery, and ought to have it all our own way when all our batteries come into play. There is only one now requiring to be finished—that in the Custom House Gardens, for four guns. That at Ludlow Castle is ready; twelve or thirteen guns, I think, there are in it; but the General won't allow it to be opened till the other one is ready, which Chesney, who was up at the Flagstaff, told me it must be by the morning.

Every one is abusing the Engineers for having promised so much more than they have been able to perform. They talked of having all the batteries ready in one night, but nobody thought it was possible; and the result has proved this, for this will be the fourth night, and it is considered by those who are judges in such matters that as much as was possible has been done with their available means.

I fancy no one here shares Mrs ———'s fears for those who go into Delhi. After the place has been well shelled for a day or two, there will probably be less opposition made by the wretches than in some of those fights when we first came here.

I told you wrong the other day about the Koodsee Bagh, where the mortar battery is. This is not the garden that we used to go to, but the one next to it. The heavy battery, however, that is to be finished to-night is in that garden, and they have had to cut down lots of those beautiful orange-trees to make room for it.

It has been a very hot day, but a refreshing shower an hour or two ago has made it considerably cooler, and there is now a pleasant breeze blowing, and thunder rumbling in the distance. I wish it would come down a good plump of rain, and it would serve, too, to put out the fire in one of our batteries, which caught fire just now, and seems inclined not to allow itself to be put out. Fortunately it is a battery in which the guns are not very much required now, and they must be removed until the battery is repaired.

Were you alarmed at all at Simla when you saw the story of the villagers attacking Murree? It seems they always have been troublesome, and in former days there was continual fighting with them, and there has been once or twice before since we took the place; so that Simla and Murree are quite different in this respect, and the recent row had nothing, apparently, to do with the mutinous proceedings below.

No further news to-day from Agra or Cawnpore. City letters say the people are trying to get away with their families, but the gates have been shut, and no one now is allowed to leave without, I suppose, paying well first, which is the meaning of the prohibition.

Past 4 P.M., and no further news. There were a few casualties yesterday, and two officers wounded—Lieutenant Murray, Engineers, and Lieutenant Eaton, 60th Rifles.

(*Diary*) 10*th September*.—Went up to the Flagstaff again this morning, and up to the first floor; but very misty, and saw little beyond smoke. One heavy battery in the Custom House Garden, of four guns, not yet ready; the other, near Ludlow Castle, up and guns in it. Loud exclamations against the Engineers for promising more than they could perform. Excessively hot; a grateful shower at noon. Look at the progress of the tomb in the evening, and then to the Flagstaff. Battery on fire this afternoon.

CAMP, DELHI CANTONMENTS, *Friday, 11th September.*

Your letter of the 8th I found lying on the table when I came back from my ride this morning. I had got up very early, as had many others, and gone to the Flagstaff to see our new heavy batteries open, which they were to have done at daybreak all together on a signal-rocket being thrown up. We were doomed, however, to disappointment; and after waiting an hour or two we ascertained that the entertainment was postponed, the batteries not being ready. They have since, however, partially opened, and the battery at Ludlow Castle has, I understand, quite demolished the Cashmere Bastion and silenced all their guns in that direction. The heavy battery in the Custom House Garden must be ready by this evening, and I hope in the morning to find that it is in full

Sketches by young officers in camp of proposed Mutiny Medals and Medal Ribbons.

operation, and finishing the rest of the work that there is to be done.

You will be very anxious to hear of the final attack, but things have progressed so much more slowly lately than was anticipated, that one cannot reckon with any certainty when the assault will be. Give us till the 15th, and I think by or before that date we shall be able to send you something satisfactory. God grant that it may be so, for all away from the actual scene of warfare must be in a painfully nervous state of excitement and suspense. We who are here, and know how satisfactorily things are going on, can easily learn the cause of what may appear to you, at a distance, some unaccountable delay; and with such people as some you have at Simla, I can easily imagine all sorts of absurd stories being in circulation. For instance, the battery catching fire yesterday; I dare say it has been made out a sad disaster, though, on the whole, I believe it to have been rather a fortunate occurrence, as the guns had pretty well finished the work required of them, and the fire making it necessary to remove them, they were sent down to the Ludlow Castle battery to take their place there; and besides, the fire has made all the officers in other batteries doubly careful, and they are now covered in the most exposed parts with hides, and water is kept close at hand in case of fire again.

The Engineers are very much blamed for misleading the General as to the time it would take to erect all these batteries. They talked of doing everything in one night, but none but themselves expected this, thinking that they might take two or three; but the fourth has already passed. They are very fine fellows the Engineers, there is not a doubt about that, but they wanted to make themselves out able to do impossibilities. Greathed, brother of the Colonel, has charge of the battery still unfinished; he is a very gallant and clever young fellow.

I am sorry to hear from Major Brooke, whom I met at the Flagstaff this morning, that poor Mrs Greathed is still very unwell; from what Mrs Brooke writes to him, he appears to think her in a very precarious state. I haven't seen Colonel Greathed for some time; he has been constantly on duty lately. Robertson, who lives with him, I got a note from just now, saying he was going to leave this evening for Kurnaul, and eventually Mussoorie. I fancy he is much vexed at having to go, but there is no help for it. He has had a very sharp attack of fever, and is dreadfully pulled down, and no chance of regaining his strength here.

Letters in from Agra this morning of the 6th and 7th; all well there then, and at Cawnpore and Lucknow by the last accounts. General Outram was pushing up to Cawnpore with all available troops, having abandoned the intention, at one time entertained, of marching *viâ* Fyzabad on Lucknow. The Goorkha troops were at Azimghur, so it is hoped some of them will march up to Cawnpore. The Indore portion of the Gwalior mutineers had left Gwalior and reached Dholpore, but without guns, and they were trying to get some from the Dholpore Raja. Colonel Cotton writes that he was on the lookout for them, if they were in the Agra direction. Mr Colvin was very ill again; we should not be surprised to hear of his death.

I got letters to-day from Captain Eden. He gives me an account of the Joudhpore Legion mutiny much the same as Arthur's, but talks of their having mutinied also at Erinpoorah, and says they made prisoners of the sergeants and their families, and the adjutant, but afterwards released them. I trust this is true; and it does not seem clear that they had plundered the station, and I hope not for Arthur's sake. George Lawrence was after the mutineers with some Europeans and Lancers, and, I hope, will come up with them. At Jeypore all was quiet, and the Raja exerting himself to the utmost in our favour.

Fortunately this has been such a nice, cool, cloudy day for our men, who have had sad hard work of it lately, poor fellows; but they are much better, the doctors say, since the work began again.

It was a mistake, it seems, about Lieutenant Murray having been wounded, though so reported by half-a-dozen. Lieutenant Lockhart of the Goorkhas, and Lieutenant Gillespie, Artillery, have been wounded, I am sorry to say; no other that I hear of.

Near four o'clock P.M., and all right here, none of the enemy's guns firing.

(*Diary*) 11*th September.*—Up very early to see the heavy batteries open, as arranged last night; but, after an hour's stay at the Flagstaff, find they are not ready. They partially open about nine, and heavy firing has been going on all day. Rode round by the Flagstaff in the evening just as usual. Some cavalry got to our rear this afternoon, but were caught, and twenty-seven (two of them Native officers) cut up.

CAMP, DELHI CANTONMENTS, *Saturday*, 12*th September*.

What a very self-sufficient fellow Hodson is, talking, or rather writing, in the way he does, for I have not heard him broach such opinions here as those he ventures to write to his wife! It is all very well abusing General Wilson for not taking Delhi, but the general impression is, amongst all those likely to know anything about the matter, that he exercised a wise discretion in waiting for the siege-train, and in using it when it came; and whether he is to blame for its having been so long on the road, I don't know. As to the Cashmere contingent with their bows and arrows (as he says), he must have known that this was not the case. They are armed (the infantry) with long flint guns, most excellent weapons, and with swords; and the men seem first-rate fellows, likely to do very good service. They had a few out the other day, and they behaved very well, two of them being wounded. The force altogether is upwards of two thousand cavalry, infantry, and artillery, and is a very welcome little addition. You may depend upon it, General Wilson has no intention whatever of waiting more than another day or two before assaulting the place; but the when is not yet settled, as it will depend on the effect of the breaching battery in the Custom House Garden, which has not yet opened (11 A.M.), but was certainly to be ready by one or two o'clock this afternoon.

The Engineers appear to have very much miscalculated matters; the delay in opening the battery to-day is from their having made the embrasures in the wrong direction, and all this had to be done afresh. The mistake was caused, it seems, by the battery being erected under the screen of a building, portions of which were found to be opposite the embrasures, and obstructed the line of fire; everything, however, is, I hope, right or nearly so by this time. The other batteries, mortars inclusive, have been playing away in grand style all this morning, and they were not very silent during the night.

The newsletter that came in last night said that there were a great many of the mutineers killed by our fire yesterday, and the wounded, according to the letter, were '*be shoomar*' (countless).

This is rather a stretch of the imagination, no doubt, but from such a heavy fire as we had upon them they must have lost many men. In the afternoon, too, there was a little skirmish with a party of their cavalry, that terminated very favourably. A party of them tried to get to our rear, when they were charged by some of the Guide and Punjab cavalry, who turned out at once on hearing the alarm, and cut up twenty-seven of them, of whom two were Native officers. On our side, Lieutenant Watson was slightly wounded in the face, and two troopers also wounded. It seems that the mutineers numbered some two or three hundred, but they cut off as hard as their horses could carry them when they saw our men coming, of whom there were not more than forty at first, more coming up after the mêlée was over.

The only officer I have heard of being wounded in the batteries since I wrote to you yesterday is Major Campbell of the Artillery. A bit of a shell wounded him in both legs. One wound is said to be very slight, the other rather severe, but no bones broken.

Did I tell you that the telegraph has been brought down here? And the office is to be established quite close to our camp, so you will have early intelligence from this place when there is anything important to communicate.

There was another letter from Agra this morning of the 5th (the one yesterday was of the 7th). All well; and the same news from Cawnpore and Lucknow, except that it is said that fifteen hundred men, in addition to those already out, were to march from Allahabad with Sir James Outram on the 5th; so they must be at Cawnpore ere this, and we may soon expect to hear of Lucknow being relieved. The report is that there are only three or four mutinous regiments before Lucknow, the rest being riff-raff of the country. I do trust that Havelock will be in good time to save the Lucknow garrison.

This morning was so very cool—quite a cold weather feeling, and there has been a nice breeze blowing all day.

You ask about the sickness. There has been a good deal, but not so much as was expected. No cholera that I hear of now, only fever; and since active operations began again, the sickness is said to be much on the decrease. I think Arthur Becher will go up to Simla after all. He had made up his mind this morning to do so.

Near 4 P.M., and all going on well. The enemy's guns, it is said, are all silenced except two which are firing across the river, and two from the Selimgurh Gate. Ours are all in full operation.

(*Diary*) 12*th September.*—Up very early again, and go to the Flagstaff; the heavy breaching battery still not ready. It seems that the embrasures were made in the wrong direction, and all had to be done over again. Great crying out, against the Engineers especially, who had the superintendence of this battery. It opens partially in the afternoon. Short ride in the evening, but nothing visible; lots of noise. Poor Fagan killed this evening in the breaching battery.

CAMP, DELHI CANTONMENTS, *Sunday,* 13*th September.*

Mrs Hodson certainly writes an amusing note. I hope she heard from her husband the next day; but you can tell her, if he has not written to-day, that he was in my tent a little while ago, and in high health and spirits, except a little cold, from which many in camp are suffering at present. He was telling me that he hopes to go on with the Movable Column under Nicholson (the hero of the last fight) when we take Delhi, to pursue the flying enemy. You see, we have settled all this to our satisfaction, though I suppose Mrs ———, when she hears of this arrangement, will still adhere to her belief that none of our party who go into Delhi will be permitted to leave the city. We shall soon now have this determined for us, and God grant us all the success that every one in our camp expects. To-morrow, or the next day at the very latest, the assault is intended to take place. The day will depend in a great measure upon the practicability of the breaches. The guns and mortars are all now hard at work, and from reports lately brought up from the batteries, all is progressing very well. We blew up two of their small magazines this morning.

Our losses yesterday were very trifling; but, I am sorry to say, one officer of Artillery—Captain Fagan—was amongst the few killed. He was a first-rate officer, and there is very great regret in camp at his loss. His poor wife is at Dalhousie with some four or five children. Poor fellow! What makes the matter worse is that he lost his life entirely from his own imprudence;

he would expose himself unnecessarily against continual remonstrances. Major Scott, in whose battery he was, was insisting upon his being more careful, when the fatal shot took effect: it was a rifle-ball in the head.

When the assault takes place, I suppose my place will be with General Wilson, who will, of course, remain with the Reserve Column, so that I shall be comparatively safe and free from danger; and may God protect me, if only for your sake and that of the dear children. But, as I told you yesterday, little or no opposition is expected on first entering the city; and the arrangements appear to be so good for overcoming any after obstacles that I trust we shall meet with very little loss. But there is not much use my saying anything on this subject now, as, in all probability, ere this reaches you you will hear the result of our attack, by electric telegraph, through Lord William Hay, to whom, no doubt, a copy of the first despatch will be sent up by Mr Barnes.

The telegraph, I think I told you, is now established in our camp, and I will try to send you a message; but I don't think there is much chance of my being able to do so, as no private messages are taken now, they say; and, in fact, there will be such confusion on the day of the assault that you must not be surprised if you get neither letter nor message from me that day. But you may be sure I shall write as soon as I can, and a happy day will it be for me when I can write and tell you that it is all settled when I am to leave for Simla. Becher, I told you, has quite determined now on going up there. He was proposing that we should go together.

I enclose a letter that came yesterday evening from Arthur, and you will be sorry to see that the scoundrels of the Legion have plundered Erinpoorah after all. Poor Arthur! I hope, however, as L. was at Aboo, that some of their most valuable articles were up there also. How very fortunate it was that he was with her! There seems every chance, I think, of the mutineers meeting with their deserts.

Nothing in to-day from Agra or Cawnpore, and from the city there is the old story of the Sepoys deserting in great numbers, and the inhabitants of the city are all leaving now the gates have been thrown open to them at last. They must think they are all going to be massacred, and I don't think the soldiers will be very particular; but General Wilson has issued a very proper order, calling upon them not to harm women or children.

Nearly 4 P.M., and no news of any kind. Our guns firing away, but we can hear none of the enemy's in reply.

(*Diary*) *Sunday*, 13*th September.*—Service at six; heavy firing all day. In the evening settled that the assault takes place the next morning.

Colonel KEITH YOUNG *to Colonel* H. B. HENDERSON.

CAMP, DELHI, 13*th September.*

When Delhi is taken, if my life is spared, I expect to be able to run up to Simla, where all my office still is. By this mail you ought to receive a telegraphic message at any rate, announcing the fall of Delhi. To-morrow the assault will probably be made, and God grant that we may be as successful as we anticipate. We have now about eight thousand men of all arms, European and Native, fit for duty—half nearly Europeans—and there are about three thousand reliable men of the Cashmere and Jheend contingents; and the enemy, though forty thousand strong at one time, have not now more than ten or twelve thousand, so we ought to beat them. Sixty guns and mortars are now playing away, preparing the way for us.

CHAPTER XIII.

ASSAULT AND CAPTURE OF DELHI.

Colonel KEITH YOUNG *to his wife.*
DELHI (IN THE CHURCH), *Monday, 14th September* (2½ P.M.).

By God's great mercy here we are, safe within the walls of Delhi, and all of our Staff party have escaped unharmed. Shute, Nicoll, and Metcalfe are now here in the veranda with me; Hodson I saw a little while ago, well. Mactier is up at the field hospital looking after the wounded, of whom, I am sorry to say, there are a good many; the only officer I have heard of as killed is Fitzgerald, Her Majesty's 75th. We have guns (the enemy's, that we took at the Water Gate) bearing on the bridge, and we are now shelling from near this some parts of the city where the mutineers still are. We hold the Cashmere Gate, the Cabul and Moree Gates, Skinner's house, and the College; and I hope the whole city will be ours before night, for the wretches have run away in great numbers.

May God watch over and protect you and the dear children, is my constant prayer.

(*Diary*) 14*th September.*—Up at 3 A.M., and soon after go down to Ludlow Castle with the General and party. Such noise and confusion! The storming parties in three columns and a reserve column. Anxious time waiting for the assault; it was rather late, coming off an hour after daybreak. I should think quite successful, but great loss on our side; few of the enemy killed, apparently. The Water Bastion a terrible smash. At the Church, and in the evening Skinner's house.

Extract copy from Mr BARNES's *letter,*
dated 14*th September* (11 A.M.).

The troops were under arms, and left camp this morning at 3 A.M. Assault at daybreak, and city successfully carried. General Wilson sent a despatch to his wife, dated City of Delhi, 10 A.M. Hard fighting going on, and the columns making slow progress. Several strong positions still to carry, and a stand will probably be made around the King and Palace.

No list of casualties.

Lord WILLIAM HAY *to Mrs* KEITH YOUNG.

SIMLA, 16*th September.*

MY DEAR MRS YOUNG,—Oblige me by sending these copies of telegrams to all Chota-Simla, including Colonel Congreve, Mrs Norman, Mrs Thomson, Wiggins, Greathed, &c.

I think it most satisfactory. The loss in the 1st is very heavy, but the rest have got well off.—Yours in haste, W. H.

Telegrams.

14*th September* (11 P.M.).

Our position is the same as the last report, 3.30 P.M., and no attempt will be made to make further progress to-night. Our mortars have been taken into the city, and are firing against the Palace, and Selimgurh, and the town. The battering guns have also been taken in to breach the magazine. The guns and mortars captured on the bastions have been turned against the mutineers. They continue to offer the most determined resistance. Our loss is very severe, especially in officers.

KILLED.
    Captain G. G. M'Barnett, 55th Native Infantry.
    Lieutenant A. W. Murray, 42nd Native Infantry.
    Lieutenant Tandy, Engineers.

DANGEROUSLY WOUNDED.
    Brigadier Nicholson.
    Captain Rosser, 6th Dragoon Guards.
    Major Jacob, 1st Fusiliers.
    Captain Greville, 1st Fusiliers.

Lieutenant Speke (doing duty).
Lieutenant Nicholson (arm amputated).

VERY SEVERELY WOUNDED.
Lieutenant A. G. Owen, 1st Fusiliers.

SEVERELY WOUNDED.
Lieutenant Chesney, Engineers.
Major Reid, Sirmoor Battalion.
Captain Boisragon, Kemaon Battalion.

SLIGHTLY WOUNDED.
Lieutenant Bond, 57th Native Infantry.
Lieutenant Shebbeare, 60th Native Infantry.
Colonel G. Campbell, Her Majesty's 52nd.
Lieutenant Wemyss, 1st Fusiliers.

15th September.

All quiet during the night; very hard fighting going on this morning. The mutineers still hold the Selimgurh battery.

15th September (9 A.M.).

We continue to occupy the city from College Garden to Cabul Gate. The enemy holds the magazine, which we are now shelling; the Palace likewise being shelled. Many of the mutineers have fled since yesterday. Our loss estimated at five hundred, thirty officers; among them seven Engineers. Major Jacob has died of his wounds.

Colonel KEITH YOUNG *to his wife.*

DELHI (SKINNER'S HOUSE), *Tuesday,* 15*th September.*

Here we are, you see, having passed a very quiet night in Skinner's house, which was found to be more comfortable than the Church, there being a regiment of Europeans there. We got our beds down and our servants, and, after a scrambling kind of dinner, were not sorry to have a good night's rest. You would be rather amused could you see us now. We have a few chairs, but no tables, and I am writing this on the top of a hat, a regular fashionable ventilator, which Hingham brought in yesterday, hat-box and all, as his lawful plunder! The General and all his party are staying here. I have brought no writing materials from camp with me, and am indebted to Maisey for this sheet of paper and a pen.

I dare say it will be two or three days yet before we are in full possession of the city and Palace, but I believe the intention is to use our artillery to clear away the scoundrels that are still in the city, and there will be no more storming like yesterday, and such dreadful loss of life. I suppose our loss could not be less than six or seven hundred killed and wounded. Amongst the former, I am sorry to say, there are six officers whose names I have heard: Tandy of the Engineers (no Artillery officers killed or wounded except Tombs—a slight contusion); Rosser, Carabineers; Murray, 42nd Native Infantry, with Guides; Bradshaw, Her Majesty's 52nd; M'Barnett, 55th, with 1st Fusiliers; and Fitzgerald, Her Majesty's 75th. Of the officers wounded, I have heard the names of Greathed, Engineers, arm broken, but will be saved; Brigadier Nicholson, dangerously, it is feared; Reid, Sirmoor Battalion, severely but not dangerously; Jacob and Greville, 1st Fusiliers, very severely; Nicholson, junior, lost his arm. There are a good many more, but nobody, I think, that you know or have heard of. Waters, of the Rifles, also is wounded.

I have not yet told you how it was that we didn't get possession of the whole of the city yesterday, as it was expected and intended we should have done. It was all owing to that wretched Cashmere contingent, which formed a part of Reid's column, which was to have cleared out the suburbs of Kissengunge and then have entered the city by the Lahore Gate. The contingent ran off immediately the enemy's guns opened on them, abandoning three of their own guns. Reid was wounded, and the column was obliged to return to Hindoo Rao's without effecting their object; and the consequence was that our columns in the city were obliged to pull up in the positions we now hold. All, however, is going on satisfactorily now. We are bringing on lots of guns and mortars, and this in the course of two or three days will clear the place very effectually and without loss to us.

Several Natives of the city—men, women, and children—have come in to pray for quarter, which has been given them, they being turned out of the city; but Sepoys who have come in to give themselves up have been told they cannot be received. I fancy, however, that this will be altered in future, and that *unconditional* surrender will be permitted. Many of the mutineers left the city last night, principally cavalry, going towards Rewaree, apparently.

An ayah came in just now to say that there are two children of Mr Skinner's concealed in the city, also two ladies, Mrs Ord and Mrs Olivia; as far as we could make out, all the men, she said, were killed.

I have just heard that Robert Pemberton, Engineers, was wounded yesterday, but very slightly—a flesh wound in the arm—and he is about his duty again to-day. Colonel Campbell, Her Majesty's 52nd, was also wounded yesterday in the wrist.

Such a packet of English letters came yesterday! I enclose one or two, and you shall have the rest to-morrow; I haven't time to send them to-day. Brind was here just now, and asked me to mention him as being quite well; if you see his sister-in-law, tell her he was going into battery, and would not have time to write. George Hall, too, was in with us yesterday evening, and asked me to say he was well, and probably wouldn't be able to write to-day, as he was on duty, but no chance of his being actively employed. Mrs Greathed's husband is quite safe, and so is Major Brooke, though he was reported wounded at first. Burnside, too, was over here a little while ago, looking very well.

I must now say good-bye; it is 2.30 P.M., and everything going on well. Lots of people coming to give themselves up, and they say that there are very few Sepoys now left in Delhi.

(*Diary*) 15*th September*.—Deal of firing last night, but we all got a good sleep. Must have had seven or eight hundred casualties yesterday. At home at Skinner's all day, writing and sleeping. Rather hot. Hard at work making a breach in the magazine, and in the evening reported practicable, and storm to be in the morning. Nothing done further towards the city; much less firing from the enemy to-day.

DELHI (SKINNER'S HOUSE), *Wednesday*, 16*th September*.

I rode up to our camp this morning, and there had the happiness to receive your letter of the 13th. All has gone on well since I wrote to you yesterday, and I was able to take up to camp the pleasing intelligence of our being in quiet possession of

(DELHI.) THE CHANDNEE CHOUK:
Main Street and "Silver Bazaar."

the magazine, which was stormed soon after daybreak, and carried with scarcely any resistance on the part of the enemy, who ran off at once on hearing the shout of our men as they entered the breach. Our whole loss was three men wounded; and the mutineers had some fifty killed. In the magazine were found about one hundred and twenty guns and mortars, with lots of shot and shell; and several mortars, which had been placed in position to fire at us, have now been turned round to play upon the Palace and Selimgurh. Other batteries are ready, too, for this purpose, and I shall not be surprised if to-morrow we find both Palace and Fort evacuated. From the former they are unable to fire guns, nothing but muskets; and the fire from the latter is very slack, not above three or four shots an hour.

You remember the great high red walls surrounding the Palace; if they do not evacuate it soon, there will be a breaching battery to knock them down, and their extreme height will rather be an advantage to us. Twenty-four hours' battering will, it is supposed, bring them entirely down. Our other posts are being gradually advanced towards the Chandnee Chouk, and I believe we have now crept up quietly to the line of the canal; but all is being done very carefully, with guns and mortars as much as possible, so as to avoid risking the lives of our soldiers when it can possibly be avoided.

While I write this, a report has just come in of the suburbs, called the Telewara and Kissengunge, having been evacuated by the enemy. This was the party that thrashed the Cashmere contingent on Monday, and their retaining their position there since then has caused some little anxiety to our camp. They have now, however, gone off, leaving five of their guns, which bullocks have been sent to bring away. Norman has just returned from the place, and he says they had entrenched themselves very strongly, so it is a very good thing they have taken themselves off without its being necessary to turn them out. The supposition is that all are going away towards their homes. We have several guns now bearing on the bridge of boats, so that all crossing the river must do so lower down; and this they will be able to do, as they have plenty of boats, but I doubt their getting much heavy luggage or guns over.

It is very unfortunate Brigadier Nicholson being wounded, as there will be great difficulty now in fixing upon a proper man to take command of the Movable Column that is to go in pursuit of the mutineers. I should not wonder if Greathed were appointed, and I think he would be the best man available. How proud poor Mrs Greathed would be! Brigadier Nicholson is in a dangerous state, but I trust, with the assistance of Mackinnon and Mactier, he may recover; his death would be a serious public loss.

I breakfasted up in camp, and then drove down with Arthur Becher in his buggy; he is so delighted with our residence that he talks of coming down and joining us. It would be much more jolly for him, I dare say, though not quite so comfortable, for we are all—nearly twenty, I think—in one large, open veranda. There are lots of rooms, but filthily dirty, and we have had only two or three partially cleared out, to sit and write and mess in; but the veranda is the grand place of assembly, and where all our beds are. Arthur Becher tells me he has sent up daily a telegraphic message to Mrs Becher, to say that all our party were well. I could not well send one myself without going up to camp; and indeed you would not receive the intelligence of us a bit sooner than you now do from Mrs Arthur, who, of course, writes and tells you and Mrs Norman immediately she gets the message.

I was in hopes of being able to tell you that a day had been fixed for my leaving here for Simla. We had fixed before, I think, on the 20th, but I fear it will hardly be so early as this, as I cannot leave until we are well in possession of city, Palace, and everything, and until matters are a little settled down. I hope, however, this will not be long after the 20th, but you shall hear immediately I can settle the day, and I shall not be long on the way up.

I succeeded yesterday in picking up a couple of those pretty spotted goats for you—plunder, of course. An Afghan chief made me a present of them. I have also got a Sepoy's medal (Rampesaud Sing, 15th Native Infantry), and one or two other trifling articles. I send enclosed two pieces of ribbon, the Jelalabad one, and the other (the blue) Mooltan, I think.

There is very good news from Agra of the 8th; the mutineers from Gwalior, the Indore portion of them, still at the Chumbal, and all right at Cawnpore and Lucknow by the latest accounts.

Mr Colvin had died of dysentery; poor man, he did not shine during our late troubles!

There was a letter from Hansi this morning with good news. The rebels had been thrashed by Van Cortlandt's force near Hansi, and the village of Jumalpore, where they had assembled in great force, was burnt by our people.

That story about Aden having been taken by the Sepoys must be false. If there was any truth in it, how did the last steamer that came here manage to coal? Who is it that sets about all these stories at Simla?

Hodson was down here just now, very well; Mactier is also here.

(*Diary*) 16*th September.*—Up at daybreak, but just too late to see the magazine stormed; but our attack was quite successful, and we had only three men wounded. Rode up to camp, breakfasted there, and then drove back with Arthur Becher. In the afternoon stroll down to College Garden, and look at Brind's battery; half-deafened with the noise. Go into magazine, but lots of bullets flying about, so do not make a long stay. As I was coming down the breach, nearly knocked over by a bullock that I had charitably loosed to allow of its going to graze. Prisoners brought in this evening.

Telegrams *received at* Simla.

Colvin died at Agra on 9th September. The magazine was stormed at daybreak 16th, by 61st Foot, wing of Belooch Battalion, and part of Wilde's Punjab Infantry. Carried with ease. We lost five or six wounded; no officers touched. Forty of enemy killed, and one hundred and twenty-five guns taken. General Wilson much fatigued and not well. Vigorous shelling going on against Palace and Selimgurh.

9 A.M.—Enemy evacuating Kissengunge suburbs. Captain Rosser* and Lieutenant Humphreys, 4th Punjab Infantry, have died of their wounds.

The following officers wounded on the 14th: Pemberton, Engineers; Gustavinsky, Sappers; Cuppage, 6th Cavalry; Bayley Her Majesty's 52nd; Shebbeare, Guides; Atkinson, Her Majesty's 52nd; Graydon, 16th Grenadiers; Speke, 65th Native Infantry;

* A mistake as to Rosser.—H. W. Norman.

Lambert, 1st Fusiliers; Elderton, 2nd Fusiliers; Gambier, 38th; Hay, 60th Native Infantry; Prior, 1st Punjab.

Colonel KEITH YOUNG *to his wife.*

DELHI, *17th September.*

This evening, I suppose, we shall get letters from you to say that you had heard of our successful entry into Delhi; but I dare say you will still be anxious till you hear of our being inside the Palace, and that all the mutineers have been destroyed or driven away. Matters are fast progressing towards this end, and we are now shelling away both Palace and Fort without their making any return whatever. They are said to have only seven artillery-men in the Fort, and these had run away, and were brought back by the King's order; and early this morning two or three shots were fired, but this soon ceased. In the Palace it is reported that they have one regiment of infantry and the King's own bodyguard. I don't envy them their present position, for the shells must penetrate everywhere in the course of a few hours. While this is going on, our troops are gradually taking possession of other parts of the city; and this morning we established a post in the Bank without any loss, and this gives us command of part of the Chandnee Chouk; and in this way, I fancy, we shall go on, gradually occupying the different parts of the city, and driving the enemy out of any place they may attempt to defend, by using our guns and mortars instead of risking the lives of our men unless absolutely necessary.

Hodson's Intelligence Department says that such mutineers as there are intend returning towards Muttra, and that there are only a very few now remaining, who are to occupy our attention as much as they can, to allow of their baggage, which they have sent off, getting ahead, in case we should pursue them. There is no doubt of the Sepoys making off, as some have been caught by our guard coming out of the Cashmere Gate disguised as women. They were immediately shot. This was this morning. So ⸺ says that lots of regiments that were staunch on the 1st August have mutinied since. He always has something agreeable and inspiriting to say. I don't think we know of any regiment having mutinied since the 1st August.

Rather an amusing incident occurred at the Head-Quarters' barrack at Skinner's house yesterday evening. A telegraphic message was brought for Norman, but as he was out it was taken to the General in case the message might be of public importance; General Wilson accordingly opened it, and with a smile closed it again, observing that the message was of private nature—in fact, telling of the birth of a little girl! Norman is indeed a first-rate officer, and glad should I be to see him made Adjutant-General of the army; and I do not think it at all impossible, for Chamberlain does not intend to remain in his present post.

Nicholson, all will be glad to hear, is better; both Mactier and Mackinnon think him so.

I saw yesterday a return of officers killed and wounded on the 14th; it amounted to the sad number of forty-seven,* but I don't think there is any one you know amongst the number except Robert Pemberton, who, I told you, was so slightly hit that he was able to go about his duty the next day.

I never saw such a strange collection of things as are being brought in, and I hope I shall be able to pick up a few portable articles to bring with me when I come. As our troops advanced this morning, and also yesterday, they found heaps of dead Sepoys. Scarcely a house, they say, that had not one or two in it; the poor wretches, probably mortally wounded, had crawled into the houses to die.

I have found it quite an agreeable change coming up here to camp to-day, there is such a noise and bustle in the city.

Past four o'clock, and no news except that people are leaving the city in great numbers.

The 20th is the day, you know, that you said that I was to write and settle as the day for coming up—and it looks very like it. I return to the city presently with Arthur Becher.

(*Diary*) 17th *September.*—Ride to the breaching battery, &c., at the Custom House Garden. It's a special wonder to me our having succeeded in overcoming all obstacles and getting inside; none but British troops could have done it, I do believe. Go on,

---

* The total casualties in the assault were 1170 killed and wounded—327 were killed and wounded from the 8th of September until the assault, and 177 were killed and wounded in the city after the assault.—H. W. NORMAN.

looking at Metcalfe's; round house to camp, and, not feeling very well, stay there. English mail in of 10th August—reached Bombay on 3rd instant. Bank occupied by us to-day. Ride down quietly in the evening to city.

TELEGRAM received at SIMLA.

DELHI, 17th September (10 A.M.).

Early this morning we occupied the Bank House, and hold city between it and magazine. Skirmishing going on, but we are fast establishing ourselves. Our guns command the bridge and Selimgurh; the latter and Palace under constant fire of shells.

The enemy are flying in hundreds towards Gwalior, *viâ* Muttra. The property of every kind left in the city immense; the number of dead Sepoys very great.

Colonel KEITH YOUNG to his wife.

DELHI, Friday, 18th September.

Here I am up in camp again, having come here to spend the day. What a very stupid telegraphic message to send up! No wonder you were all anxious at Simla, it was really enough to make you so; but you would soon have been relieved by the receipt of Arthur Becher's message to his wife, and then by getting my scrimmaging letter written on the 14th. Mrs Brooke was quite right when she said there was no danger for the staff: there certainly was very little on the day of the assault, and I don't see why there should be any at all now, if people will only keep in their proper places, which I intend to do, so you must not be under any apprehension for me; and God grant that I may soon be able to come up to see you and the dear little boys at Simla. Mrs Brooke, however, was quite wrong in her story about the heavy loss that had been sustained in the heavy breaching battery, and her friend, in stating that fifty men had been killed, must have meant in all the batteries from the day that our heavy guns first came into position; and I believe this was about the number, for Major Scott, who commanded the Custom House battery, told us that poor Fagan and two men killed were the only casualties he had—and Fagan's death, as I told you, was entirely owing to his own fault.

(DELHI.) LAHORE GATE.

You must not believe all the exaggerated stories you hear. I forget whether it is since I wrote to you yesterday that we took possession of the Bank, which we now hold, and thus command part of the Chandnee Chouk, of which Mrs Brooke has heard such a dreadful account; we have heard nothing here of the enemy having guns in it, nor do I believe it to be the case. I am afraid Mrs Brooke will have a dreadful story to tell when she hears that we tried to take the Lahore Gate this morning, and failed, having one officer, Lieutenant Briscoe (Her Majesty's 75th), and five men killed, and ten men wounded. It was a stupid business altogether, and as Greathed led the attack it ought to have been successful, but the men were seized with some strange panic and hesitated just at the time they ought to have rushed on, and hence the failure. I hope it will have this good effect, that the General will in future employ his Artillery a little more before allowing any attack to be made; if this is done, I trust there will be no more failures.

The Palace was dreadfully shelled all last night, and they were to-day to fix upon a spot for a breaching battery, which I dare say will be ready by to-morrow morning. Last night we had a welcome addition to our force of four hundred Sikh sappers, who have shown themselves most useful.

I dare say you will have seen the casualty list of the 14th. Our loss was even heavier than I supposed, amounting to eight officers and one hundred and sixty-two European privates killed, ten missing, and fifty-two officers and five hundred and ten men, Europeans, wounded, making altogether eleven hundred and fifty-five casualties; but many of the officers are slightly wounded and are already going about—young Anson, for instance, and Pemberton, and others—and no doubt many of the men are slightly wounded, but still the list is a very long one. To make up in some measure for this, I may mention that we took one hundred and fifty-five guns the other day in the magazine, and fifty-one on the 14th, making altogether two hundred and six guns taken from the enemy within the last four days. The wretches can't have many more left now; but their greatest want must be ammunition for their guns, as they could hardly have taken much out of the magazine. There are large piles of shot and shell there, which are a treasure to us, as all had to come from

Ferozepore, and one hackery only holds five, I think it is, of the large shells.

There were very satisfactory letters yesterday afternoon from Agra, Cawnpore, and Allahabad; all was going on well everywhere. The two European regiments were to reach Allahabad on the 4th, and, allowing for all delays, the force expected to be before Lucknow on the 20th, the day after to-morrow, and no fears appear to be entertained of Lucknow not holding out till then; they are said to have a party in the city favourable to them, and a messenger sent by them, who left on the 2nd instant, had reached Cawnpore. It was not said whether he brought a letter with him, but the people at Cawnpore seemed quite satisfied that all was right. General Outram had expressed his intention, when he joined at Cawnpore, of not taking the command from Havelock. The Gwalior mutineers, that portion which had left Gwalior, were still at Dholpore by the latest accounts.

Mr Colvin's death you will have heard of; the anxiety he suffered appears to have killed him. I wish they would make Frere Lieutenant-Governor, but I fear there is no chance of this.

I have just heard that Captain Rosser of the Carabineers is not dead, as was reported. Tell Mrs Greathed, if she has not heard from her husband, that I saw him this morning after the attack on the Lahore Gate, and he was quite well. Hodson was here, too, a little ago, and quite well.

Going on for four o'clock, and all right, only our guns and mortars playing away. They say that *atta* is selling in the city at two *seers* the rupee. The King wanted to come out to us, but was not permitted. Norman has just left the tent to go to the city.

(*Diary*) 18*th September*.—Rode up to camp to breakfast; just before starting, word brought in that an attack made by us on the Lahore Gate had failed, with one officer and five men killed, and ten men wounded. Bad this, and faces looking anxious. Grand shelling of the Palace all night; it ought to drive them out of it if any of the enemy are still there, which is said to be doubtful. Back to city in evening.

(DELHI.) DELHI GATE.

TELEGRAMS *received at* SIMLA.

18*th September* (8 A.M.).

Our mortars have been firing throughout the night, and must have inflicted much damage within the Palace.

2 P.M.—Our position the same as last night. We are strengthening ourselves in the Bank; our sappers are working towards the house, which commands the Burn Bastion. No suitable place yet found from which to breach the Palace, which we continue to shell. Selimgurh has only fired a few shots, and does no harm. We have received no information to-day of the movements of the rebels. Yesterday Delhi Gate of Palace was said to be open, and covered carts passing out. No certain intelligence regarding the King.

The ordnance captured is:—On the works, thirty-five; in the magazine, one hundred and seventy. Immense stores of shot and shell, and large quantities of percussion-caps, but no powder. The magazine building uninjured excepting the portion injured previously by the explosion. No increase of sickness in camp. General Nicholson not so well to-day. Lieutenants Pogson and Webb died of their wounds; Lieutenant Briscoe, 75th, killed this morning.

Rain has fallen, and made it nice and cool for the wounded.

Nothing from Delhi later than 2 P.M. of 18th. A letter from Cawnpore of 6th instant gives cheering news of Lucknow: Residency all right, and the garrison apparently supplied with food by some secret friends. The 5th and 90th Foot, and detachment of 78th, 84th, and Madras Native Infantry, expected at Cawnpore about 10th instant. General Havelock would then be able to advance on Lucknow with two thousand European infantry, three batteries of Artillery, and four thousand Sikhs.* The move was to be made immediately the reinforcements became available. Sir J. Outram accompanies, but will not take the command from General Havelock. One thousand Goorkhas are to remain at Azimghur, and two thousand at Joudhpore; the Madras Brigade marching up Trunk Road, and Her Majesty's 53rd proceeding up in carts. The Godas in Lucknow, numbering five

* The four thousand Sikhs with Havelock only existed in fiction. He had, perhaps, four hundred of the regiment of Ferozepore.—H. W. NORMAN.

thousand,* said to be fighting on our side against the insurgents. Dinapore mutineers making for Delhi *via* Banda. Numerous Europeans said to be concealed in Rohilkund by the Thakoors.

CHAMBERLAIN (*Brigadier*).

Colonel KEITH YOUNG *to his wife.*

DELHI, *Saturday*, 19*th September.*

I was so glad to find by the receipt of your letter, No. 115 of the 16th, that you had heard through Colonel Becher of our all being well on the afternoon of the 14th. It is sad to think that our letters are so long on the road, but there is no helping this, and you must be content to know that all is progressing most favourably, and that there is every prospect of our getting possession of the Palace and the rest of the city in a very short time, without any further loss of life. We have made considerable progress since yesterday in the direction of the Palace, and are now within three or four hundred yards of it; whether it will be necessary to breach the walls seems doubtful, but preparations are being made for the batteries in case it is. The impression is that both the Palace and Selimgurh are abandoned, not a gun having been fired from either all to-day, and no muskets either from the Palace walls, though our men, many of them, have been close up. I dare say we shall hear in the course of the day whether the Palace is empty or not. The report is that the King and all his family have gone out to Nizamoodeen's Tomb—you remember the place that we went with the Goughs to see? There is a large *serai* there, and lots of room to accommodate a very large party.

Our cavalry all went out this morning to reconnoitre, and they bring back word that the Bareilly mutineers, who had their camp outside the city near the Delhi Gate, had left their camp standing and fled towards Muttra; and there seems no doubt that what Sepoys are left are gradually disappearing, and parties of tens and twenties were seen this morning going over the bridge of boats, at which we have not been firing to-day, for what reason I know not, but perhaps to allow of the scoundrels clearing off

---

* I do not know what is meant by the five thousand Godas said to be fighting on our side at Lucknow. No one was fighting on the side of our small garrison.—H. W. NORMAN.

quietly. It is reported also that the principal wretches now opposing us in the city are Sikh prisoners who had escaped from the Agra jail. We are gradually creeping on towards the Lahore Gate without exposing our men, and I have not heard of a single casualty to-day. One party of the mutineers, it is said, who have left here, are making for Anoopshur, on the right bank of the Ganges, with the intention, apparently, of crossing over into Rohilkund. It does not much signify where they go, so long as they don't remain here; they will have very little chance afterwards, wherever they may be.

I told you yesterday of the news from Cawnpore, which was all confirmed by another letter received this morning, giving a very satisfactory account of affairs at Lucknow; and to-morrow was the day fixed upon for our troops to arrive there. God grant that it may be so, and that the gallant little garrison may be preserved. That effected, and the whole of Delhi in our possession, all the rest will be an easy business as far as fighting is concerned; there is nowhere for the rebels to make any serious stand against us again. Wilson, the Deputy Judge-Advocate General, got a letter yesterday from Ghazeepore, dated the 13th August, and all was well there then, and the stud had been preserved. I mention this, as I see by a paragraph in a Calcutta paper that they had heard there that all the horses had been taken away by the rebels.

I had intended to go up to camp again this morning, but it came on to rain, and I was glad I stayed, as we are getting much more comfortable than we were, half the officers here having gone away to another house, and I am sure there is no necessity for any of us being crowded as we were, for there are lots of spare houses. The one where the Rifles are is one of the best houses I have seen in India, and the very largest; the whole of the regiment is there, officers and men, and there are dozens of rooms still unoccupied. The house is beautifully furnished—chandeliers, large mirrors, couches, &c. Most of the mirrors were smashed by our troops, the Sikhs, I believe, when we first came in; it was a great pity, but there is no preventing the men committing all kinds of devastation. I was amused when I went over to the house (it belongs to a Native noble, Ahmed Allee Khan) to see most of the men of the Rifles lying on nice

Mirzapore carpets. The Prize Agents will, however, take possession of all these in time. The Agents elected are Colonel Seaton, Sir Edward Campbell, and Captain Wriford.

Past 2 P.M., and I am obliged to send my letter off from here rather earlier, the post-office being in camp. All is going on well, and I have not heard of a single casualty up to this.

(*Diary*) 19*th September.*—A stroll before breakfast. Getting on very well to-day with our operations, and gradually creeping on towards the other end of the city and camp. Burn Bastion and Lahore Gate taken without loss.

Lord WILLIAM HAY *to Mrs* KEITH YOUNG.

Sunday Evening, 20th September.

MY DEAR MRS YOUNG,—Kindly send the following to Mrs Norman:—'19th September 1857. One mortar battery continued to fire during the night towards the south of the Palace, in the direction of Durreoogunj; we have now turned them towards the Jumma Musjid. Abbot's house occupied at dawn without opposition; our advanced picket is at Khan Mahomed's house. On the right the Sappers have worked mostly towards the Burn Bastion, so as to take the guns on it. The Lahore Gate is ours. Selimgurh has not fired at all, and the town is being evacuated. King said to be in the Old Fort.' A small party will be pushed on to-day towards the Palace, with a view to seizing the gateway. All our available cavalry gone out under Brigadier Grant to reconnoitre south face of town, and it is hoped the demonstration will hurry the evacuation of the city. Captain Lowe mentions what you have doubtless heard—our failure at the Lahore Gate; but it does not appear to have been a very serious matter.—Yours sincerely, W. H.

P.S.—And, by the way, don't say that Lowe told the tale, for it is kept secret, I believe.

Colonel KEITH YOUNG *to his wife.*

DELHI, *Sunday,* 20*th September.*

Your letter of the 17th instant I received this morning, and it is delightful to think how pleased you will be when you get to-day's

(NEAR DELHI.) THE TOMB OF HAMAYOON. where the King and Princes took refuge after the capture of the city. After giving themselves up, the Princes were shot by Major Hodson who feared a rescue by the mob. Like the Jumma Musjid the Tomb is built of red sandstone and white marble.

telegraph, telling of our being in entire possession of the city, Palace, and Fort. All were evacuated this morning, or during the night, and we have now arrived at the conclusion of our labours here; but there must be a pursuing Column, which will still have something to do, but I am not aware what arrangement is to be made.

The King, unfortunately, has gone away, so I suppose the first thing will be to try and catch him; he is said to be either at Hamayoon's or Nizamoodeen's Tomb, and whether the mutineers are with him or not I don't know. I have just been all over the Palace, which is now occupied by us in large force. I went in first with George Hall, and there was an alarm of the enemy having returned and attacked the Delhi Gate. It was a small party of about twenty mutineers, who probably went, not knowing we were in possession; they wounded three of our men, and we came back to tell the General, and he sent me with such orders as he considered necessary to the officer commanding, Colonel Jones of the Rifles. All now is right and quiet everywhere and throughout the city, and all are as happy as possible.

I send you a small map of the city, which will give you an idea of our position when we first came in, and up to yesterday. Last night we took the Burn Bastion, and then the Lahore Gate, and after that all the other gates were abandoned; and we have not had a single man killed—only those three men in the place wounded.

Isn't it sad poor Greathed, the Commissioner, dying of cholera? I saw Hodson a little while ago, quite well. I hope to-morrow to tell you what day is fixed for my leaving here for Simla.

(*Diary*) 20*th September*.—Palace taken and occupied; visit it in afternoon. Selimgurh also ours, and all the town.

Brigadier CHAMBERLAIN *to* E. C. BARNES.

DELHI CITY, 20*th September* (9 A.M.).

The Burn Bastion was assaulted yesterday evening, and six guns and one mortar captured without loss. The Lahore Gateway has been occupied this morning. The Ajmere Gate and outworks do not fire; they appear deserted, and our people are going to take possession. The townspeople are all leaving the city. The mutineers blew up a magazine in their camp this morning; and our cavalry patrol, who moved out towards the southern face of the town, report that they saw no one in their camp. We hope to establish our line along the Chandnee Chouk in the course of the day. The mutineers offer much less resistance, and are evidently decreasing in numbers.

No improvement in General Nicholson's condition.* Mr Greathed died at midnight of cholera. The whereabouts of the King and Royal Family still unknown.

TELEGRAMS *received at* SIMLA.

DELHI, 20*th September* (10 A.M.).

We have taken the Ajmere Gate and outworks without opposition, securing three heavy guns and one 8-inch howitzer. We are sending up heavy mortars to the Burn Bastion to shell the portions of the town not yet in our possession. A continuous mortar fire was kept up on the town last night. On our left we hold the same position as last evening; but we have just spiked the mutineers' gun in front of the Palace. We are going to form a Column to go into the Palace.

Noon.—We have possession of the Palace, Jumma Musjid, and Ajmere Gate. Seven guns were found in position at the gateway of the Palace. HODSON.

Colonel KEITH YOUNG *to his wife.*

DELHI, *Monday,* 21*st September.*

I have arranged to leave this to-morrow morning in a dâk carriage, and hope, by God's blessing, to have a happy meeting with you and the little ones at Simla on Thursday evening. I am just going down to the city to the telegraph-office to send off a message to you to say I'm coming, and to ask you to have a pony for me at Syree, where I ought to be, if all goes right, at two or three o'clock. Seymour or Congreve would lend a pony to bring me up from Syree, but if no other is to be had send down the little black pony of Doddy's. The pony must be saddled.

All is getting on very well here, and this morning a royal salute was fired by us. The King has not given himself up, but

* General Nicholson, as is well known, died of his wounds.

is expected to do so in the course of the day. I hope, however, our soldiers will come across him, and save us further trouble with him.

(*Diary*) *21st September.*—Yesterday asked the General, who says he didn't see why I shouldn't go to Simla; determine accordingly on leaving to-morrow morning. Ride up to camp and make arrangements; return with Arthur Becher. Send off things. Go to Palace, where all are, and say good-bye. King brought in by Hodson—see the old scoundrel!

22nd September.—Pack up, breakfast, and off just at 10 A.M. Very slow work in one of those heavy penny-a-milers, and didn't get to Kurnaul till after nine. Had some eggs and tea at the dâk-bungalow, where Mackinnon pays me a visit, and then off again. At Piplee got into a doolie—slow work; a disgrace to Government that this road has not been completed.

23rd September.—Not in at Umballa till past ten. Enjoy a bathe and breakfast at the hotel very much. Ascertain that there is no horse dâk available, so lay a dâk of bearers, and on again at 1 P.M. in the doolie; rather hot work, but it seems the only way of getting over the ground without sacrificing another day, and I have promised to be at Simla to-morrow. About twelve, or nearly so, when I reach Kalka.

24th September.—Just as well that I went to Mrs Bain's, as the old lady was very civil—got up to make me a cup of tea, and had my doolie put to rights. About 1 A.M. I started; tedious work. At Kussowlie at sunrise, and at Kukree Huttee at ten, where I had breakfast. Reach Syree about half-past four, and there found Seymour's pony, which took me to Ellerslie; and then (thankful indeed ought I to be to God) I had a happy meeting with F. and the dear children.

CHAPTER XIV.

LETTERS RECEIVED AND DESPATCHED AFTER THE FALL OF DELHI.

Colonel H. B. HENDERSON *to Colonel* KEITH YOUNG.

LONDON, *9th September.*

I have been nearly the whole day at the Mansion House, busy about the Fund collecting here for the sufferers by the late Mutiny. I say *late*, though I deeply fear it is incorrect so to describe it. It is the last and most absorbing subject here with all interested in India; and oh! how I wish I could hope that by the time this letter reaches you it could be so far quelled that it could truly be called the 'late' Mutiny by you all! But it is so spread in its consequences just now, and your means of punishing it are at present so scanty, I dread to think that its murderous course will be unchecked until the troops now on the way shall be fairly up the country and falling foul of the rascals. Unless there is a break up amongst them, meantime, with your limited means, you can scarcely get possession of Delhi and put down the numbers elsewhere.

I know not what you will all think in India of the exertions made to get up a Fund for the sufferers from this Mutiny, but it is wonderful the present excitement and sympathy in England. Even those who have no friends in India are deeply anxious for news from it. The Mutiny is the subject of conversation and intense interest with every one; the atrocities committed have roused the general feeling in Europe, and India was never so much thought of as at this moment of suspense. All are eager for the mails, and all breathing vengeance on the cruel murderers of women and children.

The subscription list at the Mansion House is daily showing

an increase. To-day, at the close of the books, it stood at £17,000, and still meetings are getting up all over the country. I have undertaken a duty in which my heart is in the work; but it is very onerous just now, and I have not a moment to myself. I will endeavour to enclose a list from the *Times* of the subscribers to the Fund—£8000 goes to Lord Canning by this mail, which, with the £2000 by the last, will make £10,000 thus early remitted. It is intended to reserve, by a new resolution of another General Meeting, a part of the Funds for the sufferers who may arrive in England, ladies and children here, and others; there are many already who require aid, and much will have to be done in England. The Fund is expected to be very large. See what a handsome contribution there is from the Emperor of the French and the Garde Imperiale.

Good-night, and God bless you, my dear Keith. At times the old soldier comes about me, and I could wish I were some years younger and helping to punish the cruel wretches you have to deal with, instead of enacting Honorary Secretary only to a Fund here; but I should do little good out with you, and can only send you heartfelt good wishes.

10*th September.*—I had intended to enclose a subscription list, but I have not one available. It appears in the *Times* of the 9th (yesterday); it amounted to upwards of £16,000, and to-day the Queen has sent £1000, two other large donations bringing it up to about £20,000.—Yours anxiously and affectionately,

H. B. H.

Colonel KEITH YOUNG to Colonel H. B. HENDERSON.

SIMLA, 12*th October.*

MY DEAR H.,—This mail will bring you excellent tidings of the progress of affairs in India; and my own belief, and that indeed of all I have spoken to, is that this country, and especially Simla, will for the future be safer than it has ever been. My future movements are awaiting the orders of our new Commander-in-Chief, Sir Colin Campbell, and we know nothing at present of his movements or intentions. It is generally believed, however, that he will come up country, and that we (that is, Colonel Arthur Becher, who is up here, and myself, and other Staff officers) will join him probably at

Cawnpore, when he will march up to Umballa or Meerut and make one or other his headquarters, or perhaps he may come up to Simla; and, notwithstanding the clamour made apparently at home about the Commander-in-Chief residing at Simla, I really don't know that there is a single good reason against it, and certainly there are many in its favour—the real objection I believe to be that the Commander-in-Chief ought not to be living in a *good* climate when so many of the troops are living in a *bad* one. Whatever may be done about the Commander-in-Chief making the hills his residence, I trust that as many European troops as possible will be located in the hills. Had it not been for the three European regiments that went down from the adjacent hill stations in the highest state of health, we should never have taken Delhi: braced up as they were by the invigorating hill climate, they stood the hot weather and rains much better than the 8th, 52nd, and 61st, who had had no such advantage, and whose enfeebled constitutions were in many instances unable to bear up against the terrible wear and tear of the life in camp in the hot weather and rains.

You may imagine how delighted I was to get up here again, and after Delhi was altogether in our possession—the wretched old King, too, whom I saw when he was first brought in—I lost no time in getting away. You will see what has been going on there since I left by reference to the public papers; and so well have matters been progressing of late, that unless Sir Colin Campbell hurries up there will not be much left for either him or the troops now arriving to do, except to fix upon the proper places for locating them so as to keep the country quiet.

The Gwalior mutineers, those in Rohilkund and in Oude, are the only bodies now remaining of any importance. Penny talks of going into Rohilkund and settling matters there; and Greathed's Column, which was marching on Hatrass and Agra by the last accounts, having relieved Allyghur and sent the enemy flying in all directions, will probably be strong enough for the Gwalior scoundrels—but you will have later information from the papers than I am able to give you. I saw yesterday the last accounts hitherto received from both Showers' and Greathed's Columns, and nothing could be more satisfactory than the progress they are now making. It is only to be regretted that one Column at least was not sent off earlier after the assault, and the Bareilly mutineers might have been prevented from crossing into Rohilkund, which it is now feared they have done; but Wilson, though he took Delhi, is not quite a Sir Charles Napier. What would not such a man have been worth during the late crisis?

SIMLA, 31st October.

MY DEAR H.,—In one of the last letters I sent you I enclosed a numerical abstract of the Force before Delhi on different named dates, which I hope found its way safely, as you would have been able to judge from it how unreasonable was the clamour that was at one time raised against the Force and its commanders for not taking Delhi—just jumping over the 'garden wall,' as Mr Vernon Smith, or some member of the House, facetiously termed the defences of the city.

It is surprising what ignorance there is at home about matters out here, even amongst those to whom the best sources of information are accessible. You may have noticed, perhaps, that Colonel Sykes in the debate in Parliament (on the 11th August, I think it was) explained to the House the cause of the mutiny in the 3rd Cavalry at Meerut, stating that it was in consequence of the commanding officer attempting to force the greased cartridges on the men, the real truth being that the cartridges which the men refused to take were common blank cartridges of the same make and material exactly as had been used in the regiment for years; and before the Court-Martial was ordered, this fact was clearly ascertained by a special Court of Inquiry assembled for the purpose, before which it was satisfactorily shown that the cartridges had been made up in the regimental magazine.

Colonel H. B. HENDERSON to Colonel KEITH YOUNG.

AIX LA CHAPELLE, 20th October 1857.

MY DEAR KEITH,—Your long and welcome letter from before Delhi, of 26th August, was received here three days ago.

You seem to think that the impatient desire to get hold of Delhi was overruling, in England, all other considerations; but you may rely on it, every one whose opinion is worth having fully understood the risk and difficulty, and were rather wishing that you should hold back till fully assured of your success —though your possession of it would cause intense delight. For some weeks *all* here were *fearing* that the assault might be attempted with too few Europeans and others at your command, and were dreading what might happen when you got inside. If you could get at the mass of English newspapers, you would observe how eager they all are to praise rather than abuse; in fact, the National honour at this crisis is too much at stake to publish any abusive comments on our brave troops that sundry foreign papers would catch at, and do their best to crow at our misfortunes.

If Wilson, in September, can manage to get possession, and there is no failure in carrying out the operation, his future will be made, and he may rely on every voice crying out for his high advancement. Most anxiously shall we look out, now that it is believed you have about ten thousand men of all descriptions with you, for the anticipated attempt; but if good reason be shown, Wilson need not fear that public opinion will not be on his side though he withholds the attempt for days to come. But we do hope that when made it will be a glorious assault, to keep up the good name which at this moment the whole of Europe is liberally giving to our Indian Army for its splendid resistance of the mutineers while almost unassisted, and before the reinforcements were with you.

You may judge of this feeling from the success of our Relief Fund; its rapid increase of amount is entirely owing to the intense feeling of sympathy which has arisen on your behalf from all classes of society in Great Britain. The splendid defence of different places and the frequent exhibition of manliness and bravery are dwelt on here with pride; and even the French and other nations are admitting how much these instances uphold our honour and redeem all the blunders and mishaps of the Mutiny.

If you could see the *Times* daily you would wonder at the letters from India it so eagerly publishes; half its columns are now given to Indian matters—but the *Times* would not seek after them if it did not know the universal devouring of their contents by its readers.

Colonel KEITH YOUNG *to Colonel* H. B. HENDERSON.

SIMLA, 19*th November.*

I am still, you see, at Simla waiting till General Penny can send down a Column, and, when he can do this, all the Head-Quarters' Staff are to go down with it; but at present he is unable to detach any force in that direction, his only spare troops having gone towards Narnaul to look after the Joudhpore mutineers.

Since I commenced this I have heard that Gerrard, who commands the Column that has gone in the direction of Narnaul, has fallen in with the mutineers and defeated them, capturing six of their guns, our loss being about seventy killed and wounded, and, amongst the former, I am sorry to say Gerrard himself.

We are still here without information from Lucknow of later date than the 5th, and we are most anxiously looking out to hear that Sir Colin Campbell has advanced to the relief of Havelock. There must be a sufficiency of troops available now with Hope Grant's Column to dispose of any force the rebels can have at Lucknow.

Colonel H. B. HENDERSON *to Colonel* KEITH YOUNG.

The Relief Fund has reached £28,000, and still going on increasing; but my Honorary Secretaryship is giving me more work than I bargained for—Committees daily. But we have got General Tremenhere, and Parry Woodcock of the Civil Service, as additional Honorary Secretaries, and as they are otherwise unemployed I am now relieved from much of the care and responsibility, and am beginning to take it more easily.

I thank you for the present state of the Force at Delhi, taken at different times from May. It was shown to several about us, and finally appeared in the morning papers, where they are anxious to get all scraps of intelligence from the seat of operations.

Colonel KEITH YOUNG *to Colonel* H. B. HENDERSON.

SIMLA, 1*st December.*

I mentioned to you that all the Head-Quarters' Staff had been ordered to join Sir Colin Campbell, and we are to march with a

Column that is being sent down from Delhi; but week after week has the intended march of the Column been postponed. The day now fixed for its moving is the 10th of this month, and I fancy it is pretty certain to go about that date, unless some unexpected troubles again occur in the vicinity of Delhi; but now that the Joudhpore mutineers have been dispersed, I do not think there is much likelihood of any further rebels moving in the direction of Delhi. The Column going to Cawnpore is to escort carriage and camp followers, of which the troops there are much in want.

The King remains at Delhi for the present, and what his fate is to be we know not. I hear from Harriott (my deputy at Meerut) that he was going over that evening to conduct his trial, ordered by Government There is no doubt of the old brute's life having been guaranteed to him by Hodson, to whom he gave himself up, for I was in the Palace when the King was brought in a prisoner, and Hodson himself told me of his having promised him his life— but under what authority this was done I know not. I have not myself seen any of the papers on the subject, but I understand there are lots forthcoming to prove that the King took an active part in the rebellion, and, worse than all, he gave his approval to the Jhansi massacre. Government at one time ordered him to be sent to Calcutta, but this, General Penny said, it was impossible to do with the force at present at his disposal; perhaps if the old wretch is sent to the Cape de Verds, Ascension, or some of these places, the effect will be quite as good as hanging him.*

I must refer you to the papers for all the news about the progress made in disposing of the mutineers. We have only news from Cawnpore to the 20th of last month, and so far matters had proceeded very satisfactorily, and the loss of life on our side was not greater than might have been anticipated.

There was a talk, I heard yesterday, of our retiring from Lucknow for the present; in my opinion it would be a fatal mistake, and the effect would be very bad all over India. It is a thousand pities we ever took Oude, but we *must* keep it now at all hazards.

Severely cold weather here, and a heavy fall of snow last week, the first I have seen for many years. We (the Babas and I) had a gentle game of snowballing.

* See Appendix G.

(SIMLA.) ELYSIUM HILL.

DONALD F. M'LEOD, *Civil Service, to* Colonel KEITH YOUNG.

DHURMSÂLA, 16*th December.*

MY DEAR KEITH YOUNG,—Mr Frere has sent me the enclosed pamphlet * for transmission to you; my being up here instead of at Lahore, as he supposed, has somewhat delayed it, but I trust it will reach you in good time. I have read it with great interest, and although I think Brigadier Jacob somewhat *ultra* in his opinions, and consider some of them as impracticable, yet it contains much that I quite agree with, even to supplying the Civil Service entirely from the Army, a measure which I have long advocated myself, although I think he has been injudicious in making the suggestion here, seeing that the question is a separate one, and that for the present the reorganisation of the army is the great point in which the strength and energies of all should be concentrated. The conviction that *all* posts connected with Native regiments must in future be filled by selected officers, and be in fact Staff appointments, so that a man who secures one of these shall regard it as the fulfilment of his aims, and not, as at present, be longing to get away from his corps, appears to be now becoming very general; and I for one very sincerely hope that this principle will be adopted. It is not, however, for a moment to be supposed that Government can consent to a large proportion of officers remaining unemployed, and this portion of Brigadier Jacob's scheme appears to me altogether crude.

Another scheme, however, which I heard Sir John Lawrence broach many months ago, and which I have since seen suggested in one of the Home papers, appears to me to attain the same object, without being open to animadversion—namely, that our European regiments, of which we must ever have a large number in future, be made the magazine, so to speak, from which to select officers for Native corps, the number assigned to each of the latter being but four or five as in Irregular corps at present, and that the places of the officers so selected shall be immediately filled up in the European corps, the transfer to the Native branch being regarded as permanent when once effected.

It would be useless my entering with you on Indian politics,

---

* This pamphlet is not printed here.

as it is from your quarter that we have to look for intelligence. We have just learned of intelligence having been received, through Sindhia, of the Gwalior contingent having been very thoroughly smashed.

There is indeed occasion for the deepest thankfulness, and how loud a call is there on us all for the most humble and heartfelt gratitude for the change which has come over the state of affairs generally, through the loving mercy of our Heavenly Father, who, though He has seen fit to try and chasten us severely—as severely as any nation, except, perhaps, the Jews, was ever chastened—has not yet allowed us to be overwhelmed, but has shown us a way out of all our troubles. May we all lay deeply and solemnly to heart the solemn lessons which have been taught to us by the mysterious and tremendous events of the past few months.

CONDENSED DIARY OF
PRINCIPAL EVENTS OF THE SIEGE

CONDENSED DIARY OF PRINCIPAL EVENTS OF THE SIEGE,

FROM MONDAY THE 8TH OF JUNE TO MONDAY THE 21ST OF SEPTEMBER.

8*th June, Monday.*—Battle of Budlee-ka-Serai about five miles from Alleepore, and second fight at Ridge before Delhi—Hindoo Rao's house and Flagstaff on Ridge occupied—More than twenty guns captured—Goorkhas behave admirably—Colonel Chester killed—Our Force left Alleepore at 2 A.M., last fight over at about 9 A.M.—Tents pitched about 4 P.M. before Delhi, on parade-ground and site of ruined cantonments.

9*th June, Tuesday.*—Our guns command gateways of city—Arrival of Daly's Corps of 'Guides,' and of General Reed in infirm health—Enemy make a grand attack on Ridge at about 2 P.M.—All troops turn out, and enemy driven back—In evening another attack.

10*th June, Wednesday.*—Flag hoisted on Flagstaff Tower—Firing all day from our batteries into city—People look gloomy, and talk of necessity of assault.

11*th June, Thursday.*—Small party of Gwalior insurgents (Horse) give themselves up—City described as a perfect pandemonium—Major Martin and his Irregulars, the 4th, arrive in Camp—Some of enemy's shell fall near Head-Quarter tents, which are therefore moved.

12*th June, Friday.*—Metcalfe House occupied—Enemy again attack Ridge, and lose heavily; they surprise Flagstaff picket, and kill Captain Knox.

13*th June, Saturday.*—Arrangements made for assault on city between 1 and 2 A.M.—Delay occurs through pickets not being withdrawn in time, so assault abandoned—Enemy again attack us; party of their Cavalry get round to our left—Very hot.

14*th June, Sunday.*—Service in Camp—Enemy attack Metcalfe House; their Cavalry again get round our left flank.

15*th June, Monday.*—Attack by enemy in force at 7 A.M. on our left flank; they are driven back—Another assault planned—Council of War decided on—Talk of waiting for reinforcements—Brigadier Wilson advocates waiting—Greathed, of Engineers, wishes to assault at once.

16*th June, Tuesday.*—Enemy quiet—We are entrenching our position—Hold another Council of War—Decide to wait for all reinforcements coming up before assault is made; this will allow of insurgents being followed up and destroyed.

17*th June, Wednesday.*—In afternoon we attack a battery being erected on our right flank in village of Kissengunge—Two Columns engaged under Majors Reid and Tombs—Gun captured; village and battery burnt and destroyed—Many of enemy killed; our loss small—Wounded and sick, and ladies sent to Meerut.

18*th June, Thursday.*—Lieutenant Wheatley killed, and several men killed and wounded in or near Hindoo Rao's; Engineers blamed for this, as they had been ordered to place sandbags to protect openings—Shell falls close to mess-tent.

19*th June, Friday.*—Serious attack on our right rear by Nussereebad mutineers—People looking serious—Daly and Becher wounded—Attack repulsed—Our loss ten officers and about one hundred men killed and wounded; enemy lose heavily.

20*th June, Saturday.*—One captured gun brought in—Same force as yesterday again attack us unsuccessfully—Arrival of convoy of between two and three hundred camels with grain from Alleepore.

21*st June, Sunday.*—Service at 6 A.M.

22*nd June, Monday.*—Bridge at Bhagput broken—Hodson takes temporary command of 'Guides'—Baird Smith appointed Chief-Engineer in place of Colonel Laughton—Weather very hot.

23*rd June, Tuesday.*—Day predicted as end of our 'Raj'—Grand attack by enemy, who are unsuccessful at every point; but we suffer heavily—Generalship not good—Every one anxious—Arrival of Olpherts' Force and convoy.

24*th June, Wednesday.*—Arrival of Neville Chamberlain, new Acting Adjutant-General.

25*th June, Thursday.*—Quiet all day—Attack contemplated to-morrow.

26*th June, Friday.*—No attack from either side—Anxiety about Bhagput bridge.

27*th June, Saturday.*—Enemy again attack us: they lose four hundred killed and wounded; our loss under thirty—Arrival of convoy of two hundred camels with stores, rum, &c. from Meerut—Commencement of rains.

28*th June, Sunday.*—Arrival of Colonel Greathed with 8th King's and Rothney's Sikhs; also large convoy of stores—Part of Bhagput bridge of boats burnt—Hodson sent to report.

29*th June, Monday.*—Longfield appointed Brigadier in place of Graves, who goes away on sick leave—We cut off canal supply of water to city.

30*th June, Tuesday.*—Enemy again attack us, but are repulsed; we lose thirty or forty killed and wounded—Bridge over Jumna broken up by river rising.

CONDENSED DIARY OF PRINCIPAL EVENTS. 315

1st *July, Wednesday.*—Arrival of Bareilly mutineers in Delhi—Arrival in Camp of wing of 61st Regiment.

2nd *July, Thursday.*—Arrival of Coke's Corps, eight hundred strong; also Fenwick's Corps, 17th Irregulars—Enemy manage to put their bridge of boats together again—Executions in Camp—About eighty Poorbeahs or Oude men sent away—Arrival of Baird Smith—Assault intended this morning, but did not come off.

3rd *July, Friday.*—Party of enemy, the Bareilly Brigade, attack and partially plunder Alleepore.

4th *July, Saturday.*—Enemy from city come out to attack us, joined by Bareilly Brigade from Alleepore—Coke's Corps drives them off at about 7 A.M.

5th *July, Sunday.*—General Barnard ill with cholera: dies at 3 P.M.—General Reed to assume command of the Force.

6th *July, Monday.*—All quiet—Funeral of General Barnard—Heavy rain.

7th *July, Tuesday.*—All quiet.

8th *July, Wednesday.*—Bussye bridge over Nujufghurh canal blown up by our troops.

9th *July, Thursday.*—Enemy attack us in force—Misbehaviour of pickets of Fenwick's Corps and Carabineers—Hills and Tombs behave with great gallantry, and are recommended for Victoria Cross—Enemy lose heavily; but our loss over two hundred killed and wounded—Hodson 'taken in' by party of enemy—Arrival of convoy of stores and two or three hundred Sikh Artillerymen.

10th *July, Friday.*—Court of inquiry being held into conduct of Fenwick's Corps and Carabineers—Very rainy.

11th *July, Saturday.*—The 9th Irregulars, Fenwick's Corps, sent away to Alleepore with their arms and horses—Heavy rain during night, day foggy and misty.

12th *July, Sunday.*—All quiet—Still rainy.

13th *July, Monday.*—Convoy of ammunition and stores, &c., arrives from Raie.

14th *July, Tuesday.*—Hockin's Irregulars, the 17th, sent away from Camp—Lieutenant Campbell succeeds Fenwick in command of the 9th—Native Artillerymen disarmed two days ago—Firing going on all day; our men pursue enemy right up to city walls, and lose heavily in consequence—Chamberlain wounded.

15th *July, Wednesday.*—Enemy quiet.

16th *July, Thursday.*—General Reed ill—Brigadier Wilson to take over command—News that Sir Hugh Wheeler and his Force have been destroyed at Cawnpore—Shells fall close to Camp.

17th *July, Friday.*—Jhansi mutineers arrive in Delhi, eight hundred Infantry, some Cavalry, and three guns—One hundred and fifty of our sick and wounded sent to Umballa; Colonel Congreve also goes—General Reed leaves in evening—Wilson assumes command in Camp.

18th July, Saturday.—Arrival of large convoy of ammunition and stores, also strong party of Sikh Cavalry—Enemy attack our front and right front—Our men again follow enemy too close to walls, and lose sixty killed and wounded.

19th July, Sunday.—Residents in city reported all with us—Enemy quiet—Service in Camp.

20th July, Monday.—Nicholson telegraphs that he is anxious to join us with his Column—Major Greensill, of 75th, shot in mistake by one of our sentries.

21st July, Tuesday.—Sir John Lawrence telegraphs promising strong reinforcements from the Punjab; he is to send us about three thousand men, Europeans and Natives.

22nd July, Wednesday.—An alarm in morning, then quiet all day—Hot and rainy.

23rd July, Thursday.—Enemy attack our left front—Colonel Seaton wounded—Heavy rain.

24th July, Friday.—Hodson gives up command of 'Guides,' having got a Cavalry Corps of his own to get into order—Cool; drizzling rain all day.

25th July, Saturday.—Enemy quiet—Rain all day.

26th July, Sunday.—News of Havelock's victory over the Nana Sahib at Futtehpore; twelve guns and seven lacs of treasure taken.

27th July, Monday.—Arrival of Neemuch mutineers in Delhi—The 4th Irregulars disarmed—Arrival of large convoy.

28th July, Tuesday.—Mutineers still quiet—Rumoured internal dissensions and want of leaders; also scarcity of ammunition and money.

29th July, Wednesday.—All quiet.

30th July, Thursday.—Kemaon Force expected in Camp within two days.

31st July, Friday.—Enemy come out several thousand strong, and intend grand attack; frustrated by heavy rain.

1st August, Saturday.—Festival of the Eed; great noise in city—Arrival of Kemaon Battalion, also a convoy—Very heavy rain; Camp flooded in parts—Grand attack by enemy at Hindoo Rao's at about 6 P.M.—Still firing at 12 P.M.—Enemy's loss about one thousand; our loss between twenty and thirty killed and wounded.

2nd August, Sunday.—Service at 6 A.M.; firing going on at the time.

3rd August, Monday.—Letter from Havelock, dated 25th July, confirming massacre of Sir Hugh Wheeler and Force—Tells of Sir Henry Lawrence's death on 4th July—Havelock is advancing on Lucknow after defeating Nana Sahib three times and taking all his guns.

4th August, Tuesday.—Many mutineers are leaving city—Weather cool and pleasant.

5th August, Wednesday.—Unsuccessful attempt to destroy enemy's large bridge of boats by means of fire-rafts.

CONDENSED DIARY OF PRINCIPAL EVENTS. 317

6th August, Thursday.—Alarm sounded at 8 A.M.—Enemy come out, but do little.
7th August, Friday.—Arrival of Brigadier Nicholson—Heavy firing.
8th August, Saturday.—Powder manufactory in city blown up—Firing all night—Weather very hot and steamy.
9th August, Sunday.—Sacrament Sunday—Roar of cannon during service.
10th August, Monday.—Cannonading all day—Weather hot and steamy—Siege-train expected from Ferozepore.
11th August, Tuesday.—Very little firing—Weather cooler.
12th August, Wednesday.—Attack on enemy's outposts—Capture of four guns—Brigadier Showers slightly wounded—Enemy lose heavily; our loss about one hundred and thirteen killed and wounded.
13th August, Thursday.—Heavy cannonading, but little damage done.
14th August, Friday.—Arrival of Nicholson's Column of two thousand five hundred men, also large convoy with guns, ammunition, and treasure—Rumoured number of rebels in city about seventeen thousand—Heavy musketry firing from enemy during night.
15th August, Saturday.—Cannonading going on, otherwise all quiet—Lovely weather.
16th August, Sunday.—Attempt to spoil priming-powder of guns in one of the batteries—Special Service of Humiliation—Quiet all day—Assault to depend on arrival of siege-train.
17th August, Monday.—Hodson goes out after enemy—Successful reports from him—Two men hanged for tampering with charges of powder—All quiet—Very heavy rain.
18th August, Tuesday.—All quiet—Weather steamy and warm.
19th August, Wednesday.—All quiet—Mrs Leeson, a refugee from Delhi, comes into Camp.
20th August, Thursday.—Nicholson's Movable Column goes out to join Hodson, but has to return on account of flooded country.
21st August, Friday.—News from Brigadier Neill—Enemy's batteries fire into Metcalfe's compound and Coke's camp.
22nd August, Saturday.—Account received of Cawnpore massacre—Arrival of large quantity of shells.
23rd August, Sunday.—News of siege-train at Umballa—Reinforcements coming from Meerut—Our batteries now within six hundred yards of city walls—Weather cool.
24th August, Monday.—Return of Hodson after successful expedition.
25th August, Tuesday.—Movable Column under Nicholson, two thousand men and sixteen guns, goes out towards Nujufghurh, where two columns of enemy are said to be—Our loss in officers, up to date, is one hundred and twenty-four killed and wounded.
26th August, Wednesday.—Return of Nicholson's Movable Column—Enemy's Force completely routed: twelve guns taken, and all tents and baggage; our loss small.
27th August, Thursday.—All quiet.
28th August, Friday.—Hodson goes out with Cavalry to reconnoitre.

2 R

29th August, Saturday.—Return of Hodson with two of enemy's ammunition wagons—Arrival of five hundred carts with shells—Sir Colin Campbell coming from England as Commander-in-Chief.

30th August, Sunday.—Firing all night—Quiet during day—Siege-train at Kurnaul—Reinforcements from Meerut to arrive in Camp same time as siege-train—Chamberlain appointed *pucka* Adjutant-General.

31st August, Monday.—All quiet—Torrents of rain.

1st September, Tuesday.—Siege-train to arrive on 4th, also reinforcements from Meerut, and Cashmere troops—Very hot.

2nd September, Wednesday.—News from Captain Lumsden that the Persians have evacuated Herat.

3rd September, Thursday.—All quiet—Very hot.

4th September, Friday.—Arrival of siege-train during night, with guns and mortars harnessed to elephants—Thunder and rain.

5th September, Saturday.—Much sickness in Camp; fifty per cent. of Europeans in hospital—Very hot—Artillery and Engineers hard at work on batteries—Assault arranged for morning of 8th or 9th—Prize Agents to be appointed.

6th September, Sunday.—Arrival of Rifles and Artillery from Meerut, also Wyld's Corps of Punjab Infantry from Kurnaul—All quiet.

7th September, Monday.—Arrival of Jheend Raja's troops—First advance battery ready—Koodsee Bagh occupied without opposition.

8th September, Tuesday.—Cannonading all day—Enemy come out in force to attack new battery and drive us from Koodsee Bagh, but are repulsed on every side with great loss; we lose several officers and men—Arrival of Cashmere troops, between two and three thousand strong—Heavy mortar battery completed.

9th September, Wednesday.—Breaching batteries nearly ready; they are to be thirty feet thick—Cart with shells blown up in Camp—Enemy quiet—Very hot.

10th September, Thursday.—Batteries not yet ready—Engineers blamed for promising more than they could perform—Battery catches fire—Weather very hot and foggy.

11th September, Friday.—Batteries were all to have opened fire together at daybreak on signal rocket being thrown up; they were not ready, however—Cashmere Bastion quite demolished by our guns in afternoon—Some of enemy's Cavalry caught in our rear, and cut up—Cool, cloudy day.

12th September, Saturday.—Several of our batteries commence firing in morning, but heavy breaching battery still not ready: embrasures by mistake made in wrong direction, and have to be done over again.

13th September, Sunday.—All our batteries, with about sixty guns and mortars, hard at work—None of enemy's are replying—Assault to take place to-morrow morning—Wilson issues order not to harm women and children—Telegraph established in Camp—Our strength is about eight thousand men, and enemy's supposed to be now reduced to ten or twelve thousand; they were said to be forty thousand strong at one time—Service in Camp at 6 A.M.

14th September, Monday.—Assault commenced one hour after daybreak—We hold Cashmere, Cabul, and Moree Gates, Skinner's house, College, and Church—Water Bastion smashed—Our loss very heavy, about thirty officers and five hundred men killed and wounded; Brigadier Nicholson dangerously wounded—We are firing upon Palace and Selimgurh, and are trying to breach magazine—Enemy offer determined resistance—Major Reid fails to occupy Kissengunge; he is severely wounded—Cashmere Contingent act with cowardice and run off, abandoning their guns—Many people coming in to give themselves up—Sepoys are told they cannot be received.

15th September, Tuesday.—All quiet during night—Enemy still hold Selimgurh Fort, Palace, and magazine—Many mutineers have fled—Little firing from enemy—We are breaching magazine; storm to be to-morrow morning—Hot day.

16th September, Wednesday.—Magazine stormed soon after daybreak, and carried; enemy make little resistance—One hundred and seventy ordnance, and quantity of shot and shell, and percussion-caps in magazine, but no powder—We are now shelling Palace and Selimgurh—Telewara and Kissengunge suburbs evacuated by enemy, who leave four guns behind—Our guns command bridge of boats—News of Colvin's death.

17th September, Thursday.—Still shelling Palace and Fort—Bank occupied—Enemy flying towards Gwalior—Property of every kind in city immense—Number of dead Sepoys great—Our total loss during Assault, eleven hundred and seventy killed and wounded; of these, forty-seven are officers—Two hundred and six guns captured since 14th—Nicholson reported better.

18th September, Friday.—Palace shelled all night—No certain intelligence regarding King—Failure to take Lahore Gate, owing to panic among our men—People look anxious.

19th September, Saturday.—Palace and Selimgurh reported abandoned; we are still shelling them, also Jumma Musjid—Bareilly mutineers, who had their camp outside Delhi Gate, have fled towards Muttra—Burn Bastion and Lahore Gate taken—Seaton, Campbell, and Wriford appointed Prize Agents.

20th September, Sunday.—We have entire possession of city, including Palace and Fort—King reported to be at Hamayoon's Tomb—No improvement in Nicholson's condition—Death of Greathed, Commissioner, from cholera.

21st September, Monday.—King brought in by Hodson—Royal salute fired this morning. Colonel Keith Young leaves for Simla.

APPENDICES.

APPENDIX A. (*See page* 11.)
JOONUG AND THE RANA OF KOOYNTAL.

The following letters will best explain themselves; they were written with reference to the time when Colonel Keith Young and his family, with many others, went to Joonug, in May, and placed themselves under the protection of the Rana of Kooyntal. All the British and loyal Native troops had been ordered from Simla, which was left entirely unprotected.

No. 431.   ROBERT MONTGOMERY, ESQ., *Judicial Commissioner, Punjab, to Lieutenant* H. PASKE, *the* OFFICIATING SECRETARY *to the* CHIEF COMMISSIONER *for the Punjab.*

(No. 4501.)   LAHORE, 30*th December* 1857.

SIR,—I have the honour to forward to you in original, for the perusal of the Chief Commissioner of the Punjab, the accompanying letter, dated 23rd instant, from Colonel Keith Young, Judge-Advocate General of the Army, bringing to notice the services rendered by the Rana of Kooyntal to certain ladies and gentlemen who sought his protection during the panic at Simla, and to recommend that the Rana's services may be acknowledged in some suitable way by the Chief Commissioner.

(Signed)   ROBERT MONTGOMERY,
Judicial Commissioner.

LAHORE, 30*th December* 1857.

Ordered that a copy of the above be forwarded to Colonel Keith Young, Judge-Advocate General, for his information.

APPENDIX A.

Colonel KEITH YOUNG *to* ROBERT MONTGOMERY, ESQ., *Commissioner.*

CAMP, ALLYGHUR, *23rd December* 1857.

MY DEAR SIR,—Understanding that it is the wish of the Chief Commissioner and yourself that Native chiefs subordinate to the Punjab Government, who have exerted themselves during the late troublous times to protect our countrymen and countrywomen, should not go unrewarded, I take the liberty of bringing to your notice the very praiseworthy conduct of the Rana of Kooyntal, and I may add that I write at the request of others, who consider themselves indebted to the Rana, as well as on my own account. Enclosed is a copy of a paper that was given to him on the occasion of our visit to Joonug, the capital of his little territory.

It may be said, perhaps, that little credit is due to the Rana, as there was no sufficient reason for any one to leave Simla. This, however, were it actually so, makes *his* behaviour not the less meritorious. But subsequent events have shown that danger was to be seriously apprehended; and before I determined on leaving Simla, which was not till the day after the Nusseree battalion was known to be in a state of open mutiny, I personally consulted the chief civil and military authorities—Lord William Hay and Major-General Penny—and was told by them that all who could leave Simla ought to do so.

General Penny himself left the same day, and in the evening I, with my family and nearly all the remaining residents of that part of Simla where I was living—Colonel and Mrs Greathed, Mrs Hallifax, and Mrs Daly—was hospitably received and sheltered for the night at the Rana's house at Simla, which we left early in the morning for Joonug. This will serve to show that the Rana was not indifferent in the matter; he was ready at Simla to assist us to the utmost, and at Joonug all his available resources were placed at our disposal.

I may mention that besides those whose signatures are attached to the enclosed paper, I observed at Joonug several whose names have been omitted to be recorded—Mrs Nicoll and family, Mr Campbell (late Commissioner) and Mrs Campbell, Mrs Cholmondely, Mrs Annersley and family, and others—to all of whom I am sure it will be gratifying to find that the conduct of the Rana has been suitably acknowledged by Government.—I am, &c.,

(Signed) KEITH YOUNG (*Lieutenant-Colonel*),
Judge-Advocate General.

ROBERT MONTGOMERY, Esq.,
Commissioner.

Enclosure in Colonel KEITH YOUNG'S *Letter to Mr* R. MONTGOMERY.

To RANA SANSAR SAIN, Rana of Kooyntal.

JOONUG, *Tuesday, 19th May* 1857.

We, the undersigned, cannot leave Joonug without expressing to you our sense of the valuable kindness and assistance we have received from

APPENDIX A. 323

you during a time of great general excitement at Simla—when you voluntarily came forward and offered us all your generous protection, which we have enjoyed for several days past, and for which we all feel most grateful.

(Signed) A. Penny, Major-General.
Thos. Quin, Lt.-Col., and Family.
H. G. H. Burnside, Capt., H.M. 61st Regiment.
A. C. Yonge, Lt., H.M. 61st Regiment.
J. E. Copeland, Lt., 10th Light Cavalry.
J. H. Inglefield, Lt., 39th N. I.
J. A. Nisbett, M.D., Asst. Surgeon, Simla.
Edward F. Campbell, Bt., Capt., 60th Rifles.
Lady Campbell.
Chas. Harding, Asst. Ex. Off.
Mrs Harding.
J. W. Lawrie, Head Clerk Qr.-Master-General's Office.
Mrs Lawrie.
Keith Young, Lt.-Col., J.-A. General, and Family.
E. H. Greathed, Lt.-Col., and Mrs Greathed.
Mrs Hallifax.
John Thomas and Family, Adjt.-General's Office.
William Peskett, M.D., Civil Surgeon, Simla.
Mrs (Colonel) Pogson.
Lt.-Col. Colyear, and Family of five.
Mrs Daly.
Mrs Dean Shute.
Reginald Ouseley, Capt., 34th N. I.
Mrs Ouseley.
Mrs Scott.
Francis Peake.
R. Hay.
Captain and Mrs Andrews, Bengal Army.
M. De Baleguer, placé dans l'Inde sous les auspices de sa Majesté Napoléon III., Empereur des Français.

ROBERT MONTGOMERY, ESQ., *Judicial Commissioner for the Punjab, to Colonel* KEITH YOUNG, *Judge-Advocate General of the Army.*

LAHORE, 15*th January* 1858.

SIR,—In continuation of my docket (No. 4501) of the 30th ultimo, I have the honour to forward for your information the annexed copy of a communication from the Officiating Secretary to the Chief Commissioner, intimating how it has been proposed to reward the Rana of Kooyntal for the services rendered by him to certain residenters of

Simla, who had sought his protection during the recent disturbances.—
I have the honour to be, Sir, your most obedient servant,
(Signed) R. MONTGOMERY,
Judicial Commissioner.

Lieutenant EDWARD H. PASKE, *Officiating Secretary to the Chief Commissioner for the Punjab, to* ROBERT MONTGOMERY, ESQ., *Judicial Commissioner for the Punjab.*

LAHORE, 11*th January* 1858.

SIR,—In reply to your letter (No. 431) of the 30th ultimo, suggesting that some suitable acknowledgment should be made for the services lately rendered by the Rana of Kooyntal, I am directed to inform you that previous to the receipt of your letter, the Chief Commissioner had recommended to the Supreme Government, that the unpaid balance of a fine formerly imposed on the Rana for misconduct, and amounting to four thousand rupees, should be remitted as a reward for his services. The original enclosures of your letter are herewith returned.—I have, &c.,
(Signed) EDWARD PASKE,
Officiating Secretary to the Chief Commissioner.

APPENDIX B. (*See page* 31.)
ESCAPE OF SIR THEOPHILUS METCALFE.

The following account of Sir Theophilus Metcalfe's escape was narrated by Lieutenant Wilberforce, of the 52nd Light Infantry:

'Sir Theophilus Metcalfe accompanied our regiment to show us the best way through the city on the day of the attack on Delhi. Twice have I, Lieutenant Wilberforce, heard Sir Theophilus Metcalfe tell the story of his wonderful escape—at our mess table, and in a London drawing-room.

'When the Mutiny broke out in Delhi, Sir Theophilus Metcalfe stuck to his post until almost too late; it was not until the rebel cavalry were at the house that he escaped from a side-door, and, mounting his horse —which, owing to the forethought of his servants, stood ready saddled— rode away to seek for safety. His escape was soon noticed, and he was chased by the troopers; they gained upon him, and he realised that he must be captured. At this juncture he saw a man on the road; he told him that he was being pursued, and asked if he could suggest a way of escape. Sir Theophilus Metcalfe's own words were: "The man, on this, showed me a cave by the side of the road, and told me to enter, saying he would save me if he could. He took my horse some little distance down the road, and then returned to near the entrance of the cave. My pursuers were not far behind, for I heard their horses coming along; then I heard them interrogate my friend as to whether he had seen an Englishman on a horse go that way. He protested that he had seen no one. They then went on, but soon returned saying they had found the Sahib's horse, and that he could not be far off. One of them must have noticed the entrance to the cave, for I heard him say, 'Perhaps he is there.' My friend vehemently denied the possibility of this, and declared that for many hours he had been loitering about and had seen no one. It was evident that they did not believe him, for I heard them say, 'At any rate, we will search it.' On this my friend laughed loud, and, raising his voice so that I must hear, said, 'Ah, search the cave —do search it; but I'll tell you what you will find—a great red devil in there. He lives up at the end of the cave. You won't be able to see him, because the cave turns at the end, and the devil always stands just round the turn; he has got a great, long knife in his hand, and the moment your head appears round the corner he will slice it off, and then he will pull the body in to him and eat it. Go in—do go in; he will have such a meal.' I knew that I was intended to hear this, and to shape my action on what I had heard. I found that the cave did turn at the end at right angles for a very short distance, leaving, however, plenty of room for a man to stand. Of course, I know how superstitious Natives are, and how above all things they dread the unseen powers of darkness. I therefore drew my sword and waited. After more talking outside, my friend, who knew that the only way he could prevent them searching the cave was by frightening them, constantly urged them to go in and see the red devil. Some of them plucked up courage and entered. The cave was so narrow that they could only come up in single file. As soon as the first man came within my reach, I struck at him with all my force; the blow fell straight, his head rolled from his body, and with a yell of terror his companions fled out of the darkness. Lucky for me they did, for my sword had broken short off, and only the hilt remained in my hand. Mindful of my friend's warning, I lost no time in pulling the body of the fallen man into the recess. Their retreat out of the cave was a signal for a fresh outburst from my friend, who taunted them with, 'Go in, you will find Metcalfe there; if you don't, you will find the red devil. Did you see him? Isn't he beautiful? Don't his eyes shine bright and red? Do go back. He wants more than one; perhaps he has already got two, for if Metcalfe went in he has eaten him.' But they had had enough; nothing would induce another man to enter. One of those who fled declared he had seen the red devil— probably to excuse the shame of his own flight—and this assertion finally decided the matter, and they rode away. When night had come, my friend came to me and lodged me in his own house; and, after some days, announced to me that all was ready for my safe journey to Kurnaul. I left the man, assuring him of my gratitude, and telling him that when I had the opportunity that gratitude should be substantially expressed. When I took leave of my host, I asked him, 'Why did you save my life?' 'Because you are a just and honest man.' 'How do you know that I am a just and honest man? I have never seen you before.' 'Ah! yes you have,' was the answer; 'you decided a case against me in your court. I and all my family had fought that case through all the inferior courts, and had won by lying; but you found us out—you saw that we were lying, and you gave judgment against us. If you had given the case for me I would not have saved your life!'"'

APPENDIX C. (*See pages* 129 *and* 238.)
THE FORTIFICATIONS OF DELHI.

The following account of the strength and defences of Delhi is given in Lord Roberts's *Forty-one Years in India*, Vol. I., pages 161 and 162:

'The defences of Delhi, which remain almost unaltered up to the present day, were modernised forms of the ancient works that existed when the city fell before Lord Lake's army in 1803. These works had been strengthened and improved some years before the Mutiny by Lieutenant Robert Napier.* As described by the Commanding Engineer, the eastern face of Delhi rises on the Jumna, and at the season of the year during which our operations were carried on, the stream may be described as washing the face of the walls. The river front was therefore inaccessible to the besieging force, while at the same time the mutineers and the inhabitants of the city could communicate freely across the river by means of the bridge of boats and ferries. This rendered it impossible for us to invest Delhi, even if there had been a sufficient number of troops for the purpose. We were only able, indeed, to direct our attack against a small portion of the city wall; while throughout the siege the enemy could freely communicate with and procure supplies from, the surrounding country.

'On the river front the defences consisted of an irregular wall with occasional bastions and towers; and about one-half of the length of this face was occupied by the Palace of the King of Delhi and its outwork, the old Moghul fort of Selimghur.

'The remaining defences consisted of a succession of bastioned fronts, the connecting curtains being very long, and the outworks limited to one crown-work at the Ajmere Gate; and Martello towers, mounting a single gun, at the points where additional flanking fire to that given by the bastions themselves was required.

'The bastions were small, each mounting from ten to fourteen pieces of artillery; they were provided with masonry parapets about twelve feet in thickness, and were about sixteen feet high. The curtain consisted of a simple masonry wall or rampart sixteen feet in height, eleven feet thick at top, and fourteen or fifteen feet at bottom. This

---

* The late Field-Marshal Lord Napier of Magdala, G.C.B., G.C.S.I.

main wall carried a parapet, loopholed for musketry, eight feet in height and three feet in thickness.

'The whole of the land front was covered by a faussebraye of varying thickness, ranging from sixteen to thirty feet, and having a vertical scarp-wall eight feet high; exterior to this was a dry ditch about twenty-five feet in width. The counterscarp was simply an earthen slope, easy to descend. The glacis was very narrow, extending only fifty or sixty yards from the counterscarp, and covering barely one-half of the walls from the besiegers' view. These walls were about seven miles in circumference, and included an area of about three square miles.' (See Colonel Baird Smith's Report, dated 17th September 1857.)

APPENDIX D. (*See page* 260.)
MUTINY OF THE 50TH NATIVE INFANTRY.

The following account of the Mutiny of the 50th Native Infantry— a regiment that remained staunch for long—is not only interesting as a narrative, but will serve to show the great difficulties the officers of mutineering regiments had to face:

Letter from Colonel HAMPTON, *50th Native Infantry, to Colonel* KEITH YOUNG.

BENARES, 14*th January* 1858.

My loss of property at Nagode has regularly put me up a tree; this, however, I consider as a trifle compared to the loss of the old Regiment, which, I firmly believe, I should have saved had that dreadful traitor, Lewloll Temang, *not brought* Kerr Sing with the mutineers from Dinapore on us. The fellow had been in Kerr Sing's camp, near the Katha Pass, and arranged everything for our destruction. I was kept unacquainted with everything that was going on in the lines by old Rumdeen Sing Bahadar, of the Grenadiers, the Havildar Major, and others; my 'Long Jack,' a trump of the first water—he is a relation of Rumdeen's—through him I got the Soubahdar's report; the wretch Lewloll, with his gracious smile and his 'With God's blessing, sir,' assured me all was right in the lines, and that he would, and was, keeping me well informed of all that was going on there. I knew the villain was playing me false, but had not the power to crush him, and received his assurances as if I believed him. A most trying and anxious time I had of it for near five months, never feeling when I rose from my bed that I could calculate on returning to it. The men were sorely tried, no doubt; many left me out of funk, not knowing what to do. Had the Madras Column, with Major Erskine, come to my rescue as entreated to do, I am certain I could have hanged Lewloll, and saved the corps; or had Major Ellis, the Assistant Political Agent, roused the well-affected Punjabees and got them to side with me, and kept the ghats instead of postponing everything, I might have been at Nagode now; or had I been furnished with carriage for the men's baggage and the treasure, I might have got the Regiment away from Nagode, fallen back on Damow, where the Madras Column was, or got into the Myha Fort. But this was not to be; and remember that I was sold by the civil authorities. The real fact I believe to be, that Major Erskine was fearful that the jolly 50th would have walked into the affections of the Madrassees, and then all would have gone a regular smash, as the Regiment (52nd Native Infantry) was only kept quiet by the steadiness of the 50th. This Regiment (the 52nd) followed suit three days after.

My rascals fought well at Kujwa. A nephew of mine who was present, Anderson of the Artillery, writes: 'Yes, we pounded your regiment the other day, and they repaid the compliment pretty well; they came down to the charge twice, but it was no go—Pandy could not keep up to the scratch.' They were a fine set of men, no doubt; would that they had fought on the right side, and then I should have been proud of them. Colonel Powell, Her Majesty's 53rd, was killed on this occasion. The loss of the old Regiment is to this day like a dream to me; the men had no enmity against their officers—not one was molested, and not a shot was fired at us. I sent the families of the bandsmen off the very day of the revolt; and all the ladies with the exception of Mrs Bolton—who couldn't be persuaded to leave her son —two days before. Rupal Sing Soubahdar behaved very well, as also did Jemadar Meer-Assadady, who never flinched from his duty.

I am now sending report of the eight Native officers, twenty-two Havildars, twenty Naicks, and about two hundred Jacks who *stuck* like men to their officers. I hear that any and every man that places confidence in a black face is considered to be of unsound mind; if so, I fear my case is hopeless, for I feel that confidence in the men who accompanied us—'their officers'—in the height of the Mutiny. I would trust them to any extent. If you would like to see my report to the Commander-in-Chief giving a short detail of our misfortunes, I will send you a copy; G. O. will show you that two Havildars, one Jemadar, and 'Long Jack' have been rewarded.

Fancy that rascal Lewloll driving off in my wife's carriage; and, worse than all, he stole my little dog Lucy. I regret her loss much more than the carriage: the poor little creature followed me to the parade, and there, fearing I might lose her, I put a string round her neck and made her over to the care of my sirdar-bearer, who, the moment the men revolted, with my other servant, looted all my traps. I have lost upwards of fourteen thousand rupees by the Mutiny.

Can you for a moment fancy the fools quietly submitting to my destroying a lot of ammunition, which I did on the 15th—the day before the Mutiny? You should have seen the stew this put all hands in. The Superintendent of Nagode wrote, saying, 'For God's sake do not think of destroying your ammunition; your men will never stand it.'

APPENDIX D.

No doubt the risk was great, but I thought it necessary, and did it in the presence of all the Native officers and men, who looked rather taken aback, but they said nothing. The mutineers were at that time within sixteen miles of Nagode; and when I found they had reached Singpore, only six miles from us, I determined on moving out of the Station, it being entirely a false position. You must understand that the Banda Road leads right into the city, and had the mutineers got possession of the city our retreat would have been entirely cut off; I therefore moved from the west to the east side of it, crossing a small river which runs right under the city wall. On receiving *pucka* information from Mr Coles, the Superintendent of East Nagode, at 8 P.M., that the Insurgents were at Singpore and making arrangements to march that night on us, I went into the lines and turned the men out, sending orders to the officers to join me there; they did so in about half-an-hour, and when the men were in open column of companies I resolved on spiking two 9-pounders, left at Nagode by the Madras Regiment without gunners or Artillery. This was a difficult matter, but necessary. I had arranged with the Quartermaster-Sergeant, who came from the Artillery, to have everything ready, and to keep the two pickspikes always in his pocket. I withdrew the guard and made them fall in with their companies, and sent the Sergeant to do the needful. I heard the ring on the metal as the Sergeant drove down the spikes; and when I saw him coming back I sent the Adjutant to the right bell of arms and Matthews to the left, ordered them to smash all the arms—nearly five hundred muskets—and when they reported this nice work accomplished, shouldered, and gave the order 'Quick march!' and I can safely assure you I never saw the men step off more steadily in my life. Every man in the ranks must have heard the crack of the stocks of the muskets; not a word was uttered — you might have heard a pin drop. My impression is that no *pucka* arrangements had been made by the disaffected, and they were fearful of trying their strength. Before commencing the destruction of the arms I had loaded and capped the muskets, and having the men in open column of companies at ordered arms, the rascals were taken in a fix; it was a touch-and-go sort of an affair, but I was determined to do what I considered necessary at every risk. Well, on crossing the said river I was told by the Havildar Major that he feared matters were very bad; and sure enough they were so. The leading company advance guard was the Grenadiers, which I sent there, knowing that I had many bad men amongst the company; the next, or rather my worst company, was the right. I therefore marched left in front, and having passed over the river, continued the march for some two hundred yards, when the Grenadiers came to a halt and sat down; the officer came back and reported that the men would not advance. I went up and tried to get them on, but not an inch would they go; so after remaining in this fix for about half-an-hour, they rose in a body, went to the right-about, and returned to cantonments.

APPENDIX D.

Seeing I had lost all power over them, we made our way towards Myha, where I had a company (the 3rd). Seeing a number of the men following us, I pulled up, and was joined by some one hundred and forty, including Native officer, Havildar, Naick, and Sepoys. With these men I kept; others that had rather a dread of them went clear off to Myha, distant thirty-two miles; Mrs Bolton and her son, McMullin, and young Golding remained with me. After having gone twenty-four miles, we halted during the heat of the day at a large village, got a few chupattees and plenty of milk, started again at 3 P.M., and when within a mile or two of Myha, was met by the Adjutant, who had gone on with the men. He told me that matters were worse there than at Nagode—the company being in an open state of mutiny, and declared they would loot the city and kill all the officers. The other officers soon followed the Adjutant, and wanted to cut off to Rewah; this I could not consent to, so sent my old Soubahdar Rumdeen Sing, Geomanis Toolacdar, the Pay Havildar, and one or two others on ahead to say I was coming, and would listen to anything they had to say. This put all right. The next morning I found out that the cause offered for the disorderly conduct was that the Regiment was supposed to have received pay for August, and that they had not. I removed that cause of complaint by taking a loan from the assistant to the Superintendent of Nagode (who was on duty there) of 1800 rupees, issued pay, set my good man to work, put all right, and marched that evening at three o'clock for Ummerputtena, taking the company with me; fifteen of the fellows, however, deserted. If I could have put entire confidence in the men of the 3rd Company I would have tried a stand. The mutineers from Banda were so enraged at my having destroyed ammunition and muskets and spiked the guns, they declared their determination of following us up. This I would not have cared for much, as I had my rear open and a clear run into the Rewah territory; but I found to my disgust that the Raja of Myha was in communication with the mutineers, and had the fellow turned on us we had no chance of escape. The Raja is now in open rebellion against us.

Again, I knew well that the moment the 52nd heard that the 50th was gone they would follow suit sharp; and they did so. The Saugor Road completely shut against us by the rebel Bondeelahs, my only course therefore was to make for Mirzapore through Rewah; so off I started, but had not gone many miles when I received an official from Lieutenant Osborne, the Rewah Political Agent, telling me that I was on no consideration to bring a single man of the 50th into the Rewah territory. This was a nice mess. To quit my men I was resolved not to do, so moved on to Ummerputtena and wrote to tell Osborne of my arrival with some two hundred and sixty men—that I was willing to change my route by any pass that he could point out, either towards Mirzapore, the Soan, or Allahabad; but I claimed a passage through the Rewah territory, received a letter the next day saying I might come on—which

APPENDIX D. 331

I did—and reached Rewah the next morning after a most horrid march 'midst rain and everything disagreeable. At Rewah I found my absence would be preferred to my company, so marched again next morning through heavy rain to the dâk-bungalow, twenty-four miles; on the 24th marched on that night to Hunesenna, a large road-bungalow, twenty miles—received a letter there express from Mr Tucker the magistrate, who did not know the strength of my party, informing me that the mutineers (5th Irregular Cavalry), who had thrashed Rattray's Sikhs, were to be at Loll-gunge on the 26th.

This said Loll-gunge was my road to Mirzapore, and twenty-seven miles from Harminna, and recommended my pausing for a few days to admit of the Irregulars passing on to Banda. Well, on the receipt of this letter, I assembled the Native officers in camp and pointed out to the men if they were really loyal, and wished to prove it, now was their chance, giving them the substance of the letter. *One and all expressed the greatest desire to be led against the Irregulars.* I ordered the cartridges to be drawn and their muskets cleaned, which was immediately done; and I marched that night at 8 P.M. (the 25th September), and arrived at Loll-gunge, after a most fatiguing march of twenty-seven miles, at 9 A.M., and found to our disgust that it was a false alarm—the Cavalry had not even been heard of. I would have given the only pair of shoes I had in the world—and those were on my feet—to have had a brush between my men and the Irregulars, and feel convinced we should have given the rascals a regular pounding; it was not to be—so enough. I marched the next morning nine miles, and wrote into Mirzapore for permission to enter the Station, and, to my horror, was told that I was to be disarmed on arrival; to save which I marched the next morning and crossed the river at Narghat, where I sent my whole party away on general leave for three months, sent my arms, ammunition, &c. into the Arsenal, and reported the same to His Excellency.

Nearly all of the men have rejoined, and are anxious to behave like true men—perform any duty they may be called on to do. Curious to say, I have had a guard at Mirzapore—1st and 12th—the men behaving like trumps, and doing good service on three or four occasions with the Civilians and another guard—1st and 8th—at Allahabad, all of whom have done their duty well. I have written twice to the Fort Adjutant requesting a statement of the duty performed by these men, but can get no reply, which is most annoying, as I am only waiting for it to send in rolls to the Adjutant-General of all my men, and also of some of them that I can strongly recommend out of this general leave batch. I had put down three attempts to kick up a row, and feel convinced, even against that traitor Lewloll, I could have preserved the old corps had L. Sing and the mutineers from Dinapore not come down on me. Against their numbers and the disaffected rascals in my own ranks, I had no chance; I did my best, and could do no more.

To add to my difficulties, F—— refused to do Adjutant's duty as he heard that all Staff allowances ceased on the mutiny of a regiment; this he learnt, I believe, from some of the 40th—a very improper feeling and no mistake, and one that he never ought to have shown considering the kindness with which he had ever been treated by me. He is under arrest, and I will not say more.

I have had three letters from B——. All jolly, and delighted with his trip to England. Plowden called on me on his way to join Jung Bahadoor's force; looking, I think, far from well.

You say nothing about the Nicolls and their small children; I hope they are all well. *Every* officer, even the griffin not out of his drill, is away on temporary Staff employ. McMullin at Allahabad; glad to hear Munro has entirely recovered. Poor Barlow died at Lucknow—his poor baby lost an eye; Mrs Barlow arrived in Calcutta quite well.

What an eventful year we have had! I believe I stand about sixth from the top of the Majors. What in the world is to become of us? A Native army of some sort there must be to take Station duties, and also out duties. Not a word about going home; this dreadful affair has regularly put me up a tree. I am entitled to the Colonel's pension on the 3rd of September at latest, but think I shall have completed thirty-three years' actual service in June, as I did not take my full furlough in England, and got time of service during the voyage, coming out with recruits. My brother is trying hard to induce me to give up work; but I think I must hold on for the Major-General—in case I might meet Lewis at home!

I really must say good-night; the clock has just struck 11 P.M., time for all sober men to hug the pillow. God bless you, old fellow; and may you be preserved through all the dangers your gallant Chief is sure to push you into. You must be closer on your promotion, I think, than some three or four under me; and there are two or three Generals' steps to fill up.

The 70th clear off to China under that lucky fellow, Kennedy. I should greatly like to go to China; it is nearly the only *curious* part of the world that I have not visited.

Please give my kindest regards to Mrs Keith Young when you write, and ask her to tell my dear little friend, Doddy (Keith), that I often think of him, and that he is not to forget Joe Hampton!

I wrote in June, and twice since, but I dare say my letters have never reached you. Poor old Ripley and Colonel Chester both gone. If Colonel Becher is with you, remember me kindly to him.

I hope you will be able to read this scrawl. I have the paying up and discharging the general leave men of Regiments that have mutinied, and often have to work from 8 A.M. to 6 P.M. to get the fellows off, which will account for this being written at night.—Believe me, my dear Keith Young, ever yours most sincerely, J. HAMPTON.

Note.—The 50th Native Infantry mutinied on the 16th of September 1857.

APPENDIX E. *(See page 5.)*
THE ORIGIN OF THE SEPOYS BEING CALLED PANDIES.*

It is generally supposed that Mangul Pandy, the Sepoy of the 34th Regiment, being the *first* man in the *first* regiment to mutiny, therefore gave his name to all the Sepoys who afterwards mutinied. However, in Colonel Keith Young's Diary of January 1830, an interesting account is given of a mutiny that occurred in a regiment to which he was for a short time attached. This mutiny was soon suppressed, the ringleader being sentenced to twelve months' imprisonment. His name was Rada *Pandy*. The name of the Jemadar of the 34th Native Infantry who forbade his men to aid their officers when Mangul Pandy mutinied was also *Pandy*—Isurree Pandy. Was Pandy, therefore, a common surname among the Native soldiers, and for this reason chosen as a name by which to distinguish all Sepoys?

APPENDIX F. *(See page 263.)*
LORD LAKE AND DELHI.

In 1803, after taking the strong fort of Allyghur, Lord Lake advanced on Delhi. He encountered the enemy—the French, and Native troops under Sindhia—about six miles from the city, and after a prolonged and stubborn fight, was victorious with a loss of about four hundred killed and wounded. The enemy is estimated to have lost three thousand. Lord Lake then entered Delhi, where he was greeted as a deliverer by the inhabitants, and took undisputed possession of the city. The Mogul Emperor, Shah Alum, was treated with every respect. It was his son, Bahadoor Shah, who was destined to be the last to sit upon the throne.—*Abridged from Beveridge's History of India.*

APPENDIX G. *(See page 308.)*
THE KING AND PRINCES OF DELHI.

Bahadoor Shah, King of Delhi, last of the great Moguls, had, some thirty years before the Mutiny, lost all power as a territorial sovereign, and become a pensioner of the Company. Only in his Palace at Delhi, his authority was still absolute over a few thousand followers and dependents.

On the outbreak of the Mutiny, he allowed himself openly to be

---

* See 'Pandy' in Glossary (page 340), compiled after the above was in print.

proclaimed an independent monarch, and the city became the rallying-place of the disaffected Sepoys. He inaugurated his reign by the brutal massacre of all the Europeans, men, women, and children, who had taken refuge in the Palace.

When our troops entered Delhi, the King, with others of the royal family, fled to the tomb of Hamayoon, one of his ancestors, about five miles distant. Thence, with the promise of his own life and of that of his favourite wife, Zeenut Mahal, and their son Jamma Bukht, they were conducted by Major Hodson back to the Palace at Delhi. The next day, the 22nd September, two sons and a grandson of the King, who had also taken refuge in the tomb of Hamayoon, were being conducted to Delhi for trial, when the mob became so threatening that Major Hodson decided he had no alternative but to shoot them. This he did with his own hand, and so struck terror into the surrounding crowds and prevented a possible rescue. In the Dewan-i-Khas, the Hall of Audience in the Delhi Palace, the King's trial commenced on the 27th of January 1858, conducted by a commission of field-officers headed by Colonel Dawes of the Bengal Artillery. Major Harriott, Deputy Judge-Advocate, was the official Prosecutor. The King was found guilty of rebellion, treason, and murder, and deported a state prisoner to Rangoon, where two wives and his son Jamma Bukht were allowed to share his captivity. He died there on the 7th November 1862, aged eighty-nine.

APPENDIX H. (*See page* 9.)

THE MUTINY PREDICTED BY SIR CHARLES NAPIER.

In 1849 Sir Charles Napier wrote that it was apparent to him and to all the officers on the spot, who were conversant with Native and Sepoy habits and feelings, that a widely spread and formidable scheme of mutiny was in progress, and great danger impending; for though the Sepoys at Wazeerabad, awed by the presence of a large European force, remained passive, they were heard to say that they only waited the arrival of the relieving regiments, and would then act together.

Again he writes, from Meerut, in the same year: 'There is a report that twenty-four regiments are in league with the 41st. India is in danger of a military dictation! This is a very awkward matter.' And in a letter to Lord Dalhousie he says: 'If nothing happens, all is right; but if it turns out a preconcerted mutiny, force must be met by force. The least concession would lose us India, and justice has placed us on high ground, *thank God!* Neither your Lordship nor myself would shed a drop of blood, if it could be avoided, but a thousand lives must be taken rather than let four hundred thousand men dictate to their government unjustly—or justly either for that matter. But woe to the government that places itself in so dreadful a position!'

APPENDIX I. (*See page* 243.)
TRANSLATION OF COSSID LETTER.*

24th and *25th August.*

Up till yesterday evening General Buktawa Khan moved on to Alleepore, *via* Nujufghurh, with six Regiments of Infantry, two of Cavalry, and twelve guns, and to-day General (Namach?) left the town with an equal number, and now the total troops in the town amounts to four thousand horse and foot, including the Nussereebad detachment. The citizens will never stand against the (British) Government.

The rebels have also accompanied the above force. The rioters from Sonput have also gone with the above; they were assured that the people from other villages would join them (Buktawa Khan). The inhabitants here are of opinion that it will be most opportune for the British force to invade the town at this time; none will dare oppose them. The conspirators will take to heel, and the conspiracy will only last till Delhi is taken.

These two Generals have departed with bag and baggage with the intent of not returning here in case they are defeated at Alleepore; every man will then be free to go wherever he likes. On the day of engagement at Alleepore we could press the enemy from this side.

The Sikhs have been scattered among the different regiments. A document to Mirza Ilahi Baksh † and Zeenut Mahal Begum ‡ will even now procure the desired aid from the garrison.—*Translation by Mr M. A. Huk.*

* INDIA PAPER.—This Cossid letter is written on a paper most wonderfully thin and opaque although very tough, the secret of making which was then hidden in India. In 1841 a small fold of it was presented to the Oxford University Press, and upon it twenty-four copies were printed of the smallest Bible then in existence—the Diamond 24mo, one copy of which was presented to the Queen some years later. Experiments for producing similar paper were undertaken at the Oxford University Press mills at Wolvercote, and in 1875 an edition was published by this Press and Messrs Hamilton, Adams, & Co., exactly similar to the twenty-four copies printed in 1842.

This paper when rubbed, instead of breaking into holes, assumes a texture resembling chamois leather, and a strip only three inches wide is found able to support a quarter of a hundredweight without yielding. The secret of its manufacture is said to be known only to three living persons.

† Better known as Prince Ilahi Baksh, was the son-in-law of the old Emperor who supported the British cause.

‡ The favourite wife of the King, who had great influence in the Palace. (See Appendix G.)

GLOSSARY OF HINDOOSTANI WORDS.*

Almirah = Almāree, a wardrobe, a chest of drawers. (The word 'aumrie' is used in country districts of Scotland meaning a press or chest with drawers.)

Attar = Atā, flour, ground grain.

Bābā, (literally) 'a good person.' In some parts it is a term for boy or child.

Bāboo, a writer or clerk. In Bengal and the north of India the term is used for 'Mr,' when addressing a letter or speaking to a Hindoo.

Bearer. This proper English word is corrupted into *bahra* = (literally) 'deaf;' here it signifies a general male servant.

Be shoomar = Beshomār, countless, innumerable.

Bheestie = Bhishtee, water-carrier. A Bheestie is a Mussulman, and generally carries water in a *mashak* or bag of leather, either on his own back or on that of an ox when the bags are very large.

Box-wālla. The first part of this word is English, while the other (*wālla* = man or keeper) is Urdu; it signifies a pedlar, the proper word for which, however, is *pheriwālla*.

Buggy, a modern one-horse car or carriage.

Bundabust = Bandobast, organisation, arrangement, settlement.

Buniah = Banya, a corn-chandler.

Burra (= Barā) Simla, the 'large' or more populous part of Simla, as the Boileaugunge is called.

Charpoy = Chārpāee, a bedstead intertwined with a rope made of fibres of a special kind of grass.

Chick, a hanging screen made of thin reeds or bamboos, white or artistically coloured.

Chit, a short note written on a scrap of paper.

Chokedar = Chaukidār, a watchman.

Chota Simla, the 'small' or less populated part of Simla.

Chuprassie = Chaprāsee, an office messenger generally wearing a breastplate or buckle on which the name of his department is engraved.

Classees = Khallāsī, (technically) camp-followers for pitching tents, spreading carpets, &c.

Coss = Kos, an Indian measure of about two miles.

Cossid = Kāsid, an express messenger, a courier; also used to mean a secret, or spy's letter.

Dāk, post.

Dāk Bungalow = Dāk Banglow, a house for travellers to stay in when travelling along the main trunk roads. Such bungalows

* This Glossary has been principally compiled by Mr M. M. Huk.

are found all over the country from twelve to twenty miles apart; at some of them the post-horses were changed, hence the name.

Dhobie = Dhobī, a washerman.

Doab signifies land lying between two rivers.

Dogras = Dongars, mountaineers; a particular tribe of hillmen, generally Rajputs.

Doolie = Dolī, a kind of sedan-chair on poles, carried by two men on their shoulders.

Duffadar = Dafadar, a non-commissioned officer of a company of Sowars or Sepoys.

Eed = I'd, the Easter of Mussulmans.

Fakeer, a dervish—a man who leads what is called a holy life; there is a great variety of them.

Gerbauchs, or **Sherbachas,** curious swivel-guns of native make, used by the Cashmere troops.

Ghāt, a quay, a river landing-place.

Ghurā, a large earthen or brass water-pot.

Godas = Gondas, a tribe of cow-herds; they are of the aboriginal inhabitants of Hindoostan.

Golundāz, a gunner.

Goojurs, a tribe among the Rajputs, formerly notorious for their thieving habits.

Goojured, stolen; robbed by *Goojurs*.

Goomashta, an envoy, an agent.

Gram. The term is Anglo-Indian, and generally signifies a kind of pulse, the chick-pea (*Cicer arietinum*). The proper Urdu is *chana*.

Hackeries, Indian *chakras* or bullock-carts.

Havildar = Hawaldār, a military officer of inferior rank.

Hurkara = Harkāra, a running footman or express messenger.

'Jacks' = Jāts, a tribe among the Rajputs, agricultural and brave.

Janpan = Jhānpān, a sort of sedan-chair swung on vertically curved poles and carried by four men on their shoulders.

Janpannees = Jhānpānees or *Kahārs*, the men who carry the jhānpān.

Jemadar = Jamadār, a Native commissioned officer of the army.

Jumma Musjid, the Imperial Mosque, where Mussulmans from the town and neighbouring parts assemble for prayers in large numbers on Fridays. It was built on a high and central position in Delhi (Shāhjahānabad) by the Emperor Shāhjahān about the middle of the 17th century. It is one of the most extensive and magnificent buildings in India, and is of red sandstone and white marble; its minarets, next in height to the celebrated Kutub Minar and its domes, add a great deal to its grace. Like other buildings at Agra and Delhi the plan of the mosque was laid by Shāhjahān himself, and shows his wonderful architectural skill.

Khansamah = Khānsāma, a house-steward.

Khud, a steep precipice, an abyss.

Kitmutghur = Khidmatgār, a male domestic, a general servant.

Kootub, or **Kutub,** a small village about eleven miles south-west of Delhi. Historically it is of great importance and celebrity. For miles around it are stretched the ruins of Indraparast, the ancient capital of the Hindoos, while those of the old Mussulman Delhi, before Shāhjahān removed his capital to the present site, are to be seen all around. Most prominent among the ruins is the Kutub Minar, with the highest column standing alone in the world. It is but one of the two minarets of the most wonderful mosque which Sultan Kutbuddin (1206-1210) had formed the grand project of erecting to commemorate his victories, but he died before only a part was finished; the few middle arches are the tallest ever seen, and the fellow minarets on the opposite side are still standing in their unfinished state. The tomb of the famous Mussulman saint, Khwājā Kutbuddin, is in the village, and is visited by thousands of pilgrims. The British Political Agents to the Mogul Court used to live in Kutub; their *Kothee* or house still exists in a ruined and deserted state.

Kotwāl, the chief officer for the city; a town guard, a policeman.

Lāc, a hundred thousand.

Lattee = Lāthee, a club, a heavy stick.

Loot, plunder.

Lord-Sahib, or **-Sāhab**, a term applied to a high English official; a governor or commander-in-chief.

Lunka, (literally) 'the resplendent;' a name by which Ceylon was known to the people of India, China, &c.

Mahout = Mahāwat, an elephant driver.

Mall, the principal road used for afternoon drives.

Masaulchee = Mash'ālchee, a torch-bearer.

Mātādeen, (literally) the 'mother or goddess of faith.'

Maulchit, an Anglo-Indian term for a return note, a written answer.

Maund = Maun, an Indian measure of eighty pounds-weight.

Mem-Sahib, or **-Sāhab**, madam, lady; a term applied to European ladies.

Mistry = Mistree, a workman, a mason, a builder.

Mohur = Mohar, a gold coin, a seal.

Mohurram = Moharram, the name of the first month of the Hejra or year of the Mussulmans, who hold it sacred for the first ten days on account of the great battle fought at Koofa between Husain (son of Ali, the fourth great Caliph or successor, and Fatma, daughter of the Prophet) and Yazeed, in which Husain and his relations and followers were deprived of water for several days till he was killed. The Mussulmans greatly mourn his loss during these days.

Mohurram (= Moharram) Sabells, places built and decorated by Mussulmans during the Mohurram month for distribution of cooled water and sherbets to the thirsty. This they consider a pious act; it is done in remembrance of Husain, whose army at Koofa was cut off with water-supply by the enemy. *Page* 262.

Moonshee = Moonshi, a writer, a secretary.

Moulvi, a learned man, a doctor.

Nagas, a caste of Hindoo ascetics; a tribe of hillmen. Naga means 'a snake.'

GLOSSARY OF HINDOOSTANI WORDS.

Naick = Nayak, a Native officer of the lowest rank; a corporal.

Nimukharams = Namak Haram, rebels, disloyal men; (literally) 'breakers of the salt' (Namak = salt).

Nurzur = Nazar, a gift,—offered to a superior on state occasions.

Pâjee, stupid, silly, mean.

Pandy = Pānde, a title of the Brahmans. The descendants of King *Pandoo*, who distinguished themselves in wars, were called *Pandowas*. *See* Appendix E.

Pawn = Pān, leaves of the *Piper-betel*—chewed by Natives along with some aromatic spices.

Pergunah, (literally) 'a village that has been bestowed upon a person as a *Jāghir* or free gift for some great act.' Poonahana is a village between Bhurtpore and Delhi.

Poorbeahs = Poorbiyas, (literally) 'Eastern people.' A tribe found in Bengal, the North-west Provinces, the Punjab, and Oude.

Pucka = Pakka, (literally) 'ripe, ready, strong;' properly built, properly finished, properly confirmed; as, a *pucka* bridge, a *pucka* road, a *pucka* appointment. Pucka is the antithesis to *kutcha*.

Punkah = Pankhā, a large fan, which is suspended from the ceiling and worked by means of a rope pulled over a pulley.

Puttoo = Pattoo, a kind of thick woollen cloth, which is made into winter garments by the Natives.

Rāj, rule; government. There was a Native prophecy that British Rule would last but 100 years, and would come to an end on the centenary of the Battle of Plassy, which was fought on the 23rd of June 1757. *Pages* 80, 164.

Ressaldar = Risālahdār, the Native officer in command of a horse or lancer regiment.

Rissalah = Risālah, a troop of horse, a regiment of lancers.

Rupee, a silver coin in circulation in India originally worth 2s., now only worth about 1s. 4d.

Sahib-Logue = Sāhab Log, the English people.

Salaam = Salām, salutation, obeisance.

Seer, an Indian measure of about two pounds-weight.

Sepoy = Sepāhi, a Native foot-soldier.

Serāi, a caravanserai; a house for travellers to rest; a building with many rooms; a small mud fort.

Shamiyana = Shamyana, a canopy; a large flat tent without walls.

Sherbachas. *See* **Gerbauchs.**

Sirdar = Sardār, a chief, a headman.

Soojee, meal; porridge made of coarsely ground flour and meal.

Soubahdar, a Native commissioned officer of the army.

Sowār, a Native cavalry soldier.

Sudder Bazaar, the chief street; the principal place for selling and buying.

Syce = Saees, a groom, a horse-keeper.

Tattee, a screen, generally of grass or straw; a matted shutter.

Tattoo, a pony.

Tiffen, lunch.

Tomasha, a row, a riot; a show, an entertainment, a spectacle.

Tom-tom, a small Indian drum.

Vakeel, head-man of a village or district.

INDEX TO REGIMENTS AND CORPS—EUROPEAN AND NATIVE, CAVALRY AND INFANTRY.

EUROPEAN REGIMENTS AND CORPS.
1st Bengal Fusiliers, with 1st Brigade advancing on Delhi, 29; in Nicholson's Brigade, 191, 195, 216; in Nicholson's Movable Column, 234; capture guns, 197.
2nd Bengal Fusiliers, with 2nd Brigade advancing on Delhi, 29, 41, 215.
5th Madras Fusiliers, 126; on road to Cawnpore, 224, 227, 231, 295.
Her Majesty's—
4th Regiment, expected at Bombay, 250.
6th Dragoon Guards (Carabineers), at Meerut, 18; with General Wilson, 30, 34; with Force before Delhi, 104, 117, 119, 123, 215.
8th King's, expected before Delhi, 74, 79; arrives in Camp, 87; 126, 215.
9th Lancers, with Force advancing on Delhi, 29; 32, 34, 104, 215, 234.
32nd Regiment, at Lucknow, 137; at Cawnpore, 174, 226.
35th   ,,   arrives at Calcutta, 99.
37th   ,,   arrives at Calcutta, 99; reported 'cannibals,' 170; 231.
48th   ,,   *en route* from England, 232.
52nd Light Infantry, in Nicholson's Column, 191, 195, 202, 215.
53rd Regiment, on road to Cawnpore, 295.
57th   ,,   *en route* from England, 232.
60th Royal Rifles, at Meerut, 8, 18; with Brigadier Wilson's Force, 30, 43; a Battalion leaves England, 54; with Delhi Force, 215, 266, 297; praise of Regiment, 83, 237.
61st Regiment, expected before Delhi, 74, 87; arrives in Camp, 100, 202; 104, 126, 215; in Nicholson's Movable Column, 234; cholera in, 248; at storming of Magazine, 289.
64th Regiment, arrives at Calcutta, 99, 126.
71st   ,,   *en route* from England, 232.
75th   ,,   leaves for Umballa, 11; with Delhi Force, 29, 32, 215.
78th Highlanders, arrive at Calcutta, 99; 126; 'fiends to fight,' 170; baboo's description of, 188; expected at Cawnpore, 295.
83rd Regiment, 205.
84th   ,,   rumoured arrival at Cawnpore, 36, 82, 99, 126; 137; expected at Cawnpore, 295.
88th Regiment, *en route* from England, 53.
90th   ,,   on road to Cawnpore, 224, 227, 231, 295.

Carabineers. *See* 6th Dragoon Guards.
Naval Brigade, 247, 249, 255.

EUROPEAN AND NATIVE.
Artillery, 8, 64, 214, 264, 266, 295.
Artillery, Horse, 8, 64, 191, 214.
Engineers, 67 *et seq.*, 215, 265, 273, 274, 275, 277, 279.

NATIVE REGIMENTS AND CORPS.
1st Cavalry, rumoured mutiny of, at Mhow and Futtehpore-Sikree, 111, 114.
1st Punjab Cavalry, 106; with Force before Delhi, 215.
1st   „   Infantry. *See* 'Coke's Corps of Sikhs.'
1st Bombay Lancers, mutineers from Nussereebad, in Delhi, 71 n., 72.
2nd Cavalry, part of Gwalior Contingent, 111; at Neemuch, 256.
2nd Irregular Cavalry, suspected by Sir John Lawrence, 218.
2nd Punjab Cavalry, with Force before Delhi, 215.
2nd Grenadiers, mutineers at Calcutta, 2, 3.
2nd Punjab Infantry. *See* 'Green's Corps of Sikhs.'
3rd Light Cavalry, mutiny of, at Meerut, 7 *et seq.*; seize bridge at Delhi, 11; enter Delhi, 31.
3rd Punjab Infantry. *See* 'Henderson's Corps of Sikhs.'
4th Irregular Cavalry. *See* 'Martin's Irregulars.'
4th Native Cavalry Lancers (one squadron), with 2nd Brigade, advancing on Delhi, 29; sent to Meerut, 44.
4th Punjab Infantry. *See* 'Rothney's Corps of Sikhs.'
4th   „   Rifles. *See* 'Wilde's Corps of Sikhs.'
5th Cavalry, at Peshawar, 65.
5th Irregular Cavalry, 331.
5th Punjab Cavalry, at Alleepore, 106 n.; with Force before Delhi, 215.
5th Native Infantry, disbanded at Kurnaul, 31.
6th Native Infantry, mutiny of, at Allahabad, 85 n., 112.
8th Light Cavalry, mutiny of, at Mean Meer, 56 *et seq.*
8th Indian Cavalry, 205.
8th Irregular Cavalry, rumoured staunch at Bareilly, 46; forms part of mutinous Bareilly Brigade, 242.
8th Native Infantry, reported staunch, 252.
9th Irregular Cavalry. *See* 'Fenwick's Irregulars.'
9th Native Infantry, mutiny of, at Mean Meer, 57.
10th Light Cavalry, mutiny of, at Ferozepore, 224, 226, 241; reported in Delhi, 266.
11th Native Infantry, mutiny of, at Meerut, 85 n.
12th Bombay Native Infantry, disarmed at Nussereebad, 252, 256.
12th Irregular Cavalry, mutiny of, at Segowlie, 260.
13th   „   „   with the mutinous Bareilly Brigade, 242.
14th Irregulars, with the mutinous Bareilly Brigade, 242.

INDEX TO REGIMENTS AND CORPS. 343

14th Native Infantry, mutiny and disarming of, at Jhelum, 118, 124.
15th   „   „   mutiny of, at Nussereebad, 46.
16th   „   „   mutiny of, at Mean Meer, 57.
17th Irregular Cavalry. *See* 'Hockin's Irregulars.'
17th Bombay Native Infantry, disarmed at Aboo, 258.
18th Native Infantry, mutiny of, at Bareilly, 64, 75; with Bareilly Brigade, 109.
19th Native Infantry, mutiny of, and disbanded, at Barrackpore, 1, 2, 4, 8.
20th   „   „   mutiny of, at Meerut, 18.
21st   „   „   reported staunch, 252.
23rd   „   „   mutiny of, at Mhow, 111, 114.
26th   „   „   'bolted' from Lahore, 172; cut up by Sir John Lawrence's Sikhs, 177, 218.
27th Native Infantry, large number executed at Kolapoor, 257.
28th   „   „   with mutinous Bareilly Brigade, 109.
29th   „   „   reported staunch at Moradabad, 102; report untrue, 104; with mutinous Bareilly Brigade, 109; executions in corps at Dharwar, 256 *et seq.*
30th Native Infantry, mutiny of, at Nussereebad, 46.
31st   „   „   still staunch at Saugar, 100 n., 202, 212; splendid behaviour of, 261.
34th Native Infantry, disbanded at Barrackpore, 1 *et seq.*, 5 *et seq.*
38th   „   „   with rebels in Delhi, 109.
42nd   „   „   rumoured mutiny of, 202; nearly destroyed by Havelock, 249.
45th Native Infantry, with rebels in Delhi, 266.
46th   „   „   218.
50th   „   „   staunch at Dinapore, 4 *et seq.*; doubts of, 68, 184; 202; at Nagode, still faithful, 239; mutiny of, Appendix D.
51st Native Infantry, mutiny of, at Peshawar, 259.
52nd   „   „   mutiny of, 328, 330.
54th   „   „   mutiny of, in Delhi, 23.
60th   „   „   at Kurnaul, 26; at Rohtuck, 29, 44; accounts from, 35, 37, 52; mutiny of, 54, 57 *et seq.*
61st Native Infantry, with rebels in Delhi, 82.
64th   „   „   at Peshawar, 66, 259.
66th   „   „   officers murdered, 64.
68th   „   „   with mutinous Bareilly Brigade, 109.
70th   „   „   mutiny in, 2, 4; suggestion to send to China, 3; sent to China, 332.
72nd Native Infantry, with Neemuch rebels at Futtehpore-Sikree, 111.
* Bareilly or Rohilkund Brigade, 81, 82, 84, 100, 102, 104 *et seq.*, 109, 113, 240, 242, 243, 296.
Belooch Corps, 142, 146; ('new levies'), 202, 229, 289.
Bhopal Cavalry, 42.
Bhurtpore Contingent, 60, 69, 77, 82, 99.

* For note, see next page.

Bombay Lancers, 72.
Calcutta Militia, intended mutiny of, 2 n.
* Cashmere or Jummoo Contingent, 217 *et seq.*, 269 *et seq.*, 270, 272, 277, 281, 285, 287.
* Coke's Corps of Sikhs, (1st Punjab Infantry), 87, 100, 101, 103, 104 *et seq.*, 191, 195, 197, 198, 216, 234, 243.
Daly's Corps of Guides. *See* the 'Guides.'
* Fenwick's Irregulars, (9th Irregular Cavalry), 101, 104, 117 *et seq.*, 120 *et seq.*, 123, 125, 127, 130.
* Goorkhas, 11 *et seq.*, 14, 15, 24 *et seq.*, 26, 30, 31, 42 *et seq.*, 43, 68, 84, 104, 127, 131, 161, 295.
Green's Corps of Sikhs, (2nd Punjab Infantry), 142 n., 146, 191, 202, 204, 216, 220, 234.
* 'Guides,' the, 42, 45, 51, 54, 100 n., 216, 278.
* Gwalior Contingent, 41, 53 *et seq.*, 77, 114, 304, 310.
Henderson's Corps of Sikhs, (3rd Punjab Infantry), 142 n.
Hockin's Horse, (17th Irregular Cavalry), 106, 127.
Hodson's 'Sikh Horse,' 150, 208 *et seq.*, 215 *et seq.*, 221 *et seq.*, 230.
Hurrian Light Infantry, 41, 210.
Hyderabad Contingent, 187.
Jeypore Contingent, 60, 69.
Jhansi Force, 133, 173.
* Jheend Contingent, 38, 45, 65, 72, 86, 90, 106, 265, 268, 281.
Jhoudpore Contingent, 99.
    ,, Legion, 251 *et seq.*, 257 *et seq.*, 276, 308.
* Kemaon Battalion, 124, 131, 142, 146, 161, 169, 170, 215.
Kerowlie Contingent, 126, 206.
Kotah Contingent, 114, 126, 206.
Lind's Mooltan Horse, 215, 234.
Madras Native Infantry expected at Cawnpore, 295.
Mahidpore Contingent, 96, 111.
Martin's Irregulars, (4th Irregular Cavalry), 29, 43, 46, 81 *et seq.*, 95, 101, 113, 118, 155, 211.
Naba (or Nabha) Contingent, 45.
* Neemuch Force, 70 *et seq.*, 89, 99, 109, 114, 125 *et seq.*, 243.
Nusseree Battalion, 11, 12. *See* 'Goorkhas.'
* Olpherts' Force, 71 *et seq.*, 73, 76, 78, 79.
Rajput Horse, 159 *et seq.*
Rampore Horse, 30.
Rattray's Sikhs, 331.
Rohilkund Brigade. *See* Bareilly Brigade.
Rothney's Corps of Sikhs, (4th Punjab Infantry), 94, 215.
Saugar Brigade, 153.
Sirmoor Battalion, 30, 43, 215.
Ulwar Contingent, 126.
Wilde's Corps of Sikhs, (4th Punjab Rifles), 268, 289.

   * A more detailed Index to these Corps, &c., will be found in the General Index.

GENERAL INDEX.

(N.I.=Native Infantry; L.I.=Light Infantry; L.C.=Light Cavalry.)

ABBOT'S house, occupied after the Assault, 298.
Aboo (Mount Aboo), account of mutiny at, 251, 256 *et seq.*
Afghans, in Coke's Corps, 197; in Delhi, 222, 288.
Agents, Prize, q.v.
Agra, road open and all quiet, 42, 61, 63, 82, 88, 99, 102, 113; Neemuch mutineers expected, 109, 111, 114 *et seq.*; reported release of jail prisoners, 124; Europeans retire into the Fort, 125 *et seq.*; news from the Fort, 130, 149; severe fighting, 136 *et seq.*; account of mutiny, 206; all well, 158, 227, 294; successful expedition from, 249; illness and death of Mr Colvin, 276, 278, 289, 294.
Ahmedabad, 256.
Ahmed Allee Khan, 297.
Ajmere, 111, 112.
 Gate, 299, 300, 326.
Alexander, ——, (1st Cavalry), 111.
Alison, Captain, appointed Military Secretary on Sir Colin Campbell's Staff, 246.
Alison, Captain, (Sir Archibald), appointed A.D.C. to Sir Colin Campbell, 246.
Allahabad, mutiny at, 85; reported safe, 89, 109 *et seq.*, 113, 137; Fort at, 140; Outram expected, 227; rumoured reinforcements at, 236, 294.
Alleepore, 39; camp at, 40 *et seq.*; 59; 72; attacked by enemy and partially plundered, 104 *et seq.*; reports from, 125 *et seq.*, 278, 335.
Allen, Dr, 67.
Allyghur, all well, 63 *et seq.*, 76, 82; news of mutiny at, 111; reported European Force at, 124, 126, 137; revenue collected, 170; relief of, 304; taking of Fort by Lord Lake, 333.
Almorah, 64, 66, 125, 184.
Anderson, ——, (Artillery), 328.
Andrews, Captain F., (60th Rifles), 38, 39.
 Captain and Mrs, 323.
Annersley, Mrs, 322.
Anoopshur, 297.
Anson, General Hon. George, Commander-in-Chief, xii; letters from, 1 *et seq.*; addresses Native detachments on parade, 2; opinion of greased cartridges, *ib.*; leaves Simla, 11, 13, 16; delays departure, 19; feeling of Natives towards, 21 n.; illness, death, and funeral, 26 *et seq.*, 264; receives unmerited blame, 113; auction of things in Camp, 116, 121; 238.
Anson, Captain Hon. A. H. A., (84th Regt.), 79, 150, 177, 293.

Approaches, our, distance from walls of Delhi, 228, 229.
Army, European—
  Advisability of hill stations for, 304.
  More troops advocated, 97, 309.
  Mutiny of soldiers, (the 'White Mutiny'), xiii, xvi *et seq.*
  Sir John Lawrence on, 309.
Army, Indian, (European and Native), praise of, 306.
Army, Native—
  And Civil Service, 192, 309.
  Indiscipline of, and reorganisation necessary, 9 *et seq.*, 11, 97 *et seq.*, 166, 224, 309.
  Invaliding Rules, 10 *et seq.*, 98.
  Officers not responsible for the Mutiny, 192, 239.
  Pension Establishment, 10 *et seq.*, 98.
  Secondary position of officers, 10, 97, 166, 309.
  Seniority system, 98.
  Warning to, 6.
Army of Retribution, composition of, 29 *et seq.*, 190 *et seq.*, 213 *et seq.*; praise of, 245.
Assault on Delhi—
  Casualties during, 283 *et seq.*, 289, 291 n.
  Eve and day of, 281 *et seq.*
  Lord Lake's, 263, Appendix F.
  Opinion in England on, 306.
  Plans for final, 229, 236 *et seq.*
Assaults, intended, on Delhi, 59, 62, 78 *et seq.*, 113, 119, 245; opinions in Camp on, 60 *et seq.*, 63, 64, 72 *et seq.*; Sir John Lawrence's opinion of, 79.
Atkinson, Lieut. W., (52nd L.I.), 289.
Attacks by enemy on our Camp, 62, 70 *et seq.*, 78 *et seq.*, 85, 94, 119 *et seq.*, 128 *et seq.*, 144 *et seq.*, 163 *et seq.*, 171 *et seq.*, 269.

Attacks by us on enemy, 66, 68 *et seq.*, 196 *et seq.*
Auction in Camp, 116, 121, 148.
Aurungabad, 112.
Azimghur, 276, 295.

BABOO's description of Highlanders, 188.
Bacon, Captain, 94.
Bagot, Major, commanding Goorkhas at Jutogh, reported killed, 21; with corps at Kalka, 24 *et seq.*; ordered to Saharunpore, 26; news from, 55, 84.
Bahadoor, Jung, 143, 332.
  Khan, 65.
  Shah, King of Delhi, q.v.
Baillie, Lieut. G., (Artillery), 194.
Baillie Guard, Lucknow, still holding out, 236.
Bain, Mrs, 301.
Baird, Sir David, Bart., appointed A.D.C. to Sir Colin Campbell, 246.
Baird Smith, Colonel R., (Engineers), appointed Chief Engineer, 76; arrival in Camp, 103; 191, 215.
Baleguer, M. de, 323.
Banda, 296, 330.
  Road, 329.
Bank, Simla, people to collect at, 19 *et seq.*
  Delhi, murder of Mr Beresford at, 22; occupied after the Assault, 290, 293, 295.
Bannerman, Lieut. C. B., (Belooch Corps), 269.
Barchard, Captain C. H., (20th N.I.), 154, 213.
Bareilly, mutiny at, 44, 46; refugees at Nynee Tal, 64, 75; expedition to retake, 66.
Bareilly or Rohilkund Brigade, reported on way to Delhi, 81, 82, 84, 100; at Delhi, 102, 113; attack and plunder Alleepore,

INDEX.

104 *et seq.*; regiments composing, 109; engage our troops, 240, 242, 243; 262; flight of mutineers, 296.
Barlow, Mr and Mrs, 332.
Barnard, General Sir Henry, 27, 28, 33, 35, 41, 42; appointed to command Force advancing on Delhi, 56; opinion as to assaulting at once, 60 *et seq.*; at Councils of War, 61 *et seq.*; 66, 80, 83, 91; illness and death from cholera, 107 *et seq.*; funeral, 110; hospitality of, 116; auction of things in Camp, 121.
Barnard, Captain, A.D.C., 16, 50, 108; leaves for home, 113.
Barnes, Mr E. C., telegrams to, 154, 242, 283, 299 *et seq.*
Barrackpore, mutiny at, 1 *et seq.*, 4, 9.
Barry, ———, 112.
Bartle Frere, Mr. *See* Frere.
Bas, Mr Le, 31.
Bastion: Burn, q.v.—Water, q.v.
Batson, Dr, disguised, 45; 214.
Battalion: Kemaon, q.v.—Nusseree, q.v.—Sirmoor, q.v.
Batteries, our, before Delhi, treachery in, 209 *et seq.*, 212; distance from walls of city, 69, 228, 229; being prepared for final Assault, 248; first one ready, 268; description of, 270 *et seq.*, 273 *et seq.*; one catches fire, 273, 274, 275; one made in wrong direction, 277, 279; Engineers blamed for delay, 273, 275, 277, 279.
Baugh, Lieut., (Adjutant 34th N.I.), shot at by Mangul Pandy, 5 n.
Bayley, Captain J. A., (52nd L.I.), 289.
Baynes, Major R., (8th King's), 265, 267.
Beas, River, 131.
Becher, Colonel A. M., Quartermaster-General, accompanies Chief to Umballa, 17; begs Chief not to delay, 19; 26 n., 27, 32; wounded, 71; nature and progress of wound, 74, 76, 79, 81, 102, 125, 151, 193, 222 *et seq.*; letters to, 64, 74, 77, 88, 96, 229; 113, 213, 263, 289, 301, 303.
Becher, Mrs A. M., 24, 180, 186, 288.
Captain Septimus, letter to, 68 *et seq.*; 83, 88, 149.
Mrs James, 24.
Behar, 122.
Belaspore, 30.
Belooch Corps, 142, 146, 229, 289.
Bengal, 122.
Beresford, Mr, (Civil Service), killed in Delhi massacre, 17, 22.
Berhampore, mutiny at, 1 n., 3; 187.
Bernares, reinforcements arriving, 89; 100; mutiny of Sikh corps at, 105; letter from, 327.
Bertrand, Rev. Fred., 214.
Bhagput (Baghput), bridge of boats at, 30, 34; anxiety about, 76, 85, 86, 87 *et seq.*; truth about, 90, 102; report from, 125, 153.
Bhopal Cavalry, false, 42.
Bhurtpore, letters from, 64, 88, 206.
Contingent, 60, 69, 77, 82, 99.
Raja of, 63, 206.
Biana, 96.
Birch, C.B., Colonel R. J. H., (Military Secretary to Govt. at Calcutta), official letter from, 222.
Bishop, Lieut. H. P., (Horse Artillery), and Mrs Bishop, 161.
Bithoor, 165, 172, 174, 189.
Raja of. *See* Nana Sahib.
Blair, Colonel, 98.
Lieut. C. R., (2nd Bengal Fusiliers), 98, 101, 103, 105.
Blane, Captain Seymour J., (52nd L.I.), 216.
Boileaugunge, 11, 24.
Boisragon, Captain H. F. M., (of

1st Bengal Fusiliers, second in command of Kemaon Battalion), 284.
Bolandshur, 30, 225.
Bolton, Mrs, 328.
Bombay, Orders from, 56; message from, 187; arrival of troops at, 231; 247, 250.
Bond, Lieut. E. E. B., (of 57th N.I., attached to the 'Guides'), 284.
Bradshaw, Lieut. J. H., (52nd L.I.), 285.
Brasyer, Colonel, 100.
Bridge: Bussye, 115 *et seq.*—Gurmukteesur, 61—over Hinden River, 124, 144—Peinbaree, 241.
Bridge of boats. *See* Bhagput, *and* Jumna.
Brigade: Bareilly, or Rohilkund (*See* Bareilly)—Madras, 295—Naval, q.v.—Saugar, 153.
Brigades, changes in, 191, 194 *et seq.*; list of, 215 *et seq.*
Briggs, Captain, (71st N.I.), 113, 116, 213.
Brind, Major, (late General Sir James Brind, G.C.B.), commanding Artillery, 134, 214, 289.
Brind, Mrs, 125.
Briscoe, Mr, 155.
  Lieut. E. V., (75th Regt.), 293, 295.
British Force. *See* Force.
British Troops, 15; withdrawn from India, folly of, 16; none at Delhi, 17; reason for delay in coming out to India from home, 49; being sent from England, 167, 187, 232, 252; retake Cawnpore, 198; rumoured arrival at Calcutta, 91 *et seq.*, 99, 175; praise of, 204, 291. *See* Army, *and* Reinforcements.
Brooke, Major J. C., (8th King's), 88, 275, 286.
  Mrs, 275, 292 *et seq.*

Brown, ——, at Cawnpore, 235.
  Dr, 37, 108.
  Captain, (1st Bengal Fusiliers), 68.
Browne, Lieut. J. H., (of 33rd N.I., attached to Kemaon Battalion), 183, 200.
Budd, Lieut. S., (Artillery), 269.
Budlee-ka-Serai, battle at, 47 *et seq.*, 103, 222.
Buktawa Khan, General, King of Delhi's Commander-in-Chief, 178, 240, 335.
Bullubghur, Raja of, 37, 77; writes letter protesting fidelity, 112 *et seq.*; sends petition to the King of Delhi, 262.
Bundelkund (Bandalkhand), 68.
Bunny, Lieut. A., (Horse Artillery), 37, 51, 268.
  Mrs, 51, 268.
Burn, Colonel and Mrs H. Pelham, 244, 265.
Burn Bastion, 295; taken, 298, 299, 300.
Burnside, Captain H. G. H., (61st Regt.), 102, 215, 286, 323.
  Mrs, 241.
Busharuttgunge, 219.
Bushire, 15.
Bussee, 188.
Bussye Bridge, expedition to blow up, 115 *et seq.*
Butter, Arthur, 188, 263.

CABUL (KABUL) GATE, 282.
Calcutta, no communication with, 70, 94; troops arriving at, 49, 91 *et seq.*, 99, 175, 250; 222, 224, 234; Lord Elgin arrives at, 245, 246, 249.
Calcutta Fort, Native detachment in, 2 n.
Camels, use of, during Siege, 269.
Camp at: Alleepore, 40 *et seq.*—Guraunda, 32 *et seq.*—Kurnaul, 25 *et seq.*—Lussowlie, 36 *et seq.*—

INDEX. 349

Paniput, 33 *et seq.*—Raie, 37 *et seq.*
Camp before Delhi—
　Auction in, 116, 121, 148.
　Bazaar in, 137 *et seq.*, 193.
　Comments on life in, 62, 78, 83 *et seq.*, 85, 116, 135, 136, 137 *et seq.*, 140, 150, 170, 177, 185, 193, 195, 201, 203, 208 *et seq.*, 217, 219, 221, 227.
　Comments on the Dâk to, 51, 53, 54, 59, 67, 71, 73, 268.
　Convoys arrive in, 72, 86, 87, 119, 126, 138, 155, 169, 170 *et seq.*, 259.
　Description of, 47, 50, 238.
　Elephants and camels used in, 228, 269.
　Executions in, 103, 212.
　Explosion in, 271.
　Ladies in, 67, 220, 230.
　Mutiny in, 117 *et seq.*
　Reinforcements arrive in, 51, 78, 87, 100, 101, 119, 169, 202, 266, 268, 269.
　Shells fall in, 54, 68, 132.
　Sickness in, 103, 192, 230, 248 *et seq.*, 278.
　Siege-train and ammunition arrive in, 228, 247, 263.
　Site of, 47, 50.
　Telegraph in, 278, 280.
　Treachery in, 209 *et seq.*, 212.
　Troops sent away from, 123, 127.
　Weather in. *See* Weather, *and* Rains.
　Wounded and sick sent away from, 67, 133.
Campbell, Sir Colin, (Lord Clyde), xii, xvii; spoken of as probable Commander-in-Chief, 159, 234; appointed Commander-in-Chief, and leaves England for India, 246, 247 *et seq.*; waiting for news of, 303 *et seq.*, 307 *et seq.*
Campbell, Sir Edward, Bart., (60th

Rifles), at Simla, 14, 49, 83; ordered to rejoin corps before Delhi, 88; arrival in Camp, 105; 201, 266 *et seq.*; appointed a Prize Agent, 298, 323.
Campbell, Lady, 88, 323.
　Colonel G., (52nd L.I.), 194, 216; wounded, 284, 286.
　Lieut., (75th Regt.), to command 9th Irregulars, 127.
　Major J. H., (Artillery), 278.
　Mr and Mrs, 322.
Canal supply of water to Delhi, cut off, 89 *et seq.*, 237, 238.
Candahar, news from, 256, 259.
Canning, Lord, 4, 7; orders by, 56; news from, 132, 208; 303.
Caps, percussion, and gunpowder, scarcity of, in Delhi, 109, 113, 157, 158, 172, 173, 185, 190, 203, 258.
Carabineers, (6th Dragoon Guards), 30, 34, 39; picket fail to obey orders, 117, 119, 123.
Carlyon, Mrs, 251.
Carnegys, the, 263.
Cartridges, the greased, at Barrackpore, 1 *et seq.*, 3, 4; at Meerut, 2, 8, 9 *et seq.*; 16 *et seq.*; mentioned by Colonel Sykes in Parliament, 305.
Cash-box, theft of, 115; strange means of recovery, 117 n.
Cashmere, 201—Bastion demolished, 274 — Gate, 199, 269; capture of, 282.
Cashmere and Jummoo Contingent, 217 *et seq.*; arrival of in Camp, 269, 270; arms of, 272, 277, 281; cowardice of, 285, 287.
Cashmere, Maharajah of, 217 *et seq. See* Goolab, *and* Runbar Sing.
Casualties, our: during Siege, Assault and Capture, 47 *et seq.*, 55 *et seq.*, 68 *et seq.*, 73, 79 *et seq.*; total up to date 26th June, 84; 85, 87, 95 *et seq.*, 118 *et seq.*, 128 *et seq.*, 139, 144, 147 *et seq.*,

2 v

149, 171, 173, 175, 189 et seq., 196, 199 et seq.; number of officers killed up to date, 221, 235, 238; in fight at Nujufghurh, 240 et seq.; 243, 270, 279; during Assault, 283 et seq., 289, 291 n.; on 14th September, 293; at Lahore Gate, 293, 295.
Casualties of enemy. See Enemy.
Causes of the Mutiny. See Mutiny.
Cave-Brown, Mrs, 19.
Cawnpore, 36, 61, 82, 85, 88 et seq., 113, 121, 122, 124, 132, 137 et seq., 151, 159, 160, 170, 173.
Cawnpore, Havelock's victories at, and near, 172, 175 et seq., 179, 198, 201, 231.
Cawnpore, letters from, 175, 178, 194, 198 et seq.
    Massacre at, Native accounts of, 161, 163, 164; Havelock's, and official confirmation of, 174, 175, 177 et seq., 197, 198; Lieut. Delafosse's account of, 226, 239.
    News from General Neill at, 198, 223 et seq., 231 et seq., 267.
    Outram advancing on, 276, 278, 294, 295.
Ceylon, 15, 170.
Chalmers, Lieut. O. J., (of 3rd N.I., attached to the 'Guides'), 87.
Chamberlain, Brigadier, (now General Sir Neville), 44, 52; expected in Camp, 76, 79; made Acting Adjutant-General, 79; arrival in Camp, 80, 81; 107 et seq., 116 et seq., 123, 127; wounded, 128, 130, 134; 213; made 'pucka' Adjutant-General, 249.
Chandnee Chouk, 287, 290, 293, 300.
Changes in Brigades, 191, 194 et seq.
Chesney, Lieut. G. T., (Bengal Engineers), 67, 102, 215, 273, 284.
Chester, Colonel Charles, Adjutant-General, 1, 7, 8, 11, 13, 14; accompanies Chief to Umballa, 11, 17; letter from, 15; 26, 27 et seq., 31 et seq., 41, 43, 44; death, 47 et seq., 48 et seq., 50; funeral, 48, 49, 50; 51, 52, 58, 60, 80; monument for grave, 83, 256, 264.
Chester, Mrs, 15, 24, 43, 58, 60, 94.
    Lieut. H. D. E. W., (of 36th N.I., attached to Sirmoor Battalion), 95; wounded, 128; 216.
China Force, 99, 175, 205, 234, 245.
Chisholm, ——, (Madras Fusiliers), 235.
Cholmondley, Mrs, 322.
Chumbal (Chambal) River, 110, 262 et seq., 288.
Church, Delhi, letter from, 282.
Civil Service, the, and the Army, 192, 309.
Clarendon, Lord, promises to send reinforcements, 187.
Clarke, Longueville, 249.
Clive, ——, A.D.C., 210.
Clyde, Lord, xii, xvii. See Sir Colin Campbell.
Coel, 249.
Coghlan, Dr, 38.
Coke, Major, commanding 1st Punjab Infantry, 74 n., 101, 105, 196, 199.
Coke's Corps of Sikhs, (1st Punjab Infantry), expected in Camp, 87; arrives at Alleepore, 100; enters Camp, 101; 103; pursues enemy, 104 et seq.; to form part of Nicholson's Column, 191, 195; engages enemy, 197, 198; 216, 234, 243.
Coles, Mr, 329.
College, Cooper's Hill, 102 n.
    Delhi, 282 — Garden, 284, 289.
Collins, ——, 220.
Column: Advance, 34, 36—Greathed's, 304—Havelock's Movable, 203, 205—Hope Grant's, 307—

INDEX.

Nicholson's Movable, q.v.—Pursuing, 288, 299—Showers', 304—Wilson's, 30 et seq.

Colvin, Mr J. R., (Lieut.-Governor N.W. Provinces), news of, 56, 85, 86, 88, 90, 99, 102, 130, 208, 219, 238, 245; illness, 239, 276; death, 289, 294.

Colyear, Colonel, 323.
Mr D., 13.

Commander-in-Chief, uncertainty as to who will be appointed, 159; appointment decided on, 175; residence in the hills, 304. *See also* General Anson, Sir Colin Campbell, Lord Clyde, Sir William Gomm, Sir Patrick Grant, General Reed, Sir Hugh Rose, Lord Strathnairn, Sir Henry Somerset.

Confidence of Natives in us, and their devotion, 97, 137 et seq., 193, 200.

Congreve, Colonel, Acting Adjutant-General of Queen's Troops, 26, 27 et seq.; illness, 31, 35, 37, 68; 107, 132; leaves for Simla, 133 et seq.; 142, 143, 158 et seq., 177, 188 et seq., 234 et seq.

Contingent: Bhurtpore, q.v.—Cashmere, q.v.—Gwalior, q.v.—Hyderabad, 187—Jeypore, 69—Jheend, 99—Jhoudpore, q.v.—Jummoo, 217 et seq.—Kerowlie, 126, 206—Kotah, 114, 126, 206—Mahidpore, 96, 111—Ulwar, 126.

Convoys, arrival of in Camp, 86, 87, 119, 126, 138, 155, 169, 170 et seq., 259.

Cooper's Hill College, first President of, 102 n.

Copeland, Lieut. J. E., (10th L.C.), 323.

Corps: Belooch, q.v.—Coke's, q.v.—Daly's Guide, q.v.—Green's, q.v.—Henderson's, 142 n.—Rothney's, 94, 215—Wilde's, 268, 289.

Corps and Regiments. *See special Index, page* 341.

Cortland, General Van, and his Force, 110, 210, 228, 289.

Cossids and cossid letters, 64 n., 126, 176, 179, 225, 231, 243 et seq.; translation of, Appendix I. *See Glossary.*

Cotton, Brigadier-General, (commanding at Peshawar), 56, 65.
Colonel, (67th Regt.), to command at Agra, 208; news from, 231 et seq., 267.

Councils of War, 61 et seq., 63, 64, 68, 74.

Crimean War, troops withdrawn from India for, 16.

Crozier, Lieut. W., (75th Regt.), 139.

Cuppage, Lieut. B., (of 6th Cavalry, attached to 9th Lancers), 289.

Curtis, Lieut. P. J., (60th Rifles), 55.

Curzon, Colonel Hon. R. W. P., 3, 5, 28, 132; leaves for Simla, 134, 143, 145.

Custom House Garden Battery, 273 et seq., 277, 291.

DALHOUSIE, 279.

Dalhousie, Lord, his unwise policy, 10, 129, 268, 334.

Daly, Captain H., (of 1st Bombay Fusiliers, commanding the 'Guides'), 29, 51, 100; praise of, 68; wounded, 71; progress of wound, 74, 79, 81, 102, 128, 247.

Daly, Mrs, 12, 71, 79, 323.

Daly's Corps of Guides. *See* the 'Guides.'

Damon, ——, 328.

Daniell, Lieut. J. W., (1st Bengal Fusiliers), 130.

Darling, ——, 95.

Dashwood, Captain H. M., 112; letter from, 114 et seq.

Davidson, Lieut. A. H., (Artillery), 51.

Dawes, Colonel, (Bengal Artillery), 334.
Deesa, 83, 256.
Delafosse, Lieut., (53rd N.I.), his escape from Cawnpore and narrative of massacre, 226 et seq., 239, 265.
Delamain, Captain J. W., (56th N.I.), 50.
Delay in troops coming out to India, reason for, 49.
Delhi (Shahjahanabad)—
　Account of massacre, 22 et seq., 222.
　Assault and capture of city, 282 et seq.
　Canal supply of water cut off, 89 et seq., 237, 238.
　Entire possession of city, 299.
　First bad news from, 11, 12 et seq., 16 et seq.
　Indignation against, 164, 220.
　Intended assaults on city. See Assaults.
　King proclaimed, 19; brought in by Hodson, 301, 304; remains in city to be tried, 308; fate of King and Princes, Appendix G. See King.
　Mistaken strength and size of city and fortifications, 129, 238, 305; their true strength and size, 91 et seq., 129, 238, Appendix C.
　Newsletters from, q.v.
　Percussion-caps and gunpowder, scarcity of, 109, 157, 158, 172, 173, 185, 190, 203, 258.
　Plunder of Prime-Minister's house, 184 et seq., 189 et seq.
　Powder-factory blown up, 184.
　Residents reported for us, 55, 66, 140.
　State of city and inhabitants, 53, 55, 60, 103, 109, 113, 133, 144, 156, 160, 189, 190, 250 et seq., 258, 260, 280.
　Storming of magazine, 287.
　Strength of our Force, and of mutineers, 191, 203, 250 et seq., 281.
　Taking of city by Lord Lake, Appendix F.
Delhi Gate, 295 et seq., 299.
　Water-Gate, 282.
Dennis, Colonel J. L., (52nd L.I.), 194, 216 n.
Despatches from Brigadier Wilson, 34, 39.
Detail of Troops forming Force before Delhi, 213 et seq.
Devotion of Natives, 96 et seq., 200.
Dewan-i-Khas, the, 334.
Dharwar, 257.
Dholpore, Raja of, 63, 276.
Dhurmsala, 309.
Dinapore, letter from, 4 et seq.; mutiny at, 97, 201, 224, 231 et seq.
Dixon, Colonel, 112.
Doab, 42 et seq., 111.
Dogras, 266. See Glossary.
Donald, ——, 108.
Douglas, Captain, 17.
　Lieut., (Horse Artillery), 214.
D'Oyly, Lieut., (Artillery), 126.
Drake, Major, letter from, 217 et seq.
Drought, Major R., (60th N.I.), 147.
Dugshai, 22, 25.
Dunsford, Colonel, (of 59th N.I., commanding Jheend Contingent), 153, 208, 220.
Durand, Colonel, 205.
Durreoogunj, 298.

EARLE, Captain, 175.
Earthquake felt in Camp, 183.
East India Company, xvi.
Eaton, Lieut. K. P., (60th Rifles), 274.
Eckford, Lieut. A. H., (of 69th N.I., with Sirmoor Battalion), 120.

INDEX. 353

Eden, Captain W. F., letters from, 74 *et seq.*, 82, 96, 111 *et seq.*, 114, 159 *et seq.*, 186 *et seq.*, 204 *et seq.*, 229, 251 *et seq.*, 276.

Eden, Mrs, 111.

Edwardes, Sir Herbert, 90.

Eed, Festival of the, enemy propose to attack us on, 152; dissensions in city on, 158; attack of 1st August on, 169, 171; 178, 189. *See Glossary.*

Elderton, Lieut. A., (2nd Bengal Fusiliers), 290.

Elephants, used during Siege, 95, 203, 228, 263, 264.

Elgin, Lord, arrives at Calcutta, 245, 246, 249.

Elkington, Lieut. S. B., (61st Regt.), 240 n., 243.

Ellenborough, Lord, opinion of the Civil Service, 192; comments on speech by, 232, 235, 237 *et seq.*

Ellerslie, Colonel Keith Young's home at Simla, 1 *et seq.*; letters from, 16 *et seq.*, 301.

Elliot, Lieut. Minto, (Artillery), 39.

Ellis, Rev. Mr, 210, 212.
  Major, 327.

Emperor of the French contributes to Mutiny Fund, 303.

End of English Rule in India predicted, 80, 164.

Enemy, the—
  Casualties of, 55 *et seq.*, 68 *et seq.*, 72 *et seq.*, 80 *et seq.*, 86, 104, 119 *et seq.*, 128, 139, 144, 172, 173, 175, 184, 189 *et seq.*, 196, 198, 200, 278 *et seq.*
  Cowardice of, 105, 148, 171.
  Strength of, 191, 203, 250 *et seq.*, 281.

Enfield Rifle, the, 19, 204.

Engineers, strictures on, and excuses for, 67, 273 *et seq.*, 277, 279; praise of, 275.

England, reinforcements coming from. *See* Reinforcements, *and* British Troops.

English Press on the Mutiny, 192, 305 *et seq.*

Erinpoorah, mutiny at, 251 *et seq.*, 258, 267, 276; plunder of, 280.

Erskine, Major, 327.

Establishment, Native Army Invalid and Pension. *See* Army.

European Army. *See* Army.

Force. *See* Force.

Eve of Assault, 281.

Ewart, Major R. S., 213.

Execution: by telegraph, 7 *et seq.*
  —of mutineers and traitors in Camp, 40, 103, 212.

FAGAN, Captain R. C. H. B., (Artillery), 36, 101, 266, 271, 279 *et seq.*

Faithful, Dr, 24.
  Mrs, 94.

Fakeer, the dead, 70.

Fenwick, Captain, (of 5th Regt., in command of 9th Irregulars), 59; to be superseded, 125 *et seq.*

Fenwick's Irregulars, (9th Irregular Cavalry), with Force before Delhi, supposed staunch, 101; 104; misbehaviour in corps, 117 *et seq.*; inquiry into, 120 *et seq.*; corps sent away, 123; command of corps, 125, 127, 130.

Ferozepore, 149, 224.

Festival: of the Eed, q.v.—of the Mohurram, q.v.

Fidelity: of Punjab Regiments, 101—of the 50th N.I., 3, 328 *et seq.*

Fire-rafts, use of, to destroy bridge of boats, 178 *et seq.*, 180.

Fitzgerald, Lieut. J. R. S., (75th Regt.), 285.

Flagstaff Tower, the, 48; flag erected on, 52; 178, 273, 274.
  Picket, death of Captain Knox at, 55 *et seq.*

INDEX.

Force—
  Composition and strength of our, 29 et seq., 213 et seq., 190 et seq., 238, 281.
  China, 99, 175, 205, 234, 245.
  Enemy's. See Enemy.
  European, 126, 137, 146, 147, 150, 163.
  Havelock's. See Havelock.
  Van Cortland's, 110, 210, 228, 289.
  Wilson's, victories of, 33 et seq., 37 et seq., 39; 43.
Ford, Mr, (Civil Service), 99, 114, 159.
Fort at: Agra, 125 et seq., 130, 149—Allahabad, 140—Allyghur, 333—Calcutta, 2—Delhi (See Selimgurh)—Khooshalgurh, 99, 160—Myha, 328—Saugar, 261.
Fortifications of Delhi, size and strength of, 129, 238, Appendix C.
France, seamen of, 167.
Frazer, Mr, Commissioner at Delhi, murder of, 17, 22.
French Troops, 333.
Frere, Mr Bartle, (late Sir Bartle Frere, Bart, G.C.B., G.C.S.I.), letter from, giving opinion as to taking of Delhi, 156, 157 et seq.; praise of, 239; letter from Kurrachee, 256 et seq.; 294, 309.
Frigates 'Pearl' and 'Shannon,' 249.
Frith, Captain J. S., (Artillery), 214.
Fund, Mutiny Relief, 3 n., 253 et seq., 302 et seq., 307.
Furruckabad, 173.
Futtehpore, defeat of Nana at, 154; victory of Havelock at, 175; Havelock's Order dated at, 203.
Futtehpore-Sikree, 111, 112.
Futtyghur, reported all well, 121, 146, 151; rumoured massacre at, 153, 155 et seq., 177; 161, 202.
Futtyghur, Nawab of, 156.
Fyzabad, 148.

GABBETT, Lieut. T., (61st Regt.), 240.
Gagra (Gogari) River, 202.
Galloway, Mr and Mrs, 19, 30 et seq.
Gambier, Lieut. C. H. F., (of 38th N.I., attached to 2nd Bengal Fusiliers), 290.
Ganges, 61, 179, 297.
Garbett, Brigadier H., (Artillery), 191, 214, 225.
Garstin, Captain H. M., 30, 39, 213.
Gate: Ajmere, 299—Cabul, 282—Cashmere, 199, 269, 282—Delhi Palace, 295 et seq., 299—Lahore, 293 et seq., 298, 299—Moree, 101, 282—Water, 282.
Gerrard, Colonel, in command of Column sent to Narnaul, 307.
Ghazeeoodeen-Nugar, 30, 34, 144.
Ghazeepore, 97, 245, 297.
Gillespie, Lieut. A., (Artillery), 276.
Glazed paper, the, 1 et seq.
Glover, Toby, 149.
Goad, Major, 134, 154, 179, 181, 208, 220, 268.
Godas, 295 et seq. See Glossary.
Golding, ——, 330.
Goldney, Colonel Philip, 148, 170, 251.
  Mrs, 170.
Gomm, Sir William, xii, 136 n.
Gondepore, (Gurdaspore?), 217.
Goojurs, 76, 88, 104. See Glossary.
Goolab Sing, Maharajah of Cashmere and Jummoo, death of, 201, 217 et seq.
Goorgaon, 234.
Goorkhas, disaffected Nusseree Battalion at Jutogh, 11 et seq.; 14, 15; at Kalka, 24 et seq.; ordered to Saharunpore, 26, 31; their good behaviour, 42 et seq., 47, 68, 84, 104; rumours of, from Jutogh, 161 et seq.; with Havelock's Column, 295; with Sirmoor Battalion before Delhi, 30 et seq., 43, 127, 131.

INDEX.

355

Gordon, Colonel, 100, 105.
Gough, Lieut., (now General Sir Hugh Gough, V.C., G.C.B.—of 3rd L.C., attached to Hodson's Horse), 230.
Gough, Colonel (Sir John Bloomfield) and Mrs, 180.
Government, message from, on sending reinforcements, 187; on delay in taking Delhi, 222.
Governor-General, 2, 15; Orders by, 56; message from, 208, 224. *See also* Canning, *and* Dalhousie.
Govindghur, 204.
Gowan, General, 12, 132, 161.
Graham, Colonel and Miss, 208. Mrs, 161.
Grant, Sir Patrick, 28; appointed Commander-in-Chief in Bengal, 56; no news of, since leaving Madras, 94, 109 *et seq.*, 129, 130; rumoured arrival at Cawnpore, 154; 159, 175, 224 *et seq.*
Grant, Colonel Hope, (late General Sir Hope Grant, G.C.B.—9th Lancers), in command of Cavalry Brigade, 30; in camp at Guraunda, 33; anxious for immediate advance, 44, 73 *et seq.*; 191, 215, 298; Column commanded by, 307.
Grant, John Peter, 227.
Grant, ——, (Volunteer Cavalry), 235.
Graves, Brigadier, escapes from Delhi, 19, 23; commanding 2nd Brigade, 29; unfitness for command, 82; applies for sick leave, 88, 90.
Graydon, Captain W., (of 16th Grenadiers, attached to 1st Bengal Fusiliers), 289.
Greased cartridges, the. *See* Cartridges.
Greathed, Colonel, (commanding 8th King's), at Simla, 12, 14, 20 *et seq.*, 22; expected at Delhi from Jullunder, 82; arrives with regiment, 87; 123, 161, 184, 194, 199, 245, 256, 275, 288, 293; commanding Pursuing Column, 304; 323.
Greathed, Mrs, 12, 20, 22, 184; illness of, 256, 275, 283, 288; 323.
Greathed, Lieut. W. W. H., (Bengal Engineers), arrives at Alleepore from Agra, 42; present at Council of War held in Camp before Delhi, 63; 120, 275; wounded during Assault, 285.
Greathed, Mr Harvey, (Commissioner at Meerut), 18; does not wish Brigadier Wilson to go to Delhi, 39; arrival in Camp as Governor-General's Agent with the Army, 46; advocates immediate assault, 61; 245, 266; death from cholera at Delhi, 299 *et seq.*
Green's Corps of Sikhs, (2nd Punjab Infantry commanded by Captain—late General Sir George —Green), 142 n., 191, 202, 204, 216, 220, 234.
Greensill, Captain T. M., (24th Regt.), killed by sentry, 142 *et seq.*
Greville, Captain S., (1st Bengal Fusiliers), 50, 196.
Grindall, Captain, (8th N.I.), 213.
Guard, Baillie, (Lucknow), 236.
'Guides,' the, commanded by Captain Daly, 42, 45; arrival in Delhi Camp, 51; temporary command of, by Hodson, 67, 84; praise of corps, 52, 54, 216; 278; composition of corps, 100 n.; 278.
Gunpowder, scarcity of, in Delhi, 109, 157, 158, 172, 173, 185, 190, 203, 258.
Guns, capture of enemy's: by Wilson, 34—before Delhi, 47, 66, 71, 73 n., 196 *et seq.*, 199, 240, 241 *et seq.*, 244—during

Assault, 293 *et seq.*—by Havelock, 176, 198, 219.
Guns, enemy's superiority in, 190.
Guraunda, camp at, 32 *et seq.*; Major Olpherts at, 73.
Gurmukteesur, 61, 82, 84, 90.
Gustavinsky, Ensign L., (Punjab Sappers), 289.
Gwalior, 231, 262, 292, 294.
    Contingent, in Delhi, 41; surrender of party of, 53 *et seq.*
    Mutineers in Gwalior, Rohilkund, and Oude, 77, 89, 99, 102, 110, 111 *et seq.*, 114, 154, 158, 244, 265, 272, 289, 294, 304, 310.
Gwalior, Maharajah of, true, 63, 77, 99, 102, 111; his reported independence, 122, 124; 154, 262.

HAKEEM HASSEN OOLLAH, King of Delhi's Prime-Minister, 184 *et seq.*, 189 *et seq.*
Hall, Colonel, (commanding Joudhpore Legion), 251 *et seq.*, 257 *et seq.*
Hall, Major George, (4th Irregular Cavalry), 45 *et seq.*, 48, 51, 66 *et seq.*, 165, 174, 180, 200, 209, 286, 299.
Hall, Mrs, 27, 93, 200.
Hallifax, Brigadier, (of 75th Regt., commanding 1st Brigade), 26; illness and death at Kurnaul, 35 *et seq.*
Hallifax, Mrs, 12, 14, 21, 26, 35, 323.
    Plassy, 26.
Hamayoon's Tomb, King of Delhi's flight to, 299, 334.
Hamilton, Captain, (9th Lancers), 215.
    Octavius, Pension Paymaster, 58, 150, 180.
    Mrs, 150.
Hampton, Colonel J., (commanding 50th N.I.), letters from, 4 *et seq.*, Appendix D; 68, 202.
Hampton, Mrs, 184.
Hansi, 35, 37, 113, 289.
Hardcastle, Captain, 160.
Harding, Charles and Mrs, 323.
Harminna, 331.
Harriott, Major, (Deputy J.-A. at Meerut), 7 *et seq.*, 30; letters from, 142, 143 *et seq.*, 162 *et seq.*; 165; to conduct King of Delhi's trial, 308, 334.
Harris, Lieut. J. T., (2nd Bengal Fusiliers), 87.
Harrison, Lieut. A., (75th Regt.), 50.
Hartley, Colonel, 87, 91.
Harvey, Mr, 76; letter from, 77; 96, 205.
Hatrass, 111, 249, 304.
Haupper, (?) 173.
Havelock, Colonel, (General Sir Henry), 134; appointed Brigadier-General, 143; 156, 159; letter from, 175 *et seq.*; Morning Order to his men, 203 *et seq.*; account of victories over the Nana and others, 169, 172, 174, 175 *et seq.*, 179, 198, 203, 219 *et seq.*; marching on Lucknow, 223; decides to delay, 231; 245, 249, 267.
Hay, Lord William, Commissioner of Simla, 14, 18, 115; orders by, 48, 117, 143, 174, 180, 184, 272; 115; notes from, 179, 199, 283, 298.
Hay, Lord Frederick, 212.
    Dr and Mrs, 66.
    R., 323.
    Captain J. C., (of 60th N.I., attached to 2nd Bengal Fusiliers), 290.
Hearsay, General J. B., warrant granted to, 1 *et seq.*; additional warrant asked for, 5 *et seq.*
Henderson, Colonel H. B., letters to, 3, 9 *et seq.*, 12 *et seq.*, 91 *et seq.*, 129, 189 *et seq.*, 236 *et seq.*, 281, 303 *et seq.*, 305, 307 *et seq.*; letters from,

INDEX.

96 *et seq.*, 165 *et seq.*, 166 *et seq.*, 252 *et seq.*, 253 *et seq.*, 254, 302 *et seq.*, 305 *et seq.*, 307 *et seq.*
Henderson, H. B., (Civil Service), 9, 94.
Henderson's Corps of Sikhs, 142 n.
Herat, Persians evacuate, 256, 259.
Herbert, Colonel C., (75th Regt.), 58, 149.
Hewitt, General W. H., commanding at Meerut, 8, 18, 30, 34; allowed leave to the hills, 119; superseded, 145; 258 *et seq.*
Highlanders, Native description of, 170, 188.
Hildebrand, Lieut. E. H., (Horse Artillery), 269.
Hillersden, Mr and Mrs, 226.
Hills, Lieut. J., (Lieut.-General Sir James Hills-Johnes, V.C., G.C.B. — Artillery), wins the V.C., 118, 120, 123.
Hinden River, 124; bridge destroyed, 144.
Hindoo Princes and States, faithfulness and adherence of, 69, 82, 93.
Hindoo Rao's house on the Ridge, 45; fight at, and occupation of, 47, 48, 50, 52; attacked by enemy, 55, 171; 67; incident in, 70; 66, 77, 120, 183, 209, 285.
Hindoos and Mahomedans: in Delhi, feud between, 60, 152, 158, 160, 171—in Rohilkund, 222, 223.
Hissar, 35, 37, 228.
Hockin, Lieut., (commanding 17th Irregular Cavalry, 'Hockin's Horse'), 106, 127.
Hodson, Major W. S. R., of 'Hodson's Horse,' (Lieut.), 30, 39, 52, 64, 66; praise of, 68, 150; in temporary command of the 'Guides,' 76, 84; 72, 78, 82; goes to Bhagput, 90, 95, 102, 116; 'taken in' by the enemy, 120; gives up the 'Guides' for Cavalry Corps, 150; 157 *et seq.*, 164, 174, 201, 203;

goes out on expedition, 208; news from, 210, 211 *et seq.*, 216 *et seq.*, 221, 223, 224, 225, 229; return of, to Camp, 230; Hodson's 'Sikh Horse,' 215; the Persian *chit*, 242 *et seq.*; reconnoitres towards Nujufghurh, 245, 247; opinion upon delay in taking Delhi, 277; 279, 282, 299; telegram from, 300; takes King of Delhi prisoner, 301, 308, 334; shoots Princes, *ib.*
Hodson, Mrs, 52, 64, 66, 84, 95, 184, 279.
Hodul, 74, 99; letters from, 77, 96, 111 *et seq.*, 112, 114, 159, 229.
Hogge, Colonel C., 143, 258.
Holkar, Raja of, rumoured disaffection of his troops, 205.
Holmes, Major and Mrs, 260.
Hooshyurpore, 123.
Hope Grant, Colonel. *See* Grant.
House: Abbot's, 298—Hindoo Rao's, q.v.—India, 96, 97—Khan Mahomed's, 298—Metcalfe, q.v.— Skinner's, 282, 284.
Howell, Captain, (1st Bengal Fusiliers), 46, 50.
Hughes, Captain, (General W. T. Hughes, K.C.B.), 138 n.
Huk, Mr M. A., 335.
    Mr M. M., 337.
Humiliation, Service of, in Camp, 210.
Humphreys, Lieut., (4th Punjab Infantry), 289.
Hunesanna, 331.
Hurreepore, 15, 24.
Hurrian Light Infantry, or Hurrianas, 41, 210.
Hutchinson, Mr, 18, 19.
Huzara, 101.
Hyderabad, 112, 187.
    Contingent, mutiny of, 187.

IGNORANCE at Home and in Parliament of causes of Mutiny, 192, 239, 305 *et seq. See* Mutiny.

2 w

Ilahi Baksh, Prince, 335.
India, Empire of, no fear for, 166, 252.
    Army. *See* Army.
    Company, East, x.
    House, 97.
    Paper, description of, 335 n.
India, predicted day for fall of, 73, 78 n., 80. *See* 'Raj.'
Indiscipline of Army. *See* Army.
Indore, 111, 276.
Inglefield, Lieut., (39th N.I.), 323.
Innes, Dr J. H. K., 85.
    Lieut. F. C., (60th N.I.), 196.
Invaliding Rules of Native Army. *See* Army.
Ireland, Dr, reported killed, 240 n. ; nature of wound, 242, 272.
Isurree Pandy. *See* Pandy.

JACKSON, Lieut., (2nd Bengal Fusiliers), 82.
Jacob, Brigadier, 257 ; on reorganisation of the Indian Army and the Civil Service, 309.
Jacob, Major G. O., (1st Bengal Fusiliers), 283, 284.
Jamma Bukt, one of the King of Delhi's sons, 333 *et seq.*
Jeffries, Mrs, 108.
Jelalabad, 288.
Jennings, Rev. Mr, and Miss, massacred at Delhi, 22 *et seq.*
Jeypore, letters from, 186 *et seq.*, 251 *et seq.*
    Contingent, 60, 69, 82.
    Raja of, 276.
Jhansi, bad news from, 68, 70.
    Force, arrives in Delhi, 133, 173.
    Rissalah, 173. *See* Rissalah *in Glossary.*
Jheend Raja and Contingent, fidelity of, 38, 45, 65 ; guarding rear of Camp, 72, 86, 90, 95, 106, 220 ; arrival of in Camp, 265, 268, 281.

Jhelum, 118, 124, 153.
Jhujhur, Nawab of, 164.
Johnson, Captain, (late General Sir Edwin Johnson, G.C.B.), 43, 95, 213.
Johnson, Mr, (Civil Service), 30.
Johnston, Brigadier-General, 110, 179.
Jones, Brigadier W., (61st Regt.), 191, 215.
    Colonel C., (60th Rifles), 43, 299.
    Captain, (60th Rifles), 80.
    Lieut. E., (Engineers), 139.
    Lieut., (9th Lancers), 213.
Joonug, 12 *et seq.*, 14, 21 *et seq.*, Appendix A.
Joudhpore, (Jodhpur), 295.
    Contingent, 99.
    Legion, mutiny of, 251 *et seq.*, 257 *et seq.*, 276 ; mutineers dispersed, 307, 308.
Jullunder, mutineers from, 55, 65, 80, 104 ; Force coming from, 60 ; 131.
Jumalpore, 289.
Jumma Musjid, 158, 298, 300. *See Glossary.*
Jummoo Contingent, 217 *et seq. See* Cashmere Contingent.
    Loan, 218.
    Maharajah of. *See* Cashmere.
Jumna River, 30, 35, 45, 81, 266, 326 ; measures to destroy bridge of boats, 45, 178 *et seq.*, 180. *See* Bhagput.
Jung Bahadoor, 143, 332.
Jutogh, 11 *et seq.*, 13, 18 *et seq.*, 161.

KALKA, 24 *et seq.*
Kalpi, 184, 202.
Kama, 206.
Katha Pass, 317.
Keith Young, Colonel. *See* Young.
Kemaon Battalion, expected before Delhi, 124, 161 ; detained, 131 ; 140 ; arrival of, 169, 170 ; 215.

INDEX.

Kemp, Lieut. D., (of 5th N.I., attached to 2nd Bengal Fusiliers), 118, 120.
Kennedy, Lieut. T. G., (of 52nd N.I., attached to Guide Cavalry), 181. Colonel, (70th Regt.), 332.
Kennion, Captain T. E., (Artillery), 183.
Kenny,——, (84th Regt.), 235.
Kerowlie Contingent, desertion of, 126, 206.
Khooshalgurh, Fort of, 99, 160.
King of Delhi, (Bahadoor Shah), proclaimed, 19, 333 *et seq.*; 62 *et seq.*; anxious for terms, 104, 160, 203, 294; 153, 164, 172; proclamation by, 173; Prime-Minister and, 184, 185 *et seq.*, 187 *et seq.*, 190; 194, 255; rebel troops demand pay, 160 *et seq.*, 261 *et seq.*; 283, 290; flight of, 295, 296, 298, 299, 300 *et seq.*, 334; brought in by Hodson, 301, 304; to be tried in Delhi, 308; trial and sentence of, 334.
Kissengunge, 68, 285, 287.
Knox, Captain E. W. J., (75th Regt.), 55.
Koeg, (Kosy?), 205.
Kolapore, 256.
Koodsee Bagh, 269, 272.
Kootub, (Kutub), 194, 195, 271. *See Glossary.*
Kooyntal, Rana of, 11 *et seq.*, 21 *et seq.*; correspondence relating to, Appendix A.
Kotah Contingent, 114, 126, 206, 243.
Kujwa, 328.
Kukree Huttee, 301.
Kurnaul, 15, 17, 19; camp at, 25 *et seq.*; 138.
Kurrachee, 156; letter from, 157; 168, 256.
Kussowlie, mutiny of guard at, 13 *et seq.*; plunder of treasury, *ib.*; 22, 24, 25.

LADIES in camp, 41, 67, 220, 230.
Lahore, 44, 94, 259, 309.
Gate, failure to take, 293, 294, 298; taken, 298.
Lake, Lord, his Taking of Delhi, 263, Appendix F.
Lambert, Lieut. E. A. C., (1st Bengal Fusiliers), 290.
Lane, Mr and Mrs, 259.
Larkin, Sergeant, 41, 115.
Lascars, suspected of treachery, 209 *et seq.*, 212.
Laughton, Major, Chief Engineer, 30, 67, 76.
Mrs, 67.
Law, Captain W. G., (of 10th N.I., attached to Coke's Corps), 147.
Lawrence, Sir John, writes approval of what has been done before Delhi, 79; raising troops, 87; is not despondent, 122; 134; promises reinforcements, 142, 146; issues order to disarm Natives in Simla Bazaar, 150, 158; 154, 177, 209; 218; on the Indian Army, 309.
Lawrence, Brigadier-General Sir Henry, at Lucknow, 99, 137; reports all safe, 140; 174 n.; rumoured death of, 176 *et seq.*, 181, 182; death practically confirmed, 186; 218, 246.
Lawrence, Colonel George, 205 n.; (General), 257, 276.
Captain Richard C., (commanding Cashmere and Jummoo Contingent), 218, 270.
Lawrence School, 257.
Lawrie, Mr, 244.
Mrs, 323.
Le Bas, Mr, 31.
Leeson, Mrs, refugee from Delhi, 220; gives account of massacre, 222; 230 n.
Legion, Joudhpore, q.v.
Leisuarm, 48.
Levien, Mr, 212.

Light, Lieut. Alfred, (Artillery), 39, 50, 58; praise of, 85.
Lind's Mooltan Horse, 215, 235.
Lindsay, Major and Mrs, 226.
Lira, Superintendent, 108.
Lloyd, General, 201, 224.
Lockhart, Lieut. D. B., (of 7th N.I., attached to Sirmoor Battalion), 276.
Lollgunge, 331.
Longfield, Colonel J., (8th King's), appointed Brigadier, 90; 116, 132, 191, 215.
Loodianah, 25.
Losses. *See* Casualties.
Low, A.D.C., Lieut. R. C., (9th L.C.), 213, 240.
Lowe, A.D.C., Lieut. R. H. Drury, (74th Regt.), 28, 213, 298.
Luchman Das, 164.
Lucknow, reported safety of, 88 *et seq.*, 99; all well at, 113, 121, 137; rumoured relief of, 161; 173, 182; Havelock marching to relief of, 175, 223, 227, 231, 245, 278; the Baillie Guard holding out, 236; 265, 272, 278, 297, 308; Outram advancing towards, 278, 294, 295.
Ludlow Castle, 197, 273, 274, 275, 282.
Lugard, Colonel, 158 *et seq.*, 177.
Lumsden, Captain, (late General Sir Harry), letter from Candahar, 259.
Lumsden, Lieut. W. H., (of 10th N.I., attached to Coke's Corps), 240.
Lunka, (Ceylon), 170. *See Glossary.*
Lussowlie, camp at, 36 *et seq.*; 81, 106, 220.

McAndrew, Captain, 30; with Jheend Raja's troops, 87 *et seq.*; bad management of, at Bhagput, 90, 102; superseded, 153.
McAndrew, Lieut. J. F., (19th N.I), 8.

M'Barnett, Captain G. G., (of 55th N.I., attached to 1st Bengal Fusiliers), 285.
M'Causland, Colonel, 64, 66, 125.
Macdonald, Major, (20th N.I.), 18.
Machell, Mrs, 149.
Mackenzie, Lieut.-Colonel Murray. *See* Murray-Mackenzie.
Mackinnon, Dr, 46, 76, 108, 252.
Maclean, ——, (29th N.I.), 256.
M'Leod, Sir Donald, 94; letter from, giving opinion on reorganisation of Indian Army and Civil Service, 309 *et seq.*
Macleod, ——, (Artillery), 100.
McMullin, ——, 330.
Macpherson, Colonel J., 218.
M'Sharpley, ——, 112.
Mactier, Dr, 23, 26, 37, 47, 203, 214, 282.
Madras, troops ordered from, 15.
   Brigade, 295.
   Column, 327.
Magazine, Delhi, largest in India, 91; 203; stormed and taken, 283 *et seq.*, 286 *et seq.*, 289; number of guns found in, 287, 289, 293, 295.
Magazine on river close to Delhi, blown up, 17.
Maharajah of: Cashmere and Jummoo, 217 *et seq.* (*See* Goolab, *and* Runbar Sing)—Gwalior, q.v.
Mahidpore Contingent, 96, 111.
Mahomedans and Hindoos: in Delhi, feud between, 60, 152, 158 —in Rohilkund and Benares, 222, 223—in Simla, 221.
Mahomedans leave Agra, 137.
Mahratta country, 256.
Mahrattas, 99.
Maisey, Captain, (Deputy J.-A. General), 11, 178, 203, 213, 265.
Malaghur, Nawab of, 225.
Mangles, Mr, 239.
Mangul Pandy. *See* Pandy.
Mansfield, Colonel, (Lord Sand-

INDEX.

hurst), appointed Chief of Sir Colin Campbell's Staff, 246.
Mansion House Mutiny Relief Fund. *See* Fund.
Markunda River, 244 *et seq.*, 246.
Martin, Major R., (commanding 4th Irregular Cavalry), 27, 48, 51, 81, 93, 95, 125, 155, 211.
Martin, Mrs, 27, 93, 95, 113, 155. Mr, 36.
Martin's Irregulars, (4th Irregular Cavalry), with Delhi Force, 29, 43, 101; mutiny in corps, 81 *et seq.*, 95, 113, 118; 101; corps disarmed, 155, 211.
Massacre at: Cawnpore, q.v.—Delhi, 17, 19, 22 *et seq.*, 222—Futtyghur, 153, 177—Jhansi, q.v.—Meerut, q.v.—Shahjehanpore, 69 *et seq.*
Matadeens, 197. *See Glossary.*
Maughan, ——, 257.
Maul, Miss, 64.
Maulmein, troops ordered from, 15.
'May Day Hill,' 18.
Mayhew, Major, 83.
Mayne, Rev. Mr, 20, 88, 149.
Mayor, Lord, 253.
Mean-Meer, 56.
Meerun-ka-Serai, 194.
Meerut, court of inquiry at, xvii; the greased cartridges, and mutiny of the 3rd L.C. at, 2, 7, 8, 9 *et seq.*, 305; fighting, mutiny, and massacre at, 11, 12, 16 *et seq.*, 18, 23, 30; wounded and ladies sent to, from Camp, 67; convoy arrives from, 86; anxiety about, 39, 85, 90; news from, 124, 143 *et seq.*, 148, 169, 247, 258 *et seq.*, 334.
Meerut Division, warrant for, 8.
Melville, Sir James, 253.
Metcalfe, Sir Theophilus, Bart., escapes from Delhi, 19, 23, 31, Appendix B.; 46, 77, 234, 271, 282.
Metcalfe House, occupied, 54, 69; attacks on, 60, 85, 181, 224, 225, 292; reported mine to, 138.
Mhow, (Mahu), 114.
Mildmay, Mrs, 257.
Military and Naval resources, our, 167 *et seq.*
Mine, reported, to Metcalfe House, 138.
Mint Guard, Calcutta, attempted seduction of, 2.
Mirza Akbar Shah, 323.
    Ilahi Baksh, Prince, 335.
    Moghul, Prince, 231.
Mirzapore, 330.
Mitchell, Colonel W. St L., (commanding 19th N.I.), 2, 5.
Mitrall, 74.
Mogul Emperors, last of the, 333.
Mogul Fort. *See* Selimgurh.
Mohurram, 221, 223, 251, 259. *See Glossary.*
Money, Captain E. K., (Horse Artillery), 29, 104, 147.
Montgomery, Mr, (Sir Robert), 158, 321 *et seq.*
    Mrs, 222.
Moohurckpore, 11.
Mooltan, 52, 94.
    Horse, Lind's, 215, 235.
Moorar, 262.
Moore, Captain, (32nd Regiment), and Mrs, 226.
Moozafernugar, 29, 81, 113.
Moradabad, 44, 66, 102, 104.
Moree Bastion, battery at, 100, 101. Gate, 101, 282.
Morrieson, Major R., letters from Bhurtpore, 64 *et seq.*, 88 *et seq.*, 206 *et seq.*; 110, 111, 205.
Motto of 60th Rifles, 83. *See* Rifles.
Moule, Brigadier, 132.
Mound, the, 71, 72, 118, 119, 171.
Mountsteven, Lieut. W. H., (8th King's), 120.
Movable Column. *See* Column.
Mowatt, Colonel, 30, 31, 33, 35.

Muir, Mr, (now Sir William), 267.
Munro, ——, 332.
Murray, Lieut. A. W., (of 42nd N.I., attached to the 'Guides'), 120, 283.
Murray, Lieut., (60th Rifles), 274, 276.
Murray-Mackenzie, Lieut.-Colonel, (Horse Artillery), 101, 105, 134, 196, 214, 242.
Murree, 270, 274.
Musjid, Jumma, 158, 298, 300. *See Glossary.*
Mussorie, 150, 180.
Mutineers, execution of, 8, 103.
    Indignation against, 91 *et seq.*, 164, 252.
Mutiny, the—
    Adherence and fidelity of Native Princes and States during, 69, 82, 93. *See also Rajas of Puttiala, Ulwar, and others.*
    Conflicting opinions on, 91.
    English Press on, 192, 305 *et seq.*
    Feeling about, and indignation at Home, 165 *et seq.*, 167, 252, 302, 306.
    Havelock's confidence in our arms, for suppression of, 204.
    Ignorance in Parliament and at Home as to causes of, 192, 239, 305 *et seq.*
    Lesson of, 310.
    Officers not responsible for, 192, 239.
    Predicted by Sir Charles Napier, Appendix H.
    Revenue collected during, 170.
    Sepoys alone rebellious—not people of country, 28, 170.
Mutiny, the, causes of—
    Native fear of conversion, and breaking of caste, 21 n., 17 *et seq.*, 26 *et seq.*
    Native prophecy about end of our 'Raj,' 73, 78, 80, 164. *See Glossary.*
    Secondary position held by Native Army officers, 10, 97, 166, 309.
    Sepoys discontented with Pension Establishment, Invaliding Rules, and Seniority system, 10 *et seq.*, 98.
    Sepoys' hatred of the greased cartridges, 4 *et seq.*, 9 *et seq.*, 16 *et seq.*, 305.
Mutiny at: Aboo, 251 *et seq.*, 256 *et seq.*—Agra, 206—Allahabad, 85—Bareilly, 44, 46—Barrackpore, 1, 3, 4, 9—Berhampore, 1, 3—Cawnpore, q.v.—Delhi, q.v.—Dinapore, 97, 201, 224, 231 *et seq.*—Erinpoorah, q.v.—Ferozepore, 224—Futtyghur, q.v.—Jhansi, q.v.—Meerut, q.v.—Shahjehanpore, 69 *et seq.*, 75—Umballa, 16.
Mutiny in Camp, 117 *et seq.*
Mutiny of the 50th N.I., Appendix D.
Mutiny Relief Fund. *See Fund.*
Mutiny, the 'White,' xiii, xvi *et seq.*
Muttra, letters from, 114.
    Treasury looted, 42.
Myha, Fort, 328.
    Raja of, 330.
Mynpoorie, 159.

NABA (Nabha) Raja's fidelity, 45.
Nagas, 114. *See Glossary.*
Nagode, 184, 202, 232, 237, 327 *et seq.*
Nagpore, 112.
Nana Sahib, Raja of Bithoor, 154 *et seq.*, 163, 164, 165, 172, 173, 175, 184, 226, 239, 272.
Nana Sing, 182.
Napier, General Sir Charles, xi, xii, xv, 9, 68, 305; the Mutiny predicted by, Appendix H.
Napier, Lieut. Robert, (Lord Napier of Magdala), 326 n.
Napoleon, 167.
Narghat, 321.
Narnaul, 307.

INDEX. 363

Native—
Army. *See* Army.
Description of our soldiers, 170, 188.
Devotion to, and confidence in us, 97, 137 *et seq.*, 193, 200.
Ideas of justice, 325 *et seq.*
Insolence and cruelty, 18, 22 *et seq.*, 92, 161, 164, 184, 222, 226, 289.
Mistrust of Government and of General Anson, 17 *et seq.*, 21 n., 26 *et seq.*
Population not with rebellious Sepoys, 28, 170.
Princes' fidelity, 69, 82, 93.
Prophecy about our 'Raj.' *See* 'Raj.'
Treachery, 209 *et seq.*
Unfaithfulness, 91 *et seq.*
Naval Brigade, 247, 249, 255.
Naval and Military resources, our, 167 *et seq.*
Nawab: Syfuola Khan, 206—of Futtyghur, 156—of Jhujur, 164—of Malaghur, 225.
Nawaubgunge, letter from, 175.
Neemuch mutineers—attack Delhi Camp, 70 *et seq.*; take Fort of Khooshalgurh, 99, 160; expected at Agra, 109, 111 *et seq.*; attack Agra, 125 *et seq.*, 146; arrive in Delhi, 156, 262; fighting at Delhi, 243.
Neill, Brigadier-General, (Madras Fusiliers), commanding at Cawnpore, news from, 198; 223 *et seq.*, 231, 267.
Nepaul, (Nepal), 97, 173, 211.
Newsletters from Delhi, 62 *et seq.*, 68, 80, 109, 140, 144, 146, 147, 153, 158, 172 n. *et seq.*, 200, 203, 243 *et seq.*, 260 *et seq.*, 277 *et seq.*, Appendix I.
Nicholson, Brigadier-General John, (27th N.I.), 125; telegraphs from Punjab, 140; *en route* from Umritsur to join Force before Delhi, 151, 161; arrival in Camp, 181 *et seq.*; Column expected, 188; strength of Column, and account of Nicholson and his command, 191, 194 *et seq.*, 216; arrival of Column, 202, 204; composition of Column, *ib.*; the Movable Column, 221, 223, 234; composition of Movable Column, 234, 235; meets enemy at Nujufghurh and is victorious, 240 *et seq.*; returns to Camp, 242 *et seq.*, 244; his despatch, 261; 279; wounded at the Assault, 283, 285, 287 *et seq.*, 291, 300 n.
Nicholson, Lieut. C. J., (of 31st N.I., acting Commandant of Coke's Corps), 103, 285.
Nicoll, Captain H., (50th N.I.), 18, 19, 29, 90, 215, 230, 282.
Mrs, 14, 18, 312.
Nimukharams, 173. *See Glossary.*
Nisbett, Dr J. A., 24, 45, 89, 323.
Nixon, Mr R., 110 *et seq.*; letter to, 235.
Nizamodeen's Tomb, 296, 299.
Norman, Lieut. H. W., Assistant Adjutant-General, (now General Sir Henry), 10; accompanies Chief to Umballa, 17; 27; with Force before Delhi, 52 n., 79, 83, 117, 127, 157, 213, 261, 267, 291.
Norman, Mrs, 25, 33, 64, 83, 283, 288, 291.
Nujufghurh, 115 n.; enemy reported at, 232; Nicholson's Column sent to reconnoitre, and great victory at, 240, 241 *et seq.*; Hodson sent to reconnoitre, 245, 247.
Nullah, (Soubie Nullah), 248.
Nunda Sahib, 272.
Nusseree Battalion, 11, 12, 44 *et seq.*, 52, 68, 103 *et seq.* *See* Goorkhas.
Nussereebad Troops, mutiny of, 42,

INDEX

45, 46; attack Delhi Camp, 70 et seq.
Nynee Tal, 64, 75, 184, 208.

ODEYPORE, 257.
Old Fort or Purana Kila, at ancient Delhi, 298.
Olivia, Mrs, 286.
Olpherts, Major, (General Sir William Olpherts, V.C., K.C.B.—Horse Artillery), 73, 80, 180.
Olpherts' Force expected in Camp, 71 et seq., 73, 76; arrives, 78, 79.
Omercote, 258.
Oonao, 219.
Ord, Mrs, 286.
Order, Havelock's, to his soldiers, 203 et seq.
    Lawrence's, to disarm Bazaar people in Simla, 158.
    Wilson's, issued before the Assault, 271, 281.
Orders by the Governor-General, 56.
Osborne, Lieut., 320.
Oude, 61, 99, 170, 308; feeling of Princes of, 252.
Oung, victory at, 175.
Ouseley, Captain Reginald, (34th N.I.), and Mrs, 323.
Outram, General Sir James, expected at Allahabad, 227; appointed to Dinapore Division, 246; advancing on Cawnpore, 276, 278; will not take command of Force from Havelock, 294, 295.
Owen, Lieut. A. G., (1st Bengal Fusiliers), 196, 284.

PACKE, Lieut. C. E., (of 4th N.I., attached to 4th Sikh Infantry), 95, 101.
Palace of Delhi, 68, 77, 228, 262; shelled, 287 et seq., 290, 292 et seq.; taken, 299 et seq.
Palmer, General, 26, 28.
    Major, 247.
Pandies, 153; suggested origin of name, Appendix E. *See also Glossary.*
Pandoo Nuddee, victory at, 175.
Pandy, Isurree, Jemadar, (34th N.I.), mutiny of and sentence on, 6 et seq., 8, 333.
Pandy, Mangul, (34th N.I.), mutiny of and sentence on, 5 et seq., 333.
Paniput, 26, 29; camp at, 33 et seq., 66, 81.
Parliament, ignorant of causes of the Mutiny, 192, 305 et seq.
Paske, Lieut. Edward H., 311, 314.
Pass, Katha, 327.
Pathans, 187.
Paton, Dr, 33.
    Mr, Postmaster-General, 14.
Peacock, Mr, (Sir Barnes), 7.
Peake, Francis, 323.
'Pearl,' Frigate, 249.
Pearse, Lieut., 108.
Peel, Captain, (R.N.), 249, 255.
Peinbaree Bridge, 241.
Peishwar, the, 165, 226. *See* Nana Sahib.
Pemberton, Duncan, (Bengal Engineers), 46, 51, 66, 270.
    Robert, (Bengal Engineers), 270, 286, 293.
Penny, General A., 14; to command at Meerut, 119, 134, 162; 304, 323.
Pension Establishment, 10 et seq., 98.
Percussion-caps, scarcity of, in Delhi. *See* Caps.
Perkins, Lieut. H. G., (Horse Artillery), 38.
Persia, 2, 15.
Persians evacuate Herat, 256, 259.
Peshawar, 56, 65 et seq., 93, 173.
Peskett, Dr, 11, 19 et seq., 323.
Philipe, Mr, letter from, 13 et seq.
Piplee, 29, 31, 301.
Plowden, ——, 332.
Pogson, Lieut. W. W., (8th King's), 295.
    Mrs, 323.

Pollock, Lieut. H. T., (of 35th N.I., attached to Coke's Corps), 130.
Polwhele, Brigadier, 145, 208.
Poonahana Pergunah, 207. *See* Pergunah *in Glossary*.
Poorbeahs or Oude men, 99 *et seq.*, 119, 124, 153, 210.
Poulton, Mrs, 27, 93.
Powder, priming of, in Camp, spoilt with stones, 209 *et seq.*; charges of, tampered with, 212.
Powder manufactory in Delhi blown up, 184, 190.
Powell, Colonel, (53rd Regt.), 328.
Press, English, on the Mutiny, 192, 305 *et seq.*
Prime-Minister of Delhi, 184 *et seq.*, 189 *et seq.*
Prince: Jamma Bukt, 333 *et seq.*— Mirza Ilahi Baksh, 335—Mirza Moghul, 231.
Princes, Delhi, rumoured flight of, 194, 195; flight and death of, Appendix G.
Princes, Hindoo, loyal adherence of, 69, 82, 98. *See* Rajas of Gwalior, Puttiala, Ulwar, *and others*.
Princes of Oude, feeling towards us, 252.
Pringle, Mr, vi.
Prior, Ensign C., (attached to Coke's Corps), 290.
'Priory,' the, 95.
Prize Agents to be appointed, 263, 265, 266 *et seq.*; appointed, 298.
Proclamation to destroy offending villages, 31.
Pullen, Lieut. A., (of 36th N.I., attached to Kemaon Battalion), 120.
Pulwal, 60, 74, 76, 229.
Punishment of rebels, suggested, 252.
Punjab, (Panjab), or Sikh troops, fidelity of, 9, 101. *See* Sikhs.

Puttiala, (Patiala), Raja of, his fidelity, 13, 22, 45, 138.
Pyloo Das, 141, 164.

RAIE, 34; camp at, 37 *et seq.*; 76, 229.
Rains, commencement of, in Camp, 86 *et seq.*; 110, 121, 123 *et seq.*, 152, 164, 169, 170 *et seq.*, 250, 251.
'Raj,' our, Native prophecy about, 80, 164. *See Glossary*.
Raja of: Bithoor (*See* Nana Sahib) —Bullubghur, q.v.—Bhurtpore, 63, 206—Dholpore, 63, 276—Holkar, 205—Jeypore, 276—Jheend, q.v.—Myha, 320—Naba, 45—Puttiala, q.v.—Ulwar, q.v.
Rajpootana, (Rajputana), 206.
Rajput Horse, 159 *et seq.*
Rampore, 31—Horse, 30—Nawab of, 66.
Rana of Kooyntal. *See* Kooyntal.
Rangoon, 334.
Rashness of our troops, 81, 87, 128 *et seq.*, 129 *et seq.*, 131, 138, 147, 171, 173 *et seq.*
Rattray's Sikhs, 331.
Ravee River, 131.
Rebels. *See* Sepoys.
Reed, C.B., General T., appointed acting Commander-in-Chief, 26, 56; expected in camp at Alleepore, 45; arrives in Delhi Camp, 51; his illness, 52, 58, 80, 107; to assume command in Camp, 108; 118; takes sick leave, 131 *et seq.*; leaves for Simla, 136; appointed to Sirhind Division, 223.
Regiments and Corps. *See special Index*, page 341 *et seq.*
Reid, Major C., (Commandant Sirmoor Battalion), 30; gallant conduct of, 66; letter from, 68 *et seq.*; 120; wounded, 284, 285.
Reinforcements, 'should we wait for?' 61 *et seq.*; decide to wait for, 63 *et seq.*; reported leav-

INDEX

ing England, 53, 167 *et seq.*, 187, 231 *et seq.*; arriving at Calcutta, 91 *et seq.*, 99, 126, 175, 205; reports of various, imaginary and real, 60 *et seq.*, 71, 76, 87, 89, 92, 129, 143 *et seq.*, 147, 149, 151, 153, 161, 222, 228 *et seq.*, 230, 234, 247, 249, 255, 260; promises of, from Sir John Lawrence, 87, 142, 146, 151 n.—Arrival in Camp of : the 'Guides,' 51—Olpherts' Force, 78, 80 *et seq.*—8th King's and Rothney's Sikhs, 87, 93 *et seq.* —61st (wing of), 100—Coke's Corps and Fenwick's Corps (one wing), *ib.*—Sikh Artillerymen, 119—Kemaon Battalion, 169, 170 —Nicholson's Column, 202, 204— Green's Corps, *ib.*—52nd Foot and part of 61st, *ib.*—Belooch Corps, 'new levies,' *ib.*—Cavalry and Horse Battery, *ib.*—Rifles and Artillery from Meerut, 266— Jheend troops, 268—Wilde's, *ib.*— Cashmere Contingent, 269 *et seq.*

Relief Fund, Mutiny. *See* Fund.

Resources, our Military and Naval, 167 *et seq.*

Retribution, Army of, 29 *et seq.* *See* Army.

Revenue collected during the Mutiny, 170.

Rewah, (Rewa), 330 *et seq.*

Rewaree, 286.

Richardes, ——, 66.

'Ridge,' the, capture and occupation of, 47; attacks on, 51, 54, 56; 60, 100; description of, 238.

Rifles, the 60th, motto of, (*Celer et Audax*, 'Swift and daring'), 83. *See page* 341.

Ripley, Colonel, 17, 332.

Rissalah, Jhansi, 173. *See Glossary.*

River: Beas, 131—Chumbal, 110, 262 *et seq.*, 288—Gagra, 202— Ganges, 61, 297—Hinden, 124— Jumna, q.v.—Markunda, 244 *et seq.*, 246—Nullah, 248—Ravee, 131—Sutlej, 131, 188.

Roberts, Lieut. F. S., (Lord Roberts), 213.

Robertson, Captain Alex., (8th King's), arrives in Camp, 103; 150; ill with fever, 245; goes on sick leave, 275 *et seq.*

Rockets used by enemy, 190.

Rohilkund, (Rohilkhand), bad news from, 43 *et seq.*, 44; 61, 65, 79, 82; feud between Hindoos and Mahomedans in, 222, 223; 296, 304.

Rohilkund Brigade. *See* Bareilly Brigade.

Rohilla Chiefs, 65.

Rohtuck, 26; mutiny at, 210.

Roorkee, 76, 100.

Rose, Sir Hugh, (Lord Strathnairn), xii.

Rosser, Captain C. P., (6th Dragoon Guards), 283, 289 n., 294.

Rothney's Sikhs, 94, 215.

Rotten, Rev. J. E., 50, 60, 140, 214.

Rule, Native prophecy about our. *See* 'Raj.'

Rules, Native Invaliding and Pension, 10 *et seq.*, 98.

Runbar Sing, Maharajah of Cashmere and Jummoo, 201, 217 *et seq.*; 265.

Russell, Captain C. W., (54th N.I.), 47, 50.

SABATHOO, 24.

Sage, Brigadier, 260.

Saharunpore, 26, 31, 45, 68, 103.

Salone, 170.

Sandilands, Captain E. N., (8th King's), 194.

Saugar, (Sagar), 52, 82, 100, 202, 232.
 Brigade, 153.
 Fort at, 261.

Saunders, Mr, C. B., (Civil Service), 121, 148, 153, 268.
 Mrs, 148.

Scott, Brigadier, 247.
   Major E. W. S., (Artillery), 267.
   Dr, 107, 113, 219.
   Mrs, 323.
Sealkote, anxiety about, 124; bad news from, 125; mutineers from, 130 et seq.; mutineers disbanded, 140; 153; letter from, 217 et seq.; officers killed at, 161.
Seaton, C.B., Colonel T., (35th N.L.I.), 37; praise of, 117, 147; appointed a Prize Agent, 298.
Selimgurh, old Mogul Fort in Delhi, 279, 283, 284, 287, 289, 290, 292, 295 et seq., 298, 299, 326.
Sepoys—
   Alone rebellious, not Native population, 28, 170.
   And greased cartridges. See Cartridges.
   Cowardice of, 39, 105, 148, 171.
   Demand pay from King, 161.
   Deserting from Delhi, 220.
   Gold found on, 55, 58, 200.
Service of Humiliation in Camp before Delhi, 210.
Seymour, Captain, notes from, 48 et seq., 159.
Shah Alum, 323.
Shahjehanpore, 44, 65, 69 et seq., 75.
Shah Mull, 140.
'Shannon,' Frigate, arrives at Calcutta, 249.
Shebbeare, Lieut. R. H., (of 60th N.I., attached to the 'Guides'), 284.
Sherer, J. W., letter from, 235 et seq.
Sherriff, Lieut. D. F., (2nd Bengal Fusiliers), wounded, 196 et seq., 200, 203; death, 210.
Sherriff, Miss, 196.
Showers, Brigadier St. G. D., (2nd Bengal Fusiliers), 191, 195; wounded, 196, 199, 210; 197, 215; commanding Pursuing Column, 304.

Shumsabad, 106.
Shute, Captain D. C., 33, 37; letter from, 49; 213, 234, 282.
   Mrs, 37, 323.
Sibbald, Brigadier, 64.
Sibley, Captain, 213.
Sickness: in Camp, 103, 192, 230, 248 et seq., 265, 278—at Cawnpore, 235.
Siege-train, waiting for, 25 et seq., 29; left without guard, 32; at Kurnaul, 37; arrives in camp at Alleepore, 43; second Siege-train expected, 191 et seq., 209; at Umballa, 221, 228; 230, 234, 241, 244 et seq., 246; at Kurnaul, 248; delay in sending, 250; at Paniput, 255, 258; in Camp at Delhi, 262.
Sikhs, 59, 73, 78, 80 et seq., 87, 105, 119, 138, 297.
Simla—
   Alarm and unrest at, xiii et seq., 11 et seq., 19 et seq., 48, 141, 178, 199, 201, 221, 255 et seq., 274.
   Conflicting opinions at, on the Mutiny and fighting, 91 et seq.
   Disarming of Native Bazaar people, 103, 143, 150, 158, 174.
   Headquarters' Staff, 3 et seq., 303 et seq.
   Insolence of Natives in, 18, 184.
   Letters from, 16 et seq., 91 et seq., 303 et seq., 305, 307 et seq.
   Safety of, 198, 237.
   Special constables, 158.
   Suspicion of servants in, 115, 117, 134 et seq., 233.
   Volunteers, xiv, 161 et seq., 178.
Simpson, Brigade-Major C. F., (8th N.I.), 29, 215.
   Captain 'Tooney,' (D.A.A.-G. at Meerut), 70, 79, 169; letter to, 198 et seq.

INDEX.

Sindhia, 310, 333.
Sing, Goolab. *See* Goolab.
    Nana, 182.
    Runbar. *See* Runbar.
Singpore, 329.
Sirhind Division, warrant for, 8; 91.
Sirmoor (Sirmur) Battalion, 30, 43, 215.
Sirsa, 110.
Sketch of Army of Retribution, 29 *et seq.*
Sketches of Buktawa Khan, 178.
Skinner, Mr, children of, in Delhi, 286.
Skinner's house, Delhi, 282; letters from, 284 *et seq.*, 286 *et seq.*
Smith, Lieut., (4th Irregular Cavalry), murdered, 81 *et seq.*, 107.
    Colonel Baird. *See* Baird Smith.
    Vernon, speech by, 232, 235, 238, 305.
Smyth, Colonel G. M. C., (commanding 3rd L.C.), 7 n.
Soan, 330.
Solon, 14, 25.
Somerset, Sir Henry, to assume command as Commander-in-Chief in India, 56; 159, 175.
Sonput, (Soneput), 155, 225, 234, 237, 335.
Speke, Lieut. E., (of 5th N.I.—attached to 1st Bengal Fusiliers), 284, 289.
Spurgin, Captain, letter from, 198 *et seq.*
Spy's letters from Delhi. *See* Newsletters.
Staff, Sir Colin Campbell's, 246.
Staff, dress of, 28, 85.
Stafford, Mrs, 41, 45.
States, Hindoo, feeling of, 69, 82, 93.
Stewart, Captain Donald, (9th N.I.), arrives in Camp from Hodul, 99, 114; 159, 193, 213, 265.

Stewart, ——, (18th N.I.), 64.
Stileman, Lieut., (Carabineers), 123.
Strathnairn, Lord, vi.
Strength of: city of Delhi, 130, 157, 238, 305, Appendix C.—our Force before Delhi, 190 *et seq.*, 238, 281—enemy's Force in Delhi, 190 *et seq.*, 203, 250 *et seq.*, 281.
Stroud, Sergeant-Major, 214.
Sudder Bazaar, 138. *See Glossary.*
Suez, 49, 222, 238, 246.
Sultan, the, 49.
Sunday in Camp, 60, 108, 140, 172, 185, 210, 267, 281.
Sutlej River, 131, 188.
Sykes, Colonel, 305.
Syree, 300.

TANDY, Mr, (Volunteer Horse), 249.
    Lieut. F. S., (Engineers), 283.
Telegrams from Delhi received at Simla, 283 *et seq.*, 289, 292, 295, 299, 300.
Telegraph, execution ordered by, 7 *et seq.*
Telegraph to Camp, 31 *et seq.*, 35, 38, 40, 229, 272, 278, 280.
Telewara, 287.
Temple, Lieut. A. B., (of 49th N.I., attached to Kemaon Battalion), 183, 200.
Theft of cash-box at Simla. *See* Cash-box.
Thomas, John, 323.
Thomason, Mr, 23, 31.
Thompson, Lieut. P., (Artillery), 130.
Thomson, Colonel, 79, 213.
    Mrs, 283.
Thornhill, ——, 115.
Tireh, (Theri ?), 111.
Tomb, Hamayoon's, King of Delhi's flight to, 299, 334.
    Nizamodeen's, 296, 299.
Tombs, Major, (late Major-General Sir Harry Tombs, V.C., K.C.B.—Artillery), gallant conduct of,

INDEX.

66 n., 69; wins the V.C., 118, 123; wounded, 285.
Touch, Dr, 275.
Translation of cossid letter, Appendix I.
Travers, Captain, (second in command of 1st Punjab Infantry, Coke's Corps), 171.
Treachery in Camp, 209 *et seq.*
Treasure taken from the Nana, 154.
Treasury, at Muttra looted, 42, 114; at Kussowlie, 14, 22, 25.
Tremenere, General, 307.
Tritton, Dr, 30, 36, 200, 214.
Troops, British. *See* British Troops.
    European. *See* Army.
    Native. *See* Army.
Trunk Road, Grand, 67, 115, 231.
Tucker, Colonel, 95, 97, 166.
    Mr, 330.
Turnbull, Lieut. J. R., (75th Regt.), 213, 241.
Turner, Major Frank, (Horse Artillery), 29, 32, 37, 147, 223.
Tweeddale, Marquis of. *See* Lord William Hay.
Tytler, Colonel, letter from, 175, 194, 197.
    Captain, (38th N.I.), 214.
    Mr, 220, 230.

ULWAR Contingent, desertion of, 126.
Ulwar, Raja of: his loyalty, 114; his death, 205 *et seq.*
Umballa, letters from, 1 *et seq.*, 15; 11, 13, 16.
Ummerputtena, 330.
Umritsur, 151, 255.

VAN CORTLAND. *See* Cortland.
Vibart, Major and Mrs, 226.
Victoria Cross, 118 n.
Vivian, General, 97.
Volunteers at Simla, xiv, 161 *et seq.*, 178.
Vyse, Captain, 186.

WAGHORNE, Dr, 45.
Walker, Lieut. J. T., (late General —Bombay Engineers), 130, 247.
Walter, Ensign O. C., (of 45th N.I., attached to 2nd Bengal Fusiliers), 139.
Ward, Captain George, 155, 157, 208, 230.
Water: Bastion, 282—Gate, *ib.*
Water supply to Delhi, cut off, 89 *et seq.*, 237, 238.
Waterfield, Lieut. W. G., 11, 16.
Waters, Captain G. C. H., (60th Rifles), 200 *et seq.*, 285.
Watson, Lieut., (of 28th Bombay N.I., commanding 1st Punjab Cavalry), 278.
Watson, Mr, 111.
Wazeerabad, 334.
Weather in Camp, 78, 84, 87, 135, 165, 185, 192 *et seq.*, 202, 211, 246, 248, 250, 256, 264, 269, 273, 274. *See* Rains.
Webb, Lieut. W. R., (8th King's), 295.
Wedderburn, Mr, (Civil Service), 94.
Welchman, Colonel J., 80, 133, 135.
Wemyss, Lieut. H. M., (1st Bengal Fusiliers), 284.
Wheatly, Lieut. E. C., (of 54th N.I., attached to Sirmoor Battalion), 67.
Wheeler, General Sir Hugh, commanding at Cawnpore, 82, 89, 90, 99, 102; reported advance towards Delhi, 122, 124, 127; rumoured disaster to, 132, 137; murder of Wheeler and all his party, 138; 139, 141 *et seq.*, 144, 151; 155; Native account of massacre, 161, 163, 164; Havelock's corroboration, 174, 175, 177 *et seq.*, 197, 198; Delafosse's account, 226, 239.
Wheler, Colonel S. G., (commanding 34th N.I.), strictures on, 5 n.

'White Mutiny,' the, xiii, xvi *et seq.*
Wiggens, Colonel and Mrs, 226.
    Mrs, 283.
Wilberforce, Lieut., 324.
Wilde's Corps, (commanded by Captain—late Sir Alfred—Wilde), 268, 289.
Williams, Mr, (Commissioner at Meerut), 39, 144.
    Colonel, 226.
Willock, Miss, 94.
Wilmot, Lady Eardley, 168.
Wilson, Brigadier, (General Sir Archdale), 30; victory of, and despatch from, 33 *et seq.*, 36; second victory, 37; civilians protest against his joining Delhi Force, 39; is ordered to join Headquarters' Column, 39, 41, 42; arrives in Camp, 43; is wary and careful, 44; 46, 61; his opinion at Councils of War, 'Wait for reinforcements,' 63; opinion of strength of Delhi, 129; to command Delhi Force, 132, 133, 135; made Brigadier-General, 134; 136; opinion as to taking of Delhi, 143 *et seq.*, 201; his carefulness, 145 *et seq.*; 159, 161, 165, 191, 217; made Major-General, 223; wishes to retain command of Artillery, 225; 230; order by, 271; Hodson's strictures on, 277; not well, 289; 291, 305 *et seq.*
Wilson, Captain, (Deputy J.-A. General), 213, 297.
Woman: and dead Fakeer, 70—with rebel Sepoys, 143.
Wriford, Captain, (1st Bengal Fusiliers), 267, 298.
Wyld, Mrs, 11, 181.

YONGE, Lieut., (61st Regt.), 323.
Yorke, Lieut. J., (of 3rd N.I., attached to Kemaon Battalion), 95, 101.

Young, Arthur, 83, 156; letter from, 257 *et seq.*; 267, 276, 280.
Young, ——, (4th N.I.), 235.
    Captain J., 214.
    James Nowell, (Deputy J.-A. at Mean Meer), letter from, 56 *et seq.*
Young, C.B., Colonel Keith, joins Bengal Army, xi; appointed to 50th N.I., *ib.*; made Deputy J.-A. General of Division, *ib.*—Civil J.-A. in Sind, *ib.*—J.-A. General, Bengal, xii; commencement of friendship with Sir Henry Norman, *ib. et seq.*; receives the C.B., xvi; inquires into the 'White Mutiny,' xiii, xvi *et seq.*; his illness and death, xvi *et seq.*

Hears first rumours of the Mutiny, 1 *et seq.*; account of greased cartridges, 3, 9, 305; fears for Delhi, and for safety of Simla, 11 *et seq.*; receives orders to join Chief at Kurnaul, 14; leaves Simla, 15; arrives in camp at Kurnaul, 25 *et seq.*; hears of Chief's (General Anson) death, 26; Sketch of Army of Retribution, 29 *et seq.*; issues Proclamation, 31; hears of Wilson's victories, 33 *et seq.*, 37 *et seq.*; discussion as to Wilson joining Headquarters' Column, 39 *et seq.*; too sanguine of immediate success, 41.—In camp at : Guraunda, 32 *et seq.*—Paniput, 33 *et seq.*—Lussowlie, 36 *et seq.*—Raie, 37 *et seq.*—Alleepore, 40 *et seq.*—Describes battle of Budlee-ka-Serai and death of Colonel Chester, 47 *et seq.*, 50, 58; in Camp before Delhi, 47 *et seq.*; in city of Delhi, 282 *et seq.*; leaves Delhi for Simla, 301; expects to join Sir Colin Campbell advancing on Lucknow, 303 *et seq.*, 307 *et seq.*

INDEX.

Young, Colonel Keith (*continued*)—
Letters to Colonel H. B. Henderson, London, 3, 12 *et seq.*, 129, 236 *et seq.*, 281, 303 *et seq.*, 305, 307 *et seq.*; correspondence relating to Joonug and the Rana of Kooyntal, 311 *et seq.*
Opinion of, and comments on: General Anson, 26 *et seq.*—General Barnard, 33, 35, 52, 80, 107—Arthur Becher, 27, 32—Neville Chamberlain, 70, 107 *et seq.*, 130—Chesney, 67 —Colonel Chester, 27, 31, 33, 37, 41, 43 *et seq.*, 58—Mr Colvin, 90, 239—Captain Daly, 29, 54, 68, 76—Lord Ellenborough, 232, 235, 237 *et seq.*—Bartle Frere, 289, 294—Brigadier Graves, 82, 88—Mr Greathed, 39 *et seq.*, 61, 90—George Hall, 66, 174, 180—Major Hodson, 39, 52, 64, 66, 68, 76, 84, 102, 150—Sir John Lawrence, 122—Sir Theophilus Metcalfe, 46—Sir Charles Napier, 9, 68, 305—Brigadier Neill, 267—Nicholson, 125, 181 *et seq.*, 191, 194 *et seq.*, 288—H. W. Norman, 27, 52, 79, 117, 291—General Reed, 58, 80, 136—Major Reid, 68—Colonel Seaton, 117, 147—Vernon Smith, 232, 235, 238—Brigadier Wilson, 39 *et seq.*, 44, 52, 132, 145, 159, 191.
Opinion of—
Army, the, 9 *et seq.*
Assaulting Delhi, 39, 44, 45, 57, 59, 61 *et seq.*, 74, 83, 88, 101, 103, 109, 115, 119, 129, 185, 189, 201 *et seq.*, 229, 277, 305.
Causes of the Mutiny, 9 *et seq.*, 28.
Climate of the Hills, 304.

Young, Colonel Keith (*continued*)—
Councils of War, 61 *et seq.*, 63, 64, 74.
Disarming Native Troops, 127, 155.
Engineers, the, 67, 274 *et seq.*, 277, 279.
Cartridges, the greased, 3, 9 *et seq.*, 305.
Goorkhas, the, 127, 131.
Guide Corps, the, 51, 52, 54, 157.
Rifles, the 60th, 88, 287.
Sikhs, the, 105, 204.
Strength of enemy's position and weakness of ours, 238.
Terms for surrender of Delhi, 25.
Waiting for reinforcements, 59, 61 *et seq.*, 74, 129.
Comments upon—
Camp life, 62, 78, 83 *et seq.*, 85, 116, 135, 136, 140, 150, 177, 185, 193, 201, 203, 208 *et seq.*, 219, 221, 227; Camp 'shaves,' 209; sickness in Camp, 103, 192, 230, 248 *et seq.*, 278; weather in Camp, 78, 86, 135, 165, 202 *et seq.*, 211, 250, 264, 269, 273.
Dâk, the, 51, 53, 54, 59, 67, 71, 73, 268; letter-writing, 249 *et seq.*
Delay and vacillation in march to Delhi, 32; delay of Siege-train, 250.
Losses, our heavy, 81, 87, 128, 129 *et seq.*, 131, 136, 138, 147, 173 *et seq.*
Young, Mrs Keith, letters to London, 16 *et seq.*, 91 *et seq.*
Younghusband, Lieut., 105 *et seq.*
Yule, Major R. A., (9th Lancers), 71.

ZEENUT MAHAL, wife of the King of Delhi, 335.

Edinburgh : Printed by W. & R. Chambers, Limited.

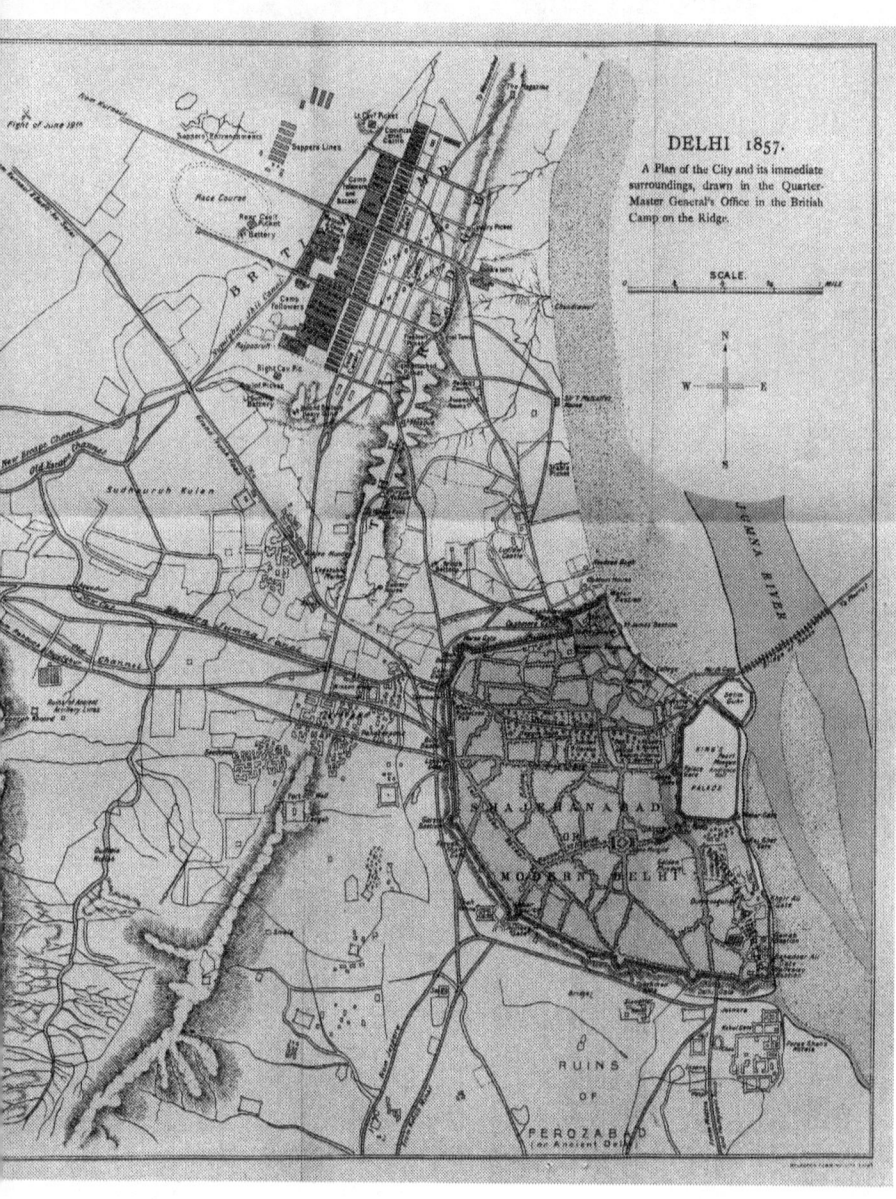

www.ingramcontent.com/pod-product-compliance
Lightning Source LLC
Chambersburg PA
CBHW031248230426
43670CB00005B/84